JOHN LENNON : WANTED BY THE FBI

The complete FBI files on John Lennon explained and illustrated

by Julien Kern

LIVERPOOL REVOLUTION

www.LIVERPOOLREVOLUTION.com

"John Lennon : Wanted by the FBI" is published by LIVERPOOL REVOLUTION (www.liverpoolrevolution.com)

Texts, research and presentation by Julien Kern.

Julien Kern is the founder of LIVERPOOL REVOLUTION, whose aim is to develop Beatles-related projects. Since 2009, we broadcast Beatles' music 8 days a week and 24 hours a day on our webradio LIVERPOOL REVOLUTION LIVE ! On this webradio you can listen to every single song ever recorded by the Beatles : studio versions, lives, rarities, alternate takes, previously unreleased material. Fab Four flavour forever on www.LIVERPOOLREVOLUTION.com

ISBN 978-2954463612

© Liverpool Revolution, 2014 – www.liverpoolrevolution.com

The images and photographs contained herein are for the sole use of educational reference for the readers. This use for educational reference falls under the "fair use" sections of U.S. copyright law.

Design, composition and illustrations by LüBA gRaPHicS

For further information on the LIVERPOOL REVOLUTION project and to listen to the ultimate non-stop Beatles webradio, go to :

www.liverpoolrevolution.com

CONTENTS

Presentation……… 5

69, pornographic year ?……… 9

War is Hoover : Wanted by the FBI, unwanted in the US……… 25
- The John Sinclair Freedom Rally, December 1970……… 45
- No more visa for Mr John Lennon, February 1972……… 96
- The MHCHAOS CIA program……… 105
- The Dick Cavett Show, May 1972……… 117
- The 1968 drug bust in London……… 128
- Deportation proceedings, March 1972……… 164
- What is going on, Mister Senator ?……… 253
- President Nixon re-elected, Beatle John still investigated……… 306
- Watergate scandal, end of war, still no Green Card for Lennon……… 329
- The Green Card, an Englishman in New York……… 334

Extortion……… 347

The dream is over……… 471

General glossary……… 487

Explanation of FOIA exemptions……… 489

Presentation

This book reproduces the most complete FBI files on John Lennon ever published. These files were filled from January 1969 to May 1983. We classified them in chronological order for a more enjoyable reading experience (the files were released by the FBI in any order, making it hard to follow the course of events). Some parts are still blacked out as they have not been declassified. When several versions of the same file were available, we chose the less blacked out. In some cases, one version shows some parts that the other doesn't and so we published both to bring you the most complete data and also for comparison purposes.

The John Lennon FBI files are a must-read document but they also form a kind of novel, and a most interesting one actually ! This novel is rooted in reality, making it a good way to catch the atmosphere of the end of the sixties / beginning of the seventies in the US. At that time there was a great deal of activism and contestation due to the war in Vietnam and these documents are frequently referring to these contestation movements and to the people and events relating to it. We also come across controversial figures like J. Edgar Hoover, director of the FBI, and Richard Nixon, who would both try to deport John Lennon at all costs and who would both have to face judicial inquiries. The Watergate scandal eventually led to Nixon's resignation as President of the United States, in August 1974, and also resulted in the conviction and incarceration of dozens of Nixon's top administration officials. As for Hoover, he proved to have used the FBI resources to reinforce his power and to harass political dissenters and activists, amass secret files on political leaders in order to gain leverage and collect evidence using illegal methods.

The John Lennon FBI files include various kinds of documents, making it very pleasant to read : you'll find reports, memos, informants testimonies, teletypes, confidential notes and also newspaper clippings, anecdotes or lyrics of songs ! And a few deleted pages information sheets...

You'll learn a lot about how the FBI was operating at that time and find out that irrationality and a kind of out of place amateurism and/or determination were sometimes what guided its actions. In some cases, a single affirmation by an informant could lead to a thorough investigation...

All in all, the John Lennon FBI files are a pleasant journey through this politically and socially troubled times. You'll come by activists like Jerry Rubin or John Sinclair, learn more about far left movements and organizations like the White Panther Party, the PCPJ, the EYSIC or the Allamuchy Tribe.

And like in any best-seller novel there is also a few sex scenes ! The John Lennon and Yoko Ono album "Two Virgins" came out in November 1968 in the US. Its cover, a photograph of John and Yoko totally naked, was declared obscene in several jurisdictions. In January 1969, this issue led to the opening of a file at the FBI.

We also added pictures and photographs to illustrate these files and make them all the more enjoyable to read through.

At the end of this book, you'll find a glossary of the many far left movements and activists mentioned on the files, as well as the explanation of the codes given by the FBI to justify why some information is still kept secret.

*And there's some little jerk in the FBI
A keepin' papers on me six feet high
It gets me down, it gets me down, it gets me down*

Song "Fingerprint File"
(The Rolling Stones)

FEDERAL BUREAU OF INVESTIGATION
FREEDOM OF INFORMATION/PRIVACY ACTS RELEASE

SUBJECT: JOHN LENNON

69, pornographic year ?

> "So I refuse to be leader, and I'll always show my genitals or do something which prevents me from being Martin Luther King or Gandhi and getting killed."
>
> John Lennon
> in *Melody Maker*, December 13, 1969

The first time the FBI investigated about John Lennon was after the release of the LP "Two Virgins", whose cover shows a nude photograph of John and Yoko holding hands. This album came out in November 1968 in the US and its cover provoked an outrage and was declared obscene in several jurisdictions. Even Apple, the own Beatles record company, had problems putting the LP out. Their albums were distributed by EMI and Capitol Records and these companies didn't want to get involved with anything regarding "Two Virgins" and its nude photographs. George Harrison recalls : "It was an Apple album, but Apple was distributed by EMI and they refused to handle it, so it was put out by Tetragrammaton in the USA."

In January 1969, this highly controversial cover led to the opening of a John Lennon file at the FBI. The first of several more to come...

It is surprising that this file begins with a teletype about a possible demonstration by students of the University of Hartford in Connecticut to protest against the suspension of the campus newspaper after it published the nude photograph used as cover for "Two Virgins". Was this really a possible threat to National Security... ?

A congressman received a letter complaining about the possible damages to the youth that could be caused by the controversial cover (showing "John Lennon of the Beatles" and "his latest flame Yoka One" (sic)) and the FBI was put on the case. Only to conclude that *"no violation with regard to obscenity exists concerning this photograph as it does not meet the criteria of obscenity from a legal standpoint"*.

This did not prevent reports tackling the issue of the relation between crime and pornography to be added to the Lennon file later that year...

The already controversial nature of the nude photograph of the front cover of the LP "Two Virgins" was emphasized by the note written by Paul McCartney : "When two great Saints meet it is a humbling experience. The long battles to prove he was a Saint."

This LP was autographed by John Lennon.

This is the back cover photograph of the LP

The LP was sold in a brown paper bag to avoid more controversy

FEDERAL BUREAU OF INVESTIGATION
U.S. DEPARTMENT OF JUSTICE
COMMUNICATION SECTION
JAN 9 1969

TELETYPE

FBI WASH DC

FBI NEW HAVEN

1006AM URGNET 1/9/69 LAL

TO DIRECTOR

FROM NEW HAVEN (100-NEW)

DEMONSTRATION; UNIVERSITY OF HARTFORD, HARTFORD, CONN., JANUARY NINE, SIXTYNINE.

SECURITY OFFICE, UNIVERSITY OF HARTFORD, HARTFORD, CONN., ADVIS INSTANT DATE STUDENTS ARE PLANNING MARCH DEMONSTRATION PROTESTING THE SUSPENSION OF THE "UNIVERSITY OF HARTFORD NEWS-LIBERATED PRESS" STUDENT PUBLICATION FOR ITS PRINTING WEDNESDAY, JANUARY EIGHT LAST, OF NUDE PHOTOGRAPHS OF BEATLE JOHN LENNON AND GIRLFRIEND YOKO ONO.

LHM FOLLOWS.

END

CKG

FBI WASH DC

X

(Rev. 5-22-64)

FBI

Date: 1/11/69

Transmit the following in _____
(Type in plaintext or code)

Via __A I R T E L__
(Priority)

TO: DIRECTOR, FBI

FROM: SAC, NEW HAVEN (100-19899) (C)

SUBJECT: DEMONSTRATION
           UNIVERSITY OF HARTFORD
           HARTFORD, CONNECTICUT
           JANUARY 9, 1969
           STAG

Re NH teletypes, 1/9/69.

Enclosed for the Bureau are 10 copies of an LHM in captioned matter.

Information was furnished to the following agencies: USA, Hartford, Conn.; 108th MI Group, Hartford, Conn.; Secret Service, New Haven, Connecticut.

AGENCY: ACSI, ONI, OSI, STATE
SEC. SER.; RAO (ISD, CD, CRD, IDIU)
DATE FORWARD: 1-15-68
HOW FORWARD: R/S
BY:

ENCLOSURE

REC-39 62-112228-32-5

17 JAN 14 1969

3 - Bureau (Encs. 10)
1 - New Haven
JAD/jbm
(4)

INT. SEC.

C. C. - Bishop

Approved: _____ Sent _____ M Per _____
         Special Agent in Charge

56 JAN 27 1969

93

UNITED STATES DEPARTMENT OF JUSTICE
FEDERAL BUREAU OF INVESTIGATION

New Haven, Connecticut

In Reply, Please Refer to
File No. NH 100-19899

January 11, 1969

DEMONSTRATION
UNIVERSITY OF HARTFORD
HARTFORD, CONNECTICUT
January 9, 1969

b7C

███████████████████████████ University of Hartford, 200 Bloomfield Avenue, Hartford, Connecticut, advised on January 9, 1969, that a group of students were planning a march from the university campus center to the administration building on January 9, 1969.

The march was to demonstrate the protest of the students over the suspension of the campus newspaper, "The UH News, Liberated Press." The press was suspended by Dean of Student Relations, EUGENE T. SWEENEY, on Wednesday, January 8, 1969, after publication of nude photographs, front and back, of Beatle JOHN LENNON holding hands with his girlfriend YOKO ONO.

b7C ███████ advised no march took place but a standing room only rally concerning the issue was held in the campus center on January 9, 1969. Present at this rally were about 200 students and five faculty members. Both the students and faculty asked and answered questions concerning the suspension and other matters which they felt should be aired at this time.

The faculty felt that guidelines should be drawn for journalistic good taste, but the students refused to agree to this. When the authorities stated that no more money was to be allocated for the publication of the paper, the students stated they had been given $2,000 previously from student government funds and additional papers would be printed.

A suggestion was made for a poll to be taken of students, faculty, and alumni concerning the paper, but the faculty did not agree with this.

ALL INFORMATION CONTAINED
HEREIN IS UNCLASSIFIED
DATE 4-8-83 BY 1678 RFP/esm

62-112228-32-5

ENCLOSURE

DEMONSTRATION
UNIVERSITY OF HARTFORD
HARTFORD, CONNECTICUT
January 9, 1969

It was decided before the end of the meeting that there would be no march or further demonstration.

PROPERTY OF THE FBI
This document contains neither recommendations nor conclusions of the FBI. It is the property of the FBI and is loaned to your agency: it and its contents are not to be distributed outside your agency.

Congress of the United States
House of Representatives
Washington, D.C.

March 5, 1969

Congressional Liaison
F.B.I.

Sir:

The attached communication is sent for your consideration. Please investigate the statements contained therein and forward me the necessary information for reply, returning the enclosed correspondence with your answer.

Yours truly,

Ancher Nelsen
M. C.

Congressman Ancher Nelsen
2329 Rayburn HOB
Washington, D.C.

Attn: Miss Olsen

RADIO ON THE GO

CLEAR CHANNEL
1050 KLOH-AM RADIO
98.7 KKLP-FM
STUDIOS IN PIPESTONE & LUVERNE, MINN.

JANUARY 31, 1969

CONGRESSMAN ANCHER NELSON

DEAR ANCHER:

YESTERDAY I RECEIVED AN ALBUM AT OUR KLOH STUDIOS WHICH CAME TO ME BECAUSE I AM IN CHARGE OF _____.

IT IS THE LATEST ALBUM OF JOHN LENNON OF THE BEATLES AND HIS LATEST FLAME YOKO ONO. THE COVER OF THE ALBUM WAS A PHOTOGRAPH OF LENNON AND ONO COMPLETELY NUDE; AND BELIEVE ME THEY DIDN'T HIDE A THING. IT IS NOW BEING SOLD TO OUR YOUNG PEOPLE ON THE RECORD STANDS. MR. NELSON, IT IS THE MOST DISCOLORED AND VULGAR DISPLAY OF GARBAGE I HAVE EVER SEEN IN MY LIFE.

ISN'T THERE SOME WAY WE CAN GET THIS ALBUM OFF THE MARKET?? IT HAS TO BE SENT IN THE MAIL TO THE STORES WHICH IN TURN SELL IT TO THE KIDS. IT DOES HAVE AN ENVELOPE OVER THE PICTURE WHEN BOUGHT IN THE STORES, SO IT IS ALSO FRAUGULENT ADVERTISING. MOST OF THE STORE MANAGERS DO NOT KNOW THIS PICTURE IS ON THE COVER BECAUSE OF THE ENVELOPE. I AM AT THIS TIME TRYING TO GET AHOLD OF ALL OF THE LOCAL MERCHANTS CARRYING THIS ALBUM AND FILLING THEM IN ON WHAT IS REALLY ON THIS ALBUM.

...YOU ASK WHY THE YOUTH OF TODAY ARE LIKE THEY ARE....THIS IS ONE OF THE PRIME REASONS. ANCHER, I SAY TO YOU, THIS HAS TO STOP..... AND I MEAN NOW!! PLEASE WRITE ME AS SOON AS YOU RECEIVE THIS LETTER AND TELL ME WHAT WE CAN DO TO GET THIS TRASH OFF OUR YOUTH MARKET.

RESPECTFULLY YOURS,

1050
AMPLITUDE
MODULATION

KLOH

98.7
FREQUENCY
MODULATION

PIPESTONE

March 10, 1969

1 - Mr. McKinnon

Honorable Ancher Nelsen
House of Representatives
Washington, D. C. 20515

My dear Congressman:

I have received your communication dated March 5, 1969, along with its enclosure, a letter to you dated January 31, 1969, from ████████.

A representative of the Department of Justice has advised that he is familiar with the photograph contained on the cover of an album by John Lennon. He stated that no violation with regard to obscenity exists concerning this photograph as it does not meet the criteria of obscenity from a legal standpoint.

Your bringing this to my attention is indeed appreciated. I am returning ████████ letter to you as requested.

Sincerely yours,

J. Edgar Hoover

Enclosure

1 - SAC, Minneapolis - Enclosure

NOTE TO SAC, MINNEAPOLIS:
Enclosed is a copy of a letter dated 1-31-69, from ████████ to Congressman Ancher Nelsen for your information.

SEE NOTE PAGE TWO

CRM:erg
(5)

NOTE:

By communication 3/5/69, Congressman Ancher Nelsen (Rep. - Minnesota) forwarded a letter sent to him from ☐ ☐. ☐ stated he is an employee of a radio station, the studio having stations in Pipestone and Luverne, Minnesota. ☐ stated the latest album of John Lennon of the Beatles contains a cover of Lennon and "his latest flame" Yoka One which depicts both completely nude.

Attorney Robert Mahony has previously reviewed the photograph contained on this record album and advised that it does not meet the criteria of obscenity from a legal standpoint. This is being confirmed in writing. We have had limited but cordial relations with Congressman Nelsen.

- 2 -

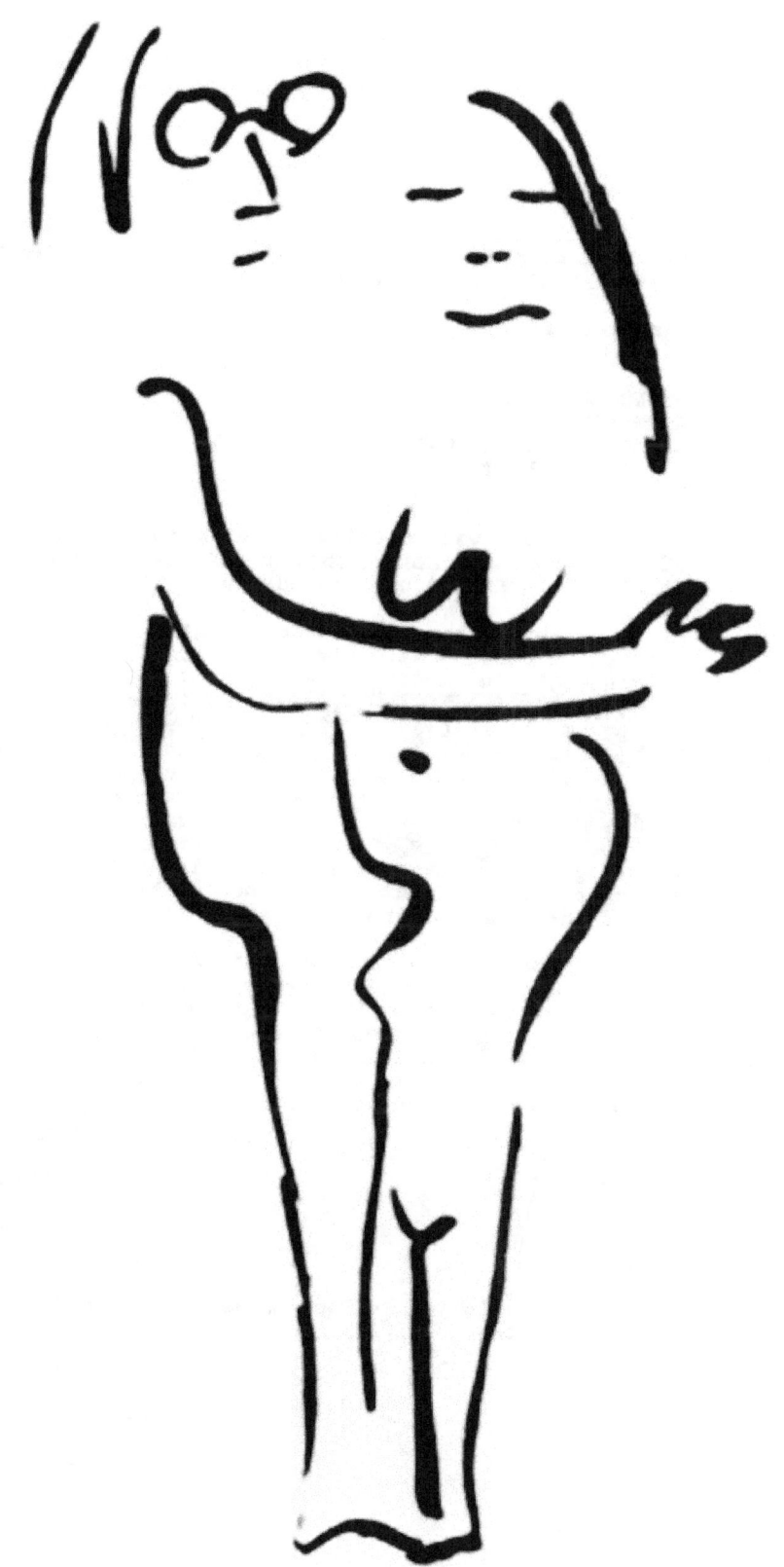

A drawing by John Lennon

Mr. Will R. Wilson
Assistant Attorney General

March 11, 1969

Director, FBI

1 - Mr. McKinnon

PHONOGRAPHIC ALBUM BY
JOHN LENNON
INTERSTATE TRANSPORTATION
OF OBSCENE MATTER

This will confirm conversation on March 7, 1969, between Mr. Robert Mahony and Special Agent Charles R. McKinnon of this Bureau.

Mr. Mahony was advised that this Bureau has received a communication from Congressman Ancher Nelsen of Minnesota forwarding a letter sent to him from ████████ identified himself in his letter as an employee of ████████ which has ████████ in ████████ Minnesota. ████████ because of his employment, has observed the cover of a phonographic album by John Lennon. This album, according to ████████ contains a nude photograph of Lennon and Yoka One. ████████ is concerned with the effect such a photograph may have on the youth in this country and requested to know what can be done to keep this photograph out of the hands of the American public.

Mr. Mahony advised he is familiar with the phonographic album by John Lennon, which cover contains the nude photograph of Lennon and Yoka One. He advised that the photograph does not meet the existing criteria of obscenity from a legal standpoint and is not a violation of the Interstate Transportation of Obscene Matter Statute. Congressman Nelsen was so advised.

CRM:emf
(4)

NOTE:

See letter to Congressman Ancher Nelsen dated 3/10/69.

These two versions of the same FBI document show the differences that can be found regarding which information is kept hidden and which is released to the public

Mr. Will R. Wilson March 11, 1969
Assistant Attorney General

Director, FBI   1 - ☐   b6
                                                                  b7C

PHONOGRAPHIC ALBUM BY
JOHN LENNON
INTERSTATE TRANSPORTATION
OF OBSCENE MATTER

      This will confirm conversation on March 7,   b6
1969, between Mr. Robert Mahony and Special Agent   b7C
☐ of this Bureau.

      Mr. Mahony was advised that this Bureau has received a communication from Congressman Ancher Nelsen of Minnesota forwarding a letter sent to him from ☐. ☐ identified himself in his letter as an employee of radio station KLOH which has studios in Pipestone and Luverne, Minnesota. ☐, because of his employment, has observed the cover of a phonographic album by John Lennon. This album, according to ☐, contains a nude photograph of Lennon and Yoka One. ☐ is concerned with the effect such a photograph may have on the youth in this country and requested to know what can be done to keep this photograph out of the hands of the American public.

      Mr. Mahony advised he is familiar with the phonographic album by John Lennon, which cover contains the nude photograph of Lennon and Yoka One. He advised that the photograph does not meet the existing criteria of obscenity from a legal standpoint and is not a violation of the Interstate Transportation of Obscene Matter Statute. Congressman Nelsen was so advised.

CRM:emf
(4)

NOTE:

See letter to Congressman Ancher Nelsen dated 3/10/69.

UNITED STATES GOVERNMENT

Memorandum

TO : Mr. Bishop DATE: 3-20-69

FROM : M. A. Jones

SUBJECT: CONGRESSMAN CHARLES E. BENNETT (D - FLORIDA)
REQUEST FOR INFORMATION REGARDING
PROPOSED LEGISLATION PROHIBITING
THE DISSEMINATION OF OBSCENE MATERIAL
TO MINORS

     By letter dated March 17th, Congressman Bennett sent a copy of H.R. 5171, which is legislation he has introduced to prohibit the dissemination of obscene material to minors. Congressman Bennett pointed out that his bill is patterned after a New York State statute which has been upheld by the Supreme Court. He also sent a copy of two other identical bills, H.R. 6186 and H.R. 7167. In his letter, Congressman Bennett requested "any information you can provide me to back up this bill." By letter of March 18th, Congressman Bennett followed up his previous letter with a request for "evidence," which would show that the rise in crime or the rise of sex crimes is attributable to pornography. He also asked if we can show that a substantial number of criminals have been exposed to pornography. He also asked if we know of any articles or research which would demonstrate a clear need for such a law as he proposes.

     We have had cordial relations with Congressman Bennett over the past several years.

RECOMMENDATION:

     That the Director restrict our assistance in this matter to provide Congressman Bennett with appropriate reprint material, and that attached letter to this effect be sent.

Enclosure

1 - Mr. DeLoach - Enclosure
1 - Mr. Bishop - Enclosure
1 - Mr. Rosen - Enclosure

War is Hoover :
Wanted by the FBI, unwanted in the US

The main issue of the FBI investigations on John Lennon were his links to pacifist and far left activist movements. The Lennons' political activism annoyed the the Nixon administration so much that they wished to kick John and Yoko out of the US by trying to prevent them from getting a proper visa. These documents are most interesting since we learn a lot about the socio-political context of the anti-war movement and also about the different methods commonly used by the FBI to conduct its investigations at that time.

After the brief pornography episode, the FBI notes and reports show that, as early as February 1970, the Bureau already kept a close watch on John Lennon's INS (Immigration and Naturalization Service) petitions and visa applications to enter the US.

But we are also made aware, in a memo, that John Lennon and George Harrison are backing the ISKC, International Society for Krishna Consciousness...

And from a newspaper clipping cut out by a federal agent, we learn that John Lennon, Yoko Ono, Jerry Rubin and David Peel (people whose names will appear more than once in the following documents) have formed the "Rock Liberation Front".

Next thing we know, Lennon is reported to have spoken "in definitive anti-law enforcement tones" during a fund raising rally to release the activist John Sinclair from prison. John Sinclair had founded the White Panther Party (WPP) and was advocating the legalization of marijuana. He was first sentenced to 10 years of prison for possession of 2 joints, but was eventually released soon after this Freedom Rally took place. The informant attending the rally also stated that Lennon "is a strong believer in the movement and the overthrow of the present society in American today (sic)". John Lennon wrote and performed a song for John Sinclair, which lyrics were included in his FBI files, along with the transcription of most speeches held during the evening. This is, indirectly, a great testimony of the atmosphere and rhetoric of the anti-war / pro marijuana / peace movements.

In some other informant report, we find this most important piece of information : "Mike Drobenare is now using his parent's car again."... !

Then there's a memo mentioning that Jerry "Rubin appeared to have his hair cut much shorter than previously shown in other photographs" and that "ALL EXTREMISTS SHOULD BE CONSIDERED DANGEROUS"...

The fact that John Lennon contributed 75,000 dollars to the Allamuchy Tribe, a far-left organization aiming at stopping Nixon from being reelected and advocating peace in Vietnam seems to have been of importance in the problems John and Yoko would pretty soon face regarding their applications for a Green Card. In the FBI files on John Lennon, this clearly marks the beginning of a flow of constant reports and memos on their peace and political activism, showing they were under close surveillance by the US administration and authorities.

There's also a memo reminding us that "All individuals involved in new left extremist activity should be considered dangerous because of their known advocacy and use of explosives, reported acquisition of firearms and incendiary devices, and known propensity for violence." Now we know !

Starting February 1972, references to John & Yoko demands to INS are systematic and information about their political activism is clearly gathered to back up a refusal. The fact that EYSIC (the new name of the Allamuchy tribe) was planning demonstrations for peace and against Nixon at the Republican Convention in August 1972 played a key role in the use of stalling tactics regarding John Lennon's visa clearances, despite the non-violent orientation of these demonstrations : Nixon wanted to be reelected at all costs (which lead to the Watergate scandal) and John Edgar Hoover, the powerful director of the FBI, hated communists/far-left movements/political dissenters. At that time, the FBI was clearly used to serve personal and political views and purposes. John Lennon was one of the victims of these drifts. The scandals would make people become aware of these issues and make things change, although the recent revelations about the NSA global surveillance programs made by former NSA consultant Edward Snowden tend to show that the issue of national security vs. personal rights is not solved yet.

The INS hearings and every information related to John Lennon's deportation case were reported in his FBI files. The Bureau was keeping a close watch on the deportation procedure and it was stated several times that it would pass on to the INS any information that could help build a case against John & Yoko, mostly anything regarding drug use, to prevent them from getting a permanent visa. We also included documents from the CIA and from Lennon's INS file to emphasize the connections between these agencies and the FBI in John Lennon's deportation case.

In 1975, a document indicates that John Lennon's attorney, Leon Wildes, had filed a suit to prosecute several people involved in the deportation case against John & Yoko, claiming it was biased and politically oriented. This proved to be true.

WAR IS HOOVER!
EVEN IF YOU DON'T WANT IT

Refers, of course, to the famous motto "WAR IS OVER ! (if you want it)" that John & Yoko had displayed on huge billboards in London, Paris, Amsterdam, Berlin, Rome, Athens, New York, Los Angeles, Montreal and Toronto in December, 1969 to voice their opposition to the war in Vietnam.

I WAS IN TORONTO last week to do an interview for WABC-FM with John and Yoko Ono Lennon; one of the reasons the Lennons were there, as you probably already know, was to announce their "peace festival."

It seems everyone and his brother is slapping together a rock festival, but this one sounds like it might headline the summer's fare, and include one unique and cozy feature. The entire stage will be in the form of a massive bed, and so this July 3, 4, and 5 the joyful noise of "rock, peace poetry, and whatever" will be coming from between the sheets. Then the Lennons would like to tuck the whole package in and take it on a world tour, especially to Russia and Czechoslovakia.

When I asked him about the Beatles as an entity, John said casually that they might never play again, then added that they feel that way every time they finish an album. On the other hand, he mentioned that it is getting increasingly hard to fit all their songs on one lp, notably since George has begun to write so prolifically. He did seem sure they would never tour again as a group. As for music, John felt they hadn't made any dynamic changes since "Sergeant Pepper," and their music should go further out again. He also denied that the Beatles are leaving the Allan Klein management, and in fact said he liked Klein, not only as a businessman but also as a person.

When asked why he comes to Canada so often, other than problems with his U. S. visa, John answered, "Because it talks to China." Another reason why he was there this time was to sign the 5000 copies of his erotic lithographs. In between writer's cramp and macrobiotic meals (served by two chefs flown in from the Caldron on the Lower East Side), the Lennons planned the next phases of their peace campaign. They just completed their billboard event in Times Square and 10 other major cities, and will present another surprise

Both John and Yoko seem unaffected that war is even more powerful a piggie now, despite all their dove flutter and commotion. "We believe in selling peace...nobody says to give up Christianity because Christ died."

Their latest angle will be a "peace poll." Letters, postcards, or any other voucher from the peace-bent will be sent to a prescribed—as yet to be announced—address. They think that maybe a mountain of this mail can be delivered to one of those masters of war who is impressed by statistics.

RECEIVED BY CODED TELETYPE

NR 045 WA CODE

8:55 PM DEFERRED 2-13-70 JDR

TO DIRECTOR
    LOS ANGELES

FROM WASHINGTON FIELD   1P

PEACE ACTION COUNCIL, IS - C. OFFICE OF ORIGIN: LOS ANGELES.

   RE LOS ANGELES TEL, FEBRUARY FIVE LAST.

[REDACTED], VISA OFFICER, VISA OFFICE, DEPARTMENT OF STATE, DETERMINED ON THIS DATE AN H PETITION (NON IMMIGRANT VISA OF TYPE ISSUED ENTERTAINERS) FILED WITH INS BY JOHN LENNON. THIS PETITION APPROVED; HOWEVER, NO INDICATION LENNON HAS APPLIED FOR VISA TO ENTER UNITED STATES.

END

FMK

FBI LOS ANGELES

☒ REMAINS UNCLASSIFIED

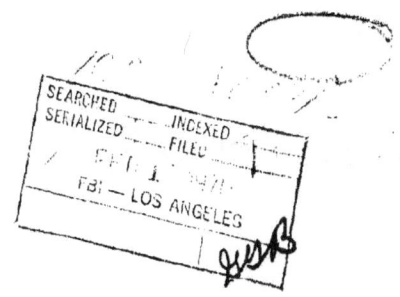

4/23/70

airtel

1 - [redacted] b6 b7C

To: SACs, New York
      Los Angeles

From: Director, FBI

JOHN LENNON [redacted] b6 b7C

INFORMATION CONCERNING

      On 4/22/70 a representative of the Department of State advised that the American Embassy in London had submitted information showing the captioned individuals planned to depart from London, England, on 4/23/70 via TWA Flight 761 which will arrive in Los Angeles at 7:15 local time. These individuals are affiliated with the Beatles musical group and Lennon will be traveling under the name Chambers while [redacted] are using the name [redacted].

      Lennon and [redacted] will remain in Los Angeles until 5/6/70 for business discussions with Capital Records and other enterprises. They will travel to New York City on 5/7/70 for further business discussions and will return to London on or about 5/16/70.

      Waivers were granted by the Immigration and Naturalization Service and the Embassy was to issue visas on 4/22/70. In this case waivers were necessary in view of the ineligibility of these three individuals to enter the U.S. due to their reputations in England as narcotic users.

FBG:kks
(8)

EX-115

REC 44 62-0-75141

SEE NOTE PAGE TWO

APR 24 1970

Tolson
DeLoach
Walters
Mohr
Bishop
Casper
Callahan
Conrad
Felt
Gale
Rosen
Sullivan
Tavel
Soyars
Tele. Room
Holmes
Gandy

MAIL ROOM ☒ TELETYPE UNIT ☐

ALL INFORMATION CONTAINED
HEREIN IS UNCLASSIFIED
DATE 4-8-83 BY 1678 RSP/cmn

This version of the document is easier to read but the name *Harrison* was erased whereas this piece of information is available on the one printed on the next page.

4/23/70

airtel

To: SACs, New York
     Los Angeles

From: Director, FBI

JOHN LENNON
GEORGE HARRISON
PATRICIA HARRISON
INFORMATION CONCERNING

    On 4/22/70 a representative of the Department of State advised that the American Embassy in London had submitted information showing the captioned individuals planned to depart from London, England, on 4/23/70 via TWA Flight 761 which will arrive in Los Angeles at 7:15 local time. These individuals are affiliated with the Beatles musical group and Lennon will be traveling under the name Chambers while the Harrisons are using the name Masters.

    Lennon and the Harrisons will remain in Los Angeles until 5/6/70 for business discussions with Capital Records and other enterprises. They will travel to New York City on 5/7/70 for further business discussions and will return to London on or about 5/16/70.

    Waivers were granted by the Immigration and Naturalization Service and the Embassy was to issue visas on 4/22/70. In this case waivers were necessary in view of the ineligibility of these three individuals to enter the U.S. due to their reputations in England as narcotic users.

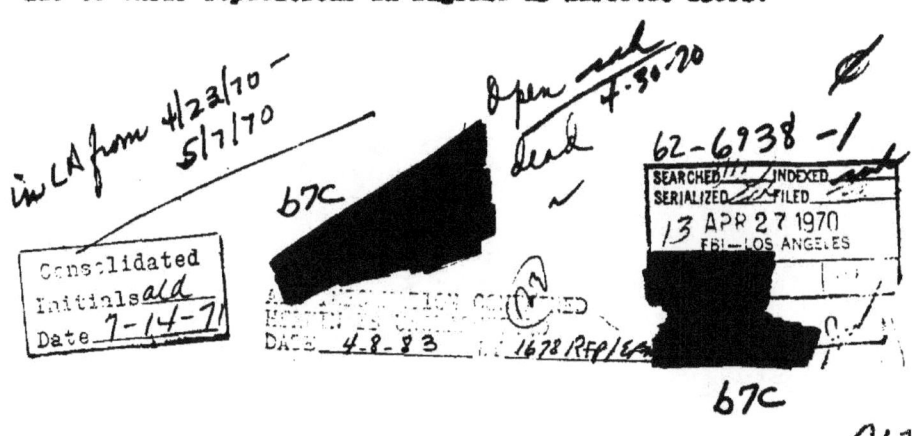

Airtel to New York
Re: John Lennon, [redacted]   b6 b7C

    While Lennon and [redacted] have shown no propensity to become involved in violent antiwar demonstrations, each recipient remain alert for any information of such activity on their part or for information indicating they are using narcotics. Submit any pertinent information obtained in form suitable for dissemination.   b6 b7C

NOTE:

    The above information was made available by [redacted] (former SA), Visa Security Office, United States Department of State.   b6 b7C

Second pages of the documents compared on the previous double page

Airtel to New York
Re: John Lennon, George Harrison, Patricia Harrison

     While Lennon and the Harrisons have shown no propensity to become involved in violent antiwar demonstrations, each recipient remain alert for any information of such activity on their part or for information indicating they are using narcotics. Submit any pertinent information obtained in form suitable for dissemination.

FD-36 (Rev. 5-22-64)

FBI

Date: 4-24-70

Transmit the following in _____
(Type in plaintext or code)

Via Airtel   VIA COURIER
_____
(Priority)

To: Director, FBI

From: Legat, Ottawa (105-0-3188)

Subject: PEACE STATION NETWORK
IS - MISCELLANEOUS
(NEW LEFT - FOREIGN INFLUENCE - CANADA)

Enclosed for the information of the Bureau are the original and two copies of RCMP letter dated 4-21-70 together with two copies of the two enclosures thereto.

There is no prior record of the captioned subject in the files of the Ottawa Office or of any of the individuals mentioned in the enclosed RCMP letter.

Note paragraph four of RCMP letter.

4 - Bureau (Enc. 7)
1 cc - Liaison Direct
1 cc - Baltimore
1 - OTT
MLI:jhc
(5)

Copy to _____ by routing slip for
☒ Info ☐ action
date 5/5/70
by _____

54 MAY 19 1970
Approved: _____
Special Agent in Charge   Sent _____

ALL CORRESPONDENCE TO
BE ADDRESSED:
COMMISSIONER
ROYAL CANADIAN MOUNTED POLICE
OTTAWA 7, CANADA

TOUTE CORRESPONDANCE DOIT
ÊTRE ADRESSÉE COMME SUIT:
LE COMMISSAIRE
GENDARMERIE ROYALE DU CANADA
OTTAWA 7, CANADA

HEADQUARTERS — DIRECTION GÉNÉRALE

YOUR NO.
VOTRE N°

OUR NO.   (b7D)
NOTRE N°

OTTAWA 7, CANADA

April 21, 1970.

CONFIDENTIAL

Mr. Moss Lee Innes,
c/o U.S. Embassy,
Ottawa, Ontario.

Dear Sir:

    Attached is a copy of a letter dated March 18, 1970 which was received from Mr. Edward MARZOA of Radio Station WJWL in Georgetown, Delaware and a copy of our reply to Mr. MARZOA dated April 21, 1970.

2.   According to the February 20, 1970 edition of the Telegram (Toronto daily newspaper), Mr. Ritchie YORKE of Toronto, Ontario was endeavouring to set up a "Peace Network", being a loose organization of radio stations aimed at promoting the July 3/5, 1970 Mosport Peace Festival at Mosport, Ontario.   (b7D)

3.   The Mosport Peace Festival was initiated by John LENNON (of Beatle fame) and his wife, while visiting Canada during December 1969. To facilitate the "peace festival", which in fact would be a youth orientated rock festival, Ritchie YORKE and John BROWER both of Toronto, Ontario, were engaged as advertising and expediting co-ordinators for promotion of the "festival". The Mosport location for the "festival" was recently vetoed by the Ontario Municipal Board and at the present time it is not certain whether the "festival" will proceed at some other location.

4.   Should Mr. MARZOA contact your Agency, you may verbally pass the information contained in paragraphs 2 and 3 to him.

Yours truly,

(J.E.M. Barrette),
Assistant Commissioner,
Director,
Security and Intelligence.

62-0-75191

ENCLOSURE

The deletions on this document were made at the request of the Canadian Security Intelligence Service.

ALL CORRESPONDENCE TO BE ADDRESSED:
THE COMMISSIONER
ROYAL CANADIAN MOUNTED POLICE
OTTAWA 7, CANADA

TOUTE CORRESPONDANCE DOIT ÊTRE ADRESSÉE COMME SUIT:
LE COMMISSAIRE
GENDARMERIE ROYALE DU CANADA
OTTAWA 7, CANADA

HEADQUARTERS – DIRECTION GÉNÉRALE

OTTAWA 7, CANADA

YOUR NO. / VOTRE N° _____

OUR NO. / NOTRE N° _____

April 21, 1970.

Mr. Edward Marzoa,
Radio Station WJWL,
Georgetown, Delaware.

Dear Sir:

    This will acknowledge receipt of your letter dated March 18, 1970 concerning the lobbying of a youth delegation under the auspices of "Peace Station Network" of 120 Avenue Road, Toronto 5, Ontario for the purpose of having WJWL broadcast 5-minute "peace" programs.

    We regret that we are unable to supply you with the information which you requested, as government policy requires us to liase with the Federal Bureau of Investigation in matters related to enquiries of this nature. We therefore suggest you redirect your enquiry to the Federal Bureau of Investigation.

Yours truly,

(S.V.M. Chisholm) Supt.

62-0-75191

ENCLOSURE

March 18, 1970

Royal Canadian Mounted Police
Montreal, Canada

Gentlemen:

WJWL has been approached by the Peace Station Network of 120 Avenue Road, Toronto 5, Ontario, Canada, to participate in a network of stations broadcasting 5-minute "peace" programs.

On a telephone listener opinion program on WJWL, I read the proposal, then solicited listener response to the question of whether WJWL should or should not air the "peace" programs.

The response was overwhelmingly against such programming. I advised the Peace Station Network to remove WJWL and our FM affiliate, WSPA from their mailing lists.

I was subsequently approached by a youth delegation with petition in hand claiming the station was unfair in refusal of time. We were abrogating the constitutionally guarantee of freedom of expression. I tried to explain that this was a Canadian organization, with no claim to any U.S. rights. Not satisfied, they claimed it was "their right to hear" that I was infringing on. Well, to head off any prolonged debate, I agreed to listen to a tape from the Peace Station Network people if they would procure one. After so reviewing same, we would make a final judgement.

The purpose of this letter is not to solicit any program recommendation from your organization. It is rather, to ascertain if the Royal Canadian Mounted Police has any information which may shed some light on the Peace Station Network. I would like to know who the officers are; what their purposes are; how they are financed; and why the Canadian base. I have my suspicions.

The decision of course is mine. I would appreciate however, something more concrete than my intuition to support whatever that decision may be.

I would appreciate an early response.

Sincerely,
WJWL

Edward Marzoa
Manager

EM/mtf

ENCLOSURE

The deletions on this document were made at the request of the Canadian Security Intelligence Service.

UNITED STATES GOVERNMENT

Memorandum

TO : DIRECTOR, FBI
ATTN: LIAISON SECTION

DATE: 8/4/70

FROM : SAC, LOS ANGELES (163-1854) (RUC)

SUBJECT: ██████████ aka
FPC ██████████

OO: Bureau

Re Bureau airtel to Los Angeles dated 7/30/70, and Los Angeles teletype to the Bureau dated 8/3/70.

Enclosed for the Bureau are six copies of a LHM dated and captioned as above.

All investigation in this matter was conducted by SA ██████████ unless otherwise indicated.

SA ██████████ contacted ██████████ (source), and ██████████

First source is ██████████. Due to nature of information furnished by this source, it is not being classified. Second source is ██████████ who was contacted by SA ██████████. Third source is ██████████ who was contacted by SA ██████████. Fourth source is ██████████ who was also contacted by SA ██████████.

All sources furnishing information had no objections to the information they furnished being disseminated to a foreign government.

Information furnished by second source advised that International Society for Krishna Consciousness (ISKC) was backed by GEORGE HARRISON and JOHN LENNON, not further identified. It appears these individuals are members of the Beatles singing group who reside in England.

No further investigation is being conducted by Los Angeles in this matter.

2 - Bureau (Encls. 6) (AM - REGISTERED)
1 - Los Angeles
(4) kaf

OFFICE COPY
Buy U.S. Savings Bonds Regularly on the Payroll Savings Plan

b7C Also Known As   O/S

"Sum and substance of Krishna is chanting name of Supreme Being". Romance and conventional courting is frowned upon. The spirit master in each city chooses mates for members. Members of ISKC do not partake in drugs, intoxicants, meat, fish, eggs, gambling or illicit sex life. Their chants are kept track of on a string of 108 beads which they repeat 16 times daily. Funds are obtained by ISKC members by begging and selling incense.

On August 3, 1970, a second source, who has furnished reliable information in the past, furnished the following information:

The Branch Manager of ISKC is Gregory Scharf who employs 75 people in Los Angeles, California. Headquarters of ISKC is 3840 North Beacon Street, Boston, Massachusetts. ISKC is backed by George Harrison and John Lennon (not further described). Assets of ISKC in Los Angeles are $250,000, and this group is described as a "meditation group".

Files of the Los Angeles Office of the FBI disclosed no information regarding Gregory Scharf.   O/S

On August 3, 1970, a third source, who has furnished reliable information in the past, furnished the following information:

The Beach Boys is a popular musical and recording group similar to the Beatles. The Beach Boys formerly enjoyed tremendous financial success, but current popularity has diminished. The Beatles and Beach Boys were interested in the philosophy of India and support the same spiritual leader, Maharishi Mahesh Yogi.

On August 3, 1970, a fourth source, who has furnished reliable information in the past, furnished the following information:

- 8 -

The end of this document is missing in the FBI files, but no reason is given. So it seems it has been lost.

UNITED STATES GOVERNMENT

Memorandum

TO : SAC, DETROIT (100- ~~CONFIDENTIAL~~ DATE: 10/5/70

FROM : SA ████████

SUBJECT: WPP - MISCELLANEOUS

FOIA/PA

DO NOT DESTROY SERIAL 323
PRIOR TO 4/86

ADMINISTRATIVE

Source is ████████

On 9/28/70, source made available an address book which she indicated belonged to ████████ who she believes is affiliated in some way with the White Panther Party. She does not know his connection with the Party but advised she felt the address book might be of some benefit. The following names, addresses, telephone numbers etc. were copied from this book. The book was returned to the source. Address book contained the following:

A.B.C. Managers Ltd.
5724 Gerrad St. East
Toronto, Ontario
416-466-53██
██-1655

GUY
644 Pitt St.
Los Angeles, Calif.
(also associated with A.B.C. Managers Ltd listed above)

Alternate U
14th St. and 5th Ave.
New York

RCP/rak
(2)

~~CONFIDENTIAL~~

100-36217-323

OCT 7 1970
DETROIT

DE 100-

YOKO & JOHN LENNON
c/o Apple Records
London, England
01-734-8232

John Aloysius Lennon 100-0-1450-2

CONFIDENTIAL

b7C
b7D

see rap slip

no subversive ref.
middle names omitted

CONFIDENTIAL

Dylan and Weberman: A Letter

WE ASK A. J. Weberman to publicly apologize to Bob Dylan for leading a public campaign of lies and malicious slander against Dylan in the past year. It is about time someone came to Dylan's defense when A. J. published articles and went on radio calling Dylan a junkie—which he never was—attacked Dylan for "deserting the movement"—when he was there before the movement and helped create it—and publicized Dylan's address and phone—exposing Bob and his wife and children to public embarrassment and abuse.

Dylan is more than a myth—he is a human being, like you and me. He has feelings and sensitivities like you and me. Who is there among us who has not had his consciousness shaped by the words and music of Bob Dylan? Yet who raised his or her voice or uttered a word to defend Dylan when A. J. Weberman began his personal campaign of slander against Dylan—in the true tradition of the sensationalistic press willing to print anything about someone famous—even organizing demonstrations at Dylan's home—for god's sake:—can't Dylan have some privacy! Can't he have some peace of mind in his own home to think and write and make music and be with his family?

Weberman took advantage of Dylan's fame. If Bob Dylan attacked A. J. Weberman, who would listen or publish it? If A. J. Weberman has some "inside gossip" or "the real truth" about Bob Dylan, everyone is all ears because everyone wants to talk about Bob Dylan. Stories spread from person to person in an ever-widening circle of exaggeration and bullshit. No one cares to find out the truth about Bob Dylan, the person. They are too busy amusing themselves by telling outlandish stories about Bob Dylan—the myth—whom they have never met.

Weberman tried to make a name for himself by attacking Dylan and proclaiming himself a Dylanologist or something like that. No one else named Weberman an expert on Dylan. Weberman calls himself an expert, and all of a sudden the press is all over him trying to get information or gossip about Dylan. Now whenever someone writes about Bob Dylan, they also interview A. J. because he is a self-proclaimed authority on Dylan's music. A. J. claims everything Dylan writes is either about Weberman or about heroin. What bullshit!

Weberman is to Dylan as Manson is to the Beatles—and Weberman uses what he interprets from Dylan's music to try and kill Dylan and build his own fame. Now A. J. Weberman takes credit for Dylan's "George Jackson" song. More egocentric bullshit. Dylan wrote it in spite of Weberman and in spite of "the movement." Dylan wrote it because he felt it.

A. J. Weberman's campaign—and the movement's complicity in it—is in the current fad of everyone in the revolution attacking each other and spreading false rumors about each other. It's time we defended and loved each other—and saved our anger for the true enemy, whose ignorance and greed destroys our planet.

—The Rock Liberation Front:
David Peel, Jerry Rubin,
Yoko Ono, John Lennon

Rock Demonstration

The Rock Liberation Front will demonstrate on Friday, December 3, from 1.30 to 3.30 p.m. against Capitol Records at their offices at 1370 Sixth Avenue (at 56th Sreet) to protest Capitol's refusal to press the Madison Square Garden Bangla Desh benefit concert at cost, so that all profits from the disc can go directly to Pakistani refugees in India. Another purpose of the demonstration is to stop Capitol from suing and/or getting an injunction against any other record company that agrees to press it at cost. For information call 477-6243.

Lennon let his followers down

By BILL GRAY
Amusement Writer

If anyone went to the John Sinclair rally Friday night in Ann Arbor for the sole purpose of seeing a rare John Lennon performance, he had to go away disappointed.

Lennon was the drawing card that brought many, if not most, of the 15,000 young people to Crisler Arena.

But almost eight hours of speeches by radical leaders, poetry by Allen Ginsberg, country rock by Commander Cody and rhythm and blues by Stevie Wonder preceded the former Beatle's appearance.

WHEN HE DID, it was brief and one major factor nearly spoiled the whole thing.

He brought Yoko.

Mrs. Lennon may be the genius that John keeps insisting she is. Possibly, if he keeps heavily hyping her, someone might believe it.

But before a singer can be judged, she must first be able to carry a tune. Yoko can't even remain on key.

This was evidenced clearly when she sang "O Sisters, O Sisters," A Women's Lib tune she claimed she wrote for the "Sisters of Ann Arbor" the day before the rally.

STANDING beside her, Lennon managed not to wince. He even kissed her when it was over.

Lennon's portion of the show was hardly worth the wait — three songs, all of which were unfamiliar to the crowd.

They were so new that Lennon had to read the lyrics from a music stand as he sang.

His tribute to Sinclair, which began, "John Sinclair, in the stir for breathing air," was played on steel guitar.

BECAUSE of the name attached to it, the song probably will become a million seller and should make Detroit Recorder's Court Judge Robert J. Colombo an antihero in the subculture. "He gave him (Sinclair) 10 (years) for two (marijuana cigarets), what else can Judge Colombo do?")

It was an interesting piece, but lacking Lennon's usual standards.

Lennon and Yoko were dressed in matching black leather jackets, unzipped to reveal "Free John Now" T-shirts. Lennon wore small circular sunglasses. He was flippant and tried to give the crowd the impression that they weren't watching a superstar, but simply the working-class hero.

PRECEDING the Lennons were David Peel and the Lower East Side, positively the worst act I've ever seen. The greasy-looking Peel sang like a deranged gorilla. The lyrics of one song consisted solely of repeating "marawanna" about 50 times.

The best rock 'n' roll of the evening was provided by some local artists. Bob Seger (formerly with the System) and Teegarden and VanWinkle combined for the evening's musical highlight.

Seger's "Looking Back" may be only a four-chord progression piece, but it's well-performed, and the lyrics should go down as the subculture's national anthem.

10a
The Detroit News
Detroit, Michigan

Date: December 13, 19
Edition:
Author: Bill Gray
Editor: Martin Hayden
Title:

Character:
or
Classification:
Submitting Office

☐ Being Investigated

Copy Sent Bureau

THE ABBIE HOFFMAN-Isaac Haber "Steal This Book" controversy has died down somewhat with Abbie's quiet departure from the scene, but nothing really has been resolved. So interest will probably be high and bidding hot when the original manuscript plus all correspondences (in Abbie's handwriting) are auctioned off this Saturday, December 18, at 4.30 in St. Peter's Church at 484 Broome Street. The book and notes are being sold with the stipulation that they must be temporarily returned when needed in any future court dispute. Will Abbie and Isaac's lawyers show up to bid against each other?

The auction is a benefit for Sun/Dance, a news magazine scheduled to debut around the first of the year. Along with the original manuscripts from books, songs, and poems, paintings, photographs, prints, and sculptures are being donated. Guest auctioneers are Jerry Rubin, Patty Oldenburg and Rip Torn, and the familiar coterie of SoHo superstars make up the list of artist-auctionees: Carl Andre, Gregory Corso, Charles Henri Ford, Allen Ginsberg, Jasper Johns, John Lennon, Gordon Matta, Robert Rauschenberg, Larry Rivers, Anne Waldman, and Andy Warhol.

THE Village Voice (NYC weekly newspaper)
12/16/71
p. 92

(From the column "Scenes" by Howard Smith)

DO NOT DESTROY - PENDING LITIGATION

FBI

Date: 12/20/71

Transmit the following in _____
(Type in plaintext or code)

Via __AIRTEL__
(Priority)

TO: DIRECTOR, FBI
FROM: SAC, DETROIT
SUBJECT: WHITE PANTHER PARTY
IS - WPP
OO: DETROIT
DEFILE 100-36217

SM - WPP (EXTREMIST)
OO: DETROIT
DEFILE 100-33198

SM - WPP (EXTREMIST)
OO: DETROIT
DEFILE 100-36335

As the Bureau is aware, ▓▓▓▓ the White Panther Party (WPP) and has continued as ▓▓▓▓ of that group since its origin despite the fact he has been incarcerated ▓▓▓▓ since 1969. His imprisonment ▓▓▓▓ has been developed in the past several years as a New Left cause in the Midwest and to some degree nationally. WPP efforts to dramatize ▓▓▓▓ situation and to advocate the liberalization of marijuana laws

4 - Bureau (RM)
2 - Indianapolis (RM)
3 - Detroit
JRC/njn
(9)

Approved: _____ Sent _____ M Per _____
Special Agent in Charge

DE 100-36217

has included many bizarre events including the mail distribution of marijuana joints to all state legislators in Michigan along with State Administration Officers, including the Governor of Michigan, State Police Officers, etc.

███████████████████████████, ██████ of the WPP, in personal papers claimed that prior to several years ago he had gotten several Michigan State Legislators on "pot" and other drugs. This claim to some extent has been corroborated by Detroit through a live informant.

b6
b7C

The above referred to "Free JOHN SINCLAIR" rallies which have been the principal activities of the WPP during the past year culminated in a large rally held at the University of Michigan field house, Ann Arbor, Michigan, 12/10/71 with speakers including a wide range of national and area New Left leaders such as RENNIE DAVIS, JERRY RUBIN, DAVE DELLINGER, WILLIAM KUNTZLER, BOBBY SEALE and Father JAMES GROPPI, representatives of the National Student Association, the National Welfare Rights Organization and a variety of other groups. Various "rock" music groups and performers including former Beatle JOHN LENNON and his wife YOKO ONO appeared.

The substance of this rally with known costs of $4,700 and an audience of 15,000 was the need to free JOHN SINCLAIR, to liberalize marijuana laws and to defeat President RICHARD NIXON in 1972.

Reference was made by one of the "Chicago Conspiracy" subjects above to the need to have JOHN SINCLAIR released so that he could arrange the rock groups for anti-administration demonstrations in 1972.

Another "Chicago Conspiracy" subject said to the effect "We will do to the GOP convention at San Diego what we did to the Democrats in 1968".

DE 100-36217

Specific rally results are being separately reported under the caption "FREEDOM RALLY, UNIVERSITY OF MICHIGAN, ANN ARBOR, MICHIGAN, 12/10/71, SPONSORED BY THE COMMITTEE TO FREE JOHN SINCLAIR, IS - NEW LEFT, WPP".

The committee sponsoring this rally was made up of several national figures such as DAVE DELLINGER, JANE FONDA and included a present and former Michigan State legislator.

JOHN SINCLAIR was released from prison on an appeal bond on order of the Michigan Supreme Court, 12/13/71. The Michigan Supreme Court announced that date they were acting in view of the passage of new Michigan State legislation regarding marijuana which liberalize the penalties for same.

In this connection the Michigan legislation passed legislation reducing marijuana possession penalty from 10 years to a misdemeanor with possible sentence ranging from 90 days to one year depending on circumstances.

As the Bureau is aware [redacted] a white revolutionary organization which has advocated violence to achieve revolutionary ends.

Information copies are furnished Indianapolis in view of the present incarceration of subject [redacted] in that division. Predictably with the WPP, emphasis will commence regarding defense interests for [redacted] who is [redacted] still incarcerated.

- 3 -

The original poster announcing the "John Sinclair Freedom Rally", a concert held in Ann Arbor, Michigan, to support John Sinclair who had been sentenced to 10 years of prison for possession of 2 joints of marijuana. He was released shortly after the event took place.

UNITED STATES GOVERNMENT
Memorandum

TO : SAC, DETROIT DATE: 12/23/71

FROM : SA

SUBJECT:

Dates of Contact
12/14/71

File #s on which contacted (Use Titles if File #s not available or when CI provides positive information)

157-3075 RPP

100-0 JOHN LENNON (Info concerning)
100-36217 WPP (RAINBOW PEOPLE'S PARTY, Ann Arbor Chapter)
100-37957 WPP (RAINBOW PEOPLE'S PARTY, Detroit Chapter)

Purpose and results of contact
☐ NEGATIVE
☒ POSITIVE
☐ STATISTIC

Informant advised that he attended the rally held in Ann Arbor on 12/10/71 to raise funds for the release of JOHN SINCLAIR from prison. Informant drove to Ann Arbor with (name unknown). Upon arriving at Ann Arbor, they met three white males and two white females (names not recalled). The individuals whom they met seemed to know a lot of people and took informant behind the podium to meet BOBBY SEALE, as he was finishing his speech.

SEALE greeted them as "brothers in the movement". Informant advised that SEALE was wearing a very expensive diamond ring and a watch that he estimated as costing at least $1,000.00. When SEALE gave his public speech or met the public, he turned the diamond ring around so that the stones could not be seen. SEALE told the informant and others in the group with him that the RPP is opening three food clinics and that

Has informant shown any indication of emotional instability, unreliability or furnishing false information? No

☒ Informant certified that he has furnished all information obtained by him since last contact.

Coverage
Security

PERSONAL DATA

b2
b7D

"If the pigs interfere with him in any way, he will open free gun clinics and distribute free guns." SEALE elaborated on this point and said "We have access to all the guns we want, and we'll kill any 'pig' that gives us trouble."

Informant noticed that SEALE had several body guards standing immediately behind him while SEALE was talking with informant and others in informant's group behind the podium. All of these body guards were carrying guns and their actions were disciplined such as that used in the military.

Informant was present for the last part of SEALE's public speech when he spoke of the Black Panther factories which produce food and clothing and the Black Panther farms. SEALE also made the following public statement: "You FBI m_____ f_____, we know you're here."

While behind the podium, informant also personally met JOHN LENNON (former member of the Beatles Band). LENNON spoke in definite anti-law enforcement tones and is a strong believer in the movement and the overthrow of the present society in American today.

Informant advised that STEVIE WONDER was present, that he entertained and made a plea for peace. Informant also saw Reverend DENNIS MOLONEY, Reverend JAMES BLAKESLIE (associate of MOLONEY), and JOHN SINCLAIR's wife (who appeared to be "stoned").

- 2 -

John & Yoko performing at the John Sinclair Freedom Rally, on December 10th, 1970

John Lennon performing his song "John Sinclair" on steel guitar

12/27/71

AIRTEL

TO: DIRECTOR, FBI

FROM: SAC, DETROIT (100-40422) (C)

FREEDOM RALLY, UNIVERSITY OF MICHIGAN,
ANN ARBOR, MICHIGAN, 12/10/71,
SPONSORED BY COMMITTEE TO FREE
JOHN SINCLAIR
SM – NEW LEFT; TRAVEL OF DEFENDENTS;
IS – WHITE PANTHER PARTY

Re Detroit teletype to Bureau, 12/11/71.

Enclosed for the Bureau are five (5) copies of a LHM setting forth information regarding captioned rally. Copies of LHM being furnished to below-listed offices for information purposes: (U)

LHM classified confidential to protect the identity of sources utilized therein whose identities if disclosed could be detrimental to the national defense interests of this nation. (U)

Sources identified as follows:

Source one is [redacted]
Source two is Intelligence Unit, Mich. State Police (U)

2 - Bureau (Enc. 5) (RM)
2 - Boston (Enc. 2) (RM)
2 - Chicago (Enc. 2) (RM)
   (1 - 176-5) (1 - 157-3315) (RM)
2 - Milwaukee (157-1785) (Enc. 2) (RM)
2 - New York (100-174910) (Enc. 2) (RM)
2 - San Francisco (176-2) (Enc. 2) (RM)
2 - WFO (1 - 100-[redacted]) (Enc. 2) (RM)
   (1 - NATIONAL STUDENT ASSOCIATION)
5 - Detroit (2 - 100-40422) (1 - 100-40452)
   (1 - 176-219) (1 - 176-68)
JBR:js
(19)

DO NOT DESTROY
PENDING LITIGATION

The following memo is, indirectly, a valuable testimony of the atmosphere and rhetoric of the anti-war / pro marijuana / peace events of these years.

CONFIDENTIAL

Re: Freedom Rally, University of Michigan,
Ann Arbor, Michigan, December 10, 1971,
Sponsored by Committee to Free
John Sinclair

Alan Ginsburg is a New York based poet and philosopher. Jane Kennedy is reportedly a Women's Liberation representative. Tabankin is the President of the National Student Association, Washington, D.C. (C)

Source two advised December 3, 1971, that the WPP has in the past made intense efforts to legalize marijuana and that Sinclair has become the symbol of that effort. (C)

On December 8, 1971, source one advised that during a second press conference by David Sinclair, Lennie Sinclair and David Fenton, all officers of WPP, Ann Arbor, it was announced that the following additional persons were scheduled to speak at the December 10, 1971, Free John Sinclair Rally; Fr. James Groppi, Robert Williams, former head, Republic of New Africa, a Black militant organization, and John Lennon and his wife, Yoko Ono. (C)

Source advised further that several national and international rock bands were scheduled for above rally. (C)

Source advised that attendance cost to the rally was set at $3.00 per person. Source advised that because of an anticipated overflow of persons at the rally hall, which hall seats 15,000 persons, the following allocation of tickets was made: (C)

   6000 - Ann Arbor, Michigan
   4000 - Detroit, Michigan
   1000 - Each Jackson, Flint, Lansing,
          Saginaw and Grand Rapids, Michigan

Source four advised December 11, 1971, that the rally began at 7:15pm, December 10, 1971, at the University of Michigan Events Building, Ann Arbor. Source advised the rally terminated at approximately 3:30am, December 11, 1971, with estimated attendance of 15,000 to 16,000 persons. (C)

- 2 -

CONFIDENTIAL

CONFIDENTIAL

Re: Freedom Rally, University of Michigan,
Ann Arbor, Michigan, December 10, 1971,
Sponsored by Committee to Free
John Sinclair

Source five advised December 13, 1971, rally was attended by an estimated 15,000 persons and terminated in the early morning hours of December 11, 1971, without any incidents. Source advised 10 off-duty Ann Arbor police officers patroled the area near the rally hall. Source advised the services of the off-duty police officers were obtained and paid for at a cost of $150.00 by the WPP at Ann Arbor, Michigan. Source advised police officers patroled only on the outside of the rally hall and were not permitted to enter rally.

Source advised the entire portion of the rally hall was patroled by so-called WPP Rangers, also known as The Psychedelic Rangers.

Source six advised December 13, 1971, University of Michigan facilities for captioned rally were obtained by unknown persons on or about November 30, 1971, at a cost of $4,000.00, which was paid for in cash and in advance. Source advised approximately five well known rock bands and/or singers performed at the rally, including John Lennon and wife Yoko Ono. Lennon formerly with group known as the Beatles. Source advised Lennon prior to rally composed the following song entitled, "John Sinclair", which song Lennon sang at the rally. Source advised this song was composed by Lennon especially for this event:

- 4 - 3

CONFIDENTIAL

~~CONFIDENTIAL~~

Re: Freedom Rally, University of Michigan
Ann Arbor, Michigan, December 10, 1971
Sponsored by Committee to Free
John Sinclair

> It ain't fair, John Sinclair
> ~~In the stir for breathing air~~
> Won't you care, for John Sinclair
> In the stir for breathing air.
> Let him be, let him free
> Let him be like you and me
>
> They gave him 10 for 2
> What more can the judges do
> Gotta, gotta, gotta, gotta, gotta
> Gotta, gotta, set him free.
>
> If he'd been a soldier man
> Shooting gooks in Vietnam
> If he was a flying man
> Dropping dope in old Siam
> He'd be free, they'd let him be,
> Breathing air, like you and me.
>
> They gave him 10 for 2
> What more can Judge Colombo do
> Gotta, gotta, gotta, gotta, gotta
> Gotta, gotta, set him free.
>
> Was he jailed for what he done
> Representing everyone
> Free John Now if we can
> From the clutches of the man
> Let him free, lift the lid
> Bring him to his wife and kids
>
> They gave him 10 for 2
> What more can Colombo, Nixon, Rockefeller, Agnew do
> Gotta, gotta, gotta, gotta, gotta
> Gotta, gotta, set him free.

(C)

On December 13, 1971, source six advised he learned from Lennie Sinclair, Officer WPP, that the Detroit Committee to Free John Sinclair netted a total of $26,000.00 from the rally. (C)

Following are verbatim speeches of William Kuntzler, Rennie Davis, Jerry Rubbin and others as indicated: (C)

- 5 - 4

~~CONFIDENTIAL~~

CONFIDENTIAL

BOB RUDNICK - MC

People have come from various parts of the planet to help get JOHN out. All right, BOBBY SEALE will be here, PHIL OAKS, JERRY RUBIN, SHEILA MURPHY, the UP, ED SANDERS, Commander CODY, RENNIE DAVIS, LENI SINCLAIR, ARCHIE SHEPP (phonetic), Father GROPPI, a special guest and then DAVID PEALE with JOHN LENNON and YOKO ONO.

The lost and found and drug help is in the north west, I think that's over there if you need it. Right now we're gonna have a tape. Ok, this is gonna be an all night long hassle, we gotta keep the aisles clear, the firemen are running around so if possible we're gonna have to keep announcing, just keep the lanes as clear as you can.

WILLIAM KUNSTLER is a little busy with a new case. He's trying to get someone else out of jail and couldn't be here, so to send a message he put it on tape and we're gonna have that in about ten seconds.

WILLIAM KUNSTLER (taped message)

I have tried everything I could to be in Ann Arbor tonight but it is impossible. But I know that so many of JOHN SINCLAIR's friends will be with you that my absence will be more keenly felt by me than by anyone else. Yet I could not let the night go by without at least making this tape, unsatisfactory as it is, to give some concrete form to my devotion to JOHN and the cause which he symbolizes and represents.

JOHN is in jail for two essential reasons; first of all he is a political person who calls into question the validity of the super state which seeks to control all of us and destroys those it cannot readily dominate. Secondly, his harsh sentence dramatizes the absurdity of our marijuana laws which are irrational, unjust and indefensible. Recently, the National Institute of Mental Health submitted to the Congress its hundred and seventy six page report "Marijuana and Health" which comes to the conclusion that quote For the bulk of smokers, marijuana does not seem to be harmful, end quote. Yet it is made a crime in every state with penalties ranging in severity from life to six months in jail. On the other hand, conventional cigarettes can be legally sold as long as they bear a legend on the package that they can cause serious illness or death.

CONFIDENTIAL

CONFIDENTIAL

We will have 20 in the next 8 months and we might have 30 in the next two years. At the same time we are going to have a quantitative increase in every major oppressed community in the country. Got to happen! Its the only way we are going to attack capitalism. To exappropriate from that capitalistic system the goods, the technology, etc. put it down in the poor oppressed communities all of us the people that are oppressed and us too and everybody processing it and giving it away free. Its the only way I know start attacking the monster of capitalism. A monster of charging people money for everything they get, we're saying the music is free, the life is free, the world is free and if it ain't, free, lets start getting our chains off now. The psychology chains and the chains of oppression. Let's get it off now. That's have the chains off of us now, cause if we don't have the chains off of us they are going to annihilate us. They are going to anniliate us by polluting this earth, the capitalists and the facists they are going to do this here. We saying the universe belongs to the people. Mars belongs to the people, and the people belong to the people, all power to the people. Thank you very much. Right on, Power to the people.

JERRY RUBIN
(first part not recorded)

.... also, PUN PLAMONDON is in jail, he is also with the Rainbow Peoples Party, he was the first person to become a fugitive and go underground in this country, and then he was caught and now's he's in jail and we ought to have this rally to free PUN PLAMONDON and to free the 2000 people who are now in jail for smoking dope, most of whom are black, and you see what people are going to feel most across the country, when they hear about this rally. Think of all the prisoners behind bars, how they are going to feel, fed shit food, isolated, treated like animals and if they do anything courageous they lose their good time, and they have to stay in jail longer and longer this rally is going to be the first prison rally all across the country demanding that they lay down the bars and let all the prisoners out. And while letting all the prisoners out, they ought to jail the judges, cause every judge, every judge should spend six months in a jail to see what its like. To see what the feeling is of being locked up, and see whather that makes you feel any more human. This is the first event of the Rock liberation front and its really incredible that JOHN LENNON and YOKO ONO are going to be here, here tonight, and should really think of what the meaning of that is. Cause it's really a commited act by people who are

CONFIDENTIAL

very involved in music, who are identifying to the culture you and I are part of. The family that you and I are part of and for them to come on this stage, and for JOHN to sing his song it ain't fair JOHN SINCLAIR and for JOHN and YOKO to sing a song about the IRA and Attica state. Its really incredible. It shows that right now we can really unite music and revolutionary politics and really build the movement all across the country. (applause). It's like a whole, it's like a whole cultural renaissance, is about to begin and if JOHN and YOKO can come here we really have to go back to high school and colleges and communitites and rebuild the movement to rebuild the revolution because all the people who say the movement and the revolution is over should see what's going on right here, because it doesn't look over to me. But there are, there are a lot of problems, for example the amount of heroin and dope that is smoked in the black and white youth communities is really serious so many young, 15, 16, 17 year old kids who are totally wiped out on downers, cause they have to find some way to get through the prison of high school and college and someway out of the prison of America, instead of building a revolutionary movement the amount of heroin that is floating around our communities, we have to drive the heroin pushers out of our communities and build (pplause). So heroin is poison and you know it gets its source from Southeast Asia, Laos, and then, it's shipped by the CIA back to the U.S. as a poison to poison us so we don't make a revolution, that's why they are pushing all this heroin into us. (applause). Also, there is like a very strange spirit among young people today, a spirit of tremendous mistrust, a spirit of which anybody who takes an action, calls a demonstration, comes forward with something is attacked by someone else, in the movement for being an ego-tripper or media freak or doing something wrong, its a total anti-leadership spirit, so the people are afraid take the initiative or afraid to take actions, not because of what the pig might do, but afraid to take, take action because of what their own brothers and sisters might say about them. Its a very strange thing that people are afraid to speak out and that's why there's such a quiet across the country, cause the moment somebody does something someone else right next to him says, I didn't like what you did. We have to give each other a chance to make mistakes, we have to give each other a chance (inaudible) because if we are our own worst critics, no one is going to do anything, we are going to be paralyzed in fear, and all the violence and hostilities that we felt against

CONFIDENTIAL

And JOHN SINCLAIR is a key person in the liberation struggle, the struggle to liberate all the people from the overt and the covert prisons, from the prisons behind bars and outside bars, and we need JOHN SINCLAIR out of prison not only for his own sake but to help in that struggle. JOHN SINCLAIR has united rock and revolution. He has united a position to political repression and to economic exploitation. His united oppossion from domestic oppression and foreign aggression and we want JOHN SINCLAIR out of prison, we want him out of prison to help us organize the music at San Diego. (applause) And we want him out of prison to organize the music in a lot of events like this one that will take place up and down the country between now and San Diego to get those other prisoners out of jail, out of the jail of the factories that they are in, out of the jail of the money system, out of the jail of the foreign policy. Now I'm just going to say one sentence about the war and I think RENNIE indicated already that NIXON's program is not for winding down the war but for winding down the anti-war movement, its the most cynical appeal to us, to say it doesn't matter that more people are being killed today than there were last month, it doesn't matter that there were more people killed last month than there were under JOHNSON, as long as they are Asians, as long as they are not Americans, but you want a real clue to that kind of syncism, I'll quote one of my political advisers, GEORGE WALLACE; GEORGE WALLACE came up with a shadow cabinet yesterday and who do you suppose was his secretary of state was, Ambassador WILLIAM PORTER who is NIXON's Ambassador to the Vietnamese peace talks. That tells you what's happening to the Vietnamese peace talks. That tells you what's happening to the war under the Nixon program. Now one last point, I also came here tonight to hear JOHN and YOKO, and so did a lot of other people, but I came here to hear JOHN and YOKO sing a song to the Liberation of JOHN SINCLAIR and the other prisoners. We have the power, we have the strength if like the Vietnamese and the Cambodian and the Laotians, we do not allow the government, visible or invisible, to pacify us, if we do not allow them to convince them that we are weak and impotent and that nothing we do will matter. Ever since 1964, the press, the dove press, mind you, and the government has been saying that the war is ending and the anti-war movement is dead, but it has never been through, and it is not through today, the war will not go away by itself, and JOHN SINCLAIR will not get free by

8
CONFIDENTIAL

Cover Sheet for Informant Report or Ma...
FD-306 (Rev. 9-30-69)

	Date prepared
SECRET	1/24/72

Date received	Received from (name or symbol number)	Received by
1/3/72	b2 b7D	b7C

Method of delivery (check appropriate blocks)

☐ in person ☐ by telephone ☐ by mail ☐ orally ☐ recording device ☒ written by Informant

If orally furnished and reduced to writing by Agent:
Date
Dictated _____ to _____
Transcribed _____
Authenticated by Informant _____

Date of Report: 2/4/72

Date(s) of activity

Brief description of activity or material
.CFJ Activity

File where original is located if not attached
b2 b7D

* INDIVIDUALS DESIGNATED BY AN ASTERISK (*) ONLY ATTENDED A MEETING AND DID NOT ACTIVELY PARTICIPATE. VIOLENCE OR REVOLUTIONARY ACTIVITIES WERE NOT DISCUSSED.

☐ Information recorded on a card index by _____ on date _____

Remarks:

All necessary action taken.

Index : JOHN LENNON

1 - Buffalo ▓▓▓▓ (RM) b7C
1 - Newark ▓▓▓▓ (RM) b7C
2 - Washington Field (RM)
  (1 - ▓▓▓▓) b7C
  (1 - ▓▓▓▓) b2 b7D
1 - New York ▓▓▓▓
1 - 100- ▓▓▓▓ (#5) b7C
1 - 105-42122 (LEM)
2 - 100-16939 (FCPJ) (#2)

b7C (3)

CLASS. EXT. BY G-3 4/19/83

DECLASSIFIED ON 5-3-83
BY 1678RFP/SBm

DO NOT DESTROY - PENDING LITIGATION

100 169939
Block Stamp 885

SECRET

231

January 4, 1972

George Vicors was in the office today. So was Mike Drobineer, Carol Cullen, Alex, Chris and Tom, and Stu Albert. All of the above, except for the first two, are members of the Alamuchie Group.

Stu Albert is living with Jerry Rubin when he's in New York. Stu, Carol and Mike are leaving for Washington on Thursday where they will stay in Carol Cullen's apartment.

Stu and Jerry are in constant contact with John Lennon. Reasons unknown (possibly financial). There will be an interim committee meeting Wednesday at 4:00 PM.

Stu will be traveling to Washington in Mike Drobineer's parents car.

SECRET

Cover Sheet for Informant Report or Material
FD-306 (Rev. 9-30-69)

Date prepared: 1/17/72

Date received: 1/6/72
Received from (name or symbol number): ___ b2, b7D
Received by: SA ___ b7C

Method of delivery (check appropriate blocks)
☐ in person ☐ by telephone ☐ by mail ☒ orally ☐ recording device ☐ written by Informant

If orally furnished and reduced to writing by Agent:
Date Dictated ___ to ___
Transcribed ___
Authenticated by Informant ___

Date of Report: 1/6/72
Date(s) of activity:

Brief description of activity or material:
PCPJ activity.

File where original is located if not attached: ___ b2, b7D

* INDIVIDUALS DESIGNATED BY AN ASTERISK (*) ONLY ATTENDED A MEETING AND DID NOT ACTIVELY PARTICIPATE. VIOLENCE OR REVOLUTIONARY ACTIVITIES WERE NOT DISCUSSED.
☐ Information recorded on a card index by ___ on date ___

Remarks:
All necessary action taken.

INDEX: JOHN LENNON

1 - Boston (100-   ) (N.H. PCPJ) (RM)
1 - Washington Field (100-   ) (DAVIS) (RM)
1 - New York ___ b2, b7D
1 - New York (100-157178) (RUBIN) (42)
1 - New York (100-   ) (J. DOHRN) (47)
1 - New York (100-158591) (SMC) (41)
1 - New York (100-148047) (SDS) (42)
2 - New York (100-169939) (PCPJ) (42)

b7C ___
(8)

DO NOT DESTROY - PENDING LITIGATION

ALL INFORMATION CONTAINED
HEREIN IS UNCLASSIFIED
DATE 5-3-83 BY ___

100-169939-892
SEARCHED ___ INDEXED ___
SERIALIZED ___ FILED ___
JAN 17 1972
FBI - NEW YORK

NY 100-169939

January 6, 1972

The New Hampshire Peoples Coalition for Peace and Justice (PCPJ) is planning a peace conference in March, time and place not yet determined. At this time, the Peach March is planned to resemble a mule train. The New Hampshire PCPJ hopes to have the peace conference sometime during the New Hampshire Presidential Primary and John Lennon, of the Beatles, Jerry Rubin, Rennie Davis and Jennifer Dohrn, of Student Mobilization Committee (SMC) are hoped to attend.

It seems that many former members of Students for a Democratic Society (SDS) are now active in the SMC.

Mike Drobenare is now using his parent's car again.

The May Day Collective has an office in Washington, D.C. (exact address unknown).

Cover Sheet for Informant Report or Material
FD-306 (Rev. 9-30-69)

SECRET

Date prepared: 1/17/72

Date received: 1/6/72
Received from (name or symbol number): ▓▓▓▓ b2 b7D
Received by: SA ▓▓▓▓ b7C

Method of delivery (check appropriate blocks)
[x] in person [ ] by telephone [ ] by mail [ ] orally [ ] recording device [ ] written by Informant

If orally furnished and reduced to writing by Agent:
Date
Dictated _____ to _____
Transcribed _____
Authenticated by Informant _____

Date of Report: 1/10/72
Date(s) of activity:

Brief description of activity or material:
PCPJ activity

File where original is located if not attached: ▓▓▓▓ b2 b7D

* INDIVIDUALS DESIGNATED BY AN ASTERISK (*) ONLY ATTENDED A MEETING AND DID NOT ACTIVELY PARTICIPATE. VIOLENCE OR REVOLUTIONARY ACTIVITIES WERE NOT DISCUSSED.

[ ] Information recorded on a card index by _____ on date _____

Remarks: Index: BOB DYLAN, JOHN LENNON
All necessary action taken.

1 - Atlanta ▓▓▓▓ (RM) b7C
1 - Buffalo ▓▓▓▓ (RM) b7C
1 - Newark ▓▓▓▓ (RM)
1 - New York ▓▓▓▓ b2, b7D
1 - New York (100- ▓▓▓) (▓▓DEN) (42)
1 - New York ▓▓▓▓ (45)
1 - New York (100-169939) (PCPJ) (42) b7C

DECLASSIFIED ON 5-3-83
BY 1678 RFP/SBM

▓▓▓▓ b7C
(7)

DO NOT DESTROY - PENDING LITIGATION

4/19/82
100-169939-893

CLASS. ▓▓▓ BY G3
REASON-▓▓▓▓ 1-2.4.2(2)(3)
DATE OF REVIEW 4/17/92

Block Stamp

SEARCHED _____ INDEXED _____
SERIALIZED _____ FILED _____
JAN 17 1972
FBI NEW YORK

SECRET

b7C

NY 100-169939

January 10, 1972

Tom Hayden is expected to be in New York City January 19 through 21, 1972. Alex Hladsky is making efforts to find speaking engagements for Hayden.

Mike Drobenare and Carrol Kitchens are presently in New York City.

Robert Greenblatt presently pays $75 per month to the New York Peoples Coalition for Peace and Justice (PCPJ) for use of one of the rooms at PCPJ Headquarters which he uses as his office. Recently Greenblatt has been spending much time at the PCPJ Office.

A male North Vietnamese exchange student at MIT named Dwon (ph) has contacted the New York PCPJ and wants to take part in anti-war activities. PCPJ has begun efforts to schedule speaking engagements for the student in New Hampshire.

PCPJ is presently planning to hold a peace concert at unknown location in New Hampshire during the New Hampshire Presidential Primary. Plans presently are to have John Lennon and Bob Dylan take part in the concert.

A peace concert has also been planned for the Boston area after the New Hampshire concert.

It appears that all of the equipment from the Washington, DC PCPJ Headquarters has now been transferred to the New York Office.

UNITED STATES GOVERNMENT

Memorandum

TO : SAC, New York (100-157178)   DATE: 1/12/72

FROM : SA [redacted] b7c

SUBJECT: JERRY CLYDE RUBIN, AKA
SM-YIP (EXTREMIST)
(Key Activist)

The subject appeared with John Lennon and Yoko Ono at a press conference taped and shown on WABC-TV "Eyewitness News" at 6:00pm on 1/11/72. The press conference was held in NYC and only Lennon was interviewed.

Rubin appeared to have his hair cut much shorter than previously shown in other photographs.

<u>ALL EXTREMISTS SHOULD BE CONSIDERED DANGEROUS.</u>

(1-100-157178)(47)

DECLASSIFIED ON 5-3-83
BY 1678 RFP/ebm

letters to the editor

A. J. Come, A. J. Go

Dear Sir:

To John, Yoko, Jerry, and David—you come to America, check out of the St. Regis Hotel, and check into the Village, where you immediately strike up a friendship with Jerry Rubin, who is into everything you want to get into.

Jerry, after all being a Yippie with Yippie tendencies, introduces you to David Peel, the "park bench singer," who just happens to be without a recording contract. Zam. David Peel breaks into Apple Records.

Now David, as far back as we can remember, you and Weberman were a duet. Remember "A. J. A. J. Weberman?" No, I guess not. I mean, when it comes to choosing between being famous or having a real friend, being famous will always win out.

John Lennon, being "the" John Lennon, met Bob Dylan and naturally they began rapping. Between the rap, Dylan must have mentioned that a guy named Alan Julius Weberman had been bothering him for the longest time. Lennon later, upon seeing Rubin and Peel, mentioned that Dylan had told him Weberman was a pest and he (Dylan) didn't know how to get rid of him. Lennon, Rubin, and Peel immediately took it upon themselves to help Dylan get rid of Weberman. Rubin called A.J. up, and who knows what they said to him. Weberman immediately wrote an apology into The Voice (Voice, December 9) who promptly misquoted him on one word which changed the context of the whole letter.

The question here is, exactly what was used to convince A. J. to mend his ways? Was it Lennon's money? Or was it Rubin's threat?

—Name withheld
Manhattan Beach

DECLASSIFIED 1678 RFP/cbm CONFIDENTIAL   2/21/72
ON 5/7/84   CODED
TELETYPE   URGENT

TO: DIRECTOR (ATTN: DID) AND SACS, NEWARK
                                      SAN DIEGO
                                      WASHINGTON FIELD

FROM: SAC, NEW YORK

ALLAMUCHY TRIBE, IS DASH NEW LEFT, CALREP

INSTANT DATE, SOURCE, WHO HAS FURNISHED RELIABLE INFORMATION IN THE PAST, ADVISED THAT THE ALLAMUCHY TRIBE IS TO OPEN AN OFFICE IN NYC DURING THE NEXT TWO WEEKS. SOURCE STATED THIS GROUP WAS FORMED FROM MEETINGS HELD AT THE PETER STUYVESANT FARM, ALLAMUCHY, NJ, DURING THE LAST MONTH. MEMBERS OF THIS GROUP, HEADED BY RENNIE DAVIS, INCLUDE STU ALPERT, J. CRAVEN. SOURCE NOTED ALL INDIVIDUALS PARTICIPATING IN THIS ENTITY WERE HARD CORE NEW LEFT ACTIVISTS FORMERLY ASSOCIATED WITH MAYDAY AND PEOPLES COALITION FOR PEACE AND JUSTICE (PCPJ). SOURCE FURTHER ADVISED THE PURPOSE OF THIS GROUP WAS TO DIRECT MOVEMENT ACTIVITIES DURING THE ELECTION YEAR TO CULMINATE WITH

1 - NEW YORK
1 - NEW YORK
1 - NEW YORK (105 42122)(STU ALPERT)
1 - NEW YORK (100 163425)(RENNIE DAVIS)
1 - NEW YORK (100 J. CRAVEN)
1 - NEW YORK (100 J. LENNON)

RTR:jl
(8)
1 - SUPERVISOR #47
1 - SUPERVISOR #42

DO NOT DESTROY - PENDING LITIGATION

ALL INFORMATION
HEREIN IS UNCLASSIFIED
CONFIDENTIAL

NY

PAGE TWO

DEMONSTRATIONS AT THE REPUBLICAN CONVENTION AUGUST NEXT. SOURCE NOTED A LARGE SUM OF MONEY HAS BEEN GIVEN TO THIS GROUP BY JOHN LENNON. JOHN LENNON IS IDENTIFIED AS FORMER MEMBER OF THE BEATLES ROCK GROUP, WHO IS CURRENTLY RESIDING IN NYC.

ADMINISTRATIVE

SOURCE IS IDENTIFIED AS ███████████████ THE NEW YORK OFFICE IS OPENING A SEPARATE CASE CAPTIONED "ALLAMUCHY TRIBE." COPY PROVIDED SAN DIEGO DUE TO INTEREST IN FORTHCOMING NATIONAL CONVENTION. INFORMATION COPY PROVIDED NEWARK.

LEADS

WASHINGTON FIELD

CONTACT SOURCES RE ACTIVITIES OF RENNIE DAVIS AND PCPJ AND FORWARD ANY INFORMATION REGARDING FORMATION OF ALLAMUCHY TRIBE.

JB 02 01-23-72 12:13 KJB

CODE PRIORITY

TO: THE PRESIDENT
TO: THE VICE PRESIDENT
TO: SECRETARY OF STATE
TO: DIRECTOR, CENTRAL INTELLIGENCE AGENCY
TO: DIRECTOR, DEFENSE INTELLIGENCE AGENCY
TO: DEPARTMENT OF THE ARMY
TO: DEPARTMENT OF THE AIR FORCE
TO: NAVAL INVESTIGATIVE SERVICE
TO: U. S. SECRET SERVICE (PID)
TO: ATTORNEY GENERAL (BY MESSENGER)

FROM: DIRECTOR, FBI

~~CONFIDENTIAL~~

PROTEST ACTIVITY AND CIVIL DISTURBANCES.

THE FOLLOWING IS A SUMMARY OF CURRENT INTELLIGENCE INFORMATION RELATING TO DEMONSTRATIONS AND CIVIL DISTURBANCES GROWING OUT OF PROTEST ACTIVITY.

END PAGE ONE

ALL INFORMATION CONTAINED
HEREIN IS UNCLASSIFIED
EXCEPT WHERE SHOWN
OTHERWISE

SECRET

The first page of this memo is missing, but here is the second :

PAGE THREE CONFIDENTIAL SECRET

ANOTHER SOURCE WHO HAS FURNISHED RELIABLE INFORMATION IN THE PAST HAS ADVISED ▓▓▓▓▓▓▓▓▓▓▓▓▓▓▓▓▓▓▓▓▓▓▓▓

▓▓▓▓▓ THE "TRIBE" IS TO BE HEADED BY RENNIE DAVIS, ONE OF THE DEFENDANTS IN THE CHICAGO SEVEN TRIALS AND WILL INCLUDE STU ALPERT AND J. CRAVEN, BOTH OF WHOM WERE ACTIVISTS IN MAY DAY COLLECTIVES AND WHO PARTICIPATED IN THE ACTIVITIES OF THE PEOPLES COALITION FOR PEACE AND JUSTICE. ACCORDING TO THE SOURCE, THE "TRIBE" WAS ORGANIZED TO DIRECT MOVEMENT ACTIVITIES DURING THE ELECTION YEAR, WHICH ACTIVITIES WILL CULMINATE WITH DEMONSTRATIONS AT THE REPUBLICAN NATIONAL CONVENTION.▓▓▓

BEATLE SINGER JOHN LENNON.

▓▓

END PAGE THREE

Does not pertain to the subject of your request.

SECRET

OPTIONAL FORM NO. 10
MAY 1962 EDITION
GSA FPMR (41 CFR) 101-11.6

UNITED STATES GOVERNMENT

Memorandum

TO : DIRECTOR, FBI (62-112678)   DATE: 1/24/72

FROM : SAC, ALBANY (100-22384)

SUBJECT: SUMMER COMMITTEE
IS-WPP
(OO: ALBANY)

Re Albany letter to Bureau dated 12/13/71.

The Newark and New Haven Divisions ascertained subscribers to automobile registrations which were included in LHM furnished Bureau with referenced letter.

Registrations of the vehicles requested were checked through sources and Albany indices with negative results regarding any phases of subversive activities regarding captioned case. As soon as results of investigation requested by Philadelphia have been received by Albany, and if there is no information received concerning individuals at Oneonta, N.Y. associating with captioned organization, this case will be closed.

Previous investigation showed members previously residing at [ ], Oneonta, N.Y., that may have been associating with the Summer Committee are no longer residing in that area.

2 - Bureau (RM)
1 - Albany
RLS:dml
(3)

EX-104

REC-22 62-112678-335

12 JAN 26 1972

Buy U.S. Savings Bonds Regularly on the Payroll Savings Plan

CLASSIFIED BY: SSA9803RDO/ss
REASON: 1.5 (C)
DECLASSIFY ON: X1

CLASSIFIED BY SSA5668LD/ss
DECLASSIFY ON: 25X1
CA# 83-1720

CLASSIFIED DECISIONS FINALIZED
BY DEPARTMENT REVIEW COMMITTEE (DRC)
DATE: 12/10/97

URGENT

TO   : DIRECTOR, FBI (ATT: DID) AND SACS, NEWARK, SAN DIEGO
          WASHINGTON FIELD

FROM   : NEW YORK (100-New)

SUBJECT : ALLAMUCHY TRIBE
          IS-NEW LEFT
          CALREP

INSTANT DATE SOURCE WHO HAS FURNISHED RELIABLE
INFORMATION IN THE PAST ADVISED AS FOLLOWS:

CAPTIONED GROUP HAS RENTED TWO STORIES OF WAREHOUSE
SPACES ON HUDSON ST. TO BE USED AS OFFICES. THIS SPACE PRESENTLY
BEING EQUIPPED WITH FURNISHINGS AND OFFICE EQUIPMENT AND WILL
BE OPERATIONAL NEAR FUTURE. ALLEGEDLY JOHN LENNON HAS
CONTRIBUTED SEVENTY FIVE THOUSAND DOLLARS AND ONE, ▮▮▮▮
FIFTEEN THOUSAND DOLLARS TO AID IN THE FORMATION OF CAPTIONED
ENTITY.

1- New York
1- New York
1- New York (100-163425)(RENNIE DAVIS)
1- New York (100-   )(JOHN LENNON)
1- New York (100-   )
1- New York (100-163260)(LNS)
1- New York
1- Supv. #42
1- Supv. #47

RTR:RAR
(9)

CLASS. & EXT BY
REASON-FCIM II, 1-2.4.2
DATE OF REVIEW

CONFIDENTIAL

NY 100-New PAGE TWO

RENNIE DAVIS PURPORTED ONE OF THE INITIAL AIMES OF THIS GROUP WOULD BE TO ATTEMPT TO PURCHASE THE LIBERATION NEWS SERVICE. DUE TO THE LNS' FINANCIAL CRISIS DAVIS PLANS TO USE LNS AS A MEDIA TOOL OF THE ALLAMUCHY TRIBE. (U)

ADMINISTRATIVE

RE NY TELETYPE, JANUARY TWENTY-ONE, LAST.

b2 b7D SOURCE IS IDENTIFIED AS [redacted]

b1 [redacted] (C) NYO IS AFFORDING CLOSE COVERAGE OF MATTER ON ADVICE OF BUREAU. (U)

CONFIDENTIAL

CONFIDENTIAL

121

FD-306 (Rev. 9-30-69)

Date prepared: 3/7/72   CONFIDENTIAL

Date received: 2/7/72
Received from (name or symbol number): [redacted] (Protect Con)
Received by: [redacted]

Method of delivery (check appropriate blocks)
[X] in person [ ] by telephone [ ] by mail [ ] orally [ ] recording device [ ] written by Informant

If orally furnished and reduced to writing by Agent:
Date
Dictated _____ to _____
Transcribed _____
Authenticated by Informant _____

Date of Report: 1/25/72
Date(s) of activity: 1/25/72

Brief description of activity or material:
Info re Election Year Strategy info and other individuals.

File where original is located if not attached: [redacted]

* INDIVIDUALS DESIGNATED BY AN ASTERISK (*) ONLY ATTENDED A MEETING AND DID NOT ACTIVELY PARTICIPATE. VIOLENCE OR REVOLUTIONARY ACTIVITIES WERE NOT DISCUSSED.

[ ] Information recorded on a card index by _____ on date _____

Remarks:
All necessary action taken.

1 - [redacted]
1 - [redacted]
1 - [redacted]
1 - [redacted]
1 - 100-175319 (JOHN LENNON)
1 - 100- (JERRY RUBIN)
1 - 100-175216 (WSMC)
1 - 100-172108 (NY SWITCHBOARD)
1 - 100-175228 (ELECTION JR INFO CAT)
1 - 105-42122 (STU ALPERT)
[redacted]
(23)

CLASS./& EXT. BY [signature]
REASON-FCIM 11. 1-2,4,
DATE OF REVIEW _____

ALL INFORMATION CONTAINED HEREIN IS UNCLASSIFIED EXCEPT WHERE SHOWN OTHERWISE.

Block Stamp:
100-175319-21
SEARCHED _____ INDEXED _____
SERIALIZED _____ FILED _____
MAR 7 1972
NEW YORK

CONFIDENTIAL

NY 100-
COPIES CONTINUED:

```
1 - 100-           (YOKO ONO)
1 - 100-174986 (NYRC)
1 -
1 -
1 -
1 - 105-100707 (RU)
1 -
1 - 100-163250 (LNS)
1 - 100-156088 (USCANLF-AIO)
1 - 100-           (RED BALLON COLLECTIVE PEOPLE)
```

CONFIDENTIAL

CONFIDENTIAL

[Tuesday January 25, 1972]

b7D

This is the first sign of tightening in the open house procedure that has prevailed.

One Michael LNU, acting as front man for Rennie Davis, John Lennon and Jerry Rubin, came to Washington Square Meth to the NY Office and had a long discussion with William Kittredge about what was going down. The office will be opened in 2 weeks - 1 month at Henderson and 10th Street and will occupy 2 floors there. The staff that was brought from Washington, DC appear to have some problems with the middle leadership (Stu Alpert and Jay Craven in particular). The staff salaries are said to be $125 per week, and Rubins pressence in the top echelon in confirmed. The bulk of the   is coming from Lennon-One.

Renner and Kittredge went to the NYLC loft to see William Smith about 8:00 p.m. and later went to Larry Levy's returning to the church at 1:30 a.m. (1/26/72) Joseph Pissarevsky was in touch with Revolutionary Union, Dia Cooper with LNS, and C. Donham with AIO. The purpose of all these meetings was to discuss a conference format that this group has cooked up and to feel out the various groups vis a vis the Red Balloon people.

FD-36 (Rev. 5-22-64)

Date: 1/28/72

Transmit the following in _____CODE_____
(Type in plaintext or code)

Via TELETYPE URGENT
(Priority)

TO: DIRECTOR, FBI (ATT:DID) & SACS,
NEWARK
PITTSBURGH
PHILADELPHIA
SAN DIEGO
WASHINGTON FIELD

FROM: SAC, NEW YORK (100-175228)

CHANGED, ELECTION YEAR STRATEGY INFORMATION CENTER (EYSIC), IS-NEW LEFT, CALREP.

TITLE "CHANGED" DUE TO GROUP BEING ORGANIZED BY RENNIE DAVIS, FORMERLY KNOWN AS ALLAMUCHY TRIBE, HAS NOW CHANGED ITS NAME AS THE PUBLIC WILL SOON BECOME AWARE OF ITS EXISTANCE AND PURPOSE (ANTI-CALREP ACTIVITIES.)

FIRST SOURCE, WHO HAS FURNISHED RELIABLE INFORMATION IN THE PAST, ADVISED THIS DATE EYSIC HAS MOVED INTO OFFICE SPACE IN THE VICINITY OF TENTH STREET AND HUDSON STREET, NYC. EYSIC WAS FORMED FOR PURPOSE OF DIRECTING NEW LEFT ACTIVITIES DURING ELECTION YEAR TO CULMINATE WITH DEMONSTRATIONS AT THE REPUBLICAN CONVENTION AUGUST, NEXT.

A SECOND SOURCE, WHO HAS FURNISHED RELIABLE INFORMATION IN THE PAST, ADVISED JANUARY TWENTY SEVEN, LAST, MEMBERS OF GROUP INCLUDE JERRY RUBIN, STU ALBERT, RENNIE DAVIS, JAY CRAVEN, CAROL CULLEN, CAROL KITCHEN,

FD-35 (Rev. 5-22-64)

FBI

Date:

Transmit the following in _____
(Type in plaintext or code)

Via _____
(Priority)

NY 100-175228
PAGE TWO

DROBENARE. MAJOR FINANCIAL BACKER APPEARS TO BE JOHN LENNON, FORMERLY OF THE BEATLES ROCK MUSIC GROUP. SOURCE ADVISED ALBERT AND RUBIN ARE IN CONSTANT CONTACT WITH LENNON REGARDING GROUP.

SECOND SOURCE ADVISED JANUARY TWENTY ONE, LAST, THAT A FACTION OF THE PEOPLES COALITION FOR PEACE AND JUSTICE (PCPJ) MET AT ALLAMUCHY, NEW JERSEY ON DECEMBER SEVENTEEN, SEVENTY ONE, THRU EIGHTEEN, SEVENTY ONE, AND THAT THEY HAVE SINCE HELD A MEETING AT A farm LOCATED IN PENN, EXACT PLACE UNKNOWN. GROUP INCLUDED BEFORE MENTIONED INDIVIDUALS.

PCPJ SELF-DESCRIBED AS ORGANIZATION CONSISTING OF OVER ONE HUNDRED ORGANIZATIONS USING MASSIVE CIVIL DISOBEDIENCE TO COMBAT WAR, RACISM, POVERY AND REPRESSION. ITS NATIONAL OFFICE LOCATED AT ONE FIVE SIX FIFTH AVE., NYC, ROOM FIVE TWO SEVEN.

ADMINISTRATIVE

RETEL TO BUREAU, JANUARY TWENTY ONE, LAST, CAPTIONED "ALLAMUCHY TRIBE, IS-NEW LEFT, CMPFP."

Approved: _____ Sent _____ M Per _____
Special Agent in Charge

FD-36 (Rev. 5-22-64)

FBI

Date:

Transmit the following in _____
(Type in plaintext or code)

Via _____
(Priority)

NY 100-175228
PAGE THREE

FIRST SOURCE IS ▮▮▮▮▮▮▮▮▮▮▮▮▮▮▮▮▮▮
SECOND SOURCE IS ▮▮▮▮▮▮▮▮▮▮▮▮▮▮▮▮

COPY OF TEL BEING SENT PITTSBURGH AND PHILADELPHIA FOR FUTURE LEAD VALUE.

NEW YORK ATTEMPTING TO LOCATE OFFICE SPACE EYSIC SO AS TO EFFECT APPROPRIATE COVERAGE.

NEWARK AT ALLAMUCHY, NEW JERSEY. IDENTIFY EXISTANCE OF PETER STUYVESANT FARM AND OCCUPANTS.

TWO. IMMEDIATELY OBTAIN TOLL CALLS FOR PHONE AT FARM FOR PAST THREE MONTHS. SUBMIT TO NEW YORK AND BUREAU, ATT: ADP UNIT - NEW LEFT, SECTION.

THREE. SURVEY SOURCES.

WASHINGTON FIELD CONTACT SOURCES REGARDING ACTIVITIES YOUR SUBJECTS DAVIS AND CULLEN CONCERNING THIS GROUP. SUTEL RESULTS OF ABOVE LEADS.

Approved: _____ Sent _____ M Per _____
Special Agent in Charge

UNITED STATES DEPARTMENT OF JUSTICE
FEDERAL BUREAU OF INVESTIGATION
Washington, D. C. 20535
January 28, 1972

CONFIDENTIAL

ALLAMUCHY TRIBE

On January 21, 1972, a confidential source advised that a group called the "Allamuchy Tribe" was planning to open an office in New York City, New York, during the following two weeks. The source stated that this group was formed from meetings held at the Peter Stuyvesant Farm, Allamuchy, New Jersey, during the Month of December, 1971.

Members of this group, headed by Rennard Cordon Davis, also known as Rennie Davis, include Stu Alpert and Jay Craven. The source noted that all of these individuals have been, or are currently affiliated with the People's Coalition for Peace and Justice (PCPJ).

The PCPJ in a press release dated March 1, 1971, described itself as being headquartered in Washington, D. C., and consisting of over one hundred organizations which are using massive civil disobedience to combat racism, poverty, repression, and war.

The source further advised that the purpose of this group was to direct New Left movement activities during the 1972 National Election Year, with plans to culminate with demonstrations at the Republican National Convention scheduled to be held at San Diego, California, during August, 1972. The source concluded by noting that a large sum of money has been given to this group by John Lennon, a former member of the Beatles rock group, and who is currently residing in New York City, New York.

CONFIDENTIAL

CONFIDENTIAL

ALLAMUCHY TRIBE

On January 24, 1972, the same source advised that the Allamuchy Tribe has rented two stories of warehouse space on Hudson Street, New York City, and anticipates utilizing this space for offices. This space is presently being equipped with furnishings and office equipment, and will be operational in the near future. Allegedly, John Lennon has contributed $75,000.00 to aid in the formation of the Allamuchy Tribe.

On January 28, 1972, a second source advised that the Allamuchy Tribe is a name coined by individuals that attended the Allamuchy, New Jersey, meetings, previously described. This second source advised that any meetings called by New Left Activists associated with Rennie Davis in the future, that deal with the topic of demonstrations surrounding the Republican National Convention, 1972, would call the participants, members of "The Allamuchy Tribe."

This second source further advised that while individual meetings concerning the Republican National Convention would be known as Allamuchy Tribe meetings, previously mentioned Rennie Davis, Stu Alpert, Jay Craven, with the additions of John Lennon, his wife, Yoko Ono Lennon, and Jerry Rubin, convicted Chicago Seven Conspiracy Trial Defendant, were getting up office space in New York City, under the name "International News Service." The alleged purpose of the group would be to spear-head tours throughout the major states holding primary elections during 1972, presenting New Left movement messages, and attempting to encourage large numbers of individuals to demonstrate at the Republican National Convention at San Diego. This second source indicated that the office space being rented in New York City has been negotiated by the previously mentioned individuals, and that while, depending upon the situation, they call themselves "The Allamuchy Tribe" or "International News Service," these two terms are often used interchangably by individuals closely involved with Rennie Davis and his current plans.

CONFIDENTIAL

ALLAMUCHY TRIBE

The second source indicated that Davis continues, at present, to reside at 1736 Lanier Place, N.W., Apartment 3, Washington, D. C., but plans to spend a great deal of time in New York City coordinating the plans of "The Allamuchy Tribe - International News Service."

Cover Sheet for Informant Report or Material
FD-306 (Rev. 9-30-69)

TO: SAC, BOSTON
FROM: SAC, NEW YORK (100-169939)
SUBJECT: PCPJ
SM-NEW LEFT

Date prepared

Date received: 2/2/72
Received from (name or symbol number): [redacted] b2 b7D
Received by: [redacted] b7c

Method of delivery (check appropriate blocks)
[X] in person [ ] by telephone [ ] by mail [ ] orally [ ] recording device [X] written by Informant

If orally furnished and reduced to writing by Agent:
Date
Dictated _____ to _____
Transcribed _____
Authenticated by Informant _____

Date of Report: 2/1/72
Date(s) of activity: 2/1/72

Brief description of activity or material
PCPJ Activity

File where original is located if not attached: [redacted] b2 b7D

* INDIVIDUALS DESIGNATED BY AN ASTERISK (*) ONLY ATTENDED A MEETING AND DID NOT ACTIVELY PARTICIPATE. VIOLENCE OR REVOLUTIONARY ACTIVITIES WERE NOT DISCUSSED.

[ ] Information recorded on a card index by _____ on date _____

Remarks:

All necessary action taken.

DECLASSIFIED ON 5-2-83
BY 1678 RFP/EBM

1 - Boston (NHPCPJ) (RM)
1 - Washington Field Office (100-   ) (R. DAVIS) (RM)
1 - New York [redacted] b2,b7D
1 - New York [redacted] (42)
1 - New York [redacted]
1 - New York [redacted] (45) b7c
1 - New York [redacted] (45)
1 - New York (100-157178) (J. RUBIN) (42)
1 - New York (100-172771) (MDC) (42)
1 - New York (100-21672) (D. DELLINGER) (42)
1 - New York (100-175319) (J. LENNON) (42)
1 - New York
[redacted] b7c
(12)

100-175319-26

ALL INFORMATION CONTAINED HEREIN IS UNCLASSIFIED EXCEPT WHERE SHOWN OTHERWISE.

SEARCHED ___ INDEXED ___
SERIALIZED ___ FILED ___
NEW YORK
b7c

February 1, 1972

Renne Davis is staying at Jerry Rubin's house. May Day is at Odds with PCPJ.

Dave Dellinger is still in a hospital in Boston. Some people in Harrisburg Committee said last Friday some government agents were around. Please find some 3" x 5" cards of key contacts in the Southwest. PCPJ is conducting a campaign of Pledge signing. The Pledge states that the signee will not support a war candidate. May Day promises that San Diego will be like Washington, but with 100 times the people.

Davis and Rubin still run May Day, but do not wish the public eye to be cast upon them so they are running the party from the background.

John Lennon is working very closely within May Day and there may be a Peace Concert next month in the Boston Garden. PCPJ refuses to pay any taxes, including the phone excise tax.

Barbara Webster will most likely be in the office Thursday (Wait for my call)

Indices Search Slip
FD-160 (Rev. 10-1-59)

TO: CHIEF CLERK
Date: 2-2-72
Subject: John Winston Lennon
Aliases: John Lennon
Address: 150 Bank St, NYC
Birth Date: 1940
Birthplace: London England
Race: —
Sex: ☒ Male ☐ Female

- ☒ Exact Spelling / All References
- ☐ Main Subversive Case Files Only
- ☐ Subversive References Only
- ☐ Main Criminal Case Files Only
- ☐ Criminal References Only
- ☐ Main Subversive (If no Main, list all Subversive References)
- ☐ Main Criminal (If no Main, list all Criminal References)
- ☐ Restrict to Locality of _____

File & Serial Number	Remarks	File & Serial Number	Remarks
see att			

Requested by: [redacted]
Squad: 42
Extension: 448
File No.: —

Searched by: 2/2/72 mg (date)

Consolidated by: b7C (date)

Reviewed by: (date)

File Review Symbols
I - Identical
NI - Not identical
? - Not identifiable
U - Unavailable reference

ALL INFORMATION CONTAINED HEREIN IS UNCLASSIFIED
DATE 6.14.82 BY [signature]

LENNON, JOHN   1/72   100-157118- b3   *appeared with Jerry Rubin*
                  1/72   -1704   *WABC-TV on 1/11/72*
                                               Rubin +2 newspaper clipping

LENNON, JOHN   12/71   100-174925-1
                                               newspaper article mentioning name only

LENNON, JOHN   1/70   100-156163-24 ✓
                                               Rubin +2
                                               not in router

LENNON, JOHN   12/71   100-161445-1516
                                               Rubin +2
                                               Jerry newsle

LENNON, JOHN   2/71   100-171160-23
                                       not in file

119

2/2/72

CODE

TELETYPE URGENT

TO: DIRECTOR, FBI AND SAC, WASHINGTON FIELD OFFICE

FROM: SAC, NEW YORK (100-175228) (P)

ELECTION YEAR STRATEGY INFORMATION CENTER (EYSIC)
SM-NL (CALREP)

ON INSTANT DATE PERSONNEL AT INS, NYC ADVISED THAT JOHN WINSTON LENNON, DOB TEN NINE FORTY, POB ENGLAND, ARRIVED NYC ON AUGUST ELEVEN SIXTY EIGHT UNDER A B DASH TWO VISITOR'S STATUS. HE LEFT THE UNITED STATES AND REENTERED NOW HOLDING H DASH ONE TEMPORARY VISA STATUS WHICH EXPIRES END OF FEBRUARY INSTANT. LENNON HAS APPLIED FOR ANOTHER B DASH TWO STATUS LEADING UPTO BECOMING A UNITED STATES CITIZEN. INS FILE LOCATED CENTRAL OFFICE INS, WDC CHARGED TO BASIS MASON TELEPHONE TWO ZERO TWO DASH SIX TWO SIX DASH ONE THREE THREE SIX. LENNONS ALIEN NUMBER A ONE SEVEN FIVE NINE SEVEN THREE TWO ONE.

NY 100-175228
PAGE TWO

HE IS PRESENTLY MARRIED TO YOKO ONO LENNON.

b7C

INS LIST NYC RESIDENCE AS SAINT REGIS HOTEL, ONE FIFTY BANK STREET. LENNON HAS SINCE MOVED TO UNKNOWN ADDRESS.

LEAD

WASHINGTON FIELD OFFICE IMMEDIATELY REVIEW INS FILE REGARDING LENNON, AND FORWARD BACKGROUND INCLUDING PHOTO OF SUBJECT TO NYO.

OPTIONAL FORM NO. 10
MAY 1962 EDITION
GSA FPMR (41 CFR) 101-11.6

UNITED STATES GOVERNMENT

Memorandum

TO : DIRECTOR, FBI DATE: 2/2/72

FROM : SAC, SPRINGFIELD (100-12659) (P)

SUBJECT: RAINBOW PEOPLE'S PARTY
EAST PEORIA, ILLINOIS
IS - NEW LEFT (EXTREMIST)

Re Springfield report of SA [ ]
dated 11/11/71, captioned " [ ]
SM - WPP (EXTREMIST)".
El Paso report of SA [ ] dated
1/18/72, captioned " [ ]
SSN [ ], SSA".

Referenced Springfield report advised of [ ]
attempt at Illinois Central College (ICC), East Peoria,
Illinois, to start a chapter of the Rainbow People's Party
i.e., the White Panther Party. [ ] was formerly a student
at Western Illinois University (WIU), Macomb, Illinois, and
had been a member of the White Panther Party there.

[ ], Dean of Student Personnel,
ICC, East Peoria, advised on 1/21/72 that there has never
been any organization on campus resembling the Rainbow
People's Party. [ ] attempted to organize
a chapter, but got absolutely no response. [ ]
further advised that [ ] is not presently registered
at ICC.

On [ ]/72 [ ] was arrested in El Paso,
Texas on a charge of "failure to have a Selective Service
Registration Card in his possession" and incarcerated at
El Paso, Texas, County Jail.

Since no White Panther Party was ever organized
at ICC, the activity was followed in Springfield files
100-12656 ([ ], SM - WPP (EXTREMIST)"and
100-12659 (WHITE PANTHER PARTY, SPRINGFIELD DIVISION.)

REC 107 62-112678-336

2 - Bureau (RM)
3 - Springfield (2 - 100-12659)
(1 - 100-12656)
BLM/jab
(5)

16 FEB 4 1972

6 1 FEB 15 1972

Buy U.S. Savings Bonds Regularly on the Payroll Savings Plan

SI 100-12659

ALL INDIVIDUALS INVOLVED IN NEW LEFT EXTREMIST
ACTIVITY SHOULD BE CONSIDERED DANGEROUS BECAUSE OF THEIR
KNOWN ADVOCACY AND USE OF EXPLOSIVES, REPORTED ACQUISITION
OF FIREARMS AND INCENDIARY DEVICES, AND KNOWN PROPENSITY
FOR VIOLENCE.

2/3/72

CODE

TELETYPE   ~~URGENT~~ NITEL

TO: DIRECTOR (ATTENTION: DOMESTIC INTELLIGENCE DIVISION)
AND SAC, NEW YORK (100-175228)

FROM: SAC, WFO (100-55361)

ELECTION YEAR STRATEGY INFORMATION CENTER (EYSIC);
INTERNAL SECURITY - NEW LEFT (CALREP).

A CONFIDENTIAL SOURCE, RELIABLE IN THE PAST, ADVISED FEBRUARY TWO, LAST, MOST STAFF MEMBERS OF PEOPLE'S COALITION FOR PEACE AND JUSTICE (PCPJ) FORMERLY OPERATING OUT OF WASHINGTON, D. C. (WDC), AND ELSEWHERE, MOST OF WHOM HAVING HAD MAY DAY COLLECTIVE CONNECTIONS, TRANSFERRED TO NEW YORK CITY (NYC) DURING MID JANUARY, SEVENTY TWO, TO INITIATE EYSIC. SOURCE INDICATED PERSONNEL TRANSFER TO NYC INITIATED BY SUGGESTION OF RENNIE DAVIS, CONVICTED CHICAGO SEVEN CONSPIRACY TRIAL DEFENDANT. SOURCE IDENTIFIED TRANSFEREES AS CAROLE SUE CULLUM, JAY CRAVEN, CHRISTINE HARRIET JOHNSON, STEWART ALPERT, NOREEN BANKS, ALLAN ALPERN, MIKE DROBINEAR, MIKE WEBER, AND WINSLOW PECK.

3 - WFO
(1 - 100-   ) (JOHN LENNON)
(1 -   )
1 - San Diego (AM)

ALL INFORMATION CONTAINED
HEREIN IS UNCLASSIFIED
DATE 6/15/   BY

WFO 100-55361

PAGE TWO

SOURCE INDICATED THESE INDIVIDUALS STAYING AT TOM HERCH'S APARTMENT, SIX HUNDRED WEST ONE HUNDRED ELEVENTH STREET, NYC. TELEPHONE NUMBER (TWO ONE TWO) SEVEN FOUR NINE FIVE EIGHT ONE SEVEN.

SOURCE STATED THAT JOHN LENNON, FORMER BEATLES ROCK SINGER MEMBER, AND HIS WIFE YOKO ONO LENNON, ARE CURRENTLY VACATIONING IN THE VIRGIN ISLANDS FOR HEALTH REASONS, AND MOST EYSIC PLANNING MEETINGS WILL BE POSTPONED UNTIL THEIR RETURN TO NYC - PROBABLY THE SECOND WEEK OF FEBRUARY, SEVENTY TWO. ACCORDING TO THE SOURCE, JOHN LENNON HAS FINANCIALLY CONTRIBUTED TO EYSIC.

ADMINISTRATIVE

RE NY TELS TO BUREAU, FEBRUARY TWO, LAST.

SOURCE UTILIZED IS ███████████████

SOURCE UTILIZED BY WFO MOST LIKELY TO REPORT ON EYSIC ACTIVITIES IN FUTURE. SOURCE CURRENTLY DIRECTED TO DEVELOP

WFO 100-55361

PAGE THREE

INFORMATION RE SAME. OTHER WFO SOURCES FAMILIAR WITH NEW LEFT ACTIVITIES CURRENTLY UNAWARE OF EYSIC.

WFO INITIATED SEARCH OF CENTRAL INS FOR JOHN AND YOKO LENNON FILES. WFO WILL REVIEW AND FURNISH RESULTS WHEN COMPLETED.

ONE COPY TO SAN DIEGO VIA AIR MAIL.

P

RECEIVED FROM
FEB 3 1972
CIA VIA COURIER

I-360
3 FEB 1972

SUBJECT: John LENNON;
Allamuchy Tribe (NL)

1. Reference is made to your teletype 003, dated 24 January 1972, Subject: Protest Activity and Civil Disturbances, reporting that former Beatles singer John LENNON had contributed a large sum of money to the "Allamuchy Tribe", headed by Rennie DAVIS.

2. It is requested that you furnish this office with any additional pertinent information concerning LENNON's relationship with the "Allamuchy Tribe" and any indications that DAVIS has received other funds for his activities from foreign sources.

Now is the time when surveillance of John Lennon by the FBI will get more and more intense. Lennon contributed to an organization advocating against the war in Vietnam and against Nixon's re-election, also planning demonstrations to disrupt the Republican Convention in August 1972. So Nixon's administration wants him out of the US and is using the FBI and the INS to achieve this goal. The deportation proceedings against the ex-Beatle will begin in March 1972. And the Bureau, led by John Edgar Hoover (or should we call him Schwarzenhoover… ?), will do everything to build a case against John Lennon.

I'LL GET YOU (OUT), JOHN LENNON !

John Edgar Schwarzenhoover

John Edgar Schwarzenhoover

John Edgar Schwarzenhoover as a young man

The three following documents clearly show that Nixon's administration was now getting involved in the Lennon case... for Internal Security reasons... :

United States Senate
COMMITTEE ON ARMED SERVICES
WASHINGTON, D.C. 20510

February 4, 1972

FEB 7 1972

Honorable William Timmons
The White House
Washington, D. C.

Dear Bill:

Find attached a memorandum to me from the staff of the Internal Security Subcommittee of the Judiciary Committee. I am a member of the subcommittee as well as the full Judiciary Committee.

This appears to me to be an important matter, and I think it would be well for it to be considered at the highest level.

As I can see, many headaches might be avoided if appropriate action be taken in time.

With kindest regards and best wishes,

Very truly,

Strom Thurmond

ST:x

Enclosure

P.S. Also find attached a memorandum entitled "John M. Thomas" concerning the Vice President about which I also talked with you. I sent the Vice President a copy of this.

JOHN LENNON

John Lennon, presently visiting in the United States, is a British citizen. He was a member of the former musical group known as "The Beatles." He has claimed a date of birth of September 10, 1940, and he is presently married to a Japanese citizen, one Yoko Ono.

The December 12, 1971, issue of the New York Times shows that Lennon and his wife appeared for about 10 minutes at about 3:00 a.m. on December 11, 1971, at a rally held in Ann Arbor, Michigan, to protest the continuing imprisonment of John Sinclair, a radical poet.

Radical New Left leaders Rennie Davis, Jerry Rubin, Leslie Bacon, Stu Albert, Jay Craven, and others have recently gone to the New York City area. This group has been strong advocates of the program to "dump Nixon." They have devised a plan to hold rock concerts in various primary election states for the following purposes: to obtain access to college campuses; to stimulate 18-year old registration; to press for legislation legalizing marihuana; to finance their activities; and to recruit persons to come to San Diego during the Republican National Convention in August 1972. These individuals are the same persons who were instrumental in disrupting the Democratic National Convention in Chicago in 1968.

According to a confidential source, whose information has proved reliable in the past, the activities of Davis and his group will follow the pattern of the rally mentioned above with reference to John Sinclair. David Sinclair, the brother of John, will be the road manager for these rock festivals.

Davis and his cohorts intend to use John Lennon as a drawing card to promote the success of the rock festivals and rallies. The source feels that this will pour tremendous amounts of money into the coffers of the New Left and can only inevitably lead to a clash between a controlled mob organized by this group and law enforcement officials in San Diego.

The source felt that if Lennon's visa is terminated it would be a strategy counter-measure. The source also noted the caution which must be taken with regard to the possible alienation of the so-called 18-year old vote if Lennon is expelled from the country.

Im/L

March 6, 1972

Dear Strom:

In connection with your previous inquiry concerning the former member of the Beatles, John Lennon, I thought you would be interested in learning that the Immigration and Naturalization Service has served notice on him that he is to leave this country no later than March 15. You may be assured the information you previously furnished has been appropriately noted.

With warm regards,

Sincerely,

William E. Timmons
Assistant to the President

Honorable Strom Thurmond
United States Senate
Washington, D. C. 20510

bcc: Mr. Harlington Wood, Department of Justice - for your information
bcc: Tom Korologos - for your information

WET:VO:jlh

John Lennon's potential links with the Irish cause were also under surveillance :

Cover Sheet for Informant Report or M...
FD-306 (Rev. ...)

Date prepared: 3/8/72

Date received: 2/14/72
Received from (name or symbol number): [redacted] b2 b7D
Received by: SA [redacted] b7C

Method of delivery (check appropriate blocks):
[X] in person [ ] by telephone [ ] by mail [ ] orally [ ] recording device [X] written by Informant

If orally furnished and reduced to writing by Agent:
Date
Dictated _____ to _____
Transcribed _____
Authenticated by Informant _____

Date of Report: 2/6/72
Date(s) of activity: 2/6/72

Brief description of activity or material:
Irish Republican Club meeting, NYC
2/6/72.

File where original is located if not attached: b2 b7D

* INDIVIDUALS DESIGNATED BY AN ASTERISK (*) ONLY ATTENDED A MEETING AND DID NOT ACTIVELY PARTICIPATE. VIOLENCE OR REVOLUTIONARY ACTIVITIES WERE NOT DISCUSSED.

[ ] Information recorded on a card index by _____ on date _____

Remarks:
All necessary action taken.

1- [redacted] b2 b7D
1-105-113426
1-105-109381 (31)
1-105-113425 (31)
1-105-115623 (31)
1-100-4013 (45)
1-100-175319 (42)
1-105-110758 (31)
1-100-164962 (45)
1-105-117501 (31)
1-105-103115 (31)
1-105-115849

(12)   b7C

ALL INFORMATION CONTAINED HEREIN IS UNCLASSIFIED
DATE 6/9/42 BY [signature]

Block Stamp:
100 175319-20
SEARCHED _____ INDEXED _____
SERIALIZED _____ FILED _____
MAR 8 1972
NEW YORK

NY 105-115849

February 6, 1972

Irish

A meeting of the committee against internment in Northern Ireland took place at the Irish Institute at 326 West 48th St., at 4:05 PM.

An amendment to the purpose of the group was made, so that the body was now not just against internment, but also for the immediate withdrawel of British troops from Northern Ireland.

A speaker from the floor asked that the purpose of the body be amended to include support for the Irish Republican Army in money and even in guns. This motion wasn't even accepted by the chair, and the gentleman declared he would leave the meeting.

A steering committee was set up after much discussion and argumentation. The original committee contained two representatives from the following clubs: Irish Republican Clubs, Northern Aid Committee, National Association for Irish Freedom, and the American Committee for Ulster Justice.

Members of the Socialist Workers Party were present, and they came into the meeting as a unit and argued the following points: "with four organizations it's packed (the steering committee)...the steering committee must be broad, the four organizations have shown that they can't cooperate freely...it is important that the steering committee be representative of all tendencies and individuals...those people who want to take responsibility will be able to do so (in the broad steering committee). There are talented people who want to do work".

The broad steering committee motion was passed.

- 2 -

NY 105-115849

A March 1 or 4th action date was proposed. The SWP people called for a mass demonstration.

It was announced that JOHN LENNON had offered entertainment. One route proposed was a march from Columbus Circle to Bryant Park, or Central Park.

Someone suggested that all British people, and all British organizations be harrassed, as the Jewish Defense League does with the Soviets.

A boycott of British goods was proposed.

It was suggested that the Irish ask the Chinese in the Hotel Roosevelt (Red Chinese) to talk to NIXON when he is in Peking. This idea was strongly put down.

Three members of the SWP (if not more) were named to the steering committee: RAY "MARKY" (1930-local of the New York Public Library System), GENE "BERTINE" of Local 1199, and NAT LONDON, formerly of the Peace Action Coalition. In all 28 names were accepted for the committee.

The Irish Republican Clubs are aware of the presence of SWP people, and they are watching them. MARY COTTER was a spokesman for the Irish group, and she's a SWP person (this occurred at a BOAC demonstration previous to this meeting), and as such served the interests of the Irish group rather than the SWP.

- 3 -

SECRET
NO FOREIGN DISSEM/NO DISSEM ABROAD

1 - Mr. R. H. Horner
1 - Mr. R. L. Shackelford
1 - Mr. R. L. Pence

CLASSIFIED DECISIONS FINAL February 7, 1972
BY DEPARTMENT REVIEW COMMITTEE (DRC)

ELECTION YEAR STRATEGY
INFORMATION CENTER (EYSIC)

Reference is made to your memorandum captioned "John Lennon; Allamuchy Tribe (NL)," dated February 3, 1972, your reference I-360.

For your information, organization formerly known as Allamuchy Tribe, led by Rennie Davis, convicted Chicago Seven Conspiracy trial defendant, was recently renamed EYSIC.

A confidential source, who has furnished reliable information in the past, has advised that John Lennon, former member of The Beatles singing group, has contributed $75,000 to assist in the formation of EYSIC, formed to direct movement activities during the coming election year to culminate with demonstrations at the Republican National Convention during August, 1972. This source advised that other leaders of EYSIC are in constant contact with Lennon.

On February 2, 1972, a representative of Immigration and Naturalization Service, New York, advised that Lennon, born October 9, 1940, in England, arrived in New York City on August 11, 1968, with B-2 visitor's visa. He left the United States and subsequently reentered holding H-1 temporary visa which expires at the end of February, 1972. Lennon has applied for a B-2 visa indicating his intention to become a United States citizen.

On February 2, 1972, a second confidential source, who has furnished reliable information in the past, advised that Lennon and his wife, Yoko Ono Lennon, are currently vacationing in the Virgin Islands for health reasons and most EYSIC planning meetings will be postponed until their return to New York City, possibly during the second week in February, 1972.

At this time, this Bureau has no additional pertinent information concerning other foreign sources of funds for the activities of EYSIC or Rennie Davis.

Original and copy to CIA
1 - John Lennon

SECRET
NO FOREIGN DISSEM/NO DISSEM ABROAD

SEE NOTE PAGE TWO

Election Year Strategy
Information Center (EYSIC)

NOTE: Per CIA letter dtd. 1/16/94 and affidavit 12/13/93 SAI w/my 1-2584

Classified "Secret - No Foreign Dissemination/No Dissemination Abroad" since information being furnished in CACTUS channel and CIA has requested that all such information be so classified. CIA has requested details of information we furnished in daily summary teletype captioned "Protest Activities and Civil Disturbances," dated 1/24/72, reporting that John Lennon contributed large sum of money to captioned organization. CIA also requested any details that other foreign sources have contributed funds to captioned organization. First source referred to in LHM is [redacted] second source is [redacted]   b2 b7D

- 2 -

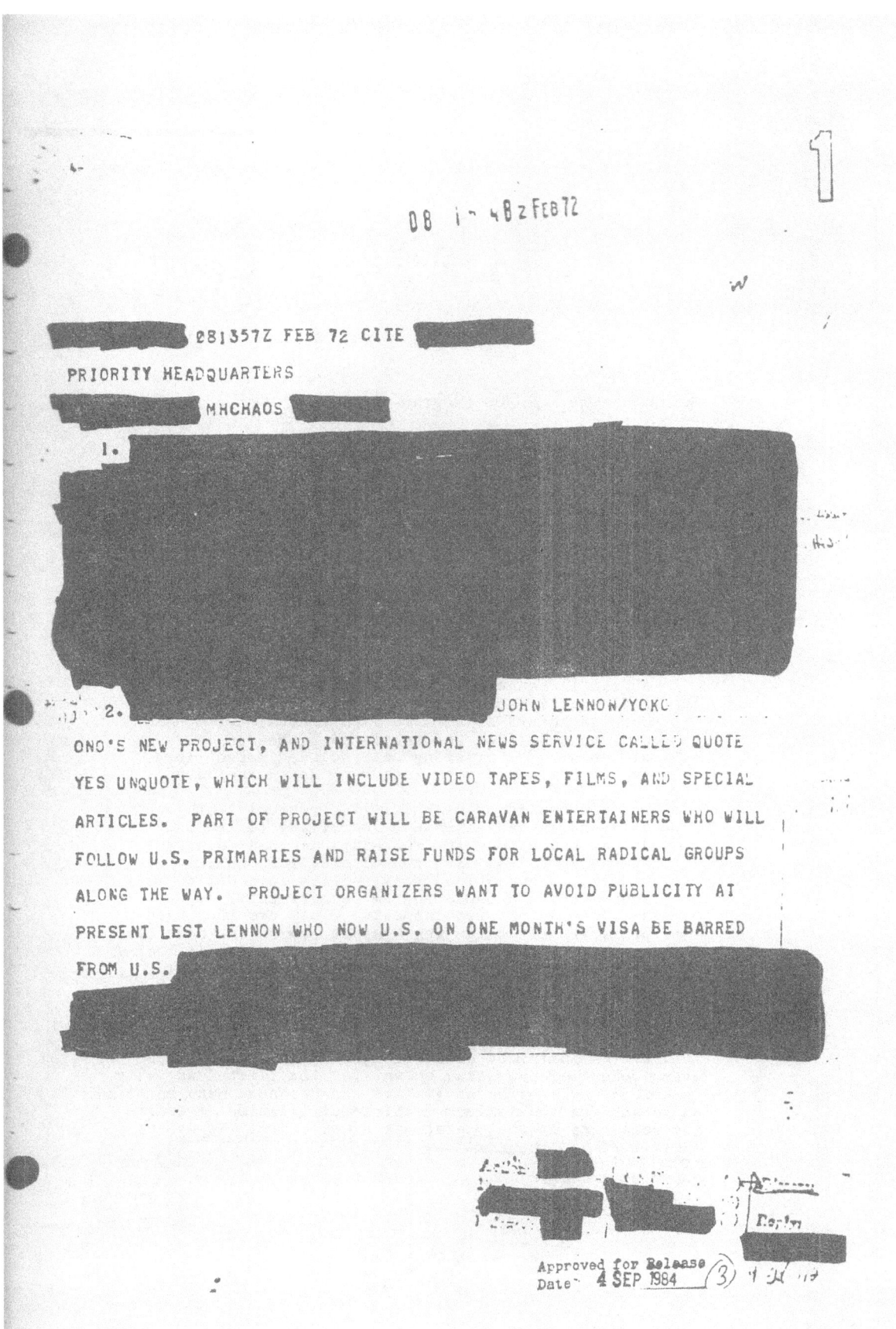

```
                  08 1-48zFEB72


         281357Z FEB 72 CITE
PRIORITY HEADQUARTERS
            MHCHAOS
   1.




   2.                              JOHN LENNON/YOKO
ONO'S NEW PROJECT, AND INTERNATIONAL NEWS SERVICE CALLED QUOTE
YES UNQUOTE, WHICH WILL INCLUDE VIDEO TAPES, FILMS, AND SPECIAL
ARTICLES. PART OF PROJECT WILL BE CARAVAN ENTERTAINERS WHO WILL
FOLLOW U.S. PRIMARIES AND RAISE FUNDS FOR LOCAL RADICAL GROUPS
ALONG THE WAY. PROJECT ORGANIZERS WANT TO AVOID PUBLICITY AT
PRESENT LEST LENNON WHO NOW U.S. ON ONE MONTH'S VISA BE BARRED
FROM U.S.
```

Approved for Release
Date 4 SEP 1984

This is a CIA document. It was issued as part of the MHCHAOS operation, code name for a secret domestic espionage project conducted by the CIA till 1976.

Here is another CIA document giving details about the MHCHAOS program:

MORI DocID: 1451843

SENSITIVE

Count 1
DO-44
8 May 73

SUBJECT: The MHCHAOS Program

1. The MHCHAOS program is a worldwide program for clandestine collection abroad of information on foreign efforts to support/encourage/exploit/manipulate domestic U.S. extremism, especially by Cuba, Communist China, North Vietnam, the Soviet Union, North Korea and the Arab fedayeen.

2. The MHCHAOS program has not and is not conducting efforts domestically for internal domestic collection purposes. Agency efforts are foreign. Foreign-oriented activity in the United States has been of two types:

   a. Selected FBI domestic sources who travel abroad in connection with their extremist activity and/or affiliations to make contact with hostile foreign powers or with foreign extremist groups have been briefed and debriefed by Headquarters officers. The briefing has included appropriate operational guidance, including defensive advice.

   b. Americans with existing extremist credentials have been assessed, recruited, tested and dispatched abroad for PCS assignments as contract agents, primarily sources offered for such use by the FBI. When abroad they collect information responsive to MHCHAOS program requirements, as well as other Agency requirements. They are thus used primarily for targeting against Cubans, Chinese Communists, the North Vietnamese, etc., as their background and their particular access permits. It should be noted that the [____] aspect of the [____] project of the East Asia Division is similar to the MHCHAOS PROGRAM.

   U.S. citizens recruited to go abroad

3. As indicated earlier, MHCHAOS is a foreign program, conducted overseas, except for the limited activity described above. The program is and has been managed so as to achieve the maximum feasible utilization of existing resources of the Operations Directorate. No assets

FULL TEXT COPY - DO NOT RELEASE

00591

SENSITIVE
SECRET

have been recuited and run exclusively for the MHCHAOS program. Instead, emphasis has been placed on the exploitation of new and old Agency assets who have a by-product capability or a concurrent capability for provision of information responsive to the program's requirements. This has involved the provision of custom-tailored collection requirements and operational guidance. This collection program is viewed as an integral part of the recruitment and collection programs of China Operations, Vietnam Operations, Cuban Operations, Soviet Bloc Division operations and Korean Branch operations. Agents who have an American "Movement" background or who have known connections with the American "Movement" are useful as access agents to obtain biographic and personality data, to discern possible vulnerabilities and susceptibilities, and to develop operationally exploitable relationships with recruitment targets of the above programs. These assets are of interest to our targets because of their connections with and/or knowledge of the American "Movement." Over the course of the MHCHAOS program, there have been approximately 20 important areas of operational interest, which at the present time have been reduced to about ten: Paris, Stockholm, Brussels, Dar Es Salaam, Conakry, Algiers, Mexico City, Santiago, Ottawa and Hong Kong.

4. The MHCHAOS program also utilizes audio operations, two of which have been implemented to cover targets of special interest.

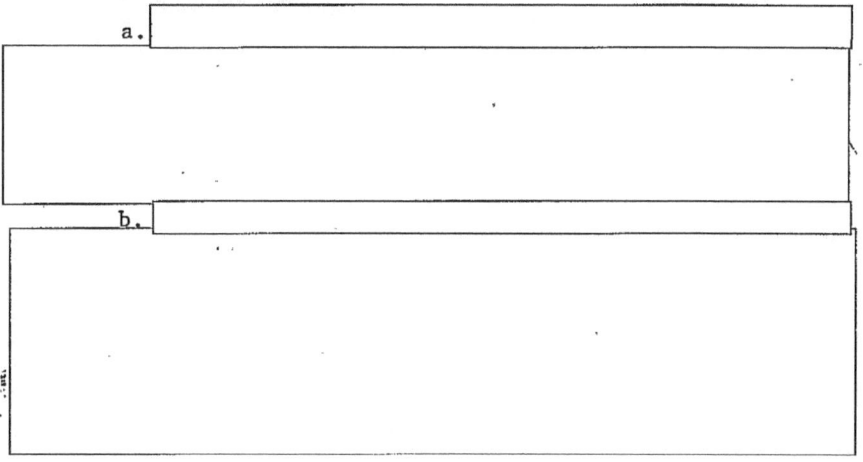

a.

b.

~~SENSITIVE~~

5. [MH]CHAOS reporting from abroad relating to the program originates in two ways: Individuals who are noted in contact with Cubans, the Chinese Communists, etc., and who appear to have extremist connections, interests or background are reported upon. Other individuals are reported upon in response to specific Headquarters requirements received from the FBI because such individuals are of active investigatory security interest to the FBI.

6. All cable and dispatch traffic related to the [MH]CHAOS program is sent via restricted channels. (It is not processed by either the Cable Secretariat or the Information Services Division.) The control and retrievability of information obtained, including information received from the FBI, is the responsibility of the Special Operations Group.

7. Information responsive to specific FBI requirements is disseminated to the FBI via special controlled dissemination channels, i.e., by restricted handling cable traffic or via special pouch and specially numbered blind memoranda.

8. Information of particular significance, when collected, has been disseminated by special memorandum over the signature of the Director of Central Intelligence to the White House (Dr. Kissinger and John Dean), as well as to the Attorney General, the Secretary of State and the Director of the FBI.

NR 010 WF CODED
5:31 PM NITEL 2-10-72 ASW
TO DIRECTOR
DOMESTIC INTELLIGENCE
NEW YORK
FROM WASHINGTON FIELD

ALL INFORMATION CONTAINED HEREIN IS UNCLASSIFIED
DATE 3/9/81 BY [signature]

ELECTION YEAR STRATEGY INFORMATION CENTER (EYSIC), IS DASH NEW LEFT, CALREP, NEW YORK FILE 100-175228, WFO FILE 100-55361. P.

JOHN WINSTO LENNON, SM DASH NEW LEFT, OO :NEW YORK, WFO FILE 100-55429. RUC.

RE NYTEL TO BUREUA, FIRST CAPTION, FEBRUARY TWO, LAST. SPECIAL CLERK [redacted] DETERMINED FEBRUARY TEN INSTANT FROM CENTRAL IMMIGRATION AND NATURALIZATION SERVICE (INS) THAT FILES REGARDING JOHN WINSTON LENNON AND WIFE YOKO ONO LENNON ARE CURRENTLY CHARGED OUT TO INS, NEW YORK CITY.

END

RESTRICTED HANDLING

D DIRECTOR, FEDERAL BUREAU OF INVESTIGATION
D FROM: DIRECTOR, CENTRAL INTELLIGENCE AGENCY

D SUBJECT: JOHN LENNON AND PROJECT "YES" (NL)
D REFERENCES: A. OUR MEMORANDUM I-360, DATED 3 FEBRUARY 1972,
      SUBJECT: JOHN LENNON; ALLAMUCHY TRIBE (NL)
   B. YOUR MEMORANDUM, DATED 7 FEBRUARY 1972, SUBJECT:
      ELECTION YEAR STRATEGY INFORMATION CENTER (EYSIC)

   A. FORMER BEATLE SINGER JOHN LENNON AND HIS WIFE YOKO ONO
ARE CURRENTLY INVOLVED IN A PROJECT CALLED QUOTE YES UNQUOTE,
DESCRIBED AS AN INTERNATIONAL NEWS SERVICE WHICH WILL INCLUDE THE
USE OF VIDEO TAPES, FILMS, AND SPECIAL ARTICLES. ALSO TO BE IN-
CLUDED IN THE PROJECT WILL BE A CARAVAN OF ENTERTAINERS, WHICH
WILL FOLLOW U.S. ELECTION PRIMARIES AND RAISE FUNDS FOR LOCAL

RESTRICTED HANDLING

RESTRICTED HANDLING

RADICAL GROUPS ALONG THE WAY.

B. PROJECT ORGANIZERS ARE SEEKING TO AVOID PUBLICITY AT PRESENT IN ORDER NOT TO JEOPARDIZE THE STAY OF JOHN LENNON, WHO IS IN THE UNITED STATES ON A ONE-MONTH VISA.

C.

D.

RICHARD OBER   CI/SO
               CI/SO
               C/CI/SO   10 FEB 72

2/13/96   9/25/97

CLASSIFIED BY SSA9PG3R00/JS   CLASSIFIED BY SSA 5668 SLD/JS
REASON: 1.5 CODE C   DECLASSIFY ON: 25X 6
DECLASSIFY ON: X6   CA# 83-1729 RMT NITEL
CA# CV83-1720   CABLEGRAM

                               1 - Mr. R.L. Shackelford
                               1 - Mr. R.L. Pence   2-11-72

TO LEGAT LONDON

FROM DIRECTOR FBI

ELECTION YEAR STRATEGY INFORMATION CENTER (EYSIC), IS - NEW LEFT.

FOR INFORMATION CAPTIONED ORGANIZATION LED BY RENNIE DAVIS, KEY ACTIVIST AND CONVICTED CHICAGO SEVEN CONSPIRACY TRIAL DEFENDANT, WAS FORMERLY NAMED ALLAMUCHY TRIBE AND HAS BEEN FORMED TO DIRECT MOVEMENT ACTIVITIES DURING COMING ELECTION YEAR TO CULMINATE WITH DEMONSTRATIONS AT REPUBLICAN NATIONAL CONVENTION, AUGUST NEXT. SOURCES ADVISE JOHN LENNON, FORMER MEMBER OF THE BEATLES SINGING GROUP, HAS CONTRIBUTED SEVENTY-FIVE THOUSAND DOLLARS TO ASSIST IN FORMATION OF EYSIC. SOURCES ADVISE EYSIC LEADERS IN CONSTANT CONTACT WITH LENNON. LENNON, BORN OCTOBER NINE, FORTY, ENGLAND, CURRENTLY IN U.S. HOLDING H DASH ONE TEMPORARY VISA WHICH EXPIRES END FEBRUARY, SEVENTY-TWO. LENNON HAS APPLIED B DASH TWO VISA INDICATING INTENTION BECOME U.S. CITIZEN.

BULHM WITH AIRTEL COVER. REQUEST PERMISSION FROM SOURCES

1 - Foreign Liaison Desk (route through for review)
1 - 100- (John Lennon)
RLP:plm
(6)

100-469910
SEE NOTE PAGE TWO

CABLEGRAM TO LONDON
RE: ELECTION YEAR STRATEGY INFORMATION CENTER (EYSIC)

TO DISSEMINATE INFORMATION OBTAINED TO U.S. STATE DEPARTMENT AND U.S. IMMIGRATION AND NATURALIZATION SERVICE (INS).

NOTE:

EYSIC, apparently dedicated to creating disruptions during Republican National Convention, obviously being heavily influenced by John Lennon, British citizen who is currently in U.S. attempting to obtain U.S. citizenship. Inasmuch as he is attempting to stay permanently in U.S., it is anticipated pertinent information concerning him will be disseminated to State and INS. (U)

FBI CURRENT INTELLIGENCE Analysis

Volume II, Number 3

February 11, 1972

ELECTION YEAR STRATEGY INFORMATION CENTER (EYSIC)

NEW "NEW LEFT" GROUP FORMED

Operating under the cumbersome title of Election Year Strategy Information Center is a new organization which has been formed to direct New Left protest activities during the 1972 election year, with these efforts geared to culminate in massive demonstrations at the Republican National Convention in San Diego in August. Before finally settling on this name, EYSIC was known both as the Allamuchy Tribe and the International News Service, names which some members of the group still occasionally use. Organizers of this band of activists are seasoned veterans of protest: Rennie Davis, Jerry Rubin, Stewart Albert, and Jay Craven. (CONFIDENTIAL)

Finances do not seem to be an immediate problem for EYSIC since John Lennon, formerly with The Beatles musical group, has reportedly contributed $75,000 to this embryonic organization. Lennon's money and name have placed him in a position of considerable influence in EYSIC--no key planning sessions are being held without Lennon (pictured at left). Lennon, a British subject, has also taken steps to acquire American citizenship. (CONFIDENTIAL)

EYSIC is headquartered in New York City in space rented in a warehouse on Hudson Street. Plans are being generated there to get EYSIC members to appear at major primary elections in 1972 to confront the candidates with the "New Left message" and to additionally encourage individuals to travel to San Diego to demonstrate in August against the Republican Party. (CONFIDENTIAL)

Airtel

SECRET   2-15-72

To: SACs, New York
        Los Angeles
        San Diego
        WFO

From: Director, FBI

PROJECT "YES"
IS - NEW LEFT

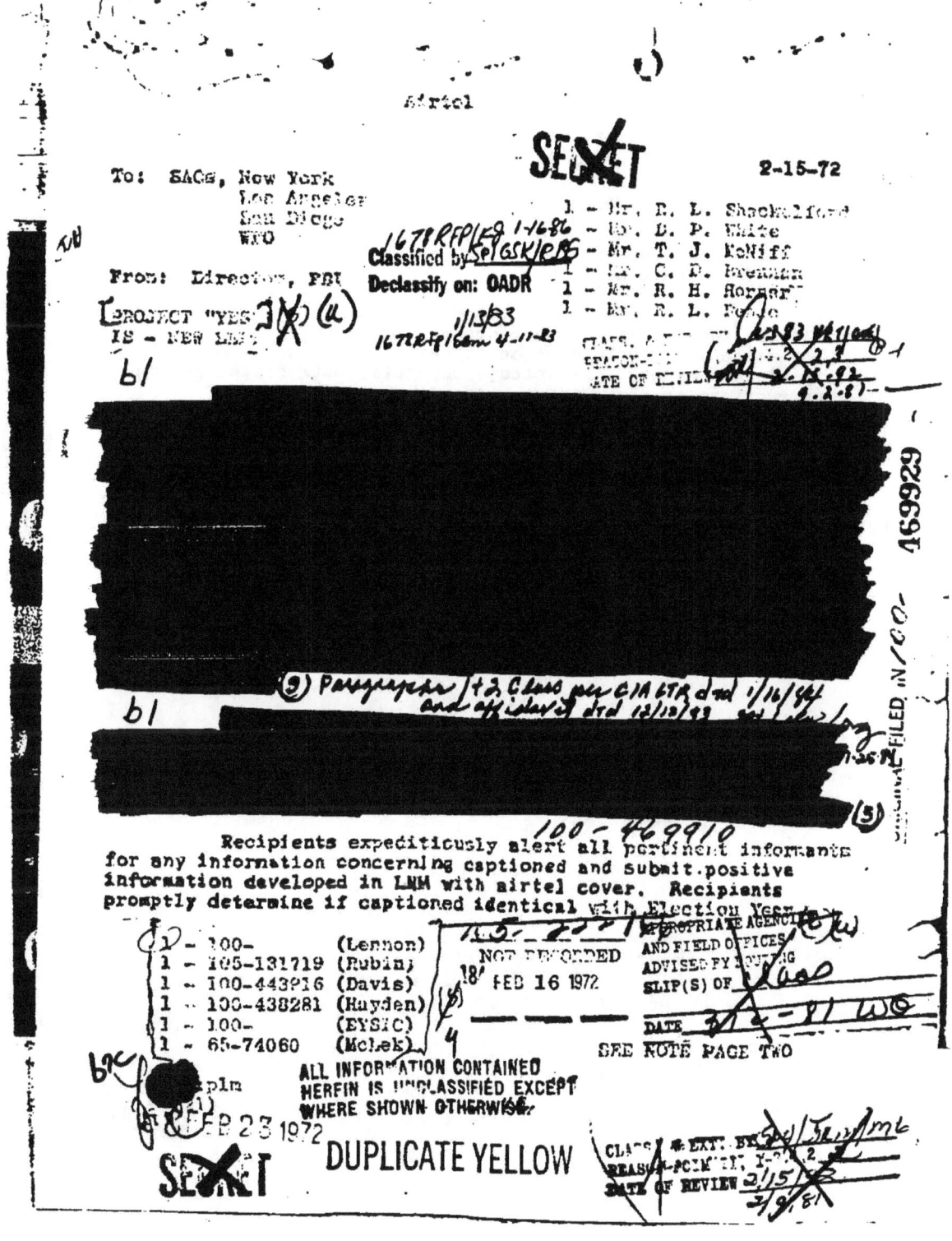

Recipients expeditiously alert all pertinent informants for any information concerning captioned and submit positive information developed in LHM with airtel cover. Recipients promptly determine if captioned identical with Election Year...

2 - 100-   (Lennon)
1 - 105-131719   (Rubin)
1 - 100-443216   (Davis)
1 - 100-438281   (Hayden)
1 - 100-   (EYSIC)
1 - 65-74060   (McLek)

ALL INFORMATION CONTAINED
HEREIN IS UNCLASSIFIED EXCEPT
WHERE SHOWN OTHERWISE

DUPLICATE YELLOW

SECRET

Airtel to New York, et al
RE: [Project "Yes"]

Strategy Information Center (FYSIC), group led by Rennie Davis allegedly aimed at creating disruptions during Republican National Convention.

Recipients are reminded that investigative instructions relating to possible disruptions during Republican National Convention must be handled on expedite basis and by mature, experienced Agents. Recipients carefully note dissemination instructions on above information from CIA

NOTE:

[redacted] Essential captioned organization be further identified expeditiously and logical investigation initiated.

John and Yoko on the Dick Cavett Show, May 1972.

On the TV show hosted by Dick Cavett, in May 1972, John and Yoko had a chance to expose their visa problems and to express some concerns about the true reasons behind it all. Here is a transcript of what they said about these issues. They clearly denied wanting to go and disrupt the Republican National Convention.

Yoko Ono had a daughter, Kyoko, with her former husband Tony Cox, an American citizen, who had run away with her and was hiding somewhere in the US. Kyoko was 8 years old in 1972.

Yoko Ono : "You see, we're really frightened now because some people feel that we have to leave this country and that puts us in a position, especially for me, that I have to choose between my husband [John Lennon] and my child."

John Lennon : "Immigration's policy has always been not to split a family. So they're saying that Mr Lennon is not eligible because I was busted in England in 1968, planted by the way, but busted, I pleaded guilty on lawyers' advise. She was 3-months pregnant and all that was a real drag, but I did it and I paid my hundred dollar fine or whatever it was. Then they say : because I'm not eligible, rather than split a family, although there's nothing against Yoko Ono, you'd both better get out. And we're saying : but if you don't want to split a family, let us stay here because her daughter's here. She has to choose between me and her daughter. (…) They're saying : no matter what, you're a criminal and you'd better go."

"This drug case, which is a possession of marijuana case, in 1968, four years ago, it was planted and the sergeant who actually came to arrest us is now suspended. There are some questions about his method of arrest. The Immigration Office is saying this is only because of the drug case and nothing else. But the strange thing is that people like Donovan, Keith Richards, Mick Jagger, George Harrison, all have exactly the same case, exactly the same record, around the same time, by the same policeman and they can come and go anytime they want." (Yoko)

For more on the 1968 drug bust in England, see pages 128 to 131.

"They're after us because we talk about peace, you know. Because we want peace, we've been saying the same thing for two years, one way or another. And we believe in it." (John)

"The only thing we promote is peace and love. There's been some rumors that we might go to San Diego to disrupt the [Republican] Convention." (Yoko)

"They think we're going to San Diego or Miami or whatever it is. We've never said we're going, we ain't going. There'll be no big jam with us and Dylan. We've never said we were going and that's it." (John)

"The reason we wanna be here is because we really dig it, we dig America, we always have. She [Yoko] loves it and she's converted me to one of those New York fanatics. I hate it when I leave New York now." (John)

John and Yoko on the Dick Cavett Show, May 1972.

FD-36 (Rev. 5-22-64)

FBI

Date: 2/17/72

Transmit the following in _____
(Type in plaintext or code)

Via   AIRTEL
(Priority)

TO: DIRECTOR, FBI

FROM: SAC, NEW YORK (100-175438) (P)

SUBJECT: CHANGED
YOUTH ELECTION STRATEGY, aka.
PROJECT "YES"
IS-NEW LEFT
(OO:NY)

Title is changed to reflect correct captioned matter.

ReBuairtel, 2/15/72.

On 2/17/72, [redacted] advised that the Youth Election Strategy is the videotape arm of the Election Year Strategy Information Center (EYSIC), which will eventually attempt to purchase the Liberation New Service in New York City. This group is controlled by JOHN LENNON, RENNIE DAVIS and JERRY RUBIN who are also the key figures in EYSIC. They will make the contacts for videotapes, films, special events and entertainers to raise money for the group to finance EYSIC's anti-calrep demonstrations.

At the present, they have no separate office in New York City, however, they are working out of the Global Village which is a media - TV type of organization.

LHM will follow.

3 - Bureau (RM)
   (1 - 100- EYSIC)
2 - Los Angeles (RM)
3 - San Diego (RM)
   (1 - 100- EYSIC)
3 - Washington Field (RM)
   (1 - 100- EYSIC)
- New York copies cont'd.
- New York

(19) trr

Approved: _____
            Special Agent in Charge

ALL INFORMATION CONTAINED
HEREIN IS UNCLASSIFIED EXCEPT
WHERE SHOWN OTHERWISE

NY 100-175483

COPIES CONT'D.

```
1 - New York (100-163425) (DAVIS)
1 - New York (100-157178) (RUBIN)
1 - New York (100-175319) (LENNON) 42
1 - New York (100-175228) (EYSIC)
1 - New York (100-174678) (CLAREP)
1 - New York (100-163250) (LNS)
1 - New York
```

These next two documents appear in Lennon's INS file. They emphasize the fact that several US administrations – including the FBI, the INS and the Department of justice – were working together to prevent John Lennon from staying on American soil :

OPTIONAL FORM NO. 10
MAY 1962 EDITION
GSA FPMR (41 CFR) 101-11.5

UNITED STATES GOVERNMENT

Memorandum

CONFIDENTIAL

A17 597 321
DATE: February 17, 1972

TO : FILE

FROM : Masil J. Mason
Immigration Examiner

SUBJECT: John W. Lennon and his wife, Yoko Ono Lennon

(b)(7)(c)

On February 16, ▮▮▮▮▮ Investigations, advised that Mr. Joel Lisker, Internal Security, Department of Justice, phone code 187 extension 4538 called regarding the subject. Mr. Lisker stated that he had information that John Lennon has contributed $75,000 to a political group known as the "Alamoochi (phonetic) Tribe" and inquired as to the type of visa Lennon has and his status in the United States.

I returned Mr. Lisker's call. He asked whether or not there would be a basis for terminating the subject's status resulting from the above political activity. He was advised that this was doubtful that the Lennons entered the United States August 13, 1971 as B-2 nonimmigrants and their stay expires February 29, 1972 and that they would not be given further extensions of stay. He was advised that Mr. Lennon was inadmissible to the United States under section 212(a)(23) for a narcotic violation but that the same was not true for Mrs. Lennon.

He was also advised that because John Lennon is inadmissible he will need to obtain a new visa before he may again enter the United States. Before such a visa may be issued the Department of State would need to recommend that this Service authorize a waiver of the subject's inadmissibility under section 212(d)(3)(A). /At that time the above information about his political activities would be taken into consideration./

/Mr. Lisker/ then requested a notice be placed on file that he be informed should Lennon again seek reentry into the United States.

TC:MJM:lmg

KEEP THIS ON TOP OF OTHER MATERIAL — UNCLASSIFIED —

~~CONFIDENTIAL~~

This document shall be declassified upon removal of classified enclosure

Buy U.S. Savings Bonds Regularly on the Payroll Savings Plan

DAC/TC

Masil J. Mason   711

XX All Regions

XX All Districts (except FKG, MAP, MEX, RIT)

CO 235.40-C
FEB 25 1972

BAXEX - 13 P-3 A17 595 321. IF JOHN WINSTON LENNON BORN 10-9-40 ENGLAND ADMITTED 8-13-71 AT NYC B-2 PURSUANT SECTION 212(d)(3) APPLIES FOR EXTENSION OF STAY, ADJUSTMENT OF STATUS, OR HAS A VISA PETITION FILED IN HIS BEHALF DEFER ACTION AND CONTACT COTRA MASON. NOTIFY ALL OFFICES AND PORTS WITHIN YOUR JURISDICTION WHO ADJUDICATE ADJUSTMENT OF STATUS EXTENSIONS OF STAY/AND PETITIONS. BENED DIDIRS BETIL ROCOMS.

LEHMANN

CC: A17 597 321

CC: CO 235.40C

TC:MJM:anb

~~SECRET~~ ~~CONFIDENTIAL~~

2-22-72

AIRTEL

TO : DIRECTOR, FBI

FROM : LEGAT, LONDON (105-5492)(P)

SUBJECT: ELECTION YEAR STRATEGY
INFORMATION CENTER (EYSIC)
IS - NEW LEFT

ReBucab 2-11-72.

Enclosed are the original and 4 copies of an LHM relating to JOHN WINSTON LENNON.

[redacted]

A copy of the LHM has been disseminated to the Visa Section, American Embassy, London.

LEAD:

④ - Bureau (Encs. 5)
1 - Foreign Liaison Desk (Enc. 1)
1 - London
WR:ejg
(C) ALL INFORMATION CONTAINED HEREIN IS UNCLASSIFIED EXCEPT WHERE SHOWN OTHERWISE.

100-175319

~~SECRET~~ ~~CONFIDENTIAL~~

The code b1 applies to documents "kept secret in the interest of national defense or foreign policy".

And here is the same document with much less blacked out sections :

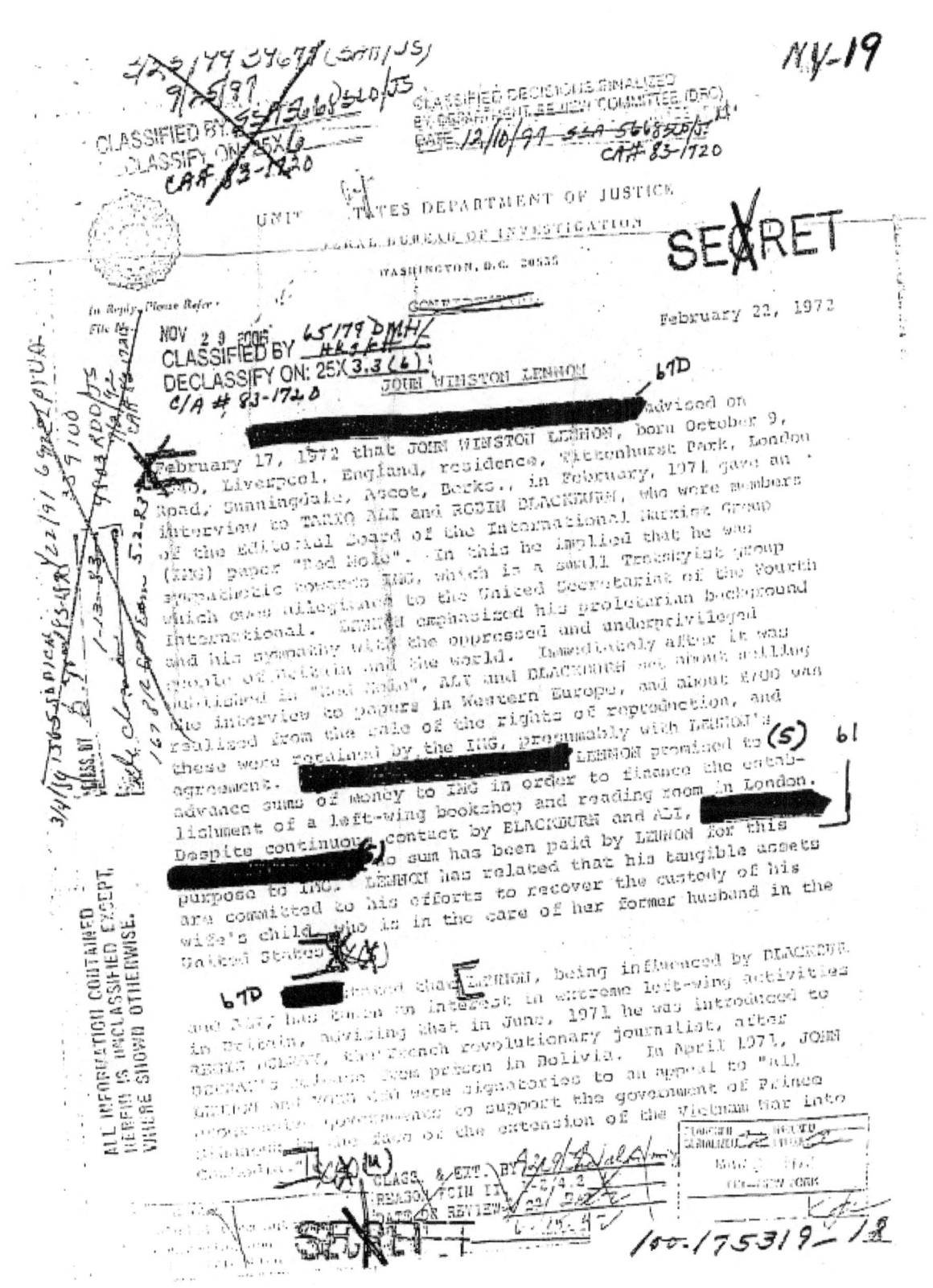

~~SECRET~~

CONFIDENTIAL

Re: JOHN WINSTON LENNON

(b7D) related

(b7D) asserted

(b7C)
(b7D)

advised on February 15, 1972 that JOHN WINSTON LENNON, born October 9, 1940 in Liverpool, England, on November 28, 1968, at Marylebone Magistrates Court, London, pleaded guilty to possessing dangerous drugs (cannabis). He was fined £150 and ordered to pay £21 costs.

The records of the Visa Section, American Embassy, London, as of February 15, 1972, revealed that JOHN LENNON last appeared at this Embassy on August 13, 1971. He was

CONFIDENTIAL   SECRET

Re: JOHN WINSTON LENNON

issued a B-1 and B-2 (business and pleasure) visa for one entry to the United States for a six-week period, after a waiver of his visa ineligibility because of his criminal conviction had been cleared with U. S. Immigration and Naturalization Service.

John & Yoko were arrested for cannabis possession on October 18, 1968. John pleaded guilty on November 28 and was sentenced to pay a £150 fine plus court costs of 20 guineas. The sentence was light but it played a great role in Nixon's administration's strategy to deport Lennon from the US and deny him a Green Card.

At the time of this drug bust, the couple was temporarily staying at Ringo Starr's flat in Montagu Square, in London. On October 18, 1968, the eight-strong police task force, led by Sergeant Norman Pilcher, entered the premises at 11.30am. It comprised two plainclothes detective sergeants, two detective constables, a policewoman and two sniffer-dog handlers, initially without their dogs.

Here is what John Lennon recalled in 1968 :

"We were lying in bed, feeling very clean and drugless, because we'd heard three weeks before that they were coming to get us - and we'd have been silly to have had drugs in the house. All of a sudden a woman comes to the front door, and rings the bell and says, 'I've got a message for you.' We said, 'Who is it? You're not the postman.' And she said, 'No, it's very personal,' and suddenly this woman starts pushing the door. She [Yoko] thinks it's the press or some fans, and we ran back in and hid. Neither of us was dressed, really; we just had vests on and our lower parts were showing.

We shut the door and I was saying, 'What is it? What is it?' I thought it was the Mafia or something. Then there was a big banging at the bedroom window, and a big super-policeman was there, growling and saying, 'Let me in, let me in!' And I said, 'You're not allowed in like this, are you?' I was so frightened. I said, 'Come round the front door. Just let me get dressed.' And he said, 'No, open the window, I'm going to fall off.'

There were some [police] at the front and some at the back. Yoko held the window while I got dressed - half-leaning out of the bathroom so they could see we weren't hiding anything. Then they started charging the door. I had a big dialogue with the policeman, saying, 'It's bad publicity if you come through the window.' And he was saying, 'Just open the window, you'll only make it worse for yourself.'

I was saying, 'I want to see the warrant.' Another guy comes on the roof and they showed me this paper, and I pretended to read it - just to try and think what to do. Then I said, 'Call the lawyer, call the lawyer,' but [Yoko] called our office instead. And I was saying, 'No, not the office - the lawyer.'

Then there was a heave on the door, so I ran and opened it, and said, 'OK. OK. I'm clean anyway,' thinking I was clean. And he says, 'Ah-ha, got you for obstruction!' And I said, 'Oh, yeah,' because I felt confident that I had no drugs.

They all came in, lots of them and a woman. I said, 'Well, what happens now? Can I call the office? I've got an interview in two hours, can I tell them that I can't come?' And he said, 'No, you're not allowed to make a phone call... Can I use your phone?' Then our lawyer came.

They [the police] brought some dogs. They couldn't find the dogs at first - and they kept ringing up, saying, 'Hello, Charlie, where are the dogs? We've been here half an hour.' And the dogs came.

I'd had all my stuff moved into the flat from my house, and I'd never looked at it. It had just been there for years. I'd ordered cameras and clothes - but my driver brought binoculars, which I didn't need in my little flat. And inside the binoculars was some hash from last year. Somewhere else in an envelope was another piece of hash. So that was it."

The police report states that 12.43 grams of cannabis resin were found in a binocular case and 1.77 more grams in an unsealed envelope. Traces of cannabis resin were also found on a can, a cigarette rolling machine and a cigarette case.

The police took John and Yoko to Paddington Green police station where they were charged with possession of cannabis and for obstructing the police in execution of a search warrant.

John pleaded guilty for possession on November 28 and was sentenced to pay a £150 fine plus court costs of 20 guineas. He was discharged on the obstruction charge. Yoko Ono was discharged on all charges.

Here is the article published on this issue in *The Times* newspaper on November 29, 1968 :

John Lennon fined £150 on drug charge

John Winston Lennon, aged 28, of The Beatles, was fined £150 with 20 guineas costs at Marleybone Magistrates' Court yesterday when he pleaded guilty to unauthorised possession of 219 grains of cannabis resin found when detectives accompanied by dogs searched his flat at Montagu Square Marleybone on October 18.

Appearing with him on remand, Mrs Yoko Ono Cox, aged 34, artist, of the same address, denied charges of unauthorised possession of the drug and willfully obstructing Detective Sergeant Norman Pilcher when he was exercising his powers under the Dangerous Drugs Act. She was discharged and Mr Lennon was also discharged on a similar charge of obstructing the officer, which he denied. The prosecution offered no evidence on those three counts.

Mr Roger Frisby, for the prosecution, told Mr John Phipps, the magistrate, that although the flat appeared to be in the joint occupation of the couple, Mr Lennon had taken full responsibility for the drugs and said Mrs Cox had nothing to do with it.

Mr Frisby said that when the officers got into the flat and told Mr Lennon that they had a search warrant they found a large quantity of drugs properly prescribed by Mr Lennon's doctor. When asked if he had any he should not have, such as cannabis, Mr Lennon shook his head. Mr Frisby said a cigarette rolling machine found on top of the bathroom mirror, a cannister originally containing film found in a bedroom and a cigarette case all bore traces of cannabis resin.

In an envelope in a suitcase was found 27.3 grains of the drug, and 191.8 grains was in a binocular case, nosed out by a dog, on the mantelshelf in the living room.

On November 8, 1972, Sgt. Norman Pilcher, who lead Lennon's drug bust, was arrested for conspiracy to pervert the course of justice after it was alleged he had committed perjury. In September 1973, Pilcher was convicted and sentenced to four years imprisonment. He was also suspected of planting evidence in several cases.

"I've never denied having been involved with drugs. There was a question raised in the Houses of Parliament : 'Why do they need forty cops to arrest John and Yoko ?' I mean, that thing was set up. *The Daily Mail* and *The Daily Express* were there before the cops came – he'd called the press. In fact, Don Short had told us, 'They're coming to get you' three weeks before. So, believe me, I'd cleaned the house out, because Jimi Hendrix had lived there before in the apartment, and I'm not stupid. I went through the whole damn house." (John Lennon, 1980)

"They got John and Yoko, and later they busted me too – and they chose Paul's wedding day to bust me on. Pilcher later emigrated to Australia, but then they extradited him and brought him back. He was charged with perjury and went to prison, but we still had trouble with our visas for years." (George Harrison)

In April 1975, John Lennon recalled this drug bust on Tom Snyder's 'Tomorrow Show' and explained why he pleaded guilty in 1968 and why he now believes the drug was planted :

John Lennon with Tom Snyder on *The Tomorrow Show*, April 1975

"In the late sixties, there was a head-hunting cop who was not very high up in the drug department in London - which was pretty new anyway. They had two dogs for the whole department. And he went round and busted every pop star he could get his hands on. And he got famous. Some of the pop stars had dope in their house and some of them didn't. It didn't matter to him. He planted it or did whatever. That's what he did to me. 'Cause at that time I didn't have any drugs.

He's in jail now by the way. He had a big drug scandal thing going. It happened after I left [England], and he was caught in Australia, trying to escape.

I at the time didn't even think he planted me. To cut a long story short, I'd just moved into an apartment and I had had everything moved from the other apartment. It was all over the place. So I thought 'oh maybe this is a bit of hash that was left over and I'd forgotten all about it'. Possibly that was what happened, you know. And I just copped a plea. He said I won't get you for obstruction if you cop a plea. And I thought : well it's a hundred dollars or whatever, it's no skin off my nose. I didn't think it would reverberate. He said I'll let your missus go.

The guy planted me and it didn't dawn on me till later, till I called a few friends who'd also been busted: did you have stuff ? One of them said : Yeah, I did have stuff, it was on the table, they didn't even notice it, they planted a whole pile in my bedroom. He had it out on the table, some marijuana. So the guy was a rip-off and he's in jail and half that drug department's in jail too.

I did just pay the fine and that was the end of it. And it went in the papers, whoopee, other pop star bites the dust, you know."

"I have a record for life because the cop who bust me and Yoko was scalp-hunting and making a name for himself." (John, 1980)

UNITED STATES GOVERNMENT

Memorandum

TO : SAC New York (100-157178)P DATE: 2/22/72

FROM : SA [redacted] b7C

SUBJECT: Jerry Rubin
SM- Youth International Party
(Extremist)
(Key Activist)
OO: NY
(100-157178)
John Winston Lennon
SM - NL
OO NY
(100-175319)

ALL INFORMATION CONTAINED
HEREIN IS UNCLASSIFIED
DATE 6/9/4? BY [redacted]

Captioned subjects will appear on the Mike Douglas Show, WCBS, New York Channel 2 TV on 2/22/72. Show begins at 4:30 pm & runs until 6:00 pm.

In view that both subjects are currently of interest to the Bureau & that New York is origin it is requested that section 14 record the show.

1 - 100-157178 (42)
1 - 100-175319 (42)
1 - Section 14 Supervisor

(3)
[initials]

100-175319-[?]

b7C

Buy U.S. Savings Bonds Regularly on the Payroll Savings Plan

Cover Sheet for Informant Report or M...
FD-306 (Rev. 9-30-69)

TO: SAC, PHILADELPHIA
FROM: SAC, NEW YORK (100-169939)
SUBJECT: PCPJ
IS - NEW LEFT

Date prepared: MAR 20 1972

Date received: 2/23/72
Received from (name or symbol number): [redacted] b2 b7D
Received by: SA [redacted] b7C

Method of delivery (check appropriate blocks):
[ ] in person [X] by telephone [ ] by mail [ ] orally [ ] recording device [ ] written by Informant

If orally furnished and reduced to writing by Agent:
Date Dictated _____ to _____
Transcribed _____
Authenticated by Informant _____

Date of Report: 2/23/72
Date(s) of activity:

Brief description of activity or material:
PCPJ activity

File where original is located if not attached: [redacted] b2 b7D

* INDIVIDUALS DESIGNATED BY AN ASTERISK * ONLY ATTENDED A MEETING AND DID NOT ACTIVELY PARTICIPATE. VIOLENCE OR REVOLUTIONARY ACTIVITIES WERE NOT DISCUSSED.

[ ] Information recorded on a card index by _____ on date _____

Remarks:
All necessary action taken.   DECLASSIFIED ON 5-2-13 BY 1678 RFp/san

7-Philadelphia (RM)
   (1-100-   )(D. BERRIGAN)(RM)
   (1-100-   )(HDC)(RM)
   (1-   )[redacted](RM)
   (1-   )[redacted](RM)
   (1-   )[redacted](RM)
   (1-   )[redacted](RM)
   (1-   )[redacted](RM)
   (1-   )[redacted](RM)
1-Boston [redacted] (RM)
1-Buffalo [redacted] (RM)
1-Newark [redacted] (RM)
1-Tampa (100-   )(FLA. PLATFORM)(RM)
1-Washington Field (100-   )(RENNIE DAVIS)(RM)
1-New York [redacted] b2
1-New York [redacted] b7D
[redacted] b7C
(20)

COPIES CONTINUED:

CLASS. & EXT. BY [redacted]
REASON-FCM II, 2.4/2
DATE OF REVIEW 3-20-97
6/12/92

ALL INFORMATION CONTAINED HEREIN IS UNCLASSIFIED EXCEPT WHERE SHOWN OTHERWISE.

Block Stamp:
100-175319-25
SEARCHED _____ INDEXED _____
SERIALIZED _____ FILED _____
FBI — NEW YORK
b7C

NY 100-169939

COPIES CONTINUED:

1-New York ███████████████(45) ⎫
1-New York ███████████████(45) ⎬ b7c
1-New York ███████████████   ⎪
1-New York (100-175319)(J. LENNON)(42)
1-New York ███████████████
1-New York (100-168469)(COMFAM)(42) ⎰ #(u)

- 1A -

CONFIDENTIAL

February 23, 1972

Daniel Berrigan will be released ~~today~~ 2/24/72 on bail. On February 24, 1972 there will be a demonstration at Danbury Prison sponsored by the Harrisburg Defense Committee.

After the demonstration at Danbury Prison there will be a "New England pilgramage for peace and freedom". This will be a march by those demonstrators at Danbury Prison to Harrisburg where they will hold a short press conference.

Berrigan will come to New York City as soon as he is released.

If one goes to Danbury to demonstrate and needs housing he may contact the following:

FRED CARPENTER
Danbury, Connecticut
telephone number 203-744-2903

Page Miller
Danbury, Connecticut
743-5037

Barbara Jenkins
Waterbury, Connecticut
757-8651

Ruth Tewksbury
Danbury, Connecticut
754-3542

The above information was issued by Tom Davidson.

The Noreen (phonetic) previously reported on is Noreen Banks of the New Hampshire Peoples Coalition for Peace and Justice (PCPJ).

ALL INFORMATION CONTAINED HEREIN IS UNCLASSIFIED EXCEPT WHERE SHOWN OTHERWISE.

CONFIDENTIAL

Mike Drobenare went to an unknown address for a meeting today, the address had phone number 431-6624.

There was a Mickey from the Peace Parade Committee (PPC) in the PCPJ office today. He is a white, male, 190 pounds, approximately 25, five feet nine inches, heavy build, shoulder length straight brown hair.

The following was found in Barbara Webster's phone book: Sue Leitner, 175 West 93rd Street, New York, New York, telephone number 865-9193, Steve Schere, PPC, telephone 343-6570; Florida Platform, Post Office Box 17521, Tampa, Florida, 33612.

The Florida Platform appears to be a mailing address for a peace organization.

The following information was also located in Webster's phone book:

As of November 15, 1970 there were 339 Prisoner of War alive in North Vietnam. Twenty have died, of that twenty, fifteen died of wounds while parachuting and five died of disease. Nine have been released.

Webster left on February 23, 1972 for Washington D.C. and will be back February 25th.

The 9000 letters being mailed by PCPJ in their fund raising effort will be mailed from the 32nd Street Westside Post Office.

Michael Drobenare is in New York City at the present time.

Alex is still in New York City and is growing a full beard.

During a conversation concerning information received at ▓▓▓▓▓▓▓▓▓▓▓▓▓▓▓▓▓▓▓▓▓▓ (name unknown) was attempting to locate ▓▓▓▓▓▓▓▓▓▓▓▓▓▓▓▓▓▓▓▓▓▓ stated that ▓▓▓▓▓▓▓▓▓▓▓▓▓▓▓▓▓▓▓▓▓▓

- 2 -

███████████ has had numerous conversations with John Lennon and his wife about becoming active in the New Left movement in the United States, and that Lennon and his wife seem uninterested. ███████████ can't seem to convince them they should become more active. ███████████ it was his opinion Lennon and his wife are passé about United States politics.

"John Lennon and his wife are passé about United States politics" : this statement didn't prevent deportation proceedings to be engaged against John Lennon in March 1972.

Cover Sheet for Informant Report or Material FD-306 (Rev. 9-30-69) TO: SAC, PHILADELPHIA FROM: SAC, NEW YORK (100-169939) SUBJECT: PCPJ SM-RA	Date prepared JUN 5 1972 CONFIDENTIAL

Date received	Received from (name or symbol number)	Received by
2/23/72	▓▓ b2 b7D	▓▓ b7C

Method of delivery (check appropriate blocks)

☐ in person ☒ by telephone ☐ by mail ☐ orally ☐ recording device ☐ written by Informant

If orally furnished and reduced to writing by Agent:

Date

Dictated _____ to _____

Transcribed _____

Authenticated by Informant _____

Date of Report: 2/23/72

Date(s) of activity:

Brief description of activity or material

PCPJ Activity

File where original is located if not attached
▓▓ b2 b7D

* INDIVIDUALS DESIGNATED BY AN ASTERISK (*) ONLY ATTENDED A MEETING AND DID NOT ACTIVELY PARTICIPATE. VIOLENCE OR REVOLUTIONARY ACTIVITIES WERE NOT DISCUSSED.

☐ Information recorded on a card index by _____ on date _____

Remarks:

All necessary action taken.

Please index STEVE SCHERZ, Peace Parade Committee, telephone number 343-6570.

```
8 - Philadelphia (RM)
    (1-100-    ) (D. BERRIGAN)
    (1-100-    ) (HDC)
    (1-         )
    (1-         )
    (1-         )
    (1-         )
    (1-         )
    (1-         )
1 - Boston           (RM)
1 - Newark           (RM)
1 - Tampa (100-  ) (FLORIDA PLATFORM) (RM)
1 - New York         (42) b2, b7D
```

DECLASSIFIED ON 5-2-83
BY 1628 RFP/jbms

ALL INFORMATION CONTAINED
HEREIN IS UNCLASSIFIED EXCEPT
WHERE SHOWN OTHERWISE.

NY 100-169939
COPIES CONTINUED:

1 - Washington Field Office (100-   ) (R. DAVIS) (RM)
1 - New York ███████████████████ (45)
1 - New York ███████████████████
1 - New York ███████████████████   b7c
1 - New York (100-175319) (J. LENNON) (42)
1 - New York ███████████████████

This document is a report on Lennon issued by the CIA :

MORI DocID: 1451843

23 FEB 1972

SUBJECT: Foreign Support For Activities Planned to Disrupt or Harass the Republican National Convention

1. There are only limited indications thus far of foreign efforts to inspire, support or take advantage of activities designed to disrupt or harass the National Convention of the Republican Party in San Diego, 21-23 August 1972.

2. Some American participants at the Soviet-controlled World Assembly for Peace and Independence of the Peoples of Indochina, held 11-13 February 1972 in Paris/Versailles, attempted unsuccessfully to include a call for international demonstrations to take place at the time of the Republican National Convention. A representative of the San Diego Convention Coalition (SDCC), one of the domestic action groups targetting on the Republican Convention, requested the American Delegations' Steering Committee at the World Assembly to include a specific call for international support of activities against the Republican convention in their proposal to the Action Commission of the World Assembly. This request, however, was dropped as too divisive by the Steering Committee, despite initial indications that the proposal would be taken to the floor of the Assembly.

3. John LENNON, a British subject, has provided financial support to Project "YES", which in turn paid the travel expenses to the World Assembly of a representative of leading antiwar activist Rennie DAVIS. (DAVIS' representative is tentatively planning to assist in preparations for disruptive actions at the San Diego Convention.) Project "YES" is an adjunct to another LENNON-supported project, the Election Year Strategy Information Center (EYSIC), of which Rennie DAVIS is a key leader, which was set up to direct New Left protest activities at the Republican National Convention. In Paris Rennie DAVIS' representative to the World Assembly met at least once with officials of the Provisional Revolutionary Government of South Vietnam; it is not known if the Republican National Convention was discussed.

00552

UNITED STATES GOVERNMENT

Memorandum

TO : Mr. E. S. Miller

FROM : [redacted]

SUBJECT: FBI CURRENT INTELLIGENCE ANALYSIS

1 - Mr. A. Rosen
1 - Mr. E. S. Miller
1 - [redacted]
1 - [redacted]
1 - [redacted]
1 - [redacted]

DATE: 2/24/72

Tolson
Felt
Rosen
Mohr
Bishop
Miller, E.S.
Callahan
Casper
Conrad
Dalbey
Cleveland
Ponder
Bates
Walkart
Walters
Soyars
Tele. Room
Holmes
Gandy

Attached is FBI Current Intelligence Analysis dated 2/25/72.

This issue highlights the Twentieth National Convention of the Communist Party, USA, which was held in Brooklyn, New York, 2/18-21/72. Two major party decisions came from the convention: the restructuring of the organization and the reinstitution of the use of party membership credentials. Party members were urged to continue supporting black militant [redacted] and were instructed to increase their participation in "peace" activities in the Nation. Criticism of President Nixon's trip to the People's Republic of China was voiced by party leaders. Reelected to head the party was Gus Hall, General Secretary.

The recent formation of Youth Election Strategy (YES) is reported. This New Left-oriented group is being formed by British musician John Lennon, New Left activist [redacted], and former Yippie leader Jerry Rubin to raise funds for proposed demonstration activities at the Republican National Convention in San Diego during August.

A planned New Left conference 3/3-5/72 is also set out. A group known as the Red Balloon Collective is attempting to form a strong national organization to bring together the fragmented elements of the New Left.

Enclosures

CPM:jan
(7)

MAILED 22
FEB 28 1972
FBI

100-422089 CONTINUED - OVER

Memorandum to Mr. E. S. Miller
Re: FBI Current Intelligence Analysis

      It is recommended that dissemination to The White House, the Vice President, and the Attorney General be made by appropriate transmittal forms. These will be hand-delivered to The White House and the Vice President by our liaison representative. Dissemination to each field office is by appropriate transmittal form. The distribution list for dissemination outside the Bureau, as approved by the Director, is attached. This dissemination is handled by the Mail Room.

ACTION:

      That the 2/25/72 issue of the FBI Current Intelligence Analysis be approved for dissemination.

- 2 -

FBI CURRENT INTELLIGENCE Analysis

Volume II, Number 4

February 25, 1972

COMMUNIST PARTY, USA (CPUSA)

CONVENTION HIGHLIGHTS

The Twentieth National Convention of the CPUSA was held February 18-21 at The Towers Hotel in Brooklyn, New York, with 254 delegates and alternates in attendance (Volume II, Numbers 2 and 3). Observers from Canada, Cuba, Chile, and Puerto Rico were also present. As in the past, there was much preconvention publicity on the importance of this meeting for the establishment of new policies for the CPUSA and on the vital roles to be played by those attending. However, the delegates' primary function was to serve again as a rubber stamp for the party hierarchy, headed by Gus Hall, General Secretary. Hall, in a three-hour speech opening the convention, reported on party accomplishments and outlined organization plans, placing stress on a new restructuring of the party. Without actually spelling it out for those at the convention, Hall's proposals were designed to appeal to the youthful element in the party while down-playing the roles of the older members. (CONFIDENTIAL)

The major development to come from the four-day convention was the establishment of a new organizational structure for the CPUSA. The Central Committee, comprised of approximately 50 members, will replace the National Committee and will be the party's most authoritative body. To run the day-to-day affairs of the CPUSA, the Central Committee will elect the Political Committee, to be made up of 7 to 9 members. Older and more experienced members will be relegated to positions on the National Council, which will have 100 members and meet semiannually to discuss party policies and operations. Four or five Regional Councils are to be established by the Central Committee to provide for local discussions of party matters; however, the resolutions of these councils will be advisory in nature and not binding on the Central Committee. (CONFIDENTIAL)

THIS DOCUMENT IS LOANED TO YOU BY THE FBI AND NEITHER IT NOR ITS CONTENTS ARE TO BE DISTRIBUTED OUTSIDE THE AGENCY TO WHICH LOANED

CONFIDENTIAL
FBI Current Intelligence Analysis

Party policy has traveled full circle concerning membership credentials. In 1948, as a security measure, party membership cards were discontinued. Twenty-four years later, a new generation of the party has demanded their use be reinstituted. Prior to the convention, this matter had produced heated debate in the party, indicating a convention battle would center on this issue. Convention delegates were not given an opportunity to discuss this issue, because National Organizational Secretary Daniel Rubin flatly announced to the assembly that a decision had been made to begin issuing membership books and dues stamps. (CONFIDENTIAL)

Reports presented at the convention boasted of the CPUSA's support of party member Angela Davis, now awaiting trial in California on murder and kidnaping charges, and the party faithful were urged to continue their protest efforts in behalf of Miss Davis. Party members were also praised for their continued work in the "peace movement" and were instructed to increase their involvement. (CONFIDENTIAL)

The high point of the convention for Gus Hall was his re-election as General Secretary, by a unanimous vote. As with his idols in the Soviet Union, Hall ran unopposed. (UNCLASSIFIED)

PARTY DISCIPLINARY ACTION

Paul Novick, 80-year-old editor of the *Morning Freiheit*, a Yiddish language communist newspaper published in New York City, was *not* expelled from the CPUSA--as had been proposed--for failing to follow the party line concerning the Mideast situation and anti-Semitism in the Soviet Union (Volume I, Number 37). Instead, the CPUSA decided to avoid a possibly devastating internal fight over this issue and delayed acting on the ouster of the long-time communist. (CONFIDENTIAL)

ADDITIONAL DEVELOPMENTS

During a convention press conference, Gus Hall strongly criticized President Nixon's trip to the People's Republic of China as an attempt to divide the socialist countries of the world. Related to this was National Chairman Henry Winston's statement relating to the President's trip: *Peace has to be found in the United States, not in China.* Not to be outdone on this general topic was James Jackson, Secretary of the International Affairs Commission, who, in a strange semantical twist, labeled Chinese Communist Party Chairman Mao Tse-tung as *anticommunist*. (CONFIDENTIAL)

CONFIDENTIAL

NEW LEFT DEVELOPMENTS

YOUTH ELECTION STRATEGY (YES)

British musician John Lennon, New Left activist Rennie Davis, and former Yippie leader Jerry Rubin are behind the recent formation of Youth Election Strategy (YES), which is to be the audio-visual arm of the Election Year Strategy Information Center (EYSIC) (Volume II, Number 3). YES plans to make arrangements for videotapes, films, and other forms of entertainment to raise funds for financing EYSIC's upcoming demonstration activities at the Republican National Convention in August. (CONFIDENTIAL)

NEW YORK NEW LEFT CONFERENCE PLANNED

A new bid is being made to bring elements of the shattered New Left under strong centralized leadership in order to revive the radical youth movement. Literature is now being distributed by a group known as the Red Balloon Collective announcing a conference will be held March 3-5 at the State University of New York in Stony Brook, New York, to form a *mass-based radical left organization which must be open to all levels and strategies to the left of electoral politics*. Appeals are being directed to various segments of the youthful subculture--communes, collectives, coffee houses, community switchboards--to gain a large and varied representation at the meetings. (UNCLASSIFIED)

In its preliminary statements, the Red Balloon Collective has been strongly critical of the New American Movement (NAM), which is attempting to form a similar group (Volume II, Number 2). NAM is condemned for having *its roots in the revolutionary American Constitution rather than Marxism* and for offering *no program of action*. The type of action the collective has in mind can be inferred from the types of persons expressing interest in the proposed new group. For example, Stewart Albert, Jay Craven, Paul Pinsky, and Rennie Davis (all formerly associated with the violence-prone May Day Collective) have been in the forefront of those indicating a desire to affiliate with the organization. (UNCLASSIFIED)

- 3 -

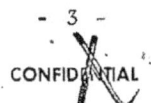

FD-36 (Rev. 5-22-64)

FBI

Date: 2/25/72

Transmit the following in _____
         (Type in plaintext or code)
Via AIRTEL
          (Priority)

TO: DIRECTOR, FBI (105-131719)

FROM: SAC, NEW YORK (100-157178)

SUBJECT: JERRY CLYDE RUBIN
     SM-YIP
     (EXTREMIST)
     (KEY ACTIVIST)
     (OO:NY)

  ReMMtel, 2/22/72 captioned, "DAVID TYRE DELLINGER, aka, ET AL (TRAVEL OF DEFENDANTS), ARL-CONSPIRACY; COC," relating that RUBIN was to appear on the Mike Douglas Show, 2/22/72.

  Enclosed for the Bureau are 10 copies of an LHM concerning RUBIN's appearance on the Mike Douglas Show, 2/22/72. Five copies of LHM are enclosed for Chicago.

  The tape recording of RUBIN's remarks on the above program is being exhibited in NY file 176-9 (JERRY CLYDE RUBIN.)

ALL INFORMATION CONTAINED HEREIN IS UNCLASSIFIED
DATE 6.14.82 BY_____

3-Bureau (Encs. 10) (RM)
 (1-176-59) (RUBIN)
2-Chicago (100-43245) (Encs. 5) (RM)
 (1-176-39) (RUBIN)
1-New York (100-175228) (EYSIC) (42)
1-New York (100-175319) (JOHN LENNON) (42)
1-New York (176-9) (RUBIN)
1-New York

WHB:ihr
(10)

100-175319-11

Approved: _____ Sent _____ M Per _____
 Special Agent in Charge

b7C

UNITED STATES DEPARTMENT OF JUSTICE

FEDERAL BUREAU OF INVESTIGATION
New York, New York
February 25, 1972

In Reply, Please Refer to
File No. Bufile (105-131719)
NYfile (100-157178)

ALL INFORMATION CONTAINED
HEREIN IS UNCLASSIFIED
DATE 6/14/82 BY

Jerry Clyde Rubin

On February 22, 1972, Jerry Rubin appeared on the Mike Douglas Television Show which was aired on Channel II, Columbia Broadcasting System, from 4:30 p.m. to 6:00 p.m. John Lennon, formerly with the Beatles musical group, and his wife were co-hosts on this show. This program was tape recorded and pertinent statements made by Rubin are included in this memorandum.

Mike Douglas introduced Jerry Rubin stating his feelings were quite negative concerning Rubin but that John Lennon wanted him on the show.

John Lennon stated that Rubin was not at all like his image as he and his wife were not like their image. He stated he found something in Rubin that was artistic.

Mike Douglas asked, "What is Jerry Rubin thinking about these days?"

Rubin stated, "Glad you asked that! We're going to support Nixon for President, because by going to China he is furthering communist revolution throughout the world, and also encouraging communism at home. Anything to get elected! Even though it's not appreciated by the right wing, it's appreciated by the left.-I'm just kidding! What he has really done is automate the war in Vietnam so that its machines killing people create a situation where 43 people can be murdered at Attica, create a situation where four kids can be killed at Kent State and people are afraid. The atmosphere of the country is one of his debts. I think the administration did this, and he is the symbol of it. And so I'm working very hard with people all over the country to defeat Nixon."

This document contains neither recommendations nor conclusions of the Federal Bureau of Investigation (FBI). It is the property of the FBI and is loaned to your agency; it and its contents are not to be distributed outside your agency.

Jerry Clyde Rubin

When questioned about the "Movement," Rubin stated that "the way the movement has changed is the pressure is so heavy that if anybody does anything, gets arrested, jailed, killed, that people are very pessimistic."

Douglas stated he had heard that Rubin was against drugs and this was the reason he was in favor of having him on the program. Rubin stated he was not against drugs but against heroin Rubin stated, "the police are the protectors of the heroin trade, and heroin is used against Black people and against some white people right now, as a killer drug. Too many young kids are taking downers and heroin, because they see no future for themselves in this country, they see no hope in changing the country, they see no decent life in which they can be creative and express themselves, so they shoot into their veins and take a pill. And that's the society's fault, as it offers no alternative. As a revolutionary movement, we've got to give an alternative."

When questioned about voting, Rubin stated that all young people should vote as a block, just like women should vote a a block. "We've got to get Nixon out of the White House because we've got to stop the automated war in Vietnam. It's power if we vote together. We shouldn't vote for any candidate that doesn't automatically withdraw everything from Vietnam. And we ought to go to both Conventions in Miami and San Diego and non-violently make our presence felt-and stand on the issues. If we do anything any other way, we'll be killed."

When questioned as to what he thinks is right in this country, Rubin stated that what's right is the fact that there are people in the country who want to change it. He stated that what he thought was beautiful about it, is that the children of America want to change the country and are going to.

FBI

Date: 2/25/72

Transmit the following in _____
(Type in plaintext or code)

Via ___AIRTEL___
(Priority)

TO: DIRECTOR, FBI

FROM: SAC, SAN DIEGO (100-16434) (P)

CALREP;
YOUTH ELECTION STRATEGY, aka
Project "Yes"
IS - NEW LEFT
(OO: New York)

Re Bureau airtel dated 2/15/72 and New York airtel dated 2/17/72.

Forwarded herewith to the Bureau are eleven (11) copies of an LHM concerning captioned organization.

Two copies are forwarded herewith to New York and one copy each to Los Angeles and Washington Field Office for information.

One copy each of this LHM is being disseminated locally at San Diego to the U.S. Secret Service; Alcohol, Tobacco and Firearms Division (ATFD); U.S. Naval Investigative Service Office (NISO); and the U.S. Attorney, San Diego.

2 - Bureau (Enc. 11) (RM)
2 - New York (100-175438) (Enc. 2) (RM)
1 - Los Angeles (Enc. 1) (Info) (RM)
1 - WFO (Enc. 1) (Info) (RM)
9 - San Diego
    (2 - 100-16434)
    (2 - 100-16372)
    (2 - 100-16200-Sub 2)
    (1 - _____)
    (1 - _____)
    (1 - 134-995A)
JHS:jam
(15)

Approved: _____ Sent _____
          Special Agent in Charge

cc
1 100-175319 (42)
   (Lennon)

ALL INFORMATION
HEREIN IS UNCLASSIFIED EXCEPT
WHERE SHOWN OTHERWISE.

100-175319-13

SD 100-16434

Dissemination of this LHM is being to NISO, San Diego, inasmuch as San Diego is home of the First Fleet and, therefore, NISO has a direct interest in developments pertaining to CALREP.

One copy of this LHM is being disseminated to the U.S. Attorney in San Diego in order that he may be apprised of developments dealing with CALREP.

Information contained in this LHM has been made available to local law enforcement agencies in San Diego, California.

The enclosed LHM is being classified "Confidential" as it contains information from documents so classified and because it contains information of a nature that its unauthorized disclosure would be prejudicial to the defense interests of the United States.

Sources mentioned in the enclosed LHM, contacted on 2/24/72, are identified as follows:

The thumbnail sketch of Youth Election Strategy, aka Project "Yes," set out in the LHM is based on information furnished

LEADS

SAN DIEGO

AT SAN DIEGO, CALIFORNIA. Will maintain contact with sources and informants and report any planned activities of captioned organization in form suitable for dissemination.

- 2 -

The last page of this document is not released because it is considered "the production of such law enforcement records or information could reasonably be expected to constitute an unwarranted invasion of personal privacy" (code (b)(7)(c)) and "could reasonably be expected to disclose the identity of confidential source" (code (b)(7)(d)).

4-750 (Rev. 4-17-85)

XXXXXX
XXXXXX
XXXXXX

FEDERAL BUREAU OF INVESTIGATION
FOIPA DELETED PAGE INFORMATION SHEET

_1_ Page(s) withheld entirely at this location in the file. One or more of the following statements, where indicated, explain this deletion.

☒ Deleted under exemption(s) _(b)(7)(c), (b)(7)(D)_ with no segregable material available for release to you.

☐ Information pertained only to a third party with no reference to you or the subject of your request.

☐ Information pertained only to a third party. Your name is listed in the title only.

☐ Documents originated with another Government agency(ies). These documents were referred to that agency(ies) for review and direct response to you.

_____ Pages contain information furnished by another Government agency(ies). You will be advised by the FBI as to the releasability of this information following our consultation with the other agency(ies).

_____ Page(s) withheld for the following reason(s):
_____
_____

☐ For your information: _____
_____

☒ The following number is to be used for reference regarding these pages:
_100-175319-13_ _pg 3_

XXXXX
XXXXX
XXXXXX

XXXXXXXXXXXXXXXXX
DELETED PAGE(S)
NO DUPLICATION FEE
FOR THIS PAGE
XXXXXXXXXXXXXXXXX

FBI/DOJ

UNITED STATES DEPARTMENT OF JUSTICE
FEDERAL BUREAU OF INVESTIGATION

San Diego, California
February 25, 1972

In Reply, Please Refer to
File No.

Title   YOUTH ELECTION STRATEGY, ALSO KNOWN AS PROJECT "YES".

Character

Reference   Memorandum dated and captioned as above at San Diego, California.

    All sources (except any listed below) used in referenced communication have furnished reliable information in the past.

This document contains neither recommendations nor conclusions of the FBI. It is the property of the FBI and is loaned to your agency; it and its contents are not to be distributed outside your agency.

UNITED STATES DEPARTMENT OF JUSTICE
FEDERAL BUREAU OF INVESTIGATION

San Diego, California
February 25, 1972

YOUTH ELECTION STRATEGY, ALSO
KNOWN AS PROJECT "YES"

On February 3, 1972, a confidential source advised that a group headed by RENNARD CORDON DAVIS, also known as Rennie Davis, is in its first phase of planning for disruption at the Republican National Convention (RNC) to be held in San Diego, California, from August 21 - August 23, 1972. According to this source, DAVIS and other associates from the People's Coalition for Peace and Justice (PCPJ) recently moved from Washington, D. C. to New York City.

RENNARD CORDON DAVIS is a convicted defendant of the so-called Conspiracy 7 Trial, Chicago, Illinois, in the period September, 1969 - February, 1970, involving those persons earlier indicted for violation of the Federal Anti-Riot Statute.

PCPJ in a press release dated March 1, 1971, described itself as being headquartered in Washington, D. C. and consisting of over 100 organizations which are using massive civil disobedience to combat racism, poverty, repression and war.

YOUTH ELECTION STRATEGY, ALSO KNOWN AS PROJECT "YES"

According to this source, the plans for San Diego include rock concerts featuring JOHN LENNON, formerly of the Beatles rock music group, and his wife, YOKO ONO, as the main crowd drawers backed up by lesser rock group talents.

It was further related by this source that dates have been reportedly been arranged in Florida and New Hampshire and the concerts will include speeches by JERRY RUBIN and RENNIE DAVIS, along with LENNON who will urge the audience to (a) register to vote; (b) work for the legalization of marijuana; and (c) get to San Diego for the GOP Convention.

This source further stated that conflicting reports make it difficult to analyze the proposed activities of JOHN LENNON at this time. While this source indicates LENNON may be coming to San Diego, other indications are that he will perform along the East Coast only and contribute a portion of his proceeds to the San Diego Convention Coalition.

> JERRY RUBIN is a convicted defendant of the so-called Conspiracy 7 Trial, Chicago, Illinois, in the period of September, 1969 - February, 1970, involving those persons earlier indicted for violation of the Federal Anti-Riot Statute.

> SDCC is a group comprised of representatives of various radical groups in San Diego, California, which was formed for active opposition to the United States Government through "serious, determined, and long term social upheaval."

The aforementioned confidential source, along with other confidential sources familiar with certain phases of New Left activity in the San Diego area, advised

YOUTH ELECTION STRATEGY, ALSO KNOWN AS PROJECT "YES"

on February 24, 1972, that information has been received in San Diego regarding proposed activities of a group headed by RENNIE DAVIS and including JOHN LENNON in connection with the RNC but no specific information has been received regarding any such activities under the name of Election Year Strategy Information Center (EYSIC) or Youth Election Strategy, also known as Project "Yes."

EYSIC is a group formed from meetings held at the Peter Stuyvesant Farm, Allamuchy, New Jersey, during December, 1971. The group is headed by RENNIE DAVIS and was organized for the purpose of directing New Left activities during the election year and to culminate with demonstrations at the 1972 RNC. On January 28, 1972, the group changed its name from Allamuchy Tribe to EYSIC.

Youth Election Strategy, also known as Project "Yes," is the video-tape arm of EYSIC which will eventually attempt to purchase the Liberation News Service in New York City. This group is controlled by JOHN LENNON, RENNIE DAVIS, and JERRY RUBIN, who are also key figures in EYSIC. They will make the contacts for video tapes, films, special events, and entertainers to raise money for the group to finance demonstrations in opposition to the RNC.

Liberation News Service (LNS) publishes news packets in New York City on a weekly basis and the packets are sold to radical New Left underground newspapers.

This document contains neither recommendations nor conclusions of the FBI. It is the property of the FBI and is loaned to your agency; it and its contents are not to be distributed outside your agency.

CONFIDENTIAL

UNITED STATES DEPARTMENT OF JUSTICE

FEDERAL BUREAU OF INVESTIGATION
New York, New York
February 28, 1972

In Reply, Please Refer to
File No.

NYfile (100-175228)

Election Year Strategy
Information Center, formerly
known as the Allamuchy Tribe

On January 21, 1972, a source, who has furnished reliable information in the past, advised that a group of individuals calling themselves the Allamuchy Tribe, met at the Peter Stuyvesant Farm in Allamuchy, New Jersey, during December, 1971. The source advised that Rennie Davis headed the group along with Stewart Albert and Jay Craven. Jay Craven and the other individuals in attendance were either members of the May Day Collective (MDC) or Peoples Coalition for Peace and Justice (PCPJ). The source further advised that the purpose of the meeting was to establish a group of individuals to coordinate New Left Movement activities during t election year, to culminate with demonstrations at the Republic National Conventions in San Diego, California during August, 1972.

Rennie Davis

On February 18, 1970, Rennie Davis, whose true name is Rennard Cordon Davis, was found guilty in United States District Court, Northern District of Illinois,

CONFIDENTIAL

GROUP I
Excluded from automatic
downgrading and
declassification

This document contains neither recommendations nor conclusions of the Federal Bureau of Investigation (FBI). It is the property of the FBI and is loaned to your agency; it and its contents are not to be distributed outside your agency.

CONFIDENTIAL

Election Year Strategy
Information Center

Chicago, Illinois, for violation of the Federal
Antiriot Law Statute in that he traveled in
interstate commerce from outside the State of
Illinois with intent to incite, organize, promote
and encourage a riot on or about August 28, 1968.
On February 20, 1970, Davis received 23 individual and
separate criminal contempt citations regarding the
above trial, and was sentenced to serve two years,
one month and nine days regarding these citations.
Davis was incarcerated February 14, 1970, Cook County
Jail, Chicago, and released on $25,000 bond on February
28, 1970, pending trial. During January, 1971, Davis
organized the MDC at Washington, D.C. to exert an
influence on the PCPJ policies concerning the planning
of a massive anti-war demonstration at Washington,
D.C. during May, 1971.

Stewart Albert

On April 25, 1966, a second source, who has
furnished reliable information in the past, advised
that Stewart Albert was arrested on April 12, 1966
at Berkeley, California, along with other Progressive
Labor Party (PLP) members while demonstrating in
front of the Berkeley City Hall.

PLP

The PLP was founded in 1962 by individuals
expelled from the Communist Party, USA, for
following the Chinese Communist line. Its
objective is the establishment of a militant
working-class movement based on Marxism-Leninism
and MAO Tse-tung thought.

MDC

The MDC in New York City (NYC) is publicly known
as an organization that participated in
demonstrations in Washington, D.C. during the
first week in May, 1971, sponsored by the PCPJ.

CONFIDENTIAL

CONFIDENTIAL

Election Year Strategy
Information Center

PCPJ

The PCPJ is self-described as an organization consisting of over 100 organizations using massive civil disobedience to combat war, racism, poverty and repression. Its National Office is located at 156 5th Avenue, NYC, Room 527.

On January 24, 1972, the first source advised that John Winston Lennon, who was formerly associated with the Beatles Music Group, donated $75,000 and ▓▓▓▓▓▓ donated $15,000 to the group to finance their activities.

Mary Boulton

Mary Boulton is the widow of the late Frank Bancroft. The now defunct "New York Journal American" in its November 28, 1952 issue, carried an article entitled, "Oust Teacher, Wife of UN Aide." This article related that the wife of Frank Bancroft, a United Nations Executive that was suspended for refusal to answer a question if he was a communist, had lost her substitute teacher's license in the State of New York. The article related that her husband had been subpoenaed by a Federal Grand Jury, later for appearance before a Senate Internal Security Subcommittee. The article further related that Mrs. Bancroft had failed to appear when she was summoned for questioning concerning a Board of Education Probe into Communism.

On January 27, 1972, a third source, who has furnished reliable information in the past, advised that during December, 1971, a group of individuals calling themselves the Allamuchy Tribe had met in Allamuchy, New Jersey to discuss plans for coordinating demonstrations at the Republican National Convention in San Diego, California in August, 1972. The group included Carole Sue Cullem, Carol Mildred Kitchens, Michael Alan Drobenare and other individuals unknown to him who were members of the PCPJ in Washington, D.C. that had traveled to New Jersey for this particular meeting. Along

CONFIDENTIAL

- 3 -

CONFIDENTIAL

Election Year Strategy
Information Center

with Stewart Albert and Rennie Davis, Jerry Rubin appeared to be in leadership at the meeting.

Jerry Rubin

On February 18, 1970, Jerry Rubin was found guilty in United States District Court, Northern District of Illinois, Chicago, Illinois for violating the Federal Antiriot Law Statute for traveling in interstate commerce from outside the State of Illinois with intent to incite riots in Chicago, Illinois during the Democratic National Conventions in August, 1968. On February 20, 1970, he was sentenced to five years imprisonment and fined $5,000. On February 28, 1970, the United States Court of Appeals, Seventh Circuit, Chicago, Illinois, ordered him released on $25,000 bond, pending appeal of his conviction.

On January 28, 1972, the first source advised that the group formerly known as the Allamuchy Tribe had changed its name to the "Election Year Strategy Information Center" (EYSIC). This change was made as to be "more effectively known, since the general public would soon become aware of its anti-Republican National Convention activities."

On February 2, 1972, the first source advised that a meeting had been held at the Washington Square Methodist Church in NYC on January 29, 1972 to further discuss officers and finances of EYSIC. The group decided that a permanent staff of officers would be set up in the near future and that the officers would receive $125 per week salary.

On February 2, 1972, a fourth source, who has furnished reliable information in the past, advised that Christine Johnson, Noreen Banks, Allan Alpern, Mike Weber, and Winslow Peck, who are all members of the PCPJ in Washington, D.C., transferred to the PCPJ office in NYC to work on the EYSIC project. All of these individuals were to stay with Thomas Hirsch at Apartment 9E1, 600 West 111th Street, NYC. Tom Hirsch is also associated with the PCPJ in NYC.

CONFIDENTIAL

CONFIDENTIAL

Election Year Strategy
Information Center

On February 17, 1972, the first source advised that individuals with EYSIC had formerly planned on using a warehouse on the corner of West 10th Street and Hudson Avenue in NYC as their headquarters. However, they had abandoned the idea due to the warehouse space being in such dilapidated condition. The source advised that at the present, Jerry Rubin, Stewart Albert and John Winston Lennon are working in office space at the Global Village, which is a TV media type of organization in NYC. They are coordinating plans to purchase the Liberation News Service (LNS) in NYC and use its wire services and mailing list to expand the activities of EYSIC. This group, a segment of EYSIC is calling itself the Youth Election Strategy (YES), and it has the financial backing of Lennon.

LNS

The LNS is self-described as an underground news wire service with headquarters in NYC which publishes news packets weekly that are sold to radical New Left underground newspapers. It was founded in 1967 and reportedly has a paid circulation over 600.

On February 23, 1972, a fifth source, who has furnished reliable information in the past, advised that the Global Village is located at 454 Broome Street, NYC. The source further advised that several members of EYSIC are making plans to form a musical band to travel to several election primaries. They will eventually travel to San Diego, California to participate in demonstrations at the Republican National Convention.

CONFIDENTIAL

FBI

Date: 2/28/72

Transmit the following in _____
(Type in plaintext or code)

Via AIRTEL
_____
(Priority)

TO: DIRECTOR, FBI

FROM: SAC, NEW YORK (100-175228) (P)

SUBJECT: ELECTION YEAR STRATEGY INFORMATION CENTER (EYSIC)
IS-NEW LEFT
(CALREP)
(OO: NY)

ReBuairtel, 1/26/72, Buairtel, 2/15/72, captioned Project "Yes" IS-NL, and NYairtel, 2/17/72, captioned Youth Election Strategy, IS-NL, OO:NY, NYfile 100-175438.

Enclosed for the Bureau are 10 copies of an LHM captioned and dated as above. Copies are being designated for those offices having PCPJ, May Day Collective, or National Political Conventions in their Divisions.

Copies of the LHM are also being designated to INS, 108 MIG, USA, SDNY, and USSS for information purposes.

2 - Bureau (Encls. 10) (RM)
1 - INS, NYC (Encl. 1) (RM)
4 - 108 MIG, NYC (Encl. 1) (RM)
1 - USA, SDNY (Encl. 1) (RM)
1 - USSS, NYC (Encl. 1) (RM)
2 - Albany (Encl. 2) (RM)
2 - Atlanta (Encl. 2) (RM)
3 - Boston (Encl. 3) (RM)
2 - Buffalo (Encl. 2) (RM)
2 - Indianapolis (Encl. 2) (EM)
2 - Los Angeles (Encl. 2) (RM)
2 - Miami (Encl. 4) (RM)
3 - San Diego (Encl. 5) (RM)
2 - San Francisco (Encl. 2) (RM)
Copies Cont'd.
1 - New York

Approved: _____ Sent _____ M Per _____
 Special Agent in Charge

NY 100-175228
COPIES CONT'D.

```
2 - Tampa (Encl. 2) (RM)
2 - Washington Field (Encl. 2) (RM)
1 - New York (105-42122) (ALBERT) (42)
1 -                                          b7C
1 -                                    (c) b1
1 - 100-174678) (CALREP) (42)
1 -                                          b7C
1 - 100-163425) (DAVIS) (42)
1 -                                          b7C
1 -
1 -
1 - 100-175319) (LENNON) (42)
1 - 100-163250) (LNS) (42)
1 - 100-172771) (MAY DAY) (42)
1 -                          (u)       b2,b7D
1 -                          (42)      b2,b7D
1 - 100-169939) (PCPJ) (42)   b7C
1 - 100-157178) (RUBIN) (42)
1 -                                          b7C
1 - 100-175438) (YES) (42)
```

Two extra copies are being sent to Miami and San Diego in event they wish to furnish appropriate Military Intelligence Groups and USSS in their Divisions copies.

b7D Captioned LHM is classified "Confidential" as to protect ▓▓▓▓▓▓▓▓▓▓▓▓▓▓▓▓ who are of continuing value and the unauthorized disclosure of their identities could impair their future effectiveness and be prejudicial to the National defense interest of the United States.

The New York Division will follow captioned matter closely and forward promptly any information developed to the Bureau and interested offices.

- 2 -

NY 100-175228

LEADS

Receiving offices who are office of origin on individuals mentioned in this LHM are requested to furnish the NYO with background, descriptive data and a current photograph of their subjects. Receiving offices are also requested to contact informants in their Divisions who are acquainted with subjects mentioned; PCPJ; and May Day Collective, activities regarding information on captioned case.

The following three documents are taken from John Lennon's INS file. They clearly show the political reasons behind the deportation proceedings initiated against him and the administration's role and involvement in the conduct of this case. Lennon's INS file contains no less than 3400 pages !

A17 597 321

March 1, 1972

(b)(6)

Mr. John W. Lennon
and Mrs. Yoko Ono Lennon
105 Bank Street
New York, N. Y.

Dear Mr. and Mrs. Lennon:

The records of this Service indicate that your temporary stay in the United States as visitors has expired on February 29, 1972.

It is expected you will effect your departure from the United States on or before March 15, 1972. Failure to do so will result in the institution of deportation proceedings.

Please notify this Service of the date, place and manner of your departure at least two days in advance of your leaving by calling Mr. Orville R. Conley at 264-5826.

Very truly yours,

SOL MARKS
District Director
New York District

cc: Leon Wildes, Esq.
515 Madison Avenue
New York, N. Y. 10022

ORC:ekw

March 2, 1972

MEMORANDUM FOR FILES:

Re: John LENNON - A17 597 321 (Conf.)
    Yoko Ono LENNON - [ ] (Conf.) (b)(6)

Associate Commissioner Greene telephonically advised today that we should immediately revoke the voluntary departure granted to John Lennon and his wife. An O.S.C. should be issued for both aliens and served upon them with a return date of March 16, 1972.

Mr. Greene further stated that under no circumstances should this office approve the I-140 filed by Lennon. This is a direction of Commissioner Farrell personally. Further action on the petition will therefore not be taken unless cleared by the undersigned with Mr. Greene.

Mr. Spivack has been advised.

SOL MARKS
District Director
New York District

cc: Mr. Spivack

This INS document shows that Nixon's administration was determined to get Lennon out of the US, no matter what : "In any event, all applications by the male subject for extension of stay or extension of voluntary departure time should be denied". Leon Wildes, Lennon's lawyer on his deportation case, explained in April 1975 (on Tom Snyder's 'Tomorrow Show') that this strategy to deny John any further time on US soil was intended to force him to either leave the US voluntarily, which he obviously didn't wish, or to apply for permanent residence, which couldn't be granted to him because of his 1968 drug bust in England for possession of marijuana.

LONG DISTANCE TELEPHONE CALL REPORT

DATE	ACTIVITY	FACILITY: FTS XXXX COMMERCIAL	AMOUNT (DO NOT FILL IN THIS BLOCK WHEN CALL IS HANDLED THROUGH A SERVICE SWITCH BOARD OR WHEN FTS IS USED.)	FILE NO.
3/1/72	50.0			CO 837-C

FROM: (NAME) (OFFICE) Carl G. Burrows, Assistant Commissioner Investigations, C. O., Washington, D. C.
TELEPHONE NUMBER CHARGED: 626-1348

TO: (NAME) (OFFICE) Sol Marks, District Director New York, New York
TELEPHONE NUMBER CALLED: 212-264-5943

CERTIFICATION: I CERTIFY THAT THIS OFFICIAL TELEPHONE CALL WAS NECESSARY IN THE INTEREST OF THE GOVERNMENT.

Carl G Burrows
SIGNATURE OF EMPLOYEE MAKING THE CALL.

APPROVAL:
SIGNATURE OF APPROVING OFFICER. (REQUIRED ON COPY ONLY.)

JUSTIFICATION: WAS THIS CALL MADE AT THE REQUEST OF THE CENTRAL OFFICE OR REGIONAL OFFICE? ☐ YES ☐ NO
IF "NO" IS CHECKED, ENTER JUSTIFICATION.

SUBJECT MATTER: Termination of stay in the United States of John W. Lennon, A17 597 321, and his wife, Yoko Ono, [redacted] (b)(6)

I advised Mr. Marks that it had been determined that no Service benefit should be granted the subjects whose extensions of stay expired yesterday, February 29, 1972. Mr. Marks is to arrange to hand deliver a letter to both subjects advising them that they must leave the United States within 15 days, with copies of the letter going to their attorney of record, Leon Wildes. In the event subjects fail to depart, Orders to Show Cause are to be issued and deportation proceedings instituted. If, however, persuasive reasons are given for the further stay in the United States of the female subject incident to the court suit for custody of her child, Kyoko, by prior marriage to Anthony D. Cox, her case may be separated from that of the male subject. In any event, all applications by the male subject for extension of stay or extension of voluntary departure time should be denied.

CC: In Duplicate - District Director, New York, New York
Personal Attention: Sol Marks - with return of CONFIDENTIAL file A17 597 321 which relates to the male subject.

~~CONFIDENTIAL~~

DC:CGB:dmw

This document shall be declassified upon removal of classified enclosure.

— *UNCLASSIFIED* —

ORIGINAL TO CASE FILE, SUBJECT FILE OR WORK FOLDER; COPY TO FINANCE

FORM G-40 (REV. 3-1-66) **UNITED STATES DEPARTMENT OF JUSTICE** Immigration and Naturalization Service

FBI

Date: 3/2/72

Transmit the following in _____
(Type in plaintext or code)

Via   AIRTEL
_____
(Priority)

TO: DIRECTOR, FBI

FROM: SAC, NEW YORK (100-175228) (P)

SUBJECT: ELECTION YEAR STRATEGY
         INFORMATION CENTER
         IS - NEW LEFT
         (CALREP)
         (OO:NY)

Re NY airtel and LHM dated 2/28/72; and San Diego airtel and LHM dated 2/25/72 captioned "YOUTH ELECTION STRATEGY IS - NL".

On 3/2/72, [redacted] Immigration Officer, Immigration and Naturalization Service, 20 West Broadway, NYC, advised that on 3/1/72 INS served notice to JOHN WINSTON LENNON and his wife YOKO ONO LENNON to be out of the United States by 3/15/72, that their visas had been recalled.

LEAD:

NEW YORK

AT NEW YORK, NEW YORK. Will keep Bureau advised

4-Bureau (RM)
2-Miami (RM)
2-San Diego (RM)
0-New York (100-175319)(LENNON)
1-New York (100-175433) (YES)
1-New York

UNITED STATES GOVERNMENT
Memorandum

TO : SAC, NEW YORK (100-175319) DATE: 3/7/72

FROM : SUPV. ███████ #311)

SUBJECT: JOHN WINSTON LENNON
SM-NL

On 3/7/72, INS Investigator ███████ telephonically advised that captioned and his wife, YOKO ONO, were served on 3/6/72, with an order to show cause as to why they should not be deported from the US as over-stayed visitors.

Review of NY indices reflects ident case file as indicated presently assigned to Rotor #42.

The foregoing is furnished for information.

1-New York
eac
(1)

ALL INFORMATION CONTAINED HEREIN IS UNCLASSIFIED
DATE 6/9/82 BY ███████

Buy U.S. Savings Bonds Regularly on the Payroll Savings Plan

Indices Search Slip
FD-160 (Rev. 10-1-59)

TO: CHIEF CLERK

Subject: John Lenon

File & Serial Number	Remarks	File & Serial Number	Remarks
162-1-Sub 7/178 p2	1/65		
501 W 47 St New York		2	
dob 1/20/29			

Searched by: 3/6/72

ALL INFORMATION CONTAINED HEREIN IS UNCLASSIFIED
DATE 6/16/82

UNITED STATES DEPARTMENT OF JUSTICE
FEDERAL BUREAU OF INVESTIGATION
Washington, D.C. 20535
March 8, 1972

CONFIDENTIAL

ELECTION YEAR STRATEGY INFORMATION CENTER

On March 1, 1972, a confidential source of the Federal Bureau of Investigation who has provided reliable information in the past, advised that Thomas Hayden, a convicted Chicago Seven conspiracy trial defendant, flew to the Washington, D.C. area on February 26, 1972, and met with Rennard Cordon Davis, another convicted Chicago Seven conspiracy trial defendant. These two individuals discussed the possibility of forming a group calling itself the "anti-war union". This was described as a coalition of individuals who, in the past, had shown leadership in various new left oriented organizations. The projected purpose of the anti-war union would be to formulate tactics in regard to movement actions during the 1972 election year primary elections, including confrontations with candidates during their speaking tours, and as a support base for the "arena stage", a recently coined description of the new left oriented "entertainment group" that would include John Winston Lennon, former "beatles" rock singer, and his wife, Yoko Ono, and function as a stimulus to encourage youths to be in the vicinity of election candidates when they are on tour.

The source indicated that currently the following organizational titles coined by Rennard Davis and his followers appear to be synonymous, and will be functioning toward the general goal of candidate harrassment and general disruption during the 1972 election year: arena stage, International News Service, Election Year Strategy Information Center (Office), the youth contingent of the People's Coalition for Peace and Justice.

This document contains neither recommendations nor conclusions of the FBI. It is the property of the FBI and is loaned to your agency it and its contents are not to be distributed outside your agency.

CONFIDENTIAL
GROUP 1
Excluded from automatic downgrading and declassification

Probably an INS memo:

JOHN WINSTON LENNON

A section 212(d)(3)(A) waiver of section 212(a)(23) was authorized for John Lennon by the Central Office on August 1, 1971. This order was based on State's recommendation that Lennon be permitted to enter for six weeks in August 1971 to edit film and consult with business associates at ABKCO Industries, 17 Broadway, New York City and Capital Records in New York City in connection with record release in September 1971, and to attend custody hearing on wife's child by former marriage in St. Thomas, Virgin Islands on September 16, 1971.

Mr. Lennon was admitted as a temporary visitor (B-2) for this purpose at New York City on August 13, 1971 with stay authorized to September 24, 1971. His stay was subsequently extended to February 29, 1972.

On March 1, 1972 the District Director in New York City notified Lennon in writing that his stay had expired on February 29, 1972 and gave him until March 15, 1972 within which to depart voluntarily without the institution of deportation proceedings. Upon learning that he did not plan to depart, the District Director notified Lennon on March 6, 1972 that this privilege of voluntary departure was revoked. Thereafter an order to show cause was issued on March 7, 1972 with hearing scheduled for March 16, 1972.

During Lennon's stay the following H-1 petitions were approved on his behalf for the purposes indicated:

1. To appear on the Dick Cavett Show on September 8, 1971.

2. To appear on the David Frost Show during the period December 16 through 21, 1971.

3. To appear on the Mike Douglas Show during period January 14 through 31, 1972.

Not FBI Doc.

FEDERAL BUREAU OF INVESTIGATION
COMMUNICATIONS SECTION

MAR 16 1972

TELETYPE

NR 028 NY CODE

440 PM URGENT 3-16-72 BGW

TO DIRECTOR

ATTN: DID

FROM NEW YORK (100-175319) 2P

Security Matter
JOHN WINSTON LENNON; SM-NEW LEFT   OO:NY

ON MARCH SIXTEENTH INSTANT MR. VINCENT SCHIANO, Immigration and Naturalization Service, New York City CHIEF TRIAL ATTORNEY, INS, NYC, ADVISE THAT JOHN LENNON AND HIS WIFE YOKO ONO APPEARED AT INS, NYC THIS DATE FOR DEPORTATION PROCEEDINGS. BOTH INDIVIDUALS THRU THEIR ATTORNEY WON DELAY OF HEARINGS. LENNON REQUESTED DELAY WHILE HE ATTEMPTED TO FIGHT A NARCOTOCS CONVICTION IN ENGLAND. YOKO ONO REQUESTED DELAY ON BASIS OF CHILD CUSTODY CASE IN WHICH SHE IS INVOLVED.

MR. SCHIANO ADVISED THAT NEW HEARINGS WOULD BE HELD ON APRIL EIGHTEEN NEXT. IF LENNON WINS OVERTHROW OF BRITISH NARCOTIC CONVICTION, INS WILL RECONSIDER THEIR ATTEMPTS

END PAGE ONE

PAGE TWO

TO DEPORT LENNON AND WIFE. SCHIANO ADVISED THERE WAS
EXTENSIVE NEWS COVERAGE AT HEARINGS BOTH INSIDE AND OUT OF
BUILDING. LENNON SPOKE WITH LOCAL UPI, AND ASSOCIATED PRESS (AP)
(United Press International)
REPRESENTATIVES WHEN HE LEFT HEARINGS AND CLAIMED HE WAS
FRAMED IN BRITISH NARCOTICS ARREST.
    NYO FOLLOWING
END New York Office

CC-MR. MILLER

John Lennon and Yoko Ono leave a brief deportation hearing in New York at the offices of the Immigration and Naturalization Service, on March 16, 1972.

John with his attorney, Leon Wildes.

FD-36

Transmit the following in _____
(Type in plaintext or code)

Via AIRTEL
(Priority)

TO: DIRECTOR, FBI

FROM: SAC, NEW YORK (100-175319) (P)

SUBJECT: JOHN WINSTON LENNON
SM-NEW LEFT
(OO:NY)

ReNYairtel and LHM captioned "ELECTION YEAR STRATEGY INFORMATION CENTER, IS-NL", dated 2/28/72 and Legat London airtel and LHM, dated 2/22/72.

Enclosed for the Bureau are 12 copies of an LHM dated and captioned as above.

A copy of this LHM has been disseminated locally at INS, NYC.

It is requested that Legat London be furnished appropriate copies of this LHM.

WFO is being furnished a copy of this LHM due to their previous interest.

(2)- Bureau (Encls. 12) (RM)
2 - Washington Field Office (Encls. 2) (RM)
1 - New York (100-175228)
1 - New York

CJL:lh
(10)

Special Agent in Charge

NY 100-175319

Sources mentioned in the attached LHM are identified as follows:

The LHM is classified "Confidential" as to protect sources ███ through ███ of continuing value, whose unauthorized disclosure could be prejudical to the security interest of the United States.

LEADS:

NEW YORK

　　AT NEW YORK, NEW YORK. Will follow deportation proceedings.

FD-323 (Rev. 11-29-61)

UNITED STATES DEPARTMENT OF JUSTICE
FEDERAL BUREAU OF INVESTIGATION
New York, New York
March 16, 1972

In Reply, Please Refer to File No.

CONF~~IDENTIAL~~

Title   John Winston Lennon

Character   Security Matter -
             New Left
Reference is made to New York Letterhead
Memorandum dated and captioned as above.

All sources (except any listed below) whose identities are concealed in referenced communication have furnished reliable information in the past.

b2
b7D

CONFI~~DENTIAL~~

This document contains neither recommendations nor conclusions of the FBI. It is the property of the FBI and is loaned to your agency; it and its contents are not to be distributed outside your agency.

CONFIDENTIAL

UNITED STATES DEPARTMENT OF
FEDERAL BUREAU OF INVESTIGATION
New York, New York
March 16, 1972

John Winston Lennon

On January 21, 1972, [redacted] advised that a group of individuals calling themselves, the Allamuchy Tribe, were to open an office in New York City within the next two weeks. The leaders of the Tribe initially were Rennard Cordon Davis and Steward Albert. The main purpose of the group was to coordinate New Left movement activities during this election year to culminate with demonstrations at the Republican National Convention in San Diego, California during August, 1972.

Rennard Cordon Davis, is a convicted defendent of the so called Conspiracy Seven Trial, Chicago, Illinois, in the period September, 1969 through February, 1970, involving those persons earlier indicted for violation of the Federal Anti-Riot Statute.

Stewart Albert: [redacted] on April 25, 1966 advised that Albert was arrested on April 12, 1966 at Berkeley, California along with other members of the Progressive Labor Party (PLP) while demonstrating in front of the Berkeley City Hall.

Progressive Labor Party

The PLP was founded in 1962 by individuals expelled from the Communist Party, USA, for following the Chinese communist line. Its objective is the establishment of a militant working class movement based on Marxism-Leninism and Mao-Tse-tung thought.

CONFIDENTIAL

Group I
Excluded from automatic
downgrading and
declassification

This document contains neither recommendations nor conclusions of the Federal Bureau of Investigation (FBI). It is the property of the FBI and is loaned to your agency; it and its contents are not to be distributed outside your agency.

ENCLOSURE 100-469910-3

CONFIDENTIAL

John Winston Lennon

On January 24, 1972, [redacted] advised that John Winston Lennon, who was formerly associated with the Beatles Music Group, donated seventy-five thousand dollars to the Allamuchy Tribe, to further their cause of New-Left activities.

On January 28, 1972, [redacted] advised that the Allamuchy Tribe had changed its name to the Election Year Strategy Information Center (EYSIC), so as to be more effectively known to the general public.

On February 2, 1972, [redacted] advised that several members of the Peoples Coalition for Peace and Justice from Washington, DC transferred to the PCPJ office in New York City to work on EYSIC.

Peoples Coalition for
Peace and Justice (PCPJ)

The PCPJ is self-described as an organization consisting of over 100 organizations using massive civil disobedience to combat war, racism, poverty and repression. Its National Office is located at 156 5th Avenue, New York City, Room 527.

On [redacted] advised that [redacted] advised that [redacted]

CONFIDENTIAL

CONFIDENTIAL

John Winston Lennon

b2
b7D
On February 15, 1972, [redacted] advised that John Lennon on November 28, 1969, pled guilty in Marylebone Magistrates Court, London, England to possession of dangerous drugs (Cannabis). He was fined L150 and ordered to pay L21 in court cost.

b7C
John Winston Lennon. On February 2, 1972, [redacted] Immigration Officer, Immigration and Naturalization Service, (INS) New York City advised that Lennon, Alien Registration Number A-17597321, first arrived in New York City on August 11, 1968 under a B-2 visitors visa. He subsequently departed the United States, and during his 1971 re-entry was granted another B-2 visa. His latest visa was due to expire on February 29, 1972.

b7C
Yoko Ono. [redacted] advised that Ono, Alien Registration Number A-19489154 was born on February 18, 1933 in Japan. She entered the United States on August 13, 1971 along with Lennon after being granted a B-2 visa.

INS has a current address of the Saint Regis Hotel, 150 Bank Street, New York City for both Lennon and his wife.

During Lennon and his wife's current stay in the United States they made a public appearance along with Jerry Rubin, on the Mike Douglas Television Show which was aired on February 22, 1972 on Channel II, Columbia Broadcasting System, in New York City.

b2
b7D
During February, 1972, [redacted] advised that Rennard Davis, Stewart Albert, Jerry Rubin and John Lennon are heavy users of narcotics. Source advised that Rubin and Davis are apparently at odds with Lennon due to his excessive use of drugs, which are referred to in the Vernacular as "Downers".

CONFIDENTIAL

- 3 -

CONFIDENTIAL

John Winston Lennon

Source advised that Lennon appears to be radically orientated, however he does not give the impression he is a true revolutionist, since he is constantly under the influence of narcotics.

Jerry Rubin, is a convicted defendent of the so called Conspiracy Seven Trial, Chicago, Illinois, in the period September, 1969 through February, 1970, involving those persons earlier indicted for violation of the Federal Anti-Riot Statute.

On March 14, 1972, Mr. Vincent Schiano, Chief Trial Attorney, INS, New York City, advised that Lennon and his wife Yoko Ono on March 6, 1972 were served with an INS order to show cause as to why they should not be deported from the United States as over-stayed visitors. Mr. Schiano advised that Lennon and his wife are scheduled to appear at INS, New York City on March 16, 1972 to answer the show cause order.

CONFIDENTIAL

- 4* -

S-113a (9-29-65)

ALL INFORMATION CONTAINED
HEREIN IS UNCLASSIFIED EXCEPT
WHERE SHOWN OTHERWISE.

Domestic Intelligence Division

INFORMATIVE NOTE
Date 3/17/72

You were previously advised that John Winston Lennon, and his wife, Yoko Ono, are in the U.S. and that Lennon is the major financial contributor to Election Year Strategy Information Center (EYSIC) which was organized to conduct disruptive demonstrations during the Republican National Convention. EYSIC has been "dying on the vine" recently due to Lennon's imminent deportation and recent dissatisfaction with Rennie Davis, militant revolutionary, who is the head of EYSIC.

Attached states that Lennon and his wife appeared at the Immigration and Naturalization Service (INS) in New York City on 3/16/72 for deportation proceedings. Both Lennon and wife won delay until 4/18/72; Lennon because he stated he was attempting to fight a narcotics conviction in England, the basis for his deportation; and Ono on the basis of a child custody case in which she is involved.

We are closely following these proceedings and you will be kept advised.

ABK:lrs/mcm

FD-36 (Rev. 5-22-64)

FBI

Date: 3/29/72

Transmit the following in _____
(Type in plaintext or code)

Via   AIRTEL
_____
(Priority)

TO: DIRECTOR, FBI

FROM: SAC, NEW YORK (100-175228) (C)

SUBJECT: ELECTION YEAR STRATEGY
         INFORMATION CENTER (EYSIC)
         IS-NEW LEFT (CALREP)
         (OO:NY)

CLASS. BY sp1 bsk/R86
         1-17-83
Declass on OADR
1678RFP/88m 4-27-83

ReNYtel dated 3/10/72.

    Enclosed for the Bureau are ten (10) copies of an LHM captioned and dated as above. Copies are being designated for Miami, San Diego and WFO who have had a previous interest.

    Copies of the LHM are also being designated to INS, 108th MIG, USA, SDNY and USSS, New York City for information purposes.

2 - Bureau (Encls. 10) (RM)
2 - Miami (Encls. 2) (RM)
2 - San Diego (Encls. 2) (RM)
2 - Washington Field Office (Encls. 2) (RM)
1 - New York (105-42122) (ALBERT) (42)
1 - New York (100-163425) (DAVIS) (42)
1 - New York (100-157178) (RUBIN) (42)
1 - New York (100-175319) (LENNON) (42)
1 - New York (100-169939) (PCPJ) (42)
1 - New York (100-
1 - New York (100-174678)(CALREP) (42)
1 - New York

100-175319-28

SEARCHED _____ INDEXED _____
SERIALIZED _____ FILED _____
MAR 30 1972

ALL INFORMATION CONTAINED
HEREIN IS UNCLASSIFIED EXCEPT
WHERE SHOWN OTHERWISE.

Approved: _____ Sent _____ M Per _____
         Special Agent in Charge

NY 100-175228

b2
b7D
     Captioned LHM is classified "Confidential", because it contains information furnished by confidential ▮▮▮▮▮▮▮▮▮▮▮▮▮▮▮ who are of continuing value; the unauthorized disclosure of which information would tend to identify them and thus be prejudicial to the national defense interest of the United States.

b2
b7D

     Due to EYSIC no longer being in existance as a functioning organization captioned case is being placed in a closed status by the NYO.

-2-

UNITED STATES DEPARTMENT OF JUSTICE

FEDERAL BUREAU OF INVESTIGATION
New York, New York
March 29, 1972

Election Year Strategy Information Center
(Formerly known as the Allamuchy Tribe)

Reference is made to Federal Bureau of Investigation (FBI), memorandum dated February 28, 1972, and captioned as above.

b7D

the Election Year Strategy Information Center (EYSIC) is no longer functioning. The organization ceased to exist approximately the first of March, 1972. Former members Jerry Rubin and Stewart Albert, upon dissolving EYSIC seem to have no definite plans regarding either the Miami Democratic National Convention or the Republican National Convention in San Diego. Rennard Cordon Davis who was also associated with EYSIC was last known to be in Florida.

> Jerry Rubin and Rennard Cordon Davis, are both convited defendents of the so called Conspiracy Seven Trial, Chicago, Illinois, in the period September, 1969 thru February, 1970; involving those persons earlier indicted for violation of the Federal Anti-Riot Statute.

Group I
Excluded from automatic downgrading and declassification

This document contains neither recommendations nor conclusions of the FBI. It is the property of the FBI and is loaned to your agency; it and its contents are not to be distributed outside your agency.

ALL INFORMATION CONTAINED HEREIN IS UNCLASSIFIED EXCEPT WHERE SHOWN OTHERWISE.

Election Year Strategy
Information Center

Stewart Albert, [redacted] that Albert was arrested on April 12, 1966, at Berkeley, California, along with other members of the Progressive Labor Party (PLP) while demonstrating in front of the Berkeley City Hall.

Progressive Labor Party

The PLP was founded in 1962 by individuals expelled from the Communist Party, USA, for following the Chinese Communist line. Its objective is the establishment of a militant working class movement based on Marxism-Leninism and MAO Tse-tung thought.

[redacted] EYSIC is no longer operational. Youth Election Strategy, which started out as a political education arm of EYSIC is presently engaged in the production of films depicting the Automated Military Machinery used in Southeast Asia by the United States Army. The films are designed so as to be shown to demonstrators at the sites of the Republican and Democratic National Conventions. The source advised that John Winston Lennon was formerly associated with EYSIC, however shortly before the organization was dissolved, Jerry Rubin and Rennard Davis were apparently at odds with Lennon due to his excessive use of drugs.

John Winston Lennon. On February 2, 1972, Mr. Raymond Connley, Immigration Officer, Immigration and Naturalization Service (INS) New York City, advised that Lennon, Alien Registration Number A-17597321, first arrived in New York City on August 11, 1968, under a B-2 visitors visa. He subsequently departed the United States, and during his 1971 re-entry was granted another B-2 visa. Lennon is married Yoko Ono, Alien Registration Number A-19489154. They both entered the United States on August 13, 1971 and their visas were due to expire on February 29, 1972.

Election Year Strategy Information
Center

On March 14, 1972, Mr. VINCENT SCHIANO, Chief Trial Attorney, INS, New York City, advised that LENNON and his wife, on March 6, 1972 were served with an INS order to show cause why they should not be deported from the United States as over stayed visitors.

Mr. SCHIANO advised on March 16, 1972, that LENNON and his wife showed at INS, New York City on this date, however their hearing was delayed until April 18, 1972.

Peoples Coalition For
Peace and Justice (PCPJ)

> The PCPJ is self-described as an organization consisting of over 100 organizations using massive civil disobedience to combat war, racisim, poverty and repression. Its National Office is locted at 156 5th Avenue, New York City, Room 527.

FD-323 (Rev. 11-29-61)

UNITED STATES DEPARTMENT OF JUSTICE
FEDERAL BUREAU OF INVESTIGATION

Atlanta, Georgia

March 31, 1972

In Reply, Please Refer to
File No.

Title   WHITE PANTHER PARTY

Character   INTERNAL SECURITY - NEW LEFT

Reference   Memorandum dated and captioned as above prepared at Atlanta.

All sources (except any listed below) whose identities are concealed in referenced communication have furnished reliable information in the past.

This document contains neither recommendations nor conclusions of the FBI. It is the property of the FBI and is loaned to your agency; it and its contents are not to be distributed outside your agency.

FD-36 (Rev. 5-22-64)

F B I

Date: 3/31/72

Transmit the following in _____ (Type in plaintext or code)

Via ___AIRTEL_____
                    (Priority)

ALL INFORMATION CONTAINED
HEREIN ... FIED
DATE 2/9/81 BY SP4/SR m/kk

TO: DIRECTOR, FBI (62-112678)

FROM: SAC, ALEXANDRIA (100-506) (P)

        WHITE PANTHER PARTY (WPP)
        IS-WPP
        (OO: DETROIT)

        CALREP JOHN O LENNON

        MIDEM

        Re Detroit airtel to the Bureau dated 3/23/72, (no copy to Miami and San Diego); and Detroit letter to the Bureau, 3/15/72.

        For the information of Miami and San Diego, referenced airtel contained information from Detroit that the White Panther Party (WPP) is not a structured organization in that WPP activities in several cities throughout the country are not contingent upon approval of the Detroit Chapter or otherwise.

(4) - Bureau (By Courier)
 2 - Chicago (RM)
 2 - Detroit (100-36217) (RM)
 2 - Miami (RM)
     (1 - 100-16553)
     (1 - 80-1353) (DEMCON)
 2 - San Diego (RM)
     (1 - 80 - CALREP)
     (1 -   )
 2 - Alexandria
     (1 - 100-506)
     (1 - 100-883) (CALREP)
RJI:1mm
(14)

Approved: _____ Sent _____ M _____ Per _____
          Special Agent in Charge

AX 100-506

On 3/31/72, Alexandria source mentioned in referenced letter who has furnished reliable information in the past concerning the WPP and who has been characterized by the Detroit Office on the basis of information furnished as "a competent observer and an efficient interviewer who obtained very factual and significant information" advised as follows:

On 3/26/72, ▮▮▮▮ told source that he had been recently contacted by one ▮▮▮▮ who is allegedly ▮▮▮▮ and who allegedly had some connection with the People's Coalition for Peace and Justice (PCPJ) in 1968, and who was said to have taken part in planning Youth International Party (YIP) demonstrations at the Democratic National Convention in Chicago.

▮▮▮▮ told source that ▮▮▮▮ related to him that he had been in contact in the recent past with individuals who were planning disruptive activities directed towards the Republican National Convention in San Diego, California, in August, 1972.

▮▮▮▮ stated that there would be no organized effort to disrupt the Democratic National Convention scheduled for Miami, Florida, in July, 1972, by this group as the Democrats are currently destroying themselves and will need no assistance from anyone to disrupt their own convention. However, "there will be a lot of trouble at the Republic National Convention in San Diego" and plans are currently being discussed but not implemented as how to best achieve this disruption. One of the primary reasons according to ▮▮▮▮ as to why no active efforts have been made to implement these plans is a lack of funds at the present time. This group consists, according to ▮▮▮▮ of people who were formerly affiliated with the PCPJ and YIP, and who have some funds left over from prior campaigns of these organizations.

-2-

AX 100-506

▓▓▓ told ▓▓▓ that many former leaders of the PCPJ and YIP have been discredited in the eyes of "rank and file" activists of these organizations as they feel that former leaders such as JERRY RUBIN have "become self-made superstars" and are only interested in obtaining fame and publicity for themselves rather than in the past stated goals of YIP and other related groups.

Leadership of PCPJ and YIP, according to ▓▓▓ is currently fragmented and the task of "picking up the pieces" and putting together an effective organization has been assumed by WPP leader JOHN SINCLAIR and a former member of the Beatles singing group, JOHN LENNON. LENNON and SINCLAIR are said to be working together and devised the following plan to obtain funds to finance activities against the Republican Convention:

A series of "rock concerts" featuring big-name established stars in the musical field as headliners and backed up with lesser known individuals and groups will be put on throughout the country. LENNON is said to have the know-how and the connections to achieve the above. These performances will provide the main source of funds needed by LENNON and SINCLAIR to carry out the disruptive tactics in San Diego.

The first such concert, according to source, is to be held in the Chrysler Arena, Ann Arbor, Michigan, in the near future. This will be, according to ▓▓▓ "the opening gun of the campaign."

Alexandria source again advised that ▓▓▓ reminde him that he desired no direct contact with the Federal Bureau of Investigation but would furnish information only to him. Additionally, for the information of the Bureau, Alexandria source still desires an interview with ▓▓▓ (Bureau refer to Alexandria airtel to Director, 3/10/72.)

AX 100-506

b7c
b7D
Additionally, the above information if disseminated outside the Bureau could tend to comprimise ████ as it is not known how many individuals have had access to it.

LEADS

CHICAGO

b7c
AT CHICAGO, ILLINOIS. Will obtain background information on ████ and advise Bureau and interested offices of any pertinent information.

DETROIT

AT DETROIT, MICHIGAN. 1. Will discreetly ascertain if a rock concert is scheduled to be held at the Chrysler Arena, Ann Arbor, in the near future.

b7c
2. Will attempt to obtain background information on ████ and advise Burea and interested offices of pertinent information developed.

3. Will through established sources ascertain if SINCLAIR and LENNON are involved in attempt to cause disruption of the Republican Convention at San Diego, California, in August, 1972.

4. Will advise Alexandria if any of the above information in the body of instant communication is verified in order to assistant Alexandria in directing its source.

ALEXANDRIA

AT ALEXANDRIA, VIRGINIA. 1. Will submit LHM regarding the above information.

2. Will maintain contact with source and await results of investigation set forth above.

-4-

UNITED STATES DEPARTMENT OF JUSTICE

FEDERAL BUREAU OF INVESTIGATION

Alexandria, Virginia

April 5, 1972

DEMONSTRATIONS DURING THE
REPUBLICAN NATIONAL CONVENTION,
SAN DIEGO, CALIFORNIA,
AUGUST, 1972

A PCPJ press release dated March 1, 1971, described the PCPJ as being headquartered in Washington, D.C., and consisting of over 100 organizations which are using massive, nonviolent, civil disobediance to combat racism, poverty, repression, and the war.

The YIP is a New York based group which was formed in early 1968 for the purpose of conducting a "Festival of Life" during the Democratic Convention (DEMCON) in August, 1968, in Chicago.

The WPP is a national white, hippie-oriented revolutionary organization which

GROUP 1
Excluded from automatic
downgrading and
declassification

100-467491-141

ENCLOSURE

RE: DEMONSTRATIONS DURING THE
REPUBLICAN NATIONAL CONVENTION
SAN DIEGO, CALIFORNIA,
AUGUST, 1972

was founded essentially to afford support to the Black Panther Party (BPP). It has advocated the published ten-point program of its own, all of which call for the unbridled personal freedom of the individual.

The BPP is a black extremist organization started in Oakland, California, in December, 1966. It advocates the use of guns and guerrilla tactics to bring about the overthrow of the U.S. Government.

John Sinclair, WPP Chairman, and a former member of the Beatles singing group, John Lennon.

Lennon and Sinclair

4-750 (Rev. 4-17-85)

XXXXXX
XXXXXX
XXXXXX

FEDERAL BUREAU OF INVESTIGATION
FOIPA DELETED PAGE INFORMATION SHEET

_1_ Page(s) withheld entirely at this location in the file. One or more of the following statements, where indicated, explain this deletion.

☒ Deleted under exemption(s) __(b)(7)(D)__ with no segregable material available for release to you.

☐ Information pertained only to a third party with no reference to you or the subject of your request.

☐ Information pertained only to a third party. Your name is listed in the title only.

☐ Documents originated with another Government agency(ies). These documents were referred to that agency(ies) for review and direct response to you.

_____ Pages contain information furnished by another Government agency(ies). You will be advised by the FBI as to the releasability of this information following our consultation with the other agency(ies).

_____ Page(s) withheld for the following reason(s):
_____
_____

☐ For your information: _____
_____

☒ The following number is to be used for reference regarding these pages:
__100-467491-141 pg.3__

XXXXXX
XXXXXX
XXXXXX

XXXXXXXXXXXXXXXXXX
DELETED PAGE(S)
NO DUPLICATION FEE
FOR THIS PAGE
XXXXXXXXXXXXXXXXXX

FBI/DOJ
303

The last page of this document is not released because it is considered "the production of such law enforcement records or information could reasonably be expected to disclose the identity of confidential source" (code (b)(7)(d)).

UNITED STATES GOVERNMENT

Memorandum

TO : DIRECTOR, FBI DATE: 4/7/72

FROM : SAC, DALLAS (100-12165)(C)

SUBJECT: WHITE PANTHER PARTY (WPP)
Fort Worth, Texas
SM - WPP

OO: DALLAS

Re Dallas letter and LHM dated 10/20/71, and Detroit airtel and LHM dated 10/13/71, captioned "WHITE PANTHER PARTY, aka Rainbow Peoples Party, IS - WPP, OO: Detroit".

Enclosed for the Bureau are eight copies of LHM dated and captioned as above. Two copies of LHM are being furnished to U.S. Secret Service, Dallas, Texas, and one copy of LHM is being furnished for the additional information of Detroit. Copies of LHM are not being designated for military agencies at their specific request.

The submission of an earlier LHM in this matter was delayed due to a lack of activity on the part of the WPP, Fort Worth.

Investigation at Arlington and Fort Worth, Texas, was conducted by SA [redacted].

[redacted] and [redacted], who were the leaders of the now defunct WPP in Fort Worth, as set out in enclosed LHM, are subjects of Dallas pending investigations, captioned "[redacted], SM - WPP (EXTREMIST)", OO: DALLAS, Dallas file 100-12162, Bureau file 100-466008; and "[redacted], aka SM - WPP (EXTREMIST)", OO: DALLAS, Dallas file 100-12164, Bureau file 100-466054. In an attempted Bureau approved interview of [redacted] on 2/2/72, [redacted] advised SA [redacted] that neither he nor [redacted] would make any statements, answer any questions or discuss anything concerning themselves,

② - Bureau (Enc. 8)(RM)
1 - Detroit (100-36217)(Enc. 1)(Info)(RM)
3 - Dallas (1 - 100-12165)
    (1 - 100-12162)
    (1 - 100-12164)

Buy U.S. Savings Bonds Regularly on the Payroll Savings Plan

DL 100-12165

their activities, or anything concerning the WPP. [____]
stated that in light of his past experiences with law enforce- b6
ment officers, "for him to answer any questions, he just gets   b7C
into trouble". [____] and [____] have been recommended
for Bureau approval for inclusion on ADEX, Category II.

   Inasmuch as the WPP in Fort Worth, completely dormant
for some time and considered to be completely defunct, no further
investigation is being conducted in this matter at this time and
this case is being closed. Sources and informants will remain
alert for any information to indicate any renewed activity or
interest in the WPP.

   <u>ALL INDIVIDUALS INVOLVED IN NEW LEFT EXTREMIST
ACTIVITY SHOULD BE CONSIDERED DANGEROUS BECAUSE OF THEIR
KNOWN ADVOCACY AND USE OF EXPLOSIVES, REPORTED ACQUISITION
OF FIREARMS AND INCENDIARY DEVICES AND KNOWN PROPENSITY FOR
VIOLENCE.</u>

2

Airtel

4/10/72

To: SAC, New York (100-175319) (Enclosures - 2)

From: Director, FBI (100-469910)

1 - Mr. Horner
1 - Mr. Preusse
1 - Mr. Shackelford
1 - Mr. Pence

JOHN WINSTON LENNON
SM - NEW LEFT

ReNYtel 3/16/72.

Enclosed for information of New York are two copies of Alexandria airtel dated 3/31/72 captioned "White Panther Party, IS - WPP; CALREP; MIDEM," which contains information from Alexandria source relating to current activities of subject.

It appears from referenced New York teletype that subject and wife might be preparing for lengthy delaying tactics to avert their deportation in the near future. In the interim, very real possibility exists that subject, as indicated in enclosed airtel, might engage in activities in U.S. leading toward disruption of Republican National Convention (RNC), San Diego, 8/72. For this reason New York promptly initiate discreet efforts to locate subject and remain aware of his activities and movements. Handle inquiries only through established sources and discreet pretext inquiries. Careful attention should be given to reports that subject is heavy narcotics user and any information developed in this regard should be furnished to narcotics authorities and immediately furnished to Bureau in form suitable for dissemination.

1 - Alexandria
1 - San Diego

RLP:mcm (9)

100-469910-4

SEE NOTE PAGE TWO   APR 10 1972

ALL INFORMATION CONTAINED
HEREIN IS UNCLASSIFIED
DATE 23/9/81 BY

Airtel to New York
RE: John Winston Lennon
100-469910

In view of subject's avowed intention to engage in disruptive activities surrounding RNC, New York Office will be responsible for closely following his activities until time of actual deportation. Afford this matter close supervision and keep Bureau fully advised by most expeditious means warranted.

NOTE:

John Lennon, former member of Beatles singing group, is allegedly in U.S. to assist in organizing disruption of RNC. Due to narcotics conviction in England, he is being deported along with wife Yoko Ono. They appeared at Immigration and Naturalization Service, New York, 3/16/72, for deportation proceedings but won delay until 4/18/72 because subject fighting narcotics conviction and wife fighting custody child case in U.S. Strong possibility looms that subject will not be deported any time soon and will probably be in U.S. at least until RNC. Information developed by Alexandria source that subject continues to plan activities directed toward RNC and will soon initiate series of "rock concerts" to develop financial support with first concert to be held Ann Arbor, Michigan, in near future. New York Office covering subject's temporary residence and being instructed to intensify discreet investigation of subject to determine activities vis a vis RNC.

- 2 -

"New York Office (...) being instructed to intensify discreet investigation of subject to determine activities vis a vis RNC [Republican National Convention]".

UNITED STATES GOVERNMENT

Memorandum

TO : SAC New York (100-175319) DATE: 4/11/72

FROM : SA [redacted] b7C

SUBJECT: John Winston Lennon
SM – New Left

b7C On this date
b7D

[redacted]

b7C
b7D

ALL INFORMATION CONTAINED
HEREIN IS UNCLASSIFIED
DATE 6/9/[--] BY [redacted]

100-175319-31
APR 11 1972
FBI — NEW YORK

NR41 NY CODE

926 PM URGENT 4-18-72 FPM

TO DIRECTOR

ATT DID

FROM NEW YORK (100-175319) 2P

JOHN WINSTON LENNON SM-NEW LEFT OONY

ON APRIL EIGHTEEN INSTANT A REPRESENTATIVE OF IMMIGRATION AND NATUPALIZATION SERVICE (INS) TWENTY WEST BROADWAY NYC ADVISED THAT SUBJECT AND WIFE YOKO ONO LENNON APPEARED BEFORE SPECIAL INQUIRY OFFICER IRA FIELDSTEEL THIS DATE FOR PURPOSE OF DEPORTATION HEARINGS. THE LENNONS WERE REPRESENTED BY THEIR ATTORNEY LEON WILDES OF NYC.

MR. WILDES, MADE COMMENTS CONCERNING THE LENNONS CHILD CUSTODY CASE IN HOUSTON, TEXAS, IN WHICH HE INDICATED THE CHILD HAD BEEN ABDUCTED BY HIS NATURAL FATHER, AND THAT THE LENNONS WERE ATTEMPTING TO LOCATE CHILD. THE ATTORNEY COMMENTED THAT HIS CLIENT FELT HE WAS BEING DEPORTED DUE TO HIS OUTSPOKEN REMARKS CONCERNING U S POLICY IN S. E. ASIA. THE ATTORNEY REQUESTED DELAY TO AS SECURE CHARACTER WITNESSES TO TESTIFY ON BEHALF OF SUBJECT. WILDES READ INTO COURT RECORD WHERE SUBJECT HAD BEEN APPOINTED ONTO THE PRESIDENTS COUNCIL FOR DRUG ABUSE AND AS WELL ONTO FACULTY OF NY UNIVERSITY IN NYC.

END PG ONE

PGTWO

SPECIAL INQUIRY OFFICER FIELDSTEEL ADVISED THAT HE WOULD MAKE TIME AVAILABLE TO HEAR CHARACTER WITNESSES AND SET HEARING FOR MAY TWO NEXT.

AFTER SUBJECT LEFT INS HE WAS MET BY GROUP OF EIGHTY FIVE SUPPORTERS INCLUDING BOTH RADIO AND TELEVISION AND PRESS REPRESENTATIVES LENNON WAS OBSERVED BY A REPRESENTATIVE OF THE FBI TO MAKE A PRESS RELEASE IN WHICH HE INFERRED INS WAS ATTEMPTING TO DEPORT HIM DUE TO HIS POLITICAL IDEAS AND PRESENT POLICY OF THE U S GOVERNMENT AS TO ALIENS WHO SPEAK OUT AGAINST THE ADMINISTRATION.

ADMINISTRATIVE

REBUAIRTEL APEIL TEN LAST. INS REPRESENTATIVE WAS VINCENT A. SCHIANO CHIEF TRIAL ATTORNEY. SA WHO OBSERVED SUBJECT WAS SA ▓▓▓ b7C ▓▓▓

FOR INFO OF BUREAU, NYCPD, NARCOTICS DIVISION IS AWARE OF SUBJECTS RECENT USE OF NARCOTICS AND ARE ATTEMPTING TO OBTAIN ENOUGH INFO TO ARREST BOTH SUBJECT AND WIFE YOKO BASED ON PD INVESTIGATION. NYO FOLLOWING. P.

END

Routing Slip
0-7 (Rev. 3-11-72)   (Copies to C[ ]s Checked)

TO: SAC:

			TO LEGAT:
☐ Albany	☐ Houston	☐ Oklahoma City	
☐ Albuquerque	☐ Indianapolis	☐ Omaha	☐ Beirut
☐ Alexandria	☐ Jackson	☐ Philadelphia	☐ Bern
☐ Anchorage	☐ Jacksonville	☐ Phoenix	☐ Bonn
☐ Atlanta	☐ Kansas City	☐ Pittsburgh	☐ Brasilia
☐ Baltimore	☐ Knoxville	☐ Portland	☐ Buenos Aires
☐ Birmingham	☐ Las Vegas	☐ Richmond	☐ Caracas
☐ Boston	☐ Little Rock	☐ Sacramento	☐ Copenhagen
☐ Buffalo	☐ Los Angeles	☐ St. Louis	☐ Hong Kong
☐ Butte	☐ Louisville	☐ Salt Lake City	☐ La Paz
☐ Charlotte	☐ Memphis	☐ San Antonio	☐ London
☐ Chicago	☐ Miami	☐ San Diego	☐ Madrid
☐ Cincinnati	☐ Milwaukee	☐ San Francisco	☐ Managua
☐ Cleveland	☐ Minneapolis	☐ San Juan	☐ Manila
☐ Columbia	☐ Mobile	☐ Savannah	☐ Mexico City
☐ Dallas	☐ Newark	☐ Seattle	☐ Ottawa
☐ Denver	☐ New Haven	☐ Springfield	☐ Paris
☐ Detroit	☐ New Orleans	☐ Tampa	☐ Rome
☐ El Paso	☐ New York City	☒ Washington Field	☐ Tel Aviv
☐ Honolulu	☐ Norfolk	☐ Quantico	☐ Tokyo

Date 4/20/72

RE: **JOHN WINSTON LENNON**
SM - NEW LEFT

☒ For information ☐ Retention optional ☐ For appropriate action ☐ Surep, by _____
☐ The enclosed is for your information. If used in a future report, ☐ conceal all sources, ☐ paraphrase contents.
☐ Enclosed are corrected pages from report of SA _____ dated _____.

Remarks:

ALL INFORMATION CONTAINED
HEREIN IS UNCLASSIFIED
DATE 6-10-82 BY _____

100-55429-9A
SEARCHED ___ INDEXED
SERIALIZED ___ FILED
APR 21 1972
WASH. F.O.

b7C

1 - Mr. R. L. Shackelford
1 - Mr. T. J. Smith (Horner)
1 - Mr. E. Pence

CODE   TELETYPE   NITEL

4-20-72

TO SACS NEW YORK (100-175319)
WFO (100-55429)
FROM DIRECTOR FBI (100-469910)

APR 20 1972
9:53 PM
TELETYPE

JOHN WINSTON LENNON, SM - NEW LEFT.

RENYTEL APRIL EIGHTEEN LAST (COPY FURNISHED WFO UNDER SEPARATE COVER).

REGARDING INFORMATION FURNISHED BY SUBJECT'S ATTORNEY TO IMMIGRATION AND NATURALIZATION SERVICE (INS) THAT SUBJECT HAD BEEN APPOINTED TO PRESIDENT'S COUNCIL FOR DRUG ABUSE AND TO FACULTY OF NEW YORK UNIVERSITY, NEW YORK EXPEDITIOUSLY CONDUCT DISCREET INQUIRIES IN ATTEMPT TO CORROBORATE THIS INFORMATION. WFO CONDUCT INQUIRY ATTEMPT CORROBORATE SUBJECT'S ALLEGED APPOINTMENT PRESIDENT'S COUNCIL FOR DRUG ABUSE, CORRECTLY KNOWN AS NATIONAL COMMISSION ON MARIJUANA AND DRUG ABUSE. RECIPIENTS SUTEL.

NEW YORK ADVISE EXTENT LIVE INFORMANT COVERAGE CONCERNING SUBJECT AND INSURE ANY INFORMATION DEVELOPED REGARDING SUBJECT'S USE OF NARCOTICS WHILE IN U.S. IMMEDIATELY DISSEMINATED TO PERTINENT LOCAL AND FEDERAL NARCOTICS OFFICIALS.

RLP:plm
(5)

NOTE: Subject, former member of Beatles singing group, allegedly in U.S. to assist organizing disruption of Republican National Convention. He is under deportation proceedings and is attempting to delay deportation mainly due to argument that wife, Yoko Ono, should have custody of child currently in U.S. At deportation hearing in New York City 4-18-72 before INS, subject's attorney made statement subject appointed to President's Council for Drug Abuse and to faculty of New York University. Subject illegally in U.S. and New York and WFO should determine immediately whether statements made by subject's attorney are true.

ALL INFORMATION CONTAINED HEREIN IS UNCLASSIFIED
DATE 3/9/81 BY

FBY ?

John & Yoko... & the FBI

Find all the "FBI"s that are hidden in the picture.

FD-36 (Rev. 5-22-64)

F B I

Date: 4/21/72

Transmit the following in ___CODE___
(Type in plaintext or code)

Via ___TELETYPE___ ___URGENT___
(Priority)

TO: DIRECTOR, FBI (100-469910) (ATTN: DID) AND SAC,
WASHINGTON FIELD (100-55429)

FROM: SAC, NEW YORK (100-175319)

JOHN WINSTON LENNON, SM - NEW LEFT

ALL INFORMATION CONTAINED
HEREIN IS UNCLASSIFIED
DATE ___ BY ___

ON APRIL TWENTY-ONE INSTANT, A SOURCE WHO IS IN A POSITION TO FURNISH RELIABLE INFORMATION ADVISED THAT SUBJECT HAS BEEN OFFERED A TEACHING POSITION WITH NEW YORK UNIVERSITY (NYU) DURING THE SUMMER. NYU HAS APPARENTLY SENT SUBJECT A LETTER REQUESTING HIS AFFIRMATIVE ANSWER REGARDING THE POSITION AND SCHOOL OFFICIALS PRESUME THAT SUBJECT WILL ACCEPT.

ADMINISTRATIVE:

REFERENCE BUREAU TELETYPE DATED APRIL TWENTY, LAST.

b7C
b7D

NYO HAS SEVERAL SOURCES IN A POSITION TO FURNISH INFORMATION ON SUBJECT'S ACTIVITIES BUT SOURCES DO NOT HAVE PERSONAL CONTACT WITH THE SUBJECT.

NYO CONTINUING INVESTIGATION ON SUBJECT. LHM FOLLOWS.

1 - NEW YORK
GGZ:JLR
(2)
1 - SUPERVISOR #42

Approved: ___ Sent ___ M Per ___
Special Agent in Charge

UNITED STATES GOVERNMENT

Memorandum

TO: Mr. E. S. Miller

FROM: R. L. Shackelford

DATE: 4-21-72

1 - Mr. A. Rosen
1 - Mr. T. E. Bishop
1 - Mr. E. S. Miller
1 - Mr. T. J. Smith (Horner)
1 - Mr. R. L. Shackelford
1 - Mr. R. L. Pence

SUBJECT: **JOHN WINSTON LENNON**
SECURITY MATTER - NEW LEFT

PURPOSE:

To advise of recent tactics of subject, New Left sympathizer already in U.S. illegally, to avoid deportation from the U.S.

BACKGROUND:

Lennon is former member of Beatles singing group in England who, despite clear ineligibility for U.S. visa due to conviction in London in 1968 for possession of dangerous drugs (marijuana), was allowed to re-enter U.S. during 1971 on visitors visa due to unexplained intervention by State Department with Immigration and Naturalization Service (INS). Visas of Lennon and wife Yoko Ono expired 2-29-72 and since that time INS has been attempting to deport the Lennons.

He has come to our attention specifically during 2-72 when information developed he had donated $75,000 to organization named Election Year Strategy Information Center, organized to disrupt Republican National Convention.

On 3-1-72 INS notified Lennons to be out of U.S. by 3-15-72. On 3-16-72 Lennons appeared at INS, New York City, for deportation proceedings and, through their attorney, won delay of hearings based on subject's attempt to fight narcotics conviction in England and wife's attempt to regain custody of child who is now living in U.S. On 4-18-72 Lennons again appeared at INS, New York City, during which appearance attorney

100-469910
Enclosures sent 4-25-72
RLP:plm (7)

CONTINUED - OVER

Memorandum to Mr. E. S. Miller
RE: John Winston Lennon
100-469910

commented that subject felt he was being deported due to his outspoken remarks regarding U.S. policy in Southeast Asia. Attorney requested delay so character witnesses could be introduced to testify on behalf of subject. Attorney also read into court record fact subject had been appointed to the President's Council for Drug Abuse, correct name National Commission on Marijuana and Drug Abuse (NCMDA), and to the faculty of New York University, New York City. As a result of these revelations, INS set new hearing date for 5-2-72, and Lennons left INS to be met by throng of supporters and news media reporters who listened to subject's press release implying he was being deported due to his political ideas and policy of the U.S. Government to deport aliens who speak out against the Administration.

OBSERVATIONS:

Irony of subject being appointed to President's Council for Drug Abuse, if true, is overwhelming since subject is currently reported heavy user of narcotics and frequently avoided by even Rennie Davis and Jerry Rubin, convicted Chicago Seven Conspiracy trial defendants, due to his excessive use of narcotics. New York City Police Department currently attempting to develop enough information to arrest both Lennons for narcotics use. WFO has contacted NCMDA under pretext and determined no information available indicating subject has been appointed to NCMDA. New York Office has confirmed that Lennon has been offered teaching position at New York University for Summer of 1972. In view of successful delaying tactics to date, there exists real possibility that subject will not be deported from U.S. in near future and possibly not prior to Republican National Convention. Subject's activities being closely followed and any information developed indicating violation of Federal laws will be immediately furnished to pertinent agencies in effort to neutralize any disruptive activities of subject. Information developed to date has been furnished as received to INS and State Department. Information has also been furnished Internal Security Division of the Department.

ACTION:

Attached for approval are letters to Honorable H. R. Haldeman at The White House and Acting Attorney General with copies to the Deputy Attorney General and Assistant Attorney General, Internal Security Division, containing information concerning Lennon.

FEDERAL BUREAU OF INVESTIGATION
COMMUNICATIONS SECTION
APR 21 1972
TELETYPE

NR003 WF CODED
947AM URGENT 4-21-72 SKA
TO DIRECTOR (100-469910)
    NEW YORK (100-175319)
FROM WASHINGTON FIELD (100-55429)

JOHN WINSTON LENNON, SM-NEW LEFT.

RE BUREAU TELETYPE APRIL TWENTY INSTANT.
NO NAME INQUIRY THIS DATE AT NATIONAL COMMISSION ON
MARIJUANA AND DRUG ABUSE (NCMDA), EIGHT ZERO ONE NINETEENTH
STREET, NORTHWEST, WASHINGTON, D.C. OF ▮▮▮▮▮▮▮▮
▮▮▮▮▮▮▮▮▮▮▮▮ NCMDA, DEVELOPED NO INFORMATION
INDICATING LENNON HAS BEEN APPOINTED TO THE NCMDA.
END
KJB FBI WA DC CLR

ALL INFORMATION CONTAINED
HEREIN IS UNCLASSIFIED
DATE 2/12/91 BY SP4/5cm/mg

9-25-97
CLASSIFIED BY SSA5668 SLD/JS
DECLASSIFY ON: 25X 6
CA# 83-1720

CLASSIFIED BY SSA9803 ROD/JS
REASON:
DECLASSIFY ON: X

April 25, 1972

BY LIAISON

1 - Mr. A. Rosen
1 - Mr. T. E. Bishop
1 - Mr. E. S. Miller
1 - Mr. R. L. Shackelford
1 - Mr. T. J. Smith (Horner)
1 - Mr. R. L. Pence

Honorable H. R. Haldeman
Assistant to the President
The White House
Washington, D. C.

Dear Mr. Haldeman

John Winston Lennon is a British citizen and former member of the Beatles singing group.

Despite his apparent ineligibility for a United States visa due to a conviction in London in 1968 for possession of dangerous drugs, Lennon obtained a visa and entered the United States in 1971. During February, 1972, a confidential source, who has furnished reliable information in the past, advised that Lennon had contributed $75,000 to a newly organized New Left group formed to disrupt the Republican National Convention. The visas of Lennon and his wife, Yoko Ono, expired on February 29, 1972, and since that time Immigration and Naturalization Service (INS) has been attempting to deport them. During the Lennons' most recent deportation hearing at INS, New York, New York, on April 18, 1972, their attorney stated that Lennon felt he was being deported due to his outspoken remarks concerning United States policy in Southeast Asia. The attorney requested a delay in order that character witnesses could testify for Lennon, and he then read into the court record that Lennon had been appointed to the President's Council for Drug Abuse (National Commission on Marijuana and Drug Abuse) and to the faculty of New York University, New York, New York.

SEE NOTE PAGE TWO

Group 1
Excluded from automatic downgrading and declassification

A second source for this FBI document enables us to get some of the blacked out information : a confidential source indicates that "Lennon has taken an interest in "extreme left-wing activities in Britain" and is known to be a sympathizer of Trotskyist communists in England" :

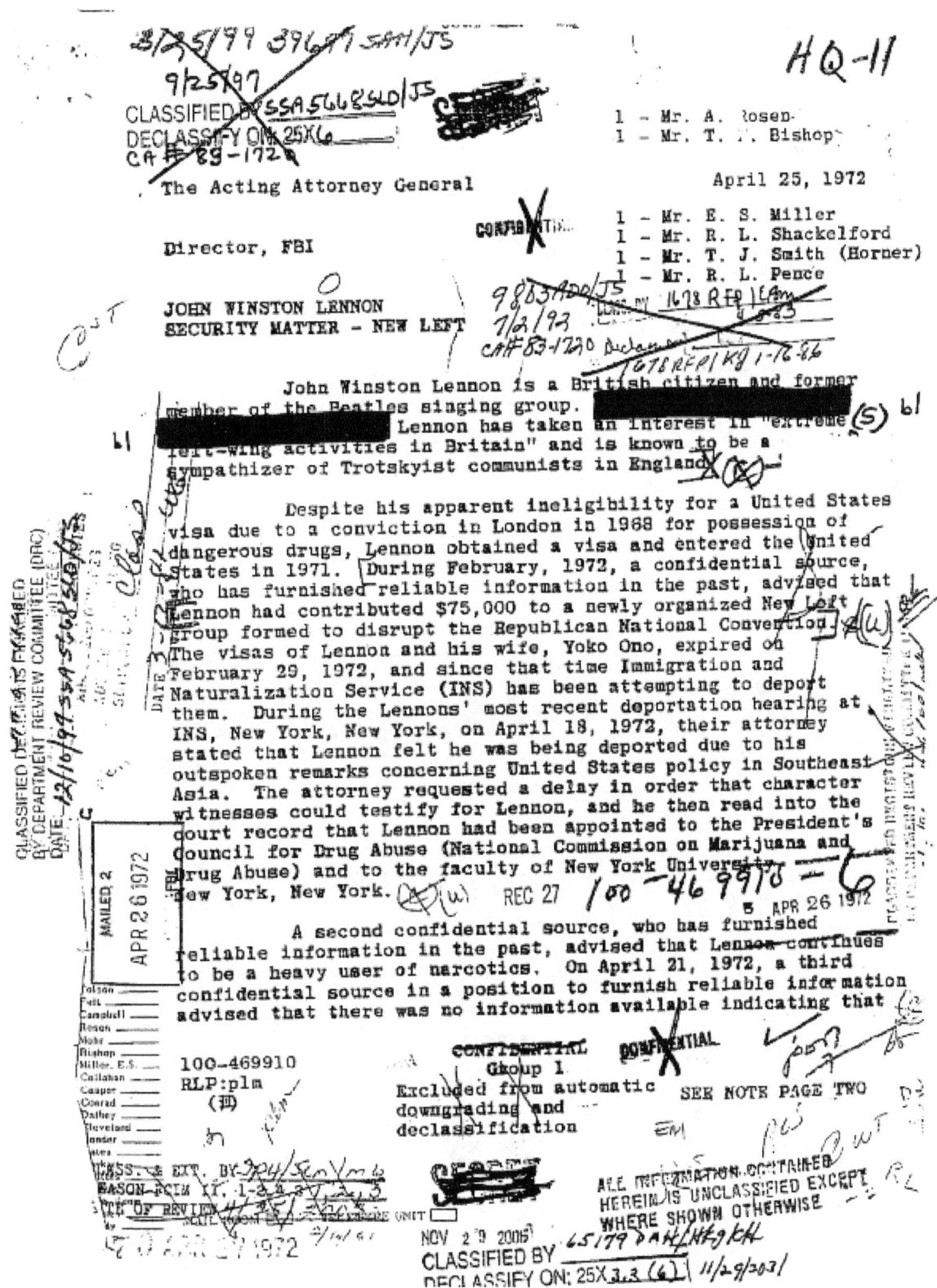

Honorable H. R. Haldeman

A second confidential source, who has furnished reliable information in the past, advised that Lennon continues to be a heavy user of narcotics. On April 21, 1972, a third confidential source in a position to furnish reliable information advised that there was no information available indicating that Lennon has been appointed to the National Commission on Marijuana and Drug Abuse. A fourth confidential source in a position to furnish reliable information advised that Lennon has been offered a teaching position at New York University for the Summer of 1972.

This information is also being furnished to the Acting Attorney General. Pertinent information concerning Lennon is being furnished to the Department of State and INS on a regular basis.

Sincerely yours,

NOTE:

Classified "Confidential" since information is contained from ▓▓▓▓ first confidential source is ▓▓▓▓ second confidential source is ▓▓▓▓ third confidential source is pretext inquiry by WFO with ▓▓▓▓ National Commission on Marijuana and Drug Abuse, Washington, D. C.; and fourth confidential source is ▓▓▓▓, New York University, New York, New York.

See memorandum R. L. Shackelford to Mr. E. S. Miller, 4/21/72, captioned "John Winston Lennon, Security Matter - New Left," and prepared by RLP:plm.

- 2 -

FD-36 (Rev. 5-22-64)

FBI

Date: 4/26/72

Transmit the following in _____
(Type in plaintext or code)

Via __AIRTEL__
(Priority)

TO: DIRECTOR, FBI (100-448910)

FROM: SAC, MILWAUKEE (100-16644)(P)

SUBJECT: YOUTH INTERNATIONAL PARTY (YIP)
IS - YIP
BU File 100-448910
MI File 100-16644

DEMONSTRATION DURING THE FORTHCOMING
POLITICAL CAMPAIGN
MI File 100-18949

MIDEM
MI File 100-19451

Re Milwaukee airtel to the Bureau, 4/18/72, bearing dual caption, "Youth International Party (YIP)," and "Demonstration During the Forthcoming Political Campaign."

5 - Bureau (RM)(AM)(Encs.13)
  (2 - 100-448910)
  (1 - 100-MIDEM)
  (1 - 100-Demonstration - Political Campaign)
  (1 - Legat, Ottawa - "For Information")
7 - Milwaukee (1 - 100-16644)(YIP - Milwaukee)
    (1 - 100-15948)(YIP - Madison)
    (1 - 100-18949)(Demonstration - Political Campaign)
    (1 - 100-19451)(MIDEM)
    (1 -
    (1 -
    (1 -
(28)

(COPIES CONTINUED PAGE 2)

Approved: _____ Sent _____ M Per _____
Special Agent in Charge

MI 100-16644

An extra copy of LHM is being furnished the Bureau in view of information set forth regarding Montreal, Quebec, Canada. If necessary, Bureau may furnish Legat, Ottawa a copy of enclosed LHM "for information" or whatever action deemed necessary.

Enclosed LHM is classified "Confidential" as it contains information furnished by a confidential source of continuing value, the unauthorized disclosure of whose identity may compromise source, thereby possibly having an adverse effect on the defense interests of this country.

O/S

Information copies of enclosed LHM are being furnished to Albany, Chicago, Detroit, Los Angeles, Miami, New York, and San Francisco in view of their divisions being mentioned in information furnished by source.

Individual concealed in enclosed LHM is identified as follows:

b2
b7D

Source is ▓▓▓▓▓▓▓

Milwaukee will follow YIP activities planned by Wisconsin YIP activists and insure that the Bureau and interested governmental agencies, along with appropriate Field Divisions, are advised on a timely basis of pertinent information developed.

3

UNITED STATES DEPARTMENT OF JUSTICE

FEDERAL BUREAU OF INVESTIGATION

Milwaukee, Wisconsin
April 26, 1972

"Confidential"

YOUTH INTERNATIONAL PARTY (YIP)

DEMONSTRATIONS DURING THE DEMOCRATIC
NATIONAL CONVENTION, JULY, 1972 -
MIAMI, FLORIDA

(Reference is made to Milwaukee memorandum dated
April 18, 1972, captioned "Youth International Party (YIP)"
and "Demonstrations During the Democratic National Convention,
July, 1972 - Miami, Florida.")

YOUTH INTERNATIONAL PARTY

The Youth International Party, also
known as Yippies, is a loosely knit,
anti-establishment, revolutionary
youth organization formed in New York
City in January, 1968.

"Confidential"

GROUP I
Excluded from automatic
downgrading and declassification

DO NOT DESTROY - PENDING LITIGATION

"This document contains neither recommendations nor conclusions
of the FBI. It is the property of the FBI and is loaned to
your agency; it and its contents are not to be distributed outside
your agency."

ALL INFORMATION CONTAINED
HEREIN IS UNCLASSIFIED
DATE _____ BY _____

"Confidential"

YOUTH INTERNATIONAL PARTY (YIP)

DEMONSTRATIONS DURING THE DEMOCRATIC
NATIONAL CONVENTION, JULY, 1972 -
MIAMI, FLORIDA

Source, who has furnished reliable information in the past, advised on April 17, 1972, that Shirley Jane Hopper traveled to New York City, from Madison, Wisconsin, on March 2, 1972, until March 6, 1972, to meet with Yippie and Zippie representatives.

The following is an account of that trip furnished by source:

Thursday - March 2, 1972

Jane Hopper took a bus to Chicago and stayed with the Halsted people. She got up early and went down to Continental Driveaway Company and made arrangements for cars to New York and back. She went to the bus station and picked up John Mattes who came down on the bus that morning.

O/S Friday - March 3, 1972

After picking John up she went and picked up the car which turned out to be a used squad car that was being sent to Brooklyn for resale.

Saturday - March 4, 1972

They arrived in New York at 3:00 AM and went to A. J. Weberman's house at 6 Bleeker Street. After getting some sleep, A. J. went over to Tom Forcade's house to get him up. He came back with Frank Rose, who lives with Tom. They decided to make a Zippie presence at the Stonybrook Conference. Jane drove out there with John, Pat Small, and Kathy Morales, (who are living with A. J.) and Frank Rose. Pat Small made a plea for the people there to join Zippie and announced that there would be a separate caucus for Zip in another room. The Zips drew off maybe a third of the people there. Most people were stopped by the campus police either coming or going. Hopper was stopped and I.D.'d while waiting to pick her friends up after the thing broke up.

"Confidential"

Confidential

YOUTH INTERNATIONAL PARTY (YIP)

DEMONSTRATIONS DURING THE DEMOCRATIC NATIONAL CONVENTION, JULY, 1972 - MIAMI, FLORIDA

Sunday, March 5, 1972

Hopper went over to the New York Switchboard and made arrangements for Zip announcements to appear in a newsletter they are planning to set up for all the underground switchboards in the next month. She went over to Rex Weiner's house. He is the editor of the "New York Ace" which is an up and coming underground paper. He seems to be an old political hand. He was very glad to see us and proposed a party that night to welcome us to New York, at his newspaper office. The party started at about 9:00 PM so Hopper had time to go eat at Tom Forcade's house. He lives in a real dump at 209 East 5th Street. His office is at 204 West 10th Street (basement). He has no legitimate phone. To call out he taps into a Hungarian person's phone. There is a girl there name Linda who acts as a servent for Tom and Frank. Linda's parrot interjects "Right On" whenever the conversation gets rousing. Tom is trying to train it to say "eat shit" whenever he argues with anyone but the bird now says it to him whenever he sees him. The cage is surrounded by small objects that Tom has thrown in response. From there Hopper went to the party. She was introduced to the elite of the radical left. Jerry Rubin rushed up to Jane and begged her to let him be a Zippie. She said we would have to iron out a few differences first and she agreed to meet with him the next day. Jane left with Forcade for a while so John, A. J., and his girl Ann mingled for a while. Frank was acting as a chauffeur dressed up in a fancy uniform. Jane got quite drunk and Jerry began to give her trouble about it.

Monday - March 6, 1972

This was Hopper's and John's last day in New York so it was packed with business meetings. Hopper had to take care of delivering the car to Brooklyn. When Hopper got back to A. J.'s, Tom was there and they were finalizing plans for the smoke-ins. They are apparently going to take place in twenty states and five foreign countries including England, Netherlands, France, Germany, and New Zealand. Debi from the Toronto Guerilla arrived to get a ride back with us as far as Erie, Pennsylvania. They left A. J.'s and went over to Jerry Rubin's house at 156 Prince Street. Stew Albert was there. Jerry told us that the bad press we were giving him had hurt him badly politically. He said he would be finished in politics unless we patched things up. They replied that they thought he was an asshole. He said that Abby was coming back next

Confidential DO NOT DESTROY - PENDING LITIGATION

246

"Confidential"

YOUTH INTERNATIONAL PARTY (YIP)

DEMONSTRATIONS DURING THE DEMOCRATIC
NATIONAL CONVENTION, JULY, 1972 -
MIAMI, FLORIDA

month and that he wouldn't let us kick him around. They told him that they would meet Abby at the airport and throw him out of the party also. He layed down on the floor close to tears. Stew said they were being too rough on him so they chewed him up in like fashion. Jerry asked us to negotiate with him and we agreed to it. We listed our bitches with him, 1. His superstar ego which enables him to appear to lead us while he does none of the work yet gets the credit; 2. Financial deals that have netted him money in the past that he made in the name of Yippie but then used for himself; 3. His b.o. and other bad habits; 4. His feud with Tom and other Zip people. He said that he would do anything and we should just tell him what we wanted. They told him they wanted money and they told him that they wanted him to get signatures for the Armstrong petition. They also told him that we would stop bad-rapping his in accordance with how well he performs his assignments. We will make no interferences in his affairs political or otherwise as long as he didn't claim leadership in Zip or Yip. He will have no decision making powers. If he or Abby want responsibilities in the new party they will have to earn them like everyone else. The fact that they are superstars and can get coverage of events does not impress us at all. They are a liability within the movement. They have turned too many people off. John and Hopper left for Madison. The only trouble they had on the way home was an incident in Pennsylvania. Their car was identified as having been involved in a burglarly. They were stopped for about an hour and then released. They were somewhere around Sharon and Mercer, Pennsylvania.

Jane and John seemed to think that Jerry was losing the friendship of John Lennon. John had thought that he was the cent of radical politics and by throwing him out we let the thought enter Lennon's head that perhaps Jerry was washed up. Lennon had a message delivered to us at Stonybrook that he would do an Armstrong benefit if we didn't let it out that he was coming. In other words, it had to be happening on its own steam before he would come. He will also come to the conventions if they are peaceful, under the same terms.

"Confidential"

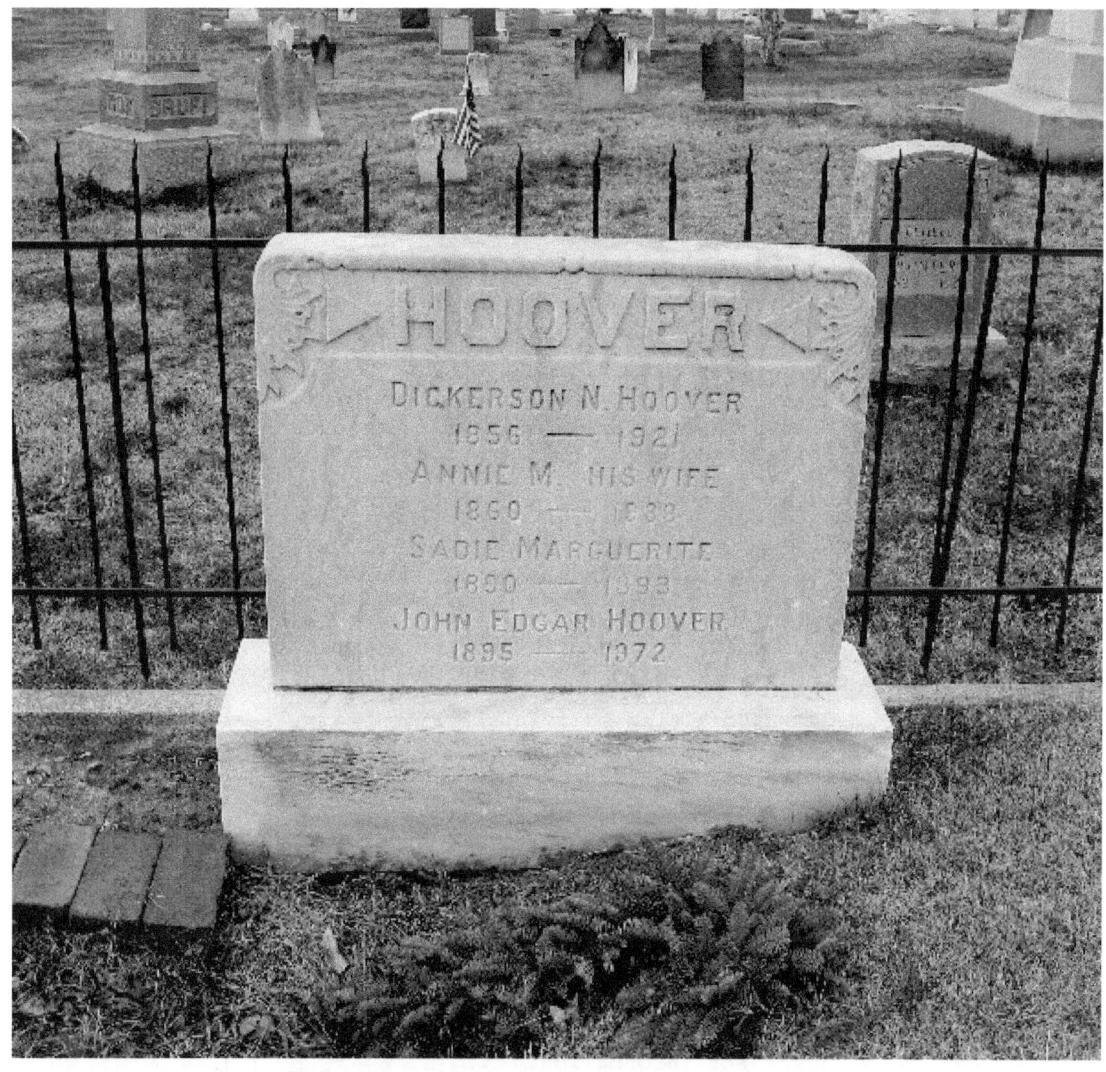

GAME hoOVER

John Edgar Hoover, director of FBI and hater of left-wing political activists, died on May 2, 1972. Nevertheless, this was not the end of John Lennon's problems with the INS.

Domestic Intelligence Division
INFORMATIVE NOTE

Date: 5-3-72

You were previously advised that both John Lennon and his wife, Yoko Ono, are in the U.S. and that Lennon is the major financial contributor to the Election Year Strategy Information Center (EYSIC) which was organized to conduct disruptive demonstrations during the Republican National Convention. EYSIC has been "dying on the vine" due to Lennon's possible deportation which he is fighting in court.

Attached states that Lennon and his wife appeared in New York City Court 5/3/72 to obtain an injunction against deportation proceedings. Immigration and Naturalization Service (INS) hearing has been delayed until 5-9-72 and the New York City Court granted a visa petition be given to subject and his wife.

INS has advised that British authorities stated that Lennon's narcotics conviction in England is not likely to be overturned. It stated a large volume of mail is being received from both supporters and non-supporters of deportation proceedings. Mayor Lindsay has publicly requested INS stop the deportation proceedings as Lennons are "distinguished artists in the music field and are an asset to U.S."

For information.

ABK:lrs

FEDERAL BUREAU OF INVESTIGATION
COMMUNICATIONS SECTION

MAY 3 1972

TELETYPE

NR022 NY CODE
408PM URGENT 5-3-72 PAC
TO DIRECTOR 100-469910
ATT DOMESTIC INTELLIGENCE DIVISION
FROM NEW YORK 100-175319 2P

Security Matters
JOHN WINSTON LENNON, SM DASH REVOLUTIONARY ACTIVITIES

ON MAY SECOND LAST A REPRESENTATIVE OF IMMIGRATION AND NATURALIZATION SERVICE (INS) NEW YORK CITY, ADVISED THAT ON PREVIOUS DAY, MAY FIRST LAST, BOTH LENNON AND WIFE YOKO ONO APPEARED IN NEW YORK CITY COURT FOR PURPOSE OF OBTAINING INJUNCTION AGAINST INS DEPORTATION PROCEEDINGS. SCHEDULED HEARING AT INS WAS DELAYED UNTIL MAY NINE NEXT. NEW YORK COURT ON MAY TWO LAST GRANTED A VISA PETITION BE GIVEN TO SUBJECT AND WIFE.

ADMINISTRATIVE

INS REPRESENTATIVE IS VINCENT A. SCHIANO CHIEF TRIAL ATTORNEY WHO FURTHER ADVISED THAT BRITISH AUTHORITIES HAVE ADVISED THAT LENNON'S NARCOTICS CONVICTION IN ENGLAND IS NOT LIKELY TO END PAGE ONE.

ALL INFORMATION CONTAINED HEREIN IS UNCLASSIFIED EXCEPT WHERE SHOWN OTHERWISE.

ALL INFORMATION CONTAINED HEREIN IS UNCLASSIFIED
DATE 2/12/81

PAGE TWO

BE OVERTURNED. SCHIANO FURTHER ADVISED LARGE VOLUME OF MAIL BEING RECEIVED BY BOTH SUPPORTERS AND NON SUPPORTERS OF DEPORTATION PROCEEDINGS. MAYOR JOHN LINDSAY, NEW YORK CITY PUBLICALLY REQUEST INS STOP DEPORTATION PROCEEDINGS AS LENNONS ARE "DISTINGUISHED ARTIST IN THE MUSIC FIELD AND ARE ASSET TO US". PENDING.

NEW YORK OFFICE FOLLOWING.

END

AND HOLD

Here is a copy of the letter sent to the INS by the mayor of New York City John Lindsay to ask that the deportation proceeding is cancelled and that John and Yoko are permitted to stay in the US :

THE CITY OF NEW YORK
OFFICE OF THE MAYOR
NEW YORK, N.Y. 10007

April 27, 1972

Hon. Raymond F. Farrell
Commissioner
Immigration and Naturalization Service
United States Department of Justice
119 D Street
N.E., Washington, D.C. 20536

Dear Commissioner Farrell:

    I am writing this letter to you on behalf of John Lennon and Yoko Ono who are currently facing deportation proceedings inititated by your Department.

    I consider it to be very much in the public interest, from the point of view of the citizens of New York as well as the citizens of the Country, that artists of their distinction be granted residence status.

    They have personally told me of their love for New York City and that they wish to make it their home. They have made me familiar with the tragic hardship involved in their desperate effort to find Yoko's 8 year old child, Kyoko. I believe this is the type of hardship that our Immigration laws must recognize and the removal of the Lennons from this Country would be contrary both to the principles of our Country as well as the humanitarian practices which should be implemented by the Department of Immigration.

    The only question which is raised against these people is that they do speak out with strong and critical voices on major issues of the day. If this is the motive underlying the unusual and harsh action taken by the Immigration and Naturalization Service, then it is an attempt to silence Constitutionally protected 1st Amendment rights of free speech and association and a denial of the civil liberties of these two people.

Hon. Raymond F. Farrell - 2 - April 27, 1972

In light of their unique past and present contribution in the fields of music and the arts, and considering their talent to be so outstanding as to be ranked among the greatest of our time in these fields, a grave injustice is being perpetuated by the continuance of the deportation proceeding.

Very truly yours,

John V. Lindsay
MAYOR

cc: Attorney General Richard G. Kleindienst
Commissioner Sol Marks
Senator Jacob Javits
Senator James Buckley

John & Yoko appearing for hearings relating to their deportation case at INS, May 1972.

UNITED STATES DEPARTMENT OF JUSTICE

FEDERAL BUREAU OF INVESTIGATION

Detroit, Michigan
May 11, 1972

Re: White Panther Party, also known as
Rainbow Peoples Party

Sources referred to herein have furnished reliable information in the past.

Set forth below is miscellaneous information developed regarding the White Panther Party (WPP), also known as the Rainbow Peoples Party (RPP) concerning miscellaneous activities and personnel of this organization during the period 1971 - 1972.

The WPP is a national white, hippie-oriented revolutionary organization which was founded essentially to afford support to the Black Panther Party (BPP). It has advocated the published ten-point program of its own, all of which call for the unbridled personal freedom of the individual.

The BPP is a black extremist organization started in Oakland, California, in December, 1966. It advocates the use of guns and guerrilla tactics to bring about the overthrow of the United States Government.

Summary Statement

The WPP which now publicly referrs to itself as the RPP, however, whose leadership among themselves continue to refer to themselves as "White Panthers", during 1971, started the end of a history of advocacy of violent action, reckless alliances with revolutionary groups and individuals throughout the country, and concerted effort to formalize a national organization under the banner of the WPP.

Re: White Panther Party, also known as
Rainbow Peoples Party

During 1971 it successfully transformed itself to the RPP as a local, unaffiliated organization, dedicated to "community organizations", retrenchment and retrospective activity with limited, calculated activity, principally dedicated to its own welfare.

It claimed success in achieving noteable support in the community on a wide variety of fronts, including local political action in the change of State Laws on marijuana and related matters, and most significant on achieving the release from prison of its Chairman, John Sinclair.

The guiding reference in its activity was furnished by ☐ early in 1971, ☐ ran to the effect that revolution today in the United States is impossible and that committed revolutionaries must emulate Chairman ☐ "Long March" to recognize that much effort and time is required to achieve success.

b6
b7C

[DE T-1
May 5, 1972.]

I. General

A. Leadership

MEMBER OF SUBJECT ORGANIZATION

The current active leadership of the WPP and persons making up the "Central Committee" of that organization are identified as follows:

John Sinclair, Chairman
David Sinclair, Chief of Staff   DAVE X SINCLAIR

☐, Member, Central Committee
☐, Member, Central Committee
☐, Member, Central Committee
☐ Member, Central Committee
☐, Member, Central Committee
☐, Member, Central Committee
☐, Member, Central Committee.

b6
b7C

[DE T-1
May 1, 1972]

- 2 -

~~CONFIDENTIAL~~

Re: White Panther Party, also known as
Rainbow Peoples Party

A source advised that the above-named individuals were included among the standing leadership and hardcore cadre of the WPP who can be assumed to share the WPP position of advocating violence to achieve revolutionary ends. Source noted that all of these individuals reside at [   ], Michigan.

b6
b7C

> DE T-1
> September 14, 1971
> May 1, 1971.

B. Location

The headquarters location for the WPP continues to be maintained at 1520 Hill Street, Ann Arbor. WPP formerly operated from this base from two adjacent mansions and a carriage house. Their base was retrenched to one of the residences when John Sinclair was in prison several years ago. Currently the WPP is negotiating for the purchase of all three of the properties mentioned and presently has some of its personnel located in the carriage house adjacent to 1520 Hill Street, and some personnel in the residence at 1510 Hill Street.

> DE T-1
> May 1, 1972.

C. Publication

The current publication of the WPP is known as the "Ann Arbor Sun" which is presently disseminated at Ann Arbor as the "Community News Service" of the RPP. It reports to be a local publication only and its content is principally local in nature, serving somewhat as a "house organ" for the WPP. Its printing run is on the order of 4,000 copies. It aims at a twice a month publication schedule, which is generally met.

> DE T-1
> May 1, 1972.

- 3 -

~~CONFIDENTIAL~~

Re: White Panther Party, also known as Rainbow Peoples Party

The former national publication of the WPP, "The Sun/Dance" was abandoned by the WPP during early 1971. The source stated that "The Sun/Dance" has reappeared recently and is being published currently by several former members of the WPP, Ann Arbor, including [   ], [   ], and [   ]". The source advised this publication is currently published on the West Coast and is run off by an organization known as the "Running-Dog-Type-Setters" located somewhere in the Bay Area of San Francisco. Source advised that the new "Sun/Dance" has no relationship with the WPP in Ann Arbor and is independently produced by personnel formerly associated with WPP leadership.

DE T-1
May 1, 1972.

D. Finances

The financial fortunes of the WPP which have been tight within the past several years became dramatically improved December, 1971, with the release of John Sinclair from prison. A large and very successful "John Sinclair Benefit" held in the field house on the campus of the University of Michigan (UM), Ann Arbor, December, 1971, grossed something on the order of $45,000.00. With John Sinclair's release from prison, shortly thereafter, he has received a constant high volume of speaking engagement requests throughout the country, many of which he has accepted, and most of which include a healthy stepeid.

As a consequence of the approved financial standing of the party through benefits, speaking engagements, and concerts, WPP Chairman has offered $130,000.00 in an attempt to purchase the property presently leased by the WPP as its headquarters.

DE T-1
February 2, 1972.

E. Aims and Purposes

A source advised that the WPP in its initiation and in the first two years of its existance, currently and

Re: White Panther Party, also known as
Rainbow Peoples Party

and openly advocated revolutionaries in the United States, completely supported efforts of the BPP and its leadership in their endeavors and consistently advocated the efforts of "Third World" forces. Its leadership in their writings and speeches openly advocated finances to achieve revolutionary ends.

This organization with its renaming into the RPP and after a year's effort to change its image, has engaged in a significant retrenchment. It exists presently only as a local organization concerned with "Community Organization" and with attempting an impact on the so-called "Youth Culture".

It is presently deeply engaged in local political activities, with some degree of success and with the release of its chairman late in 1971, it has worked in a concerted fashion on two programs: Prison Refore, and Legalization of Marijuana.

Whereas this organization philosophically was earlier oriented by Fidel Castro and BPP leadership and as its "heroes", its principle hero today is "Chairman ___".

[DE T-1
May 5, 1972.]

II. WPP Claimed Accomplishments

The WPP, Ann Arbor, continues to refer to itself as the RPP publicly, and have gained much broader public acceptance and effectiveness as a result of the name and "image" change. While maintaining the "Rainbow Peoples" stance publicly, they continue among themselves to refer to themselves as "White Panthers".

John Sinclair, Chairman, WPP, was the one responsible for the name and "Image" change. While still in prison he demanded the name RPP and the change in public stature.

- 5 -

Re: White Panther Party, also known as
Rainbow Peoples Party

His directions to "soften" the image and the rhetoric lost the WPP some of it's more militant personnel and supporters. Similarly, his demand that the WPP drop the weight of carrying or attempting to carry a national organization, lost the WPP many area supporters in other established chapters and with related groups throughout the country.

With John Sinclair's release from prison, December, 1971, he and his associates are reviewing the effectiveness of these moves, and are complimenting themselves on an excellent and effective strategy. Items for which this change is given credit, include the following:

1. Concerted Effort: The disengagement permitted most of the energies of WPP to be focused for almost a full years period of time on the imprisonment of John Sinclair, and the alleged injustice of his confinement for "two joints of Marijuana".

This concentrated focus resulted in:

a. Wide support through propaganda for liberalization of Marijuana laws in Michigan.

b. Gathered supporters to the WPP cause from among ranks of news media personnel, as well as from several State legislators.

c. Resulted in a dramatic change in Michigan narcotics legislation during 1971, for which WPP claims credit.

d. Demonstrated the pressure effectiveness of the WPP program.

e. Through the Marijuana issue, gave the WPP wide ranging and free public exposure.

f. Impacted the "youth culture" with a demonstration of the "rightness" of WPP advocacy of frontal legal assault to achieve their ends.

Re: White Panther Party, also known as
Rainbow Peoples Party

    g. Achieved the release of John Sinclair from Prison.

    h. Called attention to the need for reform in prison and corrections affairs.

    i. Made John Sinclair into an area "folk hero" to the "youth culture".

    j. Brought in an unprecedented volume of requests for Sinclair and WPP personnel to appear at "youth culture" events, concerts, etc.

    k. Brought financial support from throughout the country to the Sinclair defense funds, and more recently through speaking engagements, etc.

    l. Brought support of national "Revolutionary" leaders to John Sinclair's cause, and, indirectly, to that of the WPP.

  2. Community Action: The WPP disengagement from national affairs, permitted the concentration of local and area concerns, all of which have "blossomed" into viable, effective action programs:

    a. The Ozone House: The increasing number of "run-aways" who sought refuge at WPP commune, Ann Arbor, and the number of traveling "crashers" needing lodging there, something over a year ago, dictated the establishment of a stable, visible "crash-pad". [redacted], assisted by Ann Arbor [redacted] and WPP supporter [redacted], set up the Ozone House in downtown Ann Arbor. They established it as a living experiment of the "Ann Arbor Tribal Council" (AATC).

ARBOR, MICH
b6
b7C

They acquired a large, old, home for lease, and obtained contributions from city service clubs, and ultimately obtained a $7,000.00 annual commitment from the City of Ann Arbor to subsidize the operation.

Re: White Panther Party, also known as
Rainbow Peoples Party

The term AATC is used by the WPP whenever it wishes broad community support for an undertaking in which they either wish to avoid responsibility, or in which they feel the WPP will repel supporters.

The Ozone House operation was during 1971 a tremendous success, and after half of the year, it was apparent that the space would have to be doubled. Its existance aided the WPP Headquarters inasmuch as it cleared much of the transient traffic from that location. It enabled that commune to exert much better internal security.

b. The Drug-Help Program: [redacted], and others of the WPP leadership helped launch this program, again under the nominal auspices of the AATC. It vigorously and publicly opposed hard drugs, specifically heroin, while demanding and obtaining wide community support, financially and otherwise, for this Drug-Help program. Many organizations, including completely legitimate groups joined the AATC in this effort, which at the close of 1971 was an acknowledged success.

b6
b7C

c. The Free People's Health Clinic: [redacted], and others of the WPP leadership assisted the success of this venture, which was started by an Ann Arbor Physician, known as the "Street People's Doctor". He is regarded as a radical by such persons, and previously, when engaged in private practice, he gave free treatment to WPP and "Street People" types.

b6
b7C

He disbanded his practice and set up a Free Clinic. Numerous medical and quasi-medical personnel donated time and services to assist him in a thriving and free medical practice. Medical Students and some doctors from the UM faculty joined with their services on a part-time basis,

Re: White Panther Party, also known as
Rainbow Peoples Party

d. The Food Coop: This operation, started by
[____] of the WPP leadership, and carried
originally solely by the WPP to service itself
and area related communes, has mushroomed into
a community wide food cooperative. It is presently
promoted as a "Tribal Council" program. Participants take trucks into Detroit to the wholesale food and produce markets, where they buy
wholesale in large lots. They deliver and sell
at cost to participating Ann Arbor communes and
groups.

e. "The Ann Arbor Sun": This publication has
developed as the "Street Peoples" community news
service from Ann Arbor. It was initiated by the WPP
as the RPP, and is handled by [____] and
[____], of the WPP leadership. They are
assisted by a variety of WPP personnel, and "Street
People" assistance. It confines its interest to
area affairs and does not purport to compete with
regular area or nationally circulated underground
publications.

f. The Rock Concert Program: WPP originated and
sold the city of Ann Arbor on a summer program of
Rock Concerts in city parks, as part of a "cool
summer" project. They have obtained city and UM
support in use of city and UM campus areas to
stage weekly concerts throughout the summer months.
These have been tremendous successes for the past
several summers. Noteworthy during summer, 1971,
was the fact that the concerts were light on
"revolutionary rhetoric" and were promoted under
a broad base support, rather than solely WPP
or RPP support, ie, "Tribal Council", and Community
groups. This project is principally handled by
[____] of WPP leadership and his "UP" Band.

g. The Community School: This is the newest of
the community projects, and has not been in existance for sufficient time to evaluate its effectiveness. [____], and others at WPP Commune
envisioned it originally as a "Baby sitting"
service, to free families with small children for
employment, or other interests. It was conceived
as a "Pre-School" type of Kindergarten, with hopes
of obtaining accreditation for Kindergarten, and
primary grades. It was fashioned after an earlier
"Ann Arbor Community School", operated at Ann
Arbor in years past by Students For a Democratic
Society (SDS) at the UM. Children of radical

9

~~CONFIDENTIAL~~

Re: White Panther Party, also known as
Rainbow Peoples Party

~~CONFIDENTIAL~~

professors and professional personnel at Ann Arbor supported that venture, and it was hoped to capture that same constituency.

The Community School has obtained space at the Unitarian Church, Ann Arbor, and is now little more than a pilot program. (Characterization of SDS attached hereto).

h. Community Center: The success of all of these separate ventures, almost all operated as so called "community services" for the "Tribal Council", have drawn widening community support from area civic and church groups and from the City of Ann Arbor. This support in November enabled the AATC to secure a former large two story Automobile Agency building, which is being developed into the Community Center.

All of the above services or programs, previously operated under separate group names, are now in the process of being moved into this one new location, the Fisher Cadillac Building, located near the campus of the UM. The only exception is the Community School.

Community collection drives and financial contributions from sources noted above permitted acquisition and furnishing of this building. The building is owned by the City of Ann Arbor, purchased as a prospective spot for a future city parking structure. Until it is required for construction, the AATC will operate same on a rental basis from the City of Ann Arbor.

ORGANIZATION

Another development in community organizing, not an action project as such, but a highly successful activity in which the WPP assisted in formation, is the Radical Independent Party (RIP).

RIP was initiated several years ago by [____] of the WPP, and others from the AATC and area radicals, as an attempt to develop an alternative political vehicle.

b6
b7C

- 10 -

~~CONFIDENTIAL~~

Re: White Panther Party, also known as Rainbow Peoples Party

RIP and the WPP strongly supported candidates for local office in past several years, with the WPP claiming credit for assisting in the election of the present Mayor of Ann Arbor, as well as for the election of at least one member of the Ann Arbor City Council in the past.

RIP, now a completely independent political organization exists as a coalition of WPP, AATC, and UM campus radicals. It proposes to run candidates for most local offices at Ann Arbor, and recently obtained support of the city in its attempt at legitimizing itself for early 1972 elections. It similarly recently formed a coalition with area groups elsewhere in Michigan to form a state-wide party known as the "Human Rights/Radical Independent Party".

Through this wide variety of community projects, all effective, and well supported, the WPP, mainly through the AATC has been able to maintain steady and effective pressure on city authorities for the necessary city authorizations and support for their projects. The AATC has developed into a group with considerable political "clout", and is consulted with by city officials on a wide variety of matters.

For reasons cited above, John Sinclair and members of the Central Committee of WPP are at this time expressing satisfaction with the results of their change in strategy, and with their "Tribal Council" approach.

This period since release of Sinclair from prison is a time for celebration and self-satisfaction. No new programs are planned for launching. The leadership is most pleased with 1971 accomplishments and show no inclination to resume their previously more militant and aggressive stance.

- 11 -

~~CONFIDENTIAL~~

Re: White Panther Party, also known as
Rainbow Peoples Party

The only present indications for a change in direction is to capitalize on the release of Sinclair through publicity, and beefing up propaganda for defense of and release for [   ], [   ], and [   ].

WPP personnel show inclination to pull out of the successful AATC projects referred to above, now that they are self-sustaining, and give effort to above defense effort, as well as to the political opportunities afforded by the election year, 1972.

DE T-1
January 25, 1972.

III. Miscellaneous Activities

A. Demonstration, Washington, D.C.

Demonstrations sponsored by the Peoples Coalition For Peace and Justice (PCPJ) at Washington, D.C. October 22-26, 1971, include a variety of events including a demonstration sponsored by the PCPJ held at the Sylvin Theatre adjacent to the Washington Monument grounds on October 26, 1971. At 2:00 PM on that date, and at that place a rock group known as the "Up" was introduced as a band from Ann Arbor. Franklin Bach was observed on the bandstand as the leader of this group which dedicated its first piece to Weatherman fugitive Bernadine Dohrn and the "Weatherman Underground".

DE T-2
October 26, 1971.

The source advised that [   ], a member of the Central Committee of the WPP handles the WPP sponsored rock band known as the "Up".

DE T-1
January 25, 1972.

B. Freedom Rally

On December 10, 1971, there was held on the campus of UM, Ann Arbor, an event promoted as a "freedom rally" and

- 12 -

~~CONFIDENTIAL~~

Re: White Panther Party, also known as
Rainbow Peoples Party

~~CONFIDENTIAL~~

benefit for John Sinclair then incarcerated in the Michigan Prison at Jackson, Michigan, on a State Narcotic Charge. Complete action of the WPP leadership was directed toward arranging this rally during November and December, 1971. The rally's purpose was to promote the release of the WPP Chairman, John Sinclair, from prison and to promote a pending state charge in legislation regarding narcotics.

Jerry Rubin was of a great assistance in promoting cooperation from national movement figures in this rally and was instrumental in getting a commitment from John Lennon formerly of the "Beetles", and his wife, Yoko Ono, to attend and participate.

Additionally, all members of the "Chicago Conspiracy", except the two minor subjects and [ ], were committed to participate. [ ], [ ], and Bobbie Seale were early commitments. William Kuntsler was [ ] but taped a speech which was played at the rally.

b6
b7C

With the commitment of John Lennon, many groups of performers who volunteered to participate, had to be turned away.

The rally developed as undoubtedly one of the national organizationas successes of business affairs for the movement in recent years. It was unquestionably the most successful business event of the WPP's history. Attendance was capacity at some 16,000 persons. Gate receipts totaled in excess of $45,000.00. All participants donated their talent and time, and only some were paid for travel expenses.

In December, 1971, the Michigan State Legislature modified State Law on narcotics which action resulted in the release of John Sinclair from Michigan Prison at that time.

DE T-1
January 5, 1972.

C. Radical Independent Party (RIP)

RIP is referred to above as a political action organization developed at the UM and Ann Arbor with a

~~CONFIDENTIAL~~

- 13 -

~~CONFIDENTIAL~~

Re: White Panther Party, also known as
Rainbow Peoples Party

coalition of radicals including the WPP who worked at political effort to secure election to local offices at Ann Arbor. ▮▮▮▮ of WPP leadership serves on the original "Steering Committee" of RIP and during spring, 1972, ▮▮▮▮ of WPP leadership was elected as a candidate for an Ann Arbor City Council seat.

The RIP organization, late in 1971, in preparation for 1972 elections merged with a newly formed state-wide organization known as the Human Rights Party of Michigan which in late 1971 was granted legal status as a state-wide political party in Michigan.

On April 3, 1972, local city elections were held at Ann Arbor and two RIP or HRP candidates won election to two of the five available City Council positions. ▮▮▮▮ of the WPP who was a candidate for that position was unsuccessful, however, she obtained some 1,500 votes in a contest whose victor gained 3,000 votes.

The WPP expended considerable effort in the RIP or HRP held at Ann Arbor for this election with personnel participation by most WPP leadership including its chairman in business election hearing events.

Immediately following the election of the two successful candidates the RIP at Ann Arbor announced its prime objectives to include:

Dismissal of the Ann Arbor Police Chief, change in involvement of local narcotic violations, and establishment of control of the police department.

DE T-1
April 3, 1972.

Re: White Panther Party, also known as
Rainbow Peoples Party

D. Republican National Convention Interests

At the John Sinclair freedom rally held at UM December, 1971, referred to above, several prominent speakers, including Jerry Rubin, called for massive demonstrations during 1972 at the cite of the Republican National Convention. Speakers gave credit to John Sinclair and the WPP in that event in December, 1971, of combining "rock and revolution".

Source advised that in the months following _____ he reportedly met on several occasions with _____ and Jerry Rubin, reportedly to discuss possible demonstrations concerned with the Republican National Convention, 1972.

b6
b7C

DE T-3
December 13, 1971 and
May 1, 1972.

Cover Sheet for Informant Report or Material
FD-306 (Rev. 9-30-69)

	Date prepared
	6/6/72 CONFIDENTIAL

Date received	Received from (name or symbol number)	Received by
5/23/72	▮ (Protect) b2 b7D	SA ▮ b7C

Method of delivery (check appropriate blocks)

☐ in person ☐ by telephone ☒ by mail ☐ orally ☐ recording device ☐ written by informant

If orally furnished and reduced to writing by Agent:

Date

Dictated _____ to _____

Transcribed DECLASSIFIED BY 5/2/83
CX 1678 RFP/RBM

Authenticated by Informant _____

Date of Report: 5/13/72

Date(s) of activity: 5/13/72

Brief description of activity or material

Report on Benifit for JOHN LENNON and structure of NYRU.
b2 b7D

File where original is located if not attached: ▮

* INDIVIDUALS DESIGNATED BY AN ASTERISK (*) ONLY ATTENDED A MEETING AND DID NOT ACTIVELY PARTICIPATE. VIOLENCE OR REVOLUTIONARY ACTIVITIES WERE NOT DISCUSSED.

☐ Information recorded on a card index by _____ on date _____

Remarks:

All necessary action taken (U)

22- New York ▮
1- ▮ b2, b7D
1- 100- ▮ (JOHN LENNON)
1- 100-174832 (ATTICA DEFENSE COMMITTEE)
1- 100-156088 (ASIAN INFO OFFICE)
1- ▮
1- ▮
1- ▮
b7C
1- ▮
1- ▮
1- ▮
1- ▮
1- ▮
1- ▮
1- 100-174986 (NYRC)

Copies Continued.

b7C ▮
(22) CLASS. & EXT. BY ▮
REASON FCIM II, 1-2.4.2
DATE OF REVIEW 6/6/92

6/22/82

CLASS. BY 1678 RFP/RBM 5.2.83
Declas: OADR
ALL INFO CONTAINED HEREIN IS UNCLASSIFIED EXCEPT WHERE SHOWN OTHERWISE.

Block Stamp

100-175319-45

CONFIDENTIAL

Copies Continued.

CONFIDENTIAL

b7c
1-
1-
1-
1-
1-
1-
1-

-2-

CONFIDENTIAL

Saturday May 13, 1972

After JOHN LENNON p;ugged it on the Dick Cavett Show, the benefit concert for the Attica Defense Committee turned a larger crowd than expected. Among the people who came were OTTO PREMINGER & a party of 5 people. Security was tight. The AIO core group included RONALD ROSEN, JOSEPHINE PIZZINO (both new members of AIO), JAMES DUFFY, MAURICE WADE, and was led by WALTER TEAGUE. Also on security were WALTER APONTI (recently purged from AIO) LAWRENCE REMER, DIANE DANHAM, and STEPHEN POMERANTE. The benefit was held at the Wash. Sq. Meth Ch, began at about 20:00, was ended about 1:30 Sunday morning by a bomb threat, and neted $2,000 for the Defense Comm and $200 for the WSM Ch.

At 15:00 the NYRC had a meeting on re-organization at its hq (93 B third Ave). The meeting was fruitless. The two factions are basically these: LAWRENCE LEVY and HENRY PLATSKY want to form a more, intellectually oriented group which functions as a study group, at least at the outset. ROBERT HENES, EUGENIE S. JOSEPH, SUSAN LNU, WILLIAM SMITH, LESTER DAUM, and some unidentified members of the Prison Collective (on arm of NYRC concerned o prisoner liason) wish the group to become more action oriented feeling that any form of movement toward the study group idea is a cowardly retreat.

Other facts:

b7c
b7D

-3-

FEDERAL BUREAU OF INVESTIGATION
COMMUNICATIONS SECTION

MAY 16 1972

TELETYPE

NR 044 NY CODE

821 PM NITEL 5-16-72 KPR

TO ACTING DIRECTOR (100-469910)

FROM NEW YORK (100-175319) (P)

JOHN WINSTON LENNON. SECURITY MATTER DASH REVOLUTIONARY ACTIVITIES.

Reference teletype
RENYTEL MAY THREE LAST.

ON MAY SIXTEEN INSTANT, VINCENT SCHIANO, CHIEF TRIAL ATTORNEY, INS, NYC, ADVISED SUBJECT AND WIFE, YOKO ONO, ARE SCHEDULED FOR HEARING ON DEPORTATION PROCEEDINGS MAY SEVENTEEN NEXT.

SCHIANO ADVISED INS USING THREE KEY POINTS FOR HEARING NEXT:

ONE, CONCERNING CHILD CUSTODY CASE OF KYOKO COX, SON OF ANTHONY DAVID COX AND YOKO ONO BY PREVIOUS MARRIAGE. LENNONS CLAIM NATURAL FATHER ABDUCTED SON SHORTLY AFTER COURT IN HOUSTON, TEXAS, AWARDED LENNONS CUSTODY WITH REQUIREMENTS CHILD BE RAISED IN US. INS BELIEVES LENNONS AND COX MAY BE

END PAGE ONE

PAGE TWO

PARTY TO KEEPING CHILD HIDDEN AS TOOL OF DELAYING DEPORTATION HEARINGS. IF FACT ESTABLISHED, INS WILL GO ON PERJURY CHARGES AGAINST LENNONS.

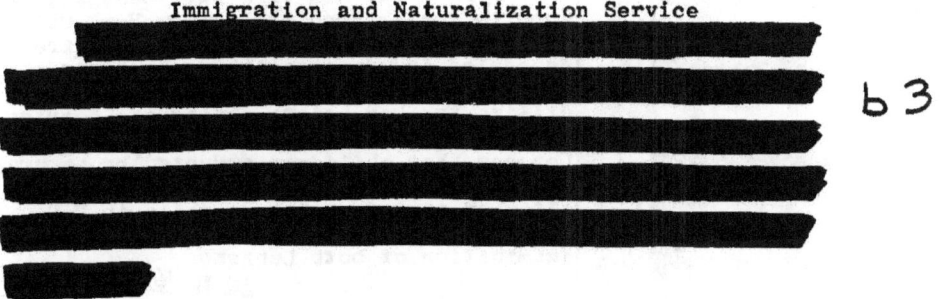

Immigration and Naturalization Service

b3

THREE, INS WILL REQUEST MENTAL EXAMINATION OF LENNONS AT LATER DATE.

END

PLS ACK FOR THREE
ACK FOR THREE TELS

MRF FBI WA DC

T's to Rosen
Miller
Wannall
Shackelford
Recer

Domestic Intelligence Division

INFORMATIVE NOTE
Date 5/17/72

You were previously advised that both John Lennon and his wife, Yoko Ono, are in the U.S. and that Lennon is the major financial contributor to the Election Year Strategy Information Center (EYSIC) which was organized to conduct disruptive demonstrations during the Republican National Convention. EYSIC has been "dying on the vine" due to Lennon's possible deportation which he is fighting in court.

Lennon and his wife have been fighting deportation proceedings in New York City. Attached states Lennon and his wife are scheduled for deportation proceedings on 5/17/72 in New York City. INS planning to utilize two key points during the hearing as follows: (1) establish claims by the Lennons that child was abducted by natural father are false; (2) establish that Lennon's claim he earned no income while in U.S. involves fraud. INS plans to request mental examination of both Lennons.

For information.

ABK:lrs/owc

ALL INFORMATION CONTAINED HEREIN IS UNCLASSIFIED EXCEPT WHERE SHOWN OTHERWISE.

Memorandum

TO: SAC, NEW YORK DATE: 5/18/72

FROM: SAC, SAN DIEGO

SUBJECT:

[redacted] was arrested by FBI Agents in San Diego for Conspiracy to Injure Government Property and Trespassing for the Purpose of Injuring Government Property during demonstrations against the Vietnam War. An address book containing approximately 395 entries was found in his possession.

1 - New York
1 - San Diego

Set forth below are addresses which appeared in ▓▓▓▓▓ address book and appear to be of possible interest to your Division. It should be noted that some names listed appear to be contacts among the revolutionary new left, while others may be associates of the subject from earlier years ▓▓▓▓▓▓▓▓▓▓▓▓▓▓▓▓▓▓▓▓▓▓ Some names are apparently contacts used to obtain publicity for the Peace Movement ▓▓▓▓▓▓▓▓▓▓

The appearance of a person's name in ▓▓▓▓▓▓ address book cannot be construed as an indictment of that individual's character nor an indication of his associations.

Information below is furnished for information purposes only, and dissemination to appropriate files is left to the discretion of receiving offices.

b7C

386. JOHN & YOKO LENNON
Old Chelsea Station
P.O. Box 654
N.Y., N.Y. 10011

✓

p3

23

FEDERAL BUREAU OF INVESTIGATION
COMMUNICATIONS SECTION

MAY 18 1972

TELETYPE

NR 026 NY CODE

1250PM URGENT 5-18-72 PAC

TO ACTING DIRECTOR 100-469910

ATT DID

FROM NEW YORK 100-175319 2P

JOHN WINSTON LENNON; SECURITY MATTER DASH REVOLUTIONARY ACTIVITIES. OFFICE OF ORIGIN: NEW YORK.

ON MAY SEVENTEEN, LAST, A REPRESENTATIVE OF IMMIGRATION AND NATURALIZATION SERVICE (INS) ADVISED THAT THE SUBJECT AND HIS WIFE YOKO ONO APPEARED AT INS HEADQUARTERS IN NEW YORK CITY THAT DATE FOR THE PURPOSE OF DEPORTATION HEARINGS.

THE CHIEF TRIAL ATTORNEY FOR INS MAINTAINED THAT THE SUBJECT WAS DEPORTABLE FROM THE UNITED STATES DUE TO HIS ONE NINE SIX EIGHT CONVICTION ON NARCOTICS CHARGES IN ENGLAND. YOKO ONO WAS ELIGIBLE TO APPLY FOR UNITED STATES CITIZENSHIP. SUBJECTS ATTORNEY LEON WILDES STATED HE WOULD FILE PETITIONS ON BEHALF OF BOTH THE SUBJECT AND HIS WIFE FOR THEM TO BECOME UNITED STATES CITIZENS.

END PAGE ONE

PAGE TWO

SPECIAL INQUIRY OFFICER IRA FIELDSTEEL CONCLUDED THE HEARINGS AND GAVE INS ATTORNEYS UNTIL JULY ONE NEXT, TO FILE LEGAL BRIEFS ON THE CASE. FIELDSTEEL COMMENTED LENNONS APPEALS COULD GO ON FOR YEARS IF THEY SO CHOOSE.

ADMINISTRATIVE

INS REPRESENTATIVE IS VINCENT SCHIANO CHIEF TRIAL ATTORNEY. ON MAY SIXTEEN, LAST, ███████████████, THIRD NARCOTICS DEISTRICT, NEW YORK POLICE DEPARTMENT ADVISED THAT HIS DEPARTMENT HAS BEEN UNABLE TO MAKE A NARCOTICS CASE ON THE LENNONS. NYPD CONTINUING. NYO FOLLOWING. NO LHM FOLLOWS.
END
RMS FBI WA DC CLR

FD-350 (Rev. 7-16-63)

(Mount Clipping in Space Below)

John and Yoko Joining Vigil Here

By MILTON ADAMS

A weekend of massive demonstrations has been scheduled to take place here and across the country by several peace groups demanding complete withdrawal of U. S. forces from Indochina.

A candlelight vigil and "procession for peace" tomorrow night in Duffy Square, at Broadway between 46th and 47th Sts., from 8 to 11 p.m., will highlight local activities.

Sponsored by the National Peace Action Coalition, the vigil is expected to attract a number of prominent members of the city's art community, and rally support for a massive demonstration scheduled for Washington on Sunday.

The two demonstrations were announced by NPAC National Coordinator Katherine Sojourner yesterday.

Supporters of the Sunday march in Washington include about 25 members of Congress, a number of local politicians, and trade union leaders from across the country.

John and Yoko

Members of the art community endorsing the Washington march and expected to attend tomorrow's vigil include John Lennon and Yoko Ono; satirist Jules Feiffer; producer Joseph Papp; writers Arthur Miller and William Styron and others.

"This Sunday in Washington, thousands of Americans will express their opposition to Nixon's latest and most dangerous escalations," said novelist Kurt Vonnegut, Jr., reading a statement signed by about 50 prominent artists.

"At this critical time, we believe it important to share some time and feeling for peace," the statement said.

On Monday, Washington demonstrators plan what they call a "blockade" of the Pentagon by blocking entrances to the building.

Plans were also announced today by the U. S. Servicemen's Fund, for a series of antiwar demonstrations at Fort Dix and more than 30 other military bases and installations across the country tomorrow.

Similar Armed Forces Day demonstrations organized by active-duty military personnel last year have forced the Pentagon to cancel official parades and ceremonies at these bases.

Such fears by officials of the Military Order of the World Wars resulted in the cancellation of New York's 23rd annual Armed Forces Day parade this week.

DO NOT DESTROY – PENDING LITIGATION

Newspaper article dated May 19, 1972, announcing peace demonstrations scheduled to take place across the USA on the next day.

The following documents are from John Lennon's INS file.

After John and Yoko exposed their visa problems on the 'Dick Cavett Show' (see pages 117 and 118), lots of people wanted to know more about what was going on. As a result, senators from all over the country received letters asking to get an update on this issue. And these senators then turned to the INS for more information.

It would have been of interest to have access to the content of these letters asking for information and explanations about Lennon's immigration case and why he wasn't granted a visa. One may wonder why, in most cases, the whole documents were withheld "to protect personal privacy", whereas on occasions some names were not even blacked out.

These letters and telegrams were answered by commissioners or associate commissioners of INS.

Only the copy of the envelope was released. The letter and its content were withheld.

WHB131 WAE057(1-003026C134)PD 05/13/72 0543
ICS IPMSFSD SFO
ZCZC 104 0 XST0074 PK NL PDF 4 EXTRA SAN FRANCISCO CALIF 13
PMS THE PRESIDENT
THE WHITE HOUSE WASHDC
BT

IT SEEMS TO ME THAT THE ACTIONS OF THE US IMMIGRATION SERVICE
IN INITIATING DEPORTATION PROCEEDINGS AGAINST MUSICIAN
JOHN LENNON AND HIS WIFE ARE CLEARLY AN ACT OF
POLITICAL REPRESSION. FOR LENNON IS MORE THAN A MUSICIAN AND
MORE THAN A CULT HERO HE IS ONE WHO HAS THROUGH HIS WRITINGS
AND PUBLIC BEHAVIOR INFLUENCED A GREAT MANY PEOPLE OVER THE
LAST FEW YEARS IN SUCH WAYS WHICH CONTRADICT MOST OF THE
POLICIES WHICH YOU ADVOCATE. THAT S HIS ONLY CRIME.

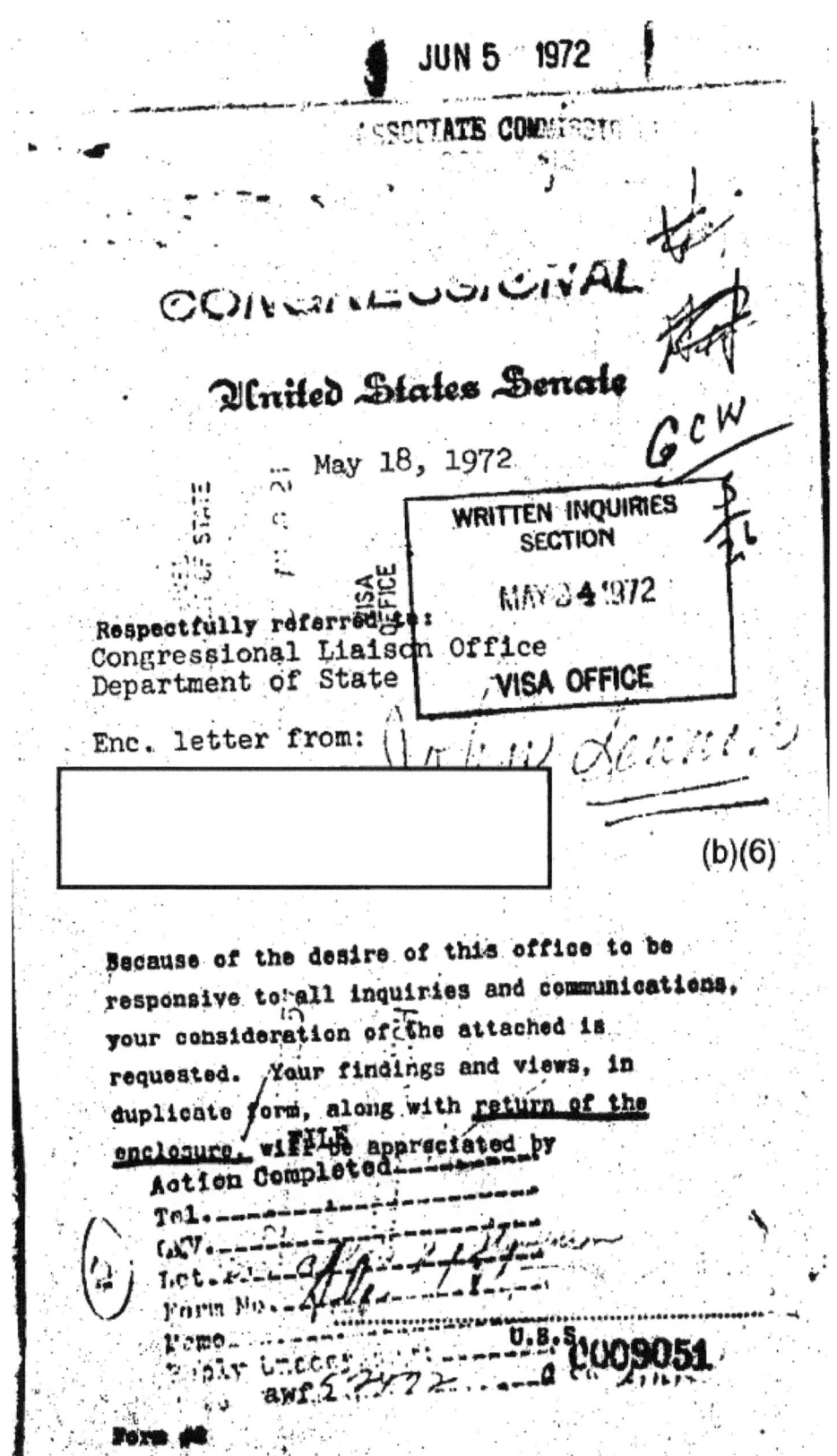

The original letter sent to Senator Stevenson and requiring information about the status of John Lennon's immigration case wasn't released to the public : "page withheld pursuant to (b)(6)", which means the disclosure of this letter "would constitute a clearly unwarranted invasion of personal privacy."

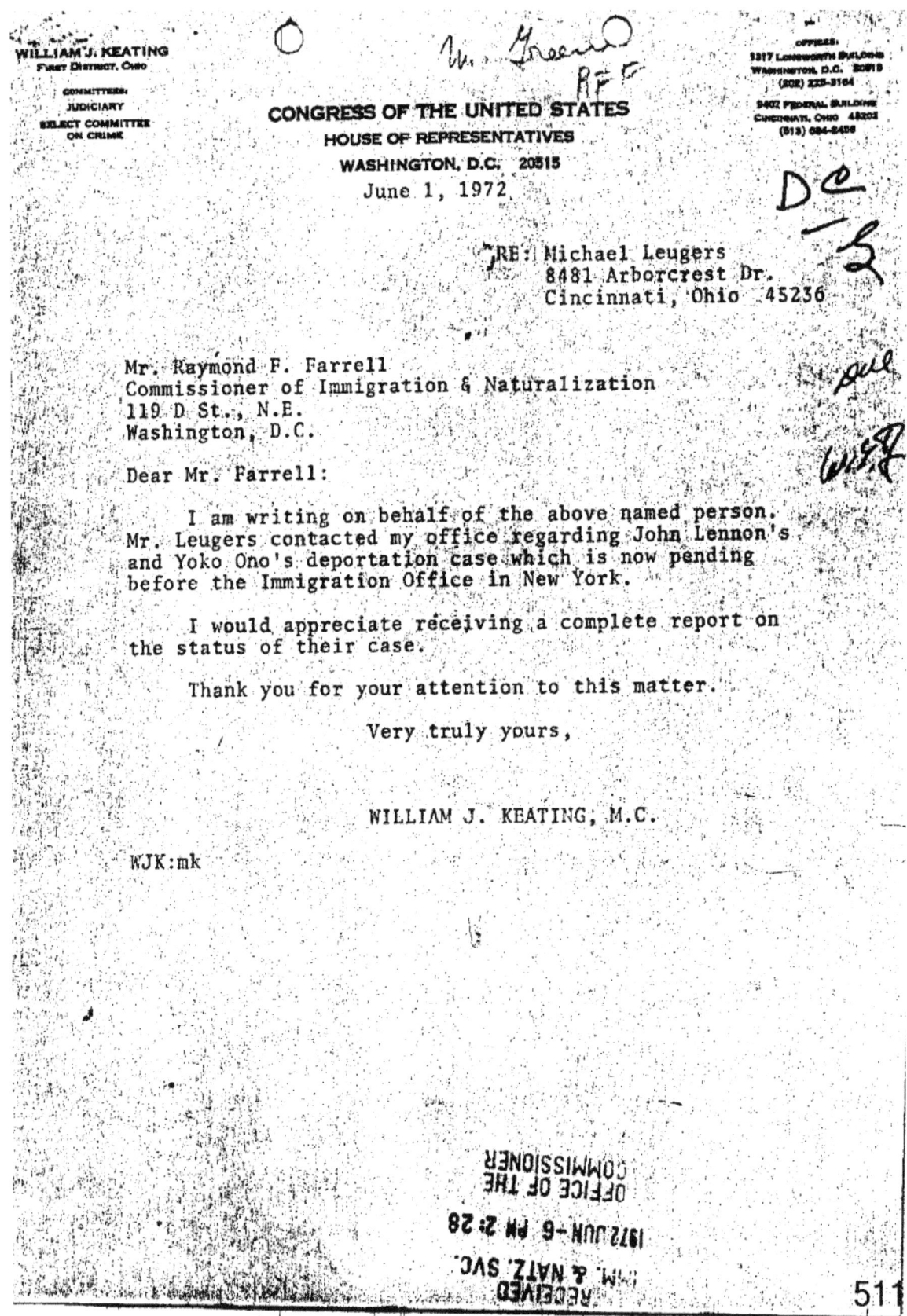

WILLIAM J. KEATING
First District, Ohio

COMMITTEES:
JUDICIARY
SELECT COMMITTEE ON CRIME

CONGRESS OF THE UNITED STATES
HOUSE OF REPRESENTATIVES
WASHINGTON, D.C. 20515

OFFICES:
1317 Longworth Building
Washington, D.C. 20515
(202) 225-3164

9402 Federal Building
Cincinnati, Ohio 45202
(513) 684-2456

June 1, 1972

RE: Michael Leugers
8481 Arborcrest Dr.
Cincinnati, Ohio 45236

Mr. Raymond F. Farrell
Commissioner of Immigration & Naturalization
119 D St., N.E.
Washington, D.C.

Dear Mr. Farrell:

I am writing on behalf of the above named person. Mr. Leugers contacted my office regarding John Lennon's and Yoko Ono's deportation case which is now pending before the Immigration Office in New York.

I would appreciate receiving a complete report on the status of their case.

Thank you for your attention to this matter.

Very truly yours,

WILLIAM J. KEATING, M.C.

WJK:mk

The letter sent to Senator Keating has been withheld, but the name and address of the sender have not been blacked out on this document.

HAROLD R. COLLIER
10TH DISTRICT, ILLINOIS

COMMITTEE:
WAYS AND MEANS

ADMINISTRATIVE ASSISTANT
MARIE HERSHEY

Congress of the United States
House of Representatives
Washington, D.C. 20515

June 1, 1972

Honorable Raymond F. Farrell
Commissioner
U. S. Immigration and Naturalization Service
119 D Street, N. E.
Washington, D. C.

Dear Ray:

I have received several letters from constituents inquiring into the deportion case of John Lennon.

At your convenience, will you provide me with an up-to-date report in this situation? It appears that many people feel that the government has dragged its feet in deporting him, probably because of his following in this country. However, I thought the charges against him were fairly well proven.

Thanks for your cooperation.

Sincerely yours,

Harold

Harold R. Collier

HRC/cdt

JUN 5 1972
ASSOCIATE COMMISSIONER

```
NR 039 NY CODE
100 PM PM URGENT 5-23-72 BGW
TO ACTING DIRECTOR (100-469910)
    ATTN: DID
    HOUSTON
FROM NEW YORK (100-175EQOL) 2P

JOHN WINSTON LENNON, SM-REVOLUTIONARY ACTIVITES (ORIGIN:
NEW YORK)

    RE NEW YORK TEL TO BUREAU MAY ONE EIGHT LAST. HOUSTON
NOT IN RECEIPT OF REFERENCED TEL.
    FOR INFORMATION OF HOUSTON, SUBJECT AND [     ]
INVOLVED IN ANTI-WAR ACTIVITES AND PLAN TO TRAVEL TO
REPUBLICAN AND DEMOCRATIC CONVENTION THIS YEAR. INS ATTEMPTING    b6
TO DEPORT [     ] ON GROUNDS OF SUBJECT'S ONE NINE SIX              b7C
EIGHT NARCOTIC CONVICTION IN ENGLAND.
    [     ] USING DELAY TACTICS IN DEPORTATION OF ATTEMTING
TO LOCATE [                    ] WHO WAS REPORTED ABDUCTED
BY [                    ]. HOUSTON COURT HAS                        b6
                                                                    b7C
[                        ]. NO PROCESS OUT ON [   ]
END PAGE ONE
```

ALL INFORMATION CONTAINED
HEREIN IS UNCLASSIFIED
DATE _____ BY _____

Here you can see what differences there can be between two versions of the same FBI document regarding which information is blacked out and which is actually released to the public.

NR 239 NY CODE
1715 PM URGENT 5-23-72 BGW
TO ACTING DIRECTOR (100-469910)
ATTN: DID
HOUSTON
FROM NEW YORK

JOHN WINSTON LENNON, SM-REVOLUTIONARY ACTIVITES (ORIGIN: NEW YORK)

RE NEW YORK TEL TO BUREAU MAY ONE EIGHT LAST. HOUSTON NOT IN RECEIPT OF REFERENCED TEL.

FOR INFORMATION OF HOUSTON, SUBJECT AND WIFE YOKO ONO INVOLVED IN ANTI-WAR ACTIVITES AND PLAN TO TRAVEL TO REPUBLICAN AND DEMOCRATIC CONVENTION THIS YEAR. INS ATTEMPTING TO DEPORT BOTH LENNONS ON GROUNDS OF SUBJECT'S ONE NINE SIX EIGHT NARCOTIC CONVICTION IN ENGLAND. BOX 442 KOUNTZE TEXAS

LENNONS USING DELAY TACTICS IN DEPORTATION OF ATTEMPTING TO LOCATE YOKO ONO'S CHILD KYOKO COX WHO WAS REPORTED ABDUCTED BY NATURAL FATHER ANTHONY DAVID COX. HOUSTON COURT HAS AWARDED CUSTODY OF CHILD TO LENNONS. NO PROCESS OUT ON COX

END PAGE ONE

ALL INFORMATION CONTAINED
HEREIN IS UNCLASSIFIED
DATE 9/9/81 BY SP4/SLR/PLG

PAGE TWO

NYO IN RECEIPT OF INFORMATION THIS DATE THAT [____] HAVE HIDDEN [____] AT RESIDENCE OF [____], [____] [____] TEXAS, ZIP [____], IN ATTEMTPS TO DELAY DEPORATION.

INS HAS ADVISED THEY WILL FILE PERJURY CHARGES AGAINST [____] IF ESTABLISHED LENNON FURNISHED FALSE INFORMATION DURING INS HEARING.

LEAD

HOUSTON

AT KOUNTZE, TEXAS. CONDUCT APPROPRIATE INVESTIGATION TO DETERMINE IF [____] IS AT ABOVE ADDRESS, AND ATTEMPT TO ESTABLISH IF [____] IN CONTACT WITH [____] IN NYC. SUTEL.

END

REC'D FBI HO KOB

CLR

PAGE TWO

NYO IN RECEIPT OF INFORMATION THIS DATE THAT LENNONS HAVE HIDDEN CHILD AT RESIDENCE OF ███████████ b7c ███████████████████████████████ IN ATTEMPTS TO DELAY DEPORATION. INS HAS ADVISED THEY WILL FILE PERJURY CHARGES AGAINST LENNONS IF ESTABLISHED LENNON FURNISHED FALSE INFORMATION DURING INS HEARING.

LEAD

HOUSTON

AT ███████████ CONDUCT APPROPRIATE INVESTIGATION TO DETERMINE IF KYOKO COX IS AT ABOVE ADDRESS, AND ATTEMPT b7c TO ESTABLISH IF ███ IN CONTACT WITH LENNONS IN NYC. SUTEL.

END

TELETYPE   IMMEDIATE

5/24/72

TO   SACS NEW YORK (100-175319)
        HOUSTON   1 - Mr. C.W. Bates
                                                 (C.A. Nuzum)
FROM   ACTING DIRECTOR FBI (100-469910)   1 - Mr. R.L. Shackelford
                                             1 - Mr. R.L. Pence

JOHN WINSTON LENNON, SM - REVOLUTIONARY ACTIVITIES.

RENYTEL MAY TWENTY-THREE LAST.

HOUSTON DISREGARD LEAD SET BY NEW YORK IN REFERENCED TELETYPE EXCEPT FOR CONTACT WITH ESTABLISHED SOURCES ONLY.

BUREAU FULLY AWARE PROGRESS OF NEW YORK OFFICE IN DEVELOPING EXCELLENT COVERAGE SUBJECT'S ACTIVITIES, HOWEVER, ASPECTS INVESTIGATION RELATING TO SUBJECT'S APPEARANCE AT INS HEARINGS AND POSSIBLE PERJURY INVOLVED IN FALSE STATEMENTS MADE BY SUBJECT STRICTLY RESPONSIBILITY OF INS. INFORMATION DEVELOPED BY NEW YORK SHOULD BE IMMEDIATELY, IF NOT ALREADY, FURNISHED TO INS. ALL SUBSEQUENT INFORMATION DEVELOPED REGARDING SUBJECT'S VIOLATIONS OF FEDERAL AND LOCAL LAWS INCLUDING NARCOTICS OR PERJURY, SHOULD LIKEWISE BE DISSEMINATED WITHOUT DELAY TO PERTINENT AGENCIES.

Lennon is former member of Beatles singing group in England who, despite clear ineligibility for U.S. visa due to narcotics conviction in England in 1968, was allowed to reenter U.S. during 1971 on visitors visa. Visas of Lennon and wife, Yoko Ono, expired 2/72 and since that time Immigration and Naturalization Service (INS) has been attempting to deport Lennons. New York Office following activities of Lennon closely

Information developed by our

NOTE CONTINUED - OVER

ALL INFORMATION CONTAINED HEREIN IS UNCLASSIFIED EXCEPT WHERE SHOWN OTHERWISE

Teletype to New York and Houston
RE: John Winston Lennon
100-469910

CONFIDENTIAL

NOTE CONTINUED:

sources that Lennon donated $75,000 to organization formed to disrupt Republican National Convention. Lennons using delaying tactics to avoid deportation claiming that they must locate Ono's child by former marriage who was reported abducted by natural father Anthony Cox. New York developed information that Lennons actually have child hidden at certain residence in Houston Division for purpose of delaying deportation. INS considering filing perjury charges against Lennons if information can be established they furnished false information during hearing. New York has set urgent lead for Houston Division to attempt to locate Ono's child and attempt to establish if person keeping child is in contact with Lennons. Actual location of Ono's child and subsequent prosecution for perjury in this instance is responsibility of INS and Houston being instructed to disregard lead except for contact with established sources only. In view of possible court proceedings, active investigation by FBI in this area could result in FBI Agents testifying which would not be in Bureau's best interest and could result in considerable adverse publicity.

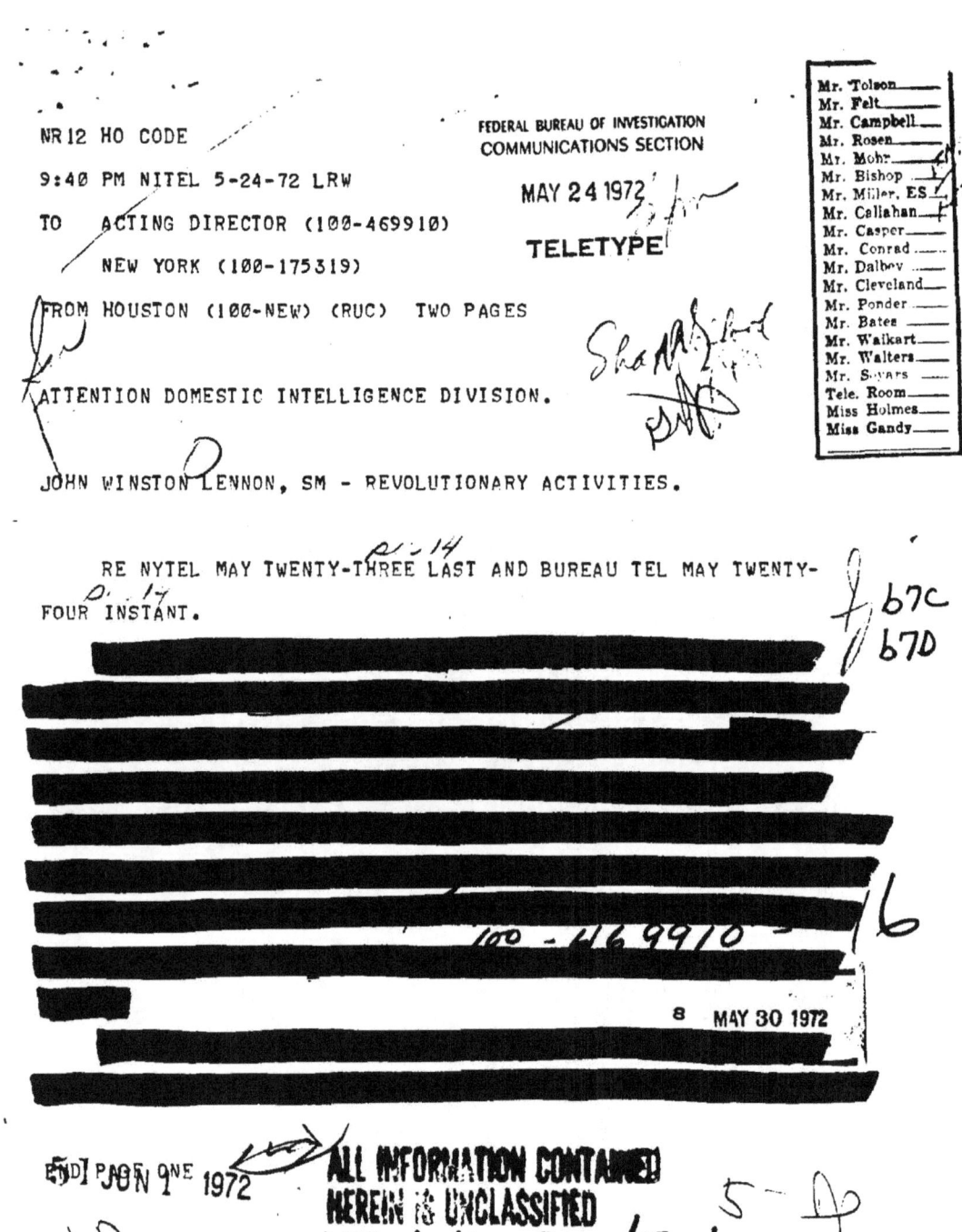

As you can see with these two documents (continued on the next pages), there are sometimes major differences regarding what information is made available to the public for the same FBI document coming from two different sources

NR 12 HO CODE

9:40 PM NITEL 5-24-72 LRW

TO   ACTING DIRECTOR (100-469910)

     NEW YORK (100-175319)

FROM HOUSTON (100-NEW) (RUC)   TWO PAGES

ATTENTION DOMESTIC INTELLIGENCE DIVISION.

ALL INFORMATION CONTAINED HEREIN IS UNCLASSIFIED DATE 2/15/91 BY [signature]

JOHN WINSTON LENNON, SM - REVOLUTIONARY ACTIVITIES.

RE NYTEL MAY TWENTY-THREE LAST AND BUREAU TEL MAY TWENTY-FOUR INSTANT.

ON MAY TWENTY-FOUR, SEVENTY-TWO, [redacted], [redacted], ESTABLISHED SOURCE, STATED [redacted]. [redacted] IS [redacted], ABOUT [redacted] YEARS OF AGE, HIPPIE TYPE, WHO TRAVELS TO OTHER COUNTRIES INCLUDING ENGLAND. [redacted] STATED HE SEES HER OCCASIONALLY IN [redacted] BUT HAS NEVER SEEN [redacted] FITTING DESCRIPTION OF [redacted] WITH HER. [redacted], [redacted], FORMER [redacted], [redacted], HAS QUESTIONABLE REPUTATION IN COMMUNITY.

ON MAY TWENTY-FOUR, SEVENTY-TWO, [redacted], [redacted], TEXAS, STATED HE HAS KNOWN [redacted]

b6
b7C
b7D

100-12734-9

Searched
Serialized
Indexed
Filed

END PAGE ONE

No Blue copy,
Approved by Supv.

HO 100-NEW
PAGE TWO

b7C
b7D

IN VIEW OF INSTRUCTIONS IN REBUTEL, NO FURTHER INQUIRY BEING MADE BY HOUSTON DIVISION.

E N D
KJB FBI WA DC CLXX   REC THREE TELS
CLR

HO 100-NEW

PAGE TWO

WELL FOR YEARS. VERIFIED THAT THE FAMILY HAS QUESTIONABLE REPUTATION AND IS KNOWN TO BE SOMEWHAT RADICAL. STATED FAMILY CAPABLE OF [   ], BUT HE HAS NEVER SEEN [   ] FITTING [   ] DESCRIPTION. HE RECENTLY SAW [   ] AT THE [   ] BUT SHE DID NOT HAVE [   ] WITH HER.

b6
b7C

IN VIEW OF INSTRUCTIONS IN REBUTEL, NO FURTHER INQUIRY BEING MADE BY HOUSTON DIVISION.

E N D

KJB FBI WA DC CLXX   REC THREE TELS

CLR

NY-JMC

```
FD-36 (Rev. 5-22-64)
                                    FBI

                                    Date: 5/25/72

Transmit the following in _____
                              (Type in plaintext or code)
Via      AIRTEL
      _____
                              (Priority)
```

TO: ACTING DIRECTOR, FBI (100-469910)

FROM: SAC, NEW YORK (100-175319) (P)

SUBJECT: JOHN WINSTON LENNON
           SM-REVOLUTIONARY ACTIVITIES
           (OO:NY)

ReButel and Houston teletype both dated 5/24/72.

On 5/25/72, Mr. VINCENT SCHIANO, Chief Trial Attorney, INS, NYC, advised that his agency is in receipt of a letter from ▓▓▓▓▓▓▓▓▓▓ dated 5/19/72, which states the following: b7c

"I can no longer remain silent, I know the whereabouts of KYOKO COX, and I wish to be of assistance. I am willing to help..."

The letter was signed ▓▓▓▓▓▓▓▓▓▓ b7c

SCHIANO advised that he will contact his headquarters in Washington this date and advise the appropriate official, Mr. CARL BURROWS, who is in charge of INS Investigation of the above information. He will request INS officials in Texas to contact ▓▓▓▓▓▓▓▓▓▓ concerning her letter.

  b7c

② - Bureau (RM)
1 - Houston (INFO) (RM)
3 - Miami (RM)
    (1 - MIDEM)
    (1 - MIREP)
1 - New York
CJL:slb
(8)

100-469910- 15

MAY 27 1972

Approved: _____   Sent _____ M Per _____
         Special Agent in Charge

These two documents (continued on the next pages) from John Lennon's FBI files come from two different sources and were not blacked out the same way.

5/25/72

AIRTEL

TO: ACTING DIRECTOR, FBI (100-469910)

FROM: SAC, NEW YORK (100-175319) (P)

SUBJECT: JOHN WINSTON LENNON
SM-REVOLUTIONARY ACTIVITIES
(OO:NY)

ReButel and Houston teletype both dated 5/24/72.

On 5/25/72, Mr. VINCENT SCHIANO, Chief Trial Attorney, INS, NYC, advised that his agency is in receipt of a letter from [   ], [   ], dated 5/19/72, which states the following:

The letter was signed [   ]

SCHIANO advised that he will contact his headquarters in Washington this date and advise the appropriate official, [   ], who is in charge of INS Investigation of the above information. He will request INS officials in [   ] to contact [   ], concerning [   ] letter.

2 - Bureau (RM)
1 - Houston (INFO) (RM)
3 - Miami (RM)
  (1 - MIDEM)
  (1 - MIREP)
1 - New York
CJL:slb
(8)

ALL INFORMATION CONTAINED
HEREIN IS UNCLASSIFIED
DATE _____ BY _____

NY 100-175319

SCHIANO also advised that he has considered requesting INS to place the subject and YOKO ONO on bond pending the outcome of their deportation proceedings and to restrict their travel. He has received information that the LENNONs are planning a large rock concert in Miami during the Conventions and that the rock concert was to be held in front of the Convention Hall.

b7c

The above information is being furnished in view of possibility ▬▬▬▬ may contact the Houston Office. ▬▬▬ name should be appropriately indexed.

- 2*-

NY 100-175319

        ☐ also advised that he has considered requesting INS to place the subject and ☐ on bond pending the outcome of their deportation proceedings and to restrict their travel. He has received information that ☐ are planning a large rock concert in Miami during the Conventions and that the rock concert was to be held in front of the Convention Hall.

b6
b7C

        The above information is being furnished in view of possibility ☐ may contact the Houston Office. ☐ name should be appropriately indexed.

b6
b7C
b7D

-2*-

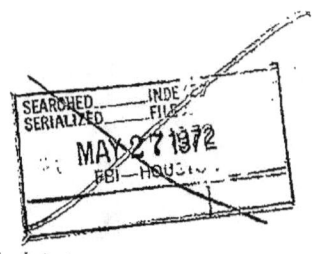

UNITED STATES GOVERNMENT

Memorandum

TO : SAC, New York (100-170471)   6/2/72

FROM : SA [redacted]   b7C

SUBJECT: NATIONAL PEACE ACTION COALITION (NPAC)
IS-C (TROTSKYIST)
OO: NY

The attached flyer was obtained from unidentified individual by SA [redacted] at an anti-war demonstration on 5/20/72 at Duffy Sq, NYC, NY.

CLASS. & EXT. BY 4/19/82
REASON-FCIM II 4.2(2)(3)
DATE OF REVIEW

DO NOT DESTROY — PENDING LITIGATION

100-170471-1360

DECLASSIFIED ON 5-3-83
BY 1628 RFP/SBm

Buy U.S. Savings Bonds Regularly on the Payroll Savings Plan

Join us Saturday night, May 20, 1972 – 8 to 11 p
in Duffy Square, Broadway between 46th & 47th

fo

CANDLELIGHT VIGIL AI
PROCESSION FOR PEA

STOP THE BLOCKADE NOW!
STOP THE BOMBING NOW!
U.S. OUT OF S.E. ASIA NOW!

ALL INFORMATION CONTAINED
HEREIN IS UNCLASSIFIED
DATE 5-3-83 BY 1670

on the
the Emergency M
on Washington Sunday, Ma

"This Sunday in Washington thousands of Americans of all ages will express their opposition – legally and peacefully – to Nixon's latest and most dangerous escalations. At this critical time we members of New York's community of the arts believe it important to share with you some time and feeling for peace.

"Join us Saturday night, May 20, 1972 – 8 to 11 p.m., in Duffy Square. And, remember, you . . . we . . . are not alone!"

Rae Allen
David Amram
Peter Boyle
Joseph Chaikin
Gavin Cort
Ossie Davis
Ruby Dee
Jules Feiffer
Gene Frankel
Ben Gazzara
Bernard Gersten
Jack Gilford

Lee Grant
Tammy Grimes
John Hammond
Barbara Harris
Jon Hendricks
Jules Irving
Anne Jackson
Jill Krementz
John Lahr
Lynn and Burton Lane
Madeline Lee

John Lennon and Yoko Ono
Viveca Lindfors
Paul Lipson
Helen Lynd
Monica McCall
Charles Marvan
Arthur Miller
Anais Nin
Jerry and Marta Orbach
Joseph Papp
Estelle Parsons

Muriel Rukeyser
Janice Rule
Robert Ryan
Isiah Sheffer
William Styron
Barbara Tarbuck
Harold Taylor
Jean-Claude Van Italie
Kurt Vonnegut, Jr.
Gerald and Greta Walker
Eli Wallach

March on Washington Information

TRANSPORTATION

Bus tickets: $10 round trip. Train tickets: $15 round trip. Buses leave Manhattan, Queens, Brooklyn, Bronxt at 6:00 a.m. Buses leave D.C. at 6:00 p.m. Train leaves Penn Station at 7:00 a.m., and leaves D.C. at 6:00 p.m. Make checks payable to "NPAC TRANSPORTATION FUND."

DEMONSTRATION DETAILS

Assemble: 10:00 a.m. at the Ellipse.

March: Noon on Pennsylvania Avenue.

Rally: 1:00 p.m. on the Capitol Steps, west side.

For more information, to volunteer, or to purchase tickets, contact: NATIONAL PEACE ACTION COALIT 150 Fifth Avenue, New York, N.Y. 10011. (212) 741-2018. Urgent – we need money now to help pay for M

FD-36 (Rev. 5-22-64)

FBI

Date: 6/5/72

Transmit the following in _____
(Type in plaintext or code)

Via AIRTEL
(Priority)

ALL INFORMATION CONTAINED
HEREIN IS UNCLASSIFIED
DATE 2/12/81 BY SP4/SEA

TO: ACTING DIRECTOR, FBI (100-469910)
                              (100-469601)

FROM: SAC, MIAMI (100-NEW) (P)
                   (80-1353) (P)

SUBJECT: JOHN WINSTON LENNON
         SM - REVOLUTIONARY ACTIVITIES
         (OO: NEW YORK)

         MIDEM

    Re New York airtel to the Bureau dated 5/25/72, under first caption above.

    New York airtel indicated information was received from VINCENT SCHIANO, Chief Trial Attorney, INS, New York City, on 5/25/72, to the effect that he had received information that subject LENNON and his wife, YOKO ONO, are planning a large rock concert in Miami during the conventions and that the rock concert was to be held in front of the convention hall.

                    LEAD

NEW YORK

4 - Bureau (RM)
    (2 - 100-469910)
    (2 - 100-469601)
2 - New York (RM) (100-175319)
3 - Miami
    (2 - 100-NEW)
    (1 - 80-1353)
JCB:mly
(9)

REC-117

100-46990-17

JUN 8 1972

Approved: _____ Sent _____ M Per _____
           Special Agent in Charge
57 JUN 19 1972

MM 100-NEW
80-1353

At New York, New York

Will re-contact Attorney SCHIANO for source and accuracy of above information. New York thereafter requested to place this information in LHM form under caption Demonstrations at Democratic and Republican National Conventions.

OPTIONAL FORM NO. 10
MAY 1962 EDITION
GSA FPMR (41 CFR) 101-11.6

UNITED STATES GOVERNMENT

Memorandum

TO : SAC, HOUSTON (100-12734)　　　　　　　DATE: 6/8/72

FROM : SA [   ] b6 b7C

SUBJECT: JOHN WINSTON LENNON
SM - RA

On 6/8/72, [   ], INS, advised an investigator of INS intended to interview [   ] at [   ], and he wished to be advised whether this investigation would interfere with any investigation being conducted by this office.　　　　　　　　　　　　　　　　　b6 b7C b7D

[   ] was advised that this action by his service would in no manner interfere with any pending FBI investigation.　　　　　　　　　　　　　　　　　b6 b7C

ALL INFORMATION CONTAINED
HEREIN IS UNCLASSIFIED
DATE 6-10-82 BY [signature]

BP:jam
(1)

100-12734-5
SEARCHED____ INDEXED____
SERIALIZED____ FILED____
JUN 8 1972
FBI HOUSTON

Buy U.S. Savings Bonds Regularly on the Payroll Savings Plan

This is the front cover of John and Yoko's LP "Some Time in New York City". This album came out in June 1972 and certainly didn't help to solve Lennon's visa problems as it had a strong political flavor with songs like "John Sinclair" (see page 48), "Attica State" (about the riots that had taken place at Attica prison in 1971) or "Angela" (about Angela Davis, a black activist who was abusively jailed and kept in prison for her alleged involvement in a shooting).

This cover also shows an altered photo of Richard Nixon and Mao Zedong dancing nude together. Not such a good way to be left alone by Nixon's administration…

4-94 (Rev. 1-4-67)

Immigration and Naturalization - General	39-0-A
(SUBJECT)	(FILE NO.)

ALL SERIALS, EXCEPT THOSE REMAINING IN FILE AND THOSE LISTED AS CHANGED ON THIS SHEET WERE "SKIPPED" OR WERE REMOVED FROM FILE AND DESTROYED IN ACCORDANCE WITH AUTHORITY CONTAINED IN 66-19087-47

39-0-A (Newspaper clipping N.Y. Compass 5/26/50) CT 100-372020-1
39-0-A Times Herald 3/19/52 CT 105-51210-A

(TAB CARD IN THE NUMBERING UNIT INDICATES ACTION TAKEN)

DATE July, 1974

INITIALS Purge

Search Slip
FD-160 (Rev. 3-23-71)

TO: CHIEF CLERK			Date	
Subject			Social Security Account #	
Aliases				
Address		Birth Date	Birthplace	Race	Sex ☐ Male ☐ Female

☐ Exact Spelling ☐ Main Criminal Case Files Only ☐ Restrict to Locality of
☐ All References ☐ Criminal References Only
☐ Main Subversive Case Files Only ☐ Main Subversive (If no Main, list all Subversive References)
☐ Subversive References Only ☐ Main Criminal (If no Main, list all Criminal References)

File & Serial Number	Remarks	File & Serial Number	Remarks
John W. Lennon 87-12615-7 p.11		100-52854 Sub I-2 p.5	
John Lennon 100-55361-2 p.1			
174-318-309 p.5			
174-318-308 p.7			
100-52854 Sub I-12 p.55			

Requested by	Squad	Extension	File No.
Searched by		(date)	
Consolidated by		(date)	
Reviewed by		(date)	

File Review Symbols
I - Identical   ? - Not identifiable
NI - Not identical   U - Unavailable reference

ALL INFORMATION CONTAINED
HEREIN IS UNCLASSIFIED
DATE 4/15/82 BY _____

John & Yoko Wait & Wait

A decision in the deportation proceedings against former Beatle John Lennon and his Japanese-born wife, Yoko Ono may not be reached until September, the U.S. Immigration and Naturalization Service said yesterday.

The government and the defense were to have submitted briefs by July 1, but they are still waiting for a transcript of the May 17 hearing.

Special inquiry officer Ira Fieldsteel, who is hearing the case, will be away in August, and so a decision is not expected until September.

The government wants to deny Lennon permanent residence here because of a 1968 marijuana conviction in England.

PacTel Appeals Refund

Pacific Telephone & Telegraph asked the U.S. Supreme Court yesterday to stop a $145 million refund to its customers which was ordered by the California Supreme Court Tuesday. The California court denied Pacific Tel's $143 million rate increase.

P. BL 30
7/14/72
Daily News
New York, N.Y.

100-175319-
46
203

Lennon Decision Delayed

NEW YORK (AP)—A decision in the deportation proceedings against former Beatle John Lennon and his wife, Yoko Ono, may not be reached until September, the United States Immigration and Naturalization Service reported today.

The government was awaiting a transcript of a May 17 hearing in the case before submitting its brief. Special Inquiry Officer Ira Fieldsteel, in charge of the case, had set July 1 as the final date for both sides to submit briefs supporting their cases.

Fieldsteel will be away for the month of August, immigration officials reported, saying they do not expect a decision until September.

The Lennons are seeking permanent residence in the U.S., but the government has balked over granting residence to Lennon, on grounds of a 1968 narcotics conviction in England.

DATE 7-14-72
PAGE B-2

X THE WASHINGTON POST & TIMES HERALD
___ THE EVENING STAR
___ THE SUNDAY STAR
___ THE WASHINGTON DAILY NEWS
___ WASHINGTON AFRO AMERICAN

FD-36 (Rev. 5-22-64)

FBI

Date: 7/21/72

Transmit the following in _____
(Type in plaintext or code)

Via ___AIRTEL___
(Priority)

TO: ACTING DIRECTOR (100-469910)

FROM: SAC, MIAMI (100-16733) (P)

JOHN WINSTON LENNON
SM - RA
(OO: NEW YORK)

MIREP

Re Miami airtel to Bureau, 6/5/72.

The New York Office is requested to furnish any results regarding the information set forth in referenced airtel obtained to date to the Bureau and Miami in a form suitable for dissemination under caption "Demonstrations At Democratic and Republican National Conventions", with a copy for Miami file 100-16733.

**ALL INFORMATION CONTAINED
HEREIN IS UNCLASSIFIED
DATE 2/12/81 BY sp/sw/mc**

EX-104
REC-65
100-469910-19

4 - Bureau (2-100-469910)(RM)
   (2-100-469601)
2 - New York (100-175314) (RM)
2 - Miami (1-100-16733)
   (1-80-1374)
WED/fp

15 JUL 27 1972

Approved _____ Sent _____ M Per _____
Special Agent in Charge

FBI

Date: 7/27/72

Transmit the following in _____
(Type in plaintext or code)

Via ___AIRTEL___

TO: ACTING DIRECTOR, FBI)(100-469910)

FROM: SAC, NEW YORK (100-175319) (P)

SUBJECT: JOHN WINSTON LENNON
SM - REVACT
(OO: NY)

MIREP

ReNYairtel, dated 5/25/72, and Miami airtel, dated 6/5/72.

Attached are 5 copies for the Bureau, and seven copies for Miami, of an LHM dated and captioned as above.

Miami should note that LENNON is reportedly a "heavy user of narcotics" known as "downers". This information should be emphasized to local Law Enforcement Agencies covering MIREP, with regards to subject being arrested if at all possible on possession of narcotics charge.

Local INS has very loose case in NY for deporting subject on narcotics charge involving 1968 arrest in England.

INS has stressed to Bureau that if LENNON were to be arrested in US for possession of narcotics he would become more likely to be immediately deportable.

2 - Bureau (Encls. 5) (RM)
2 - Miami (Encls. 7) (RM)
1 - New York

ALL INFORMATION CONTAINED
HEREIN IS UNCLASSIFIED EXCEPT
WHERE SHOWN OTHERWISE

NY 100-175319

Captioned LHM is classified "Confidential" because it contains information furnished by [Confidential Sources] through ███ who are of continuing value; the unauthorized disclsoure of which information would tend to identify them and thus be prejudicial to the natioal defense interest of the US.

LHM is so classified by SA ███

FD-323 (Rev. 11-29-61)

UNITED STATES DEPARTMENT OF JUSTICE
FEDERAL BUREAU OF INVESTIGATION
New York, New York
July 27, 1972

In Reply, Please Refer to
File No.

~~CONFIDENTIAL~~

Title   John Winston Lennon

Character   Security Matter - Revolutionary
Reference   Activity
                  is made to letterhead memorandum,
dated and captioned as above at New York.

       All sources (except any listed below) whose identities
are concealed in referenced communication have furnished reliable
information in the past.

CONFIDENTIAL

This document contains neither recommendations nor conclusions of the FBI. It is the property
of the FBI and is loaned to your agency; it and its contents are not to be distributed outside
your agency.

UNITED STATES DEPARTMENT OF JUSTICE

FEDERAL BUREAU OF INVESTIGATION

New York, New York
July 27, 1972

John Winston Lennon

On January 21, 1972, ███████ advised a group of individuals calling themselves the Allamuchy Tribe were to open an office in New York City within the next two weeks. The leaders of the tribe were Rennard Cordon Davis and Stewart Albert.

Lennon, who was formerly associated with the Beatles music group reportedly donated $75,000 dollars to the tribe. The main purpose of the group was to coordinate New Left Movement activities during this election year to culminate with demonstrations at the Republican National Convention during August, 1972.

Rennard Cordon Davis is a convicted defendant of the so-called Conspiracy Seven Trial, at Chicago, Illinois, in the period September, 1969 through February, 1970, unvolving those persons earlier indicted for violation of the Federal Anti-Riot Laws.

Stewart Albert - ███████ on April 25, 1966, advised that Albert was arrested on April 12, 1966, at Berkeley, California along with other members of the Progressive Labor Party (PLP) while demonstrating in front of the Berkeley City Hall.

ALL INFORMATION CONTAINED HEREIN IS UNCLASSIFIED EXCEPT WHERE SHOWN OTHERWISE.

100-469910-

~~CONFIDENTIAL~~

John Winston Lennon

The PLP was founded in 1962 by individuals expelled from the Communist Party, USA, for following the Chinese communist line. Its objective is the establishment of a militant working class movement based on Marxism-Leninism and MAO Tse-tung thought.

On March 10, 1972, the first source advised that the Allamuchy Tribe which had changed its name to the Election Year Strategy Information Center had ceased functioning.

During February, 1972, ███ advised that Rennard Davis, Stewart Albert, and John Lennon are heavy users of narcotics. Source advised that Davis is apparently at odds with Lennon due to Lennon's excessive use of drugs.

On May 17, 1972, Mr. Vincent Schiano, Chief Trial Attorney, Immigration and Naturalization Service (INS), New York City advised that Lennon and his wife Yoko Ono appeared at INS Headquarters in New York City on that date for the purpose of deportation hearings. INS maintains that Lennon is deportable from the United States due to his failure to "timely renew his visitors visa", which expired during February, 1972, and in particular, his 1968 Narcotics conviction in England.

On July 27, 1972, Mr. Anthony DiVito, Attorney, INS, New York City advised that INS is still in the exchange of briefs stage with Lennon's Attorney and no definite decision has been reached as to when Lennon will be deported.

Attached is a memorandum, including descriptive data and photograph of Lennon.

~~CONFIDENTIAL~~

- 2* -

John Winston Lennon

John Winston Lennon, a former member of the Beatles Rock Music Group is presently the subject of deportation hearing by the Immigration and Naturalization Service.

Lennon is described as follows:

Name:	John Winston Lennon
Race:	White
Date of Birth:	October 9, 1940
Place of Birth:	Liverpool, England
Hair:	Brown to Blond
Weight:	160 pounds
Height:	Approximately six feet
Build:	Slender
Nationality:	English
United States Residence:	105 Bank Street New York City
Arrest Record:	1968 Narcotics Arrest, in England for Possession of Dangerous Drugs (Cannabis) Pled Guilty

Note that the man appearing on the image illustrating the memo on "John Winston Lennon" isn't John Lennon at all, although they both do have round glasses... The man is in fact David Peel. And "The Pope smokes dope" is the title of one of his LPs. It was produced by John Lennon and came out in April 1972 on Apple Records, the record company founded by the Beatles.

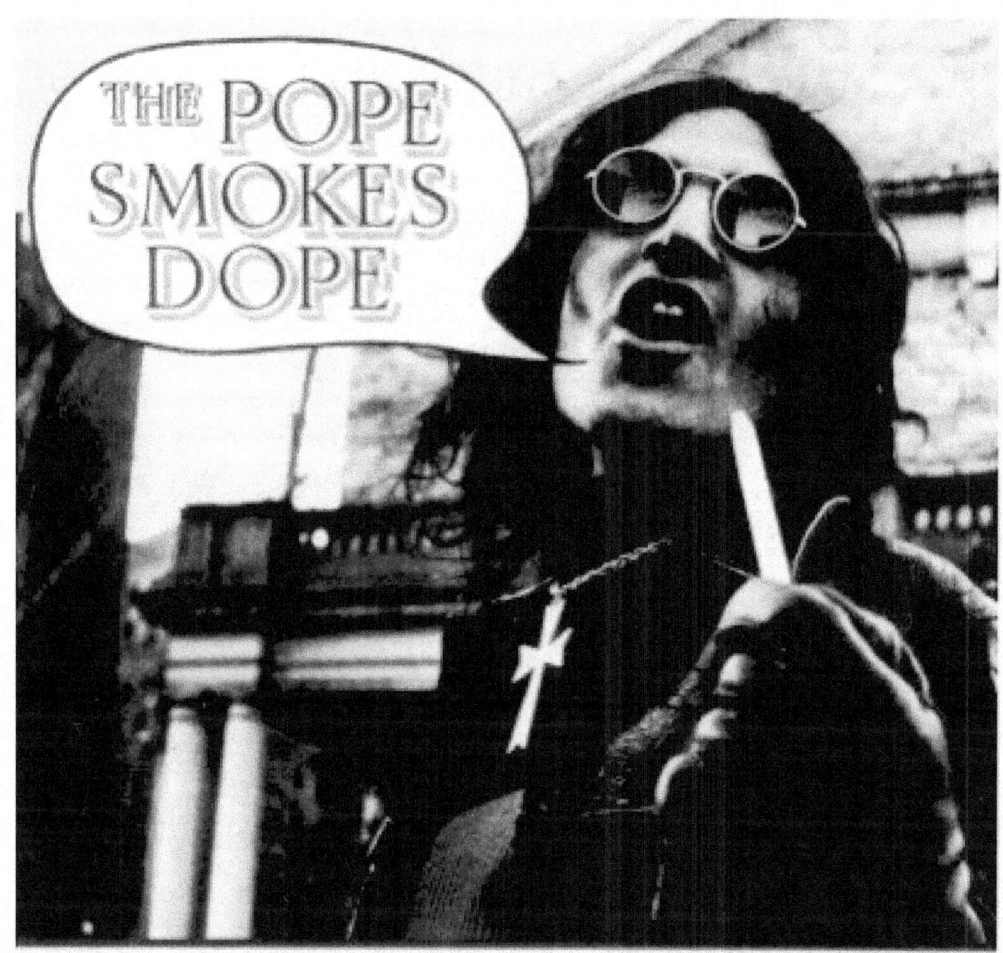

UNITED STATES GOVERNMENT

Memorandum

TO: ACTING DIRECTOR, FBI (62-112678)   DATE: 8/1/72

FROM: SAC, SAN FRANCISCO (100-61875) ~~CONFIDENTIAL~~

SUBJECT: RAINBOW PEOPLE'S PARTY
(formerly the White Panther Party)
IS - WPP

OO: DETROIT

Enclosed for Detroit is a xeroxed copy of the May 19, 1972 issue of "GRASS ROOTS", self described as the National Publication of the People's Party, which has its National Office at 1404 M Street NW, Washington, D.C. 20005. Enclosed item was xeroxed from a copy made available by ▓▓▓▓ on 6/8/72, as having been Received by ▓▓▓▓. Xeroxed copy of this and other items made available by ▓▓▓▓ were furnished to the Bureau, WFO and St. Louis by SF Letter to Bureau dated 7/31/72, captioned: PEOPLE'S PARTY, IS - NEW LEFT.

Although enclosed item undoubtedly received wide distribution and needs no classification, any mention that it was received by ▓▓▓▓ must be classified to protect the sensitive relationship between ▓▓▓▓ and ▓▓▓▓ and such mention should be avoided, since ▓▓▓▓ is a valuable source who furnishes information on a continuing basis, which is not otherwise available.

Enclosed item, on pages 10 through 13 sets forth an article by LOWELL YOUNG, captioned:"A TIME OF TRIAL FOR THE PEOPLE'S PARTY", in which he deplores the fact that some potential and actual supporters of the People's Party have decided to support McGovern's candidacy. LOWELL spends some time discussing the captioned organization and its having united with the Youth International Party and deplores the fact that"ABBIE HOFFMAN, JERRY RUBIN, JOHN SINCLAIR, GENIE PLAMONDON"and the entire Rainbow People's Party of Michigan have come out in support of George McGovern's candidacy". YOUNG's article appears to be of interest and is set out in xeroxed form as the following four pages of instant letter.

6 - Bureau (RM)
  (2 - 62-112678)
  (2 - 100-448910; Y.I.P.)
  (1 - 105-184368; RU)
  (1 - ▓▓▓▓)
3 - Detroit (100-36217) (RM)
3 - New York (RM)
  (1 - 100-162260;Y.I.P.)
4 - San Francisco (1 - 100-61875)
  (1 - ▓▓▓▓)(1 - ▓▓▓▓Y.I.P.)(1 - 100-61281;RU)
JES/jes
(16)

OPINION

AN OPEN FORUM FOR THE PEOPLE'S PARTY

A TIME OF TRIAL FOR THE PEOPLE'S PARTY

By Lowell Young

"My candidacy is the only way to avoid a fourth party on the left in 1972." — George McGovern

The George McGovern candidacy for the Democratic nomination for President has been transformed from an invisible campaign supported by only a faithful few into a lavishly financed campaign of a front-runner. From the beginning, McGovern's campaign has been an attempt to co-opt a fourth party on the left by adopting the left's issues and rhetoric as his own. His initial strong stands in opposition to the war and in favor of amnesty for all draft evaders and exiles, legalization of marijuana, abortion on demand, and the shifting of the burden of taxation from the poor and the working class onto the shoulders of the super-rich and the corporations were all designed to rally all possible fourth party constituents to his cause. And, for the moment, he has partially succeeded.

Recently, Abbie Hoffman, Jerry Rubin, John Sinclair, Genie Plamondon, and the entire Rainbow People's Party of Michigan have come out in support of George McGovern's candidacy. Abbie Hoffman and Jerry Rubin founded the Youth International Party (YIP) in early 1967. Their perfection of the use of guerrilla theater was designed to gain media attention in order to try to educate the American people about the hypocrisy of the present system.

To strengthen their organization and broaden their base of support, they united YIP with the Michigan based White Panther Party. The White Panther Party was founded by John Sinclair and "Pun" Plamondon with the intention of it becoming

SF 100-61785

the white counterpart of the Black Panther Party. But, that never came to be due to the different forms of oppression the different constituencies of the Black and White Panther Parties are subjected to. Black people are oppressed racially and materially; so the ten-point program of the Black Panther Party related to those forms of political oppression by making political demands for "land, bread, housing, clothing, education, justice, and peace." The white people Sinclair and Plamondon were attempting to organize were primarily culture-oriented; so the ten-point program of the White Panther Party related primarily to their cultural oppression by demanding an open society where free dope, free sex, and free rock music abounded. (They did make political references as well, the principle ones being the right of armed self-defense and complete support for the ten-point program of the Black Panther Party.)

While their followers were primarily culturally oriented, Sinclair and Plamondon were themselves very political. They were thought to believe that the perverted system of values in this country was a direct outgrowth of the undemocratic political system and the competitive economic system. By primarily relating to their followers' cultural oppression now, they supposedly hoped to educate them to the system's role in that oppression later. They were therefore viewed as very dangerous by the power structure and were moved against. Plamondon was framed on a charge of attempting to blow-up a Federal Building in Ann Arbor and is still in jail today. Sinclair was given a ten year jail sentence for possessing two joints and wasn't released until early this Spring.

The Rainbow People's Party was founded by Sinclair as the successor to the White Panther Party. It concentrated its efforts on local community organizing in the Ann Arbor area and linked-up with the state-wide Human Rights Party. Five Rainbow candidates, including "Pun" Plamondon's wife Genie, ran for Ann Arbor city council seats in April under the Human Rights Party banner. Part of the agreement between the two parties was that neither would support any Democratic candidates. But, two weeks after two of their candidates got elected, Sinclair, Genie Plamondon, and the rest of the Rainbow Party broke the agreement and announced their support for George McGovern.

ST 100-61785

CONFIDENTIAL

12/
But they are not alone. Such "radical" entertainers as Joan Baez and John Lennon have also come out in support of Mc-Govern. Also, Gore Vidal, Secretary of State in the People's Party Shadow Cabinet, and an individual with the means to provide the party with much needed economic assistance, never came across with a cent and at the May 4th Moratorium rally in New York City announced his support for George McGovern.

The defections by potential members and, worse yet, by people within the party itself, makes this a period of extreme darkness for the People's Party. But, that proverbial light at the end of the tunnel is coming into view; and the reason is George McGovern himself.

As his chances of getting the nomination have become better, McGovern has found it necessary to broaden his base of support by moving to the right. He is making an attempt to win over the reactionary labor leaders currently in the Humphrey camp. He is talking more about the economic issues relevant to George Wallace's alienated constituency than about the political or cultural issues relevant to his own alienated constituency.

George McGovern has a history of backing off on strong stands he might initially take. He initially agreed to introduce a bill on the floor of the Senate calling for Statehood for the Colony of Columbia, but at the last moment changed his mind, much to the embarrassment and anger of Julius Hobson and the D.C. Statehood Party. He initially agreed to run a slate of delegates in Chicago as a challenge to Mayor Daley in the Illinois Primary, but, after a twenty minute talk in the Mayor's office, agreed not to challenge Daley, much to the chagrin of his Chicago supporters. During the recent Nebraska primary, McGovern was accused of harboring "radical" views regarding the issues of marijuana, amnesty, and abortion. He immediately changed his previously stated positions. Now, he is opposed to the legalization of marijuana, says that abortion is a matter for the states to deal with, and that all draft evading cases should be dealt with on an individual basis.

- 4 -

SF 100-61785

"Radicals" who support George McGovern do not have a clear understanding of the true nature of this society and the ruling system responsible for the current oppressive conditions. We in the People's Party have a general understanding of the problem, but by no means do we possess a specific or a clearly thought out understanding to the point that we can serve as that force which will educate and awaken the unconscious and mislead (by McGovern on down) masses of the American people.

In order to develop that specific and clearly thought out understanding, we must turn our energies inward - i.e., concentrate on educating those of us already committed to building the People's Party so that we can begin to make crystal clear the differences between what we must advocate and the "New Populism" of George McGovern and the left-wing of the Democratic Party. They advocate reforming the present capitalist system; we must advocate replacing the present capitalist system with Socialism. But, <u>in order to talk about Socialism to others, we must first have a complete understanding of Socialism ourselves</u>.

Our attempts at recruitment should center upon those groups and individuals politically educated enough to contribute to this period of internal development. This doesn't mean that we should be closed to those who through their own bitter experience decide that they should join the party. In the immediate future, as McGovern's move to the right - and thus his duplicity - becomes more blatant, the People's Party can expect an influx of McGovern's more radical supporters, including, hopefully, all those mentioned above. The doors should and <u>will</u> be open to them.

The further one looks into the future the brighter that light at the end of the darkness becomes. If McGovern gets the nomination, wins the election, and then proceeds to carry on Johnson's and Nixon's policies (since he can't do any different because of the nature of the system); then for many millions of the American people that will be it. They will be through with the Democratic Party and the capitalist system, and they will turn to the only <u>mass-based, independent</u> political party calling for Socialism: the People's Party!

SAC, Detroit (100-36217)   8/9/72

Acting Director, FBI (62-112678)

WHITE PANTHER PARTY
IS - WPP

On page 2 of 5/26 - 6/9/72 issue of the "Ann Arbor Sun," published by the Rainbow People's Party (RPP), 1520 Hill Street, Ann Arbor, there is set forth the identities of the editorial committee and staff of this publication. Although White Panther Party (WPP) adopted the name RPP in 1971, to reportedly soften the previous revolutionary image of the organization, nevertheless, with the recent release from prison of the two top leaders in WPP, John Sinclair and Lawrence Plamondon, the potential for return to revolutionary tactics on the part of WPP membership remains strong.

The "Sun" editorial committee consists of Mike Brady, John Collins, Ann Hoover, Kathy Kelley, Mike Minnich, Linda Ross and Walden Simper.

ALL INDIVIDUALS INVOLVED IN NEW LEFT EXTREMIST ACTIVITY SHOULD BE CONSIDERED DANGEROUS BECAUSE OF THEIR KNOWN ADVOCACY AND USE OF EXPLOSIVES, REPORTED ACQUISITION OF FIREARMS AND INCENDIARY DEVICES, AND KNOWN PROPENSITY FOR VIOLENCE.

UNITED STATES GOVERNMENT

Memorandum

TO : ACTING DIRECTOR, FBI (100-469910) DATE: 8/30/72

FROM : SAC, NEW YORK (100-175319) (P*)

SUBJECT: JOHN WINSTON LENNON
SM-REVACT
(OO: NY)

Re NY airtel and LHM, 7/27/72.

Referenced communications set forth background information as requested by Miami in view of MIREP activities in that city, August 21-24, 1972.

Case Agent traveled to Miami as a member of the Weatherman Task Group (WTG). The subject was not observed by the case agent and based on informant coverage it is believed that the subject did not travel to Miami for the Republican National Convention as he had previously planned.

On August 28, 1972, Mr. VINCENT SCHIANO, Chief Trial Attorney, INS, NYC, advised that no information has come to his attention to indicate the subject traveled to Miami.

For the past several months there has been no information received to indicate that the subject is active in the New Left.

Sources; ████████ all advised during the month of July, 1972, that the subject has fallen out of the favor of activist JERRY RUBIN, STEWART ALBERT, and RENNIE DAVIS, due to subject's lack of interest in committing himself to involvement in anti-war and New Left activities.

In view of this information the New York Division is placing this case in a pending inactive status. When information concerning subject's tentative deportation is received such information will be sent to the Bureau.

2-Bureau (RM)
1-New York

CJL:jas
(3)

REC-24 100-469910-20

EX-104

21 SEP 1 1972

Buy U.S. Savings Bonds Regularly on the Payroll Savings Plan

A "National Committee for John and Yoko" was created to support John Lennon and his wife Yoko Ono after the beginning of the deportation proceedings. Many artists and celebrities pleaded for them to be allowed to stay in the USA.

UNITED STATES GOVERNMENT

Memorandum

TO : Acting Director, FBI DATE: 9/12/72

FROM : Legat, London (105-5492) (P)

SUBJECT: JOHN WINSTON LENNON
SM-NEW LEFT

OO - NYC

Re NYairtel to Bureau dated 3/16/72.

Enclosed are 2 copies of a self-explanatory letter dated ▓▓▓▓▓▓▓▓▓▓▓▓▓▓▓▓▓▓▓▓▓▓▓▓▓▓▓▓▓ classified Secret. (U)

Bureau is requested to have the NYO fully identify the "International Committee for John and Yoko" (U)

Incorporate results in LHM.

2 - Bureau (2 encls)
1 - Foreign Liaison Desk
1 - London
WAK:rn
(4)

EX-116 00-469910-22

REC-110   SEP 18 1972

ALL INFORMATION CONTAINED
HEREIN IS UNCLASSIFIED, EXCEPT
WHERE SHOWN OTHERWISE.

Buy U.S. Savings Bonds Regularly on the Payroll Savings Plan

100-469910-22

UNITED STATES GOVERNMENT

Memorandum

TO : ACTING DIRECTOR, FBI (100-469910) DATE: 9/28/72

FROM : SAC, MIAMI (100-16733) (P)

SUBJECT: JOHN WINSTON LENNON
SM - REVOLUTIONARY ACTIVITIES
(OO: NEW YORK)

Re New York airtel and LHM to Miami, 7/27/72.

Copies of referenced LHM were disseminated to the Miami Beach Police Department in connection with the dissemination program in the MIDEM case. The Miami Beach Police Department and other local authorities have furnished no information to indicate the presence of the subject in Miami Beach, Florida, at any time during the summer of 1972.

The following informants were alerted concerning the subject but were unable to furnish information which would indicate his presence in Miami Beach:

ALL INFORMATION CONTAINED HEREIN IS UNCLASSIFIED EXCEPT WHERE SHOWN OTHERWISE.

On 8/22/72 and 8/23/72 approximately 1,200 individuals were arrested in Miami Beach by local authorities during protest demonstrations against the Republican National Convention. The records relating to these arrests were photographed by the Miami Office and the film is currently being processed by the FBI Laboratory. When the arrest records become available, they will be reviewed

2 - Bureau (RM)
2 - New York (100-175319) (RM)
1 - Miami
WED/jah
(5)

100-469910-2

REC 64

EX-117

OCT 2 1972

Buy U.S. Savings Bonds Regularly on the Payroll Savings Plan

MM 100-16733

to determine whether subject may have been arrested during the above conventions.

OPTIONAL FORM NO. 10
5010-104-01

UNITED STATES GOVERNMENT

Memorandum

TO : SAC New York (100-175319) DATE: 10-3-72

FROM : SA ████████ 42
b7C

SUBJECT: John Winston Lennon
SM - ReAct
OO: NY

b7C ████████ On 10-3-72 Bureau Supervisor ████████ advised telephonically that captioned case should remain in a pending inactive status until such time as the subject is either deported from the US or until such time as his activities warrant case being reopened.

ALL INFORMATION CONTAINED
HEREIN IS UNCLASSIFIED
DATE 6-9-82 BY ████████

100-175319-52
SEARCHED____ INDEXED____
SERIALIZED____ FILED____
OCT 3 1972
FBI — NEW YORK

209

4-750 (Rev. 4-17-85)

FEDERAL BUREAU OF INVESTIGATION
FOIPA DELETED PAGE INFORMATION SHEET

_1_ Page(s) withheld entirely at this location in the file. One or more of the following statements, where indicated, explain this deletion.

☒ Deleted under exemption(s) _(b)(1)_ with no segregable material available for release to you.

☐ Information pertained only to a third party with no reference to you or the subject of your request.

☐ Information pertained only to a third party. Your name is listed in the title only.

☐ Documents originated with another Government agency(ies). These documents were referred to that agency(ies) for review and direct response to you.

_____ Pages contain information furnished by another Government agency(ies). You will be advised by the FBI as to the releasability of this information following our consultation with the other agency(ies).

_____ Page(s) withheld for the following reason(s):

☐ For your information:

☒ The following number is to be used for reference regarding these pages:
_100-175319-53_

XXXXXXXXXXXXXXXXX
DELETED PAGE(S)
NO DUPLICATION FEE
FOR THIS PAGE
XXXXXXXXXXXXXXXXX

210 FBI/DOJ

The non-disclosure of this document is "specifically authorized under criteria by an executive order to be kept secret in the interest of national defense or foreign policy" (code (b)(1)).

4-750 (Rev. 4-17-85)

FEDERAL BUREAU OF INVESTIGATION
FOIPA DELETED PAGE INFORMATION SHEET

__1__ Page(s) withheld entirely at this location in the file. One or more of the following statements, where indicated, explain this deletion.

☒ Deleted under exemption(s) _(b)(2), (b)(7)(c), (b)(7)(D)_ with no segregable material available for release to you.

☐ Information pertained only to a third party with no reference to you or the subject of your request.

☐ Information pertained only to a third party. Your name is listed in the title only.

☐ Documents originated with another Government agency(ies). These documents were referred to that agency(ies) for review and direct response to you.

_____ Pages contain information furnished by another Government agency(ies). You will be advised by the FBI as to the releasability of this information following our consultation with the other agency(ies).

_____ Page(s) withheld for the following reason(s):

☐ For your information:

☒ The following number is to be used for reference regarding these pages:
_100-175319-58_

XXXXXXXXXXXXXXXXXX
DELETED PAGE(S)
NO DUPLICATION FEE
FOR THIS PAGE
XXXXXXXXXXXXXXXXXX

This document is not released because it is considered "the production of such law enforcement records or information could reasonably be expected to constitute an unwarranted invasion of personal privacy" (code (b)(7)(c) and "could reasonably be expected to disclose the identity of confidential source" (code (b)(7)(d)). It is also material "related solely to the internal personnel rules and practices of an agency" (code (b)(2)).

UNITED STATES GOVERNMENT

Memorandum

TO : ACTING DIRECTOR, FBI (100-469910)   DATE: 10-24-72

FROM : SAC, MIAMI (100-16733) (RUC)

SUBJECT: JOHN WINSTON LENNON
SM - RA

(OO: New York)

Re Miami letter to Bureau, 9-28-72.

A review of records relating to the individuals arrested in Miami Beach, Florida, on 8/22 and 23/72, in connection with protest demonstrations against the Republican National Convention, failed to reflect that the subject was one of those arrested.

Inasmuch as there is no indication that the subject ever appeared in Miami Beach during either of the national political conventions in July and August, 1972, no further investigation is being conducted by Miami.

2-Bureau (RM)
2-New York (100-175319) (RM)
1-Miami
WED/al
(5)

ST-114

ALL INFORMATION CONTAINED
HEREIN IS UNCLASSIFIED
DATE 2/19/91 BY SP4/Sm/prk

REC-63 100-469910-23

3 OCT 27 1972

NOV 3 1972

Buy U.S. Savings Bonds Regularly on the Payroll Savings Plan

So it seems John Lennon didn't disrupt the Republican National Convention or threaten National Security of the US in any way… And that he wasn't even in Miami at the time.

And John Lennon did not prevent President Nixon from being reelected either.

Richard Nixon during the 1972 presidential election campaign

Nixon was ahead in most polls and was reelected on November 7, 1972 in one of the largest landslide election victories in American history. He defeated democrat McGovern with over 60 percent of the popular vote.

Routing Slip
FD-4 (Rev. 12-22-69)

To: ☑ Director
Att.: ~~[redacted]~~

Date: 11/22/72
FILE: Lon 105-5492
Title: JOHN WINSTON LENNON
SM - NEW LEFT

☐ SAC
☐ ASAC
☐ Supv.
☐ Agent
☐ SE
☐ IC
☐ CC
☐ Steno
☐ Clerk _____ ☐ Rotor #:

RE: Lonlet 9/12/72

DECLASSIFIED ON 4-27-84
BY 1673Bfp/Ebm

ACTION DESIRED

☐ Acknowledge
☐ Assign ___ Reassign ___
☐ Bring file
☐ Call me
☐ Correct
☐ Deadline ___
☐ Deadline passed
☐ Delinquent
☐ Discontinue
☐ Expedite
☐ File
☐ For information
☐ Handle
☐ Initial & return
☐ Leads need attention
☐ Return with explanation or notation as to action taken.

☐ Open Case
☐ Prepare lead cards
☐ Prepare tickler
☐ Return assignment card
☐ Return file
☐ Search and return
☐ See me
☐ Serial # ___
  ☐ Post ☐ Recharge ☐ Return
  ☐ Send to ___
☐ Submit new charge out
☐ Submit report by ___
☐ Type

Please expedite.

SAC
Office: J. T. Minnich
Legat, London

ALL INFORMATION CONTAINED
HEREIN IS UNCLASSIFIED EXCEPT
WHERE SHOWN OTHERWISE.

100- 469910-22
NOT RECORDED
1 DEC 5 1972

57 DEC 8 1972

FD-36 (Rev. 5-22-64)

FBI

Date: 12/8/72

Transmit the following in _____
(Type in plaintext or code)

Via AIRTEL
(Priority)

TO: ACTING DIRECTOR, FBI (100-469910)

FROM: SAC, NEW YORK (100-175319)(C)

SUBJECT: JOHN WINSTON LENNON
SM - RA
(OO:NY)

ReLegat, London letter, 9/12/72; NYlet, 8/30/72.

Enclosed for the Bureau are ten copies of an LHM captioned "International Committee for John and Yoko,", dated as above. Appropriate copies should be made available to Legat, London, as per their request.

In view of subject's inactivity in Revolutionary Activities and his seemingly rejection by NY Radicals, captioned case is being closed in the NY Division.

In event other information comes to New York's attention indicating subject is active with Revolutionary groups, the case will be re-opened at that time and the Bureau advised accordingly.

The Special Agent of the FBI who contacted INS was SA ███████ b7C

② - Bureau (RM) (Encls. 10)
1 - New York

CJL:eps
(4)

ALL INFORMATION CONTAINED HEREIN IS UNCLASSIFIED EXCEPT WHERE SHOWN OTHERWISE

Approved: _____ Sent _____ M Per _____
Special Agent in Charge

NY 100-175319

Sources referred to in LHM are:

b2 (c) b1
b7D (c) b1
(c) b1

-2-

UNITED STATES DEPARTMENT OF JUSTICE

FEDERAL BUREAU OF INVESTIGATION

In Reply, Please Refer to File No.

NYfile 100-175319
Bufile 100-469910

New York, New York
December 8, 1972

ALL INFORMATION CONTAINED
HEREIN IS UNCLASSIFIED
DATE 2/19/91 BY SP4/SR04/mb

International Committee For John and Yoko

On December 8, 1972, Mr. Vincent Schiano, Chief Trial Attorney, Immigration and Naturalization Service (INS), 20 West Broadway, New York City, New York, advised a representative of the Federal Bureau of Investigation (FBI) that the "International Committee for John and Yoko," has been established to campaign for John Winston Lennon and Yoko Ono Lennon who are currently appealing their deportation case in the United States.

John Winston Lennon

On February 2, 1972, Mr. Raymond Connley, INS, New York City, advised that Lennon, Alien Registration Number A-17597321, first arrived in the United States through New York City on August 11, 1968, under a B-2 visitors visa. He subsequently departed the United States and re-entered in 1971. Lennon is married to Yoko Ono Lennon, Alien Registration Number A-19489154. They both entered the United States together on August 13, 1971, and their visas were due to expire on February 29, 1972.

This document contains neither recommendations nor conclusions of the Federal Bureau of Investigation (FBI). It is the property of the FBI and is loaned to your agency; it and its contents are not to be distributed outside your agency; nor duplicated within your agency.

100-469910- 24

ENCLOSURE

International Committee for
John and Yoko

     Mr. Schiano advised that the International Committee for John and Yoko is located at Number One White Street, New York City, and in addition he understands they use Post Office Box 693 Radio City Station, New York City.

     Mr. Schiano further advised that the Lennons deportation is still being appealed by their attorney.

     During the months of September, October, and November, 1972, sources of the FBI who are familiar with Revolutionary Type Activities in the New York City area could not furnish additional information concerning this organization or the Lennon's activities.

2/13/96
FBI INFO
CLASSIFIED BY: SSA 9803RDD/JS
REASON: 1.5 (b)
DECLASSIFY ON: X5

CA# 83-1720

ST-123 REC-71 100-469910-?

CA# 83-1720
CLASSIFIED DECISIONS FINALIZED
BY DEPARTMENT REVIEW COMMITTEE (DRC)
DATE: 12/10/97   SSA SLD/JS

MCT-26 22 AUG 10 1976

Notice of Classification Action
Cross Ref. File # only
File # 100-469910-25
Classified by: 1678 RFP/eam 4-6-83
Declass on: OADR
Classified decisions finalized by DRC 2/2/96

ENCLOSURE 100-46910-25

HQ-33

Routing Slip
0-7 (Rev. 4-28-72)   (Copies to Offices Checked)

TO: SAC:
- [ ] Albany
- [ ] Albuquerque
- [ ] Alexandria
- [ ] Anchorage
- [ ] Atlanta
- [ ] Baltimore
- [ ] Birmingham
- [ ] Boston
- [ ] Buffalo
- [ ] Butte
- [ ] Charlotte
- [ ] Chicago
- [ ] Cincinnati
- [ ] Cleveland
- [ ] Columbia
- [ ] Dallas
- [ ] Denver
- [ ] Detroit
- [ ] El Paso
- [ ] Honolulu
- [ ] Houston
- [ ] Indianapolis
- [ ] Jackson
- [ ] Jacksonville
- [ ] Kansas City
- [ ] Knoxville
- [ ] Las Vegas
- [ ] Little Rock
- [ ] Los Angeles
- [ ] Louisville
- [ ] Memphis
- [ ] Miami
- [ ] Milwaukee
- [ ] Minneapolis
- [ ] Mobile
- [ ] Newark
- [ ] New Haven
- [ ] New Orleans
- [ ] New York City
- [ ] Norfolk
- [ ] Oklahoma City
- [ ] Omaha
- [ ] Philadelphia
- [ ] Phoenix
- [ ] Pittsburgh
- [ ] Portland
- [ ] Richmond
- [ ] Sacramento
- [ ] St. Louis
- [ ] Salt Lake City
- [ ] San Antonio
- [ ] San Diego
- [ ] San Francisco
- [ ] San Juan
- [ ] Savannah
- [ ] Seattle
- [ ] Springfield
- [ ] Tampa
- [ ] Washington Field
- [ ] Quantico

TO LEGAT:
- [ ] Beirut
- [ ] Bern
- [ ] Bonn
- [ ] Brasilia
- [ ] Buenos Aires
- [ ] Caracas
- [ ] Copenhagen
- [ ] Hong Kong
- [ ] La Paz
- [ ] London
- [ ] Madrid
- [ ] Managua
- [ ] Manila
- [ ] Mexico City
- [ ] Ottawa
- [ ] Paris
- [ ] Rome
- [ ] Singapore
- [ ] Tel Aviv
- [ ] Tokyo

RE: _____ Date _____ 1973

- [✓] For information
- [ ] Retention optional
- [ ] For appropriate action
- [ ] Surep, by _____
- [ ] The enclosed is for your information. If used in a future report, [ ] conceal all sources, [ ] paraphrase contents.
- [ ] Enclosed are corrected pages from report of SA _____ dated _____

Remarks:

4-19-83   1678 RFP KEAm

b7C   62-6938-2

Enc.
Bufile
Urfile   (info)

4-750 (Rev. 4-17-85)

FEDERAL BUREAU OF INVESTIGATION
FOIPA DELETED PAGE INFORMATION SHEET

__2__ Page(s) withheld entirely at this location in the file. One or more of the following statements, where indicated, explain this deletion.

☒ Deleted under exemption(s) __(b)(3), (b)(7)(c)__ with no segregable material available for release to you.

☐ Information pertained only to a third party with no reference to you or the subject of your request.

☐ Information pertained only to a third party. Your name is listed in the title only.

☐ Documents originated with another Government agency(ies). These documents were referred to that agency(ies) for review and direct response to you.

_____ Pages contain information furnished by another Government agency(ies). You will be advised by the FBI as to the releasability of this information following our consultation with the other agency(ies).

_____ Page(s) withheld for the following reason(s):

☐ For your information: _____

☒ The following number is to be used for reference regarding these pages:
__62-6938-2   Los Angeles__

XXXXXXXXXXXXXXXXXX
DELETED PAGE(S)
NO DUPLICATION FEE
FOR THIS PAGE
XXXXXXXXXXXXXXXXXX

FBI/DOJ

The following two pages of this file are withheld as it is considered that "the production of such law enforcement records or information could reasonably be expected to constitute an unwarranted invasion of personal privacy" (code (b)(7)(c)). Information is also withheld pursuant to statute, including visa and tax records (code (b)(3)).

ALL INFORMATION CONTAINED
HEREIN IS UNCLASSIFIED
DATE 2/19/81 BY SP4/SAM/MB

A054
D A
LENNON 6-17
DAY LD

NEW YORK (UPI) -- FORMER BEATLE JOHN LENNON, FIGHTING A 1972 DEPORTATION ORDER, HAS FILED SUIT AGAINST THE JUSTICE DEPARTMENT, FORMER ATTORNEY GENERAL JOHN N. MITCHELL AND OTHER OFFICIALS, CHARGING THEY SINGLED HIM OUT FOR "IMPROPER SELECTIVE PROSECUTION."

LEON WILDES, LENNON'S ATTORNEY, SAID MONDAY HE HAS DOCUMENTS SHOWING LENNON'S DEPORTATION WAS ORDERED FROM WASHINGTON BECAUSE OF A SENATE INTERNAL SECURITY COMMITTEE REPORT WHICH SOUGHT TO LINK LENNON WITH PLANS TO DISRUPT THE 1972 REPUBLICAN NATIONAL CONVENTION.

IN 1973, NEW YORK IMMIGRATION DIRECTOR SOL MARKS SAID AT A NEWS CONFERENCE HE MADE THE DECISION TO PROCEED AGAINST LENNON HIMSELF.

WILDES SAID MARKS SAID IN A DEPOSITION LAST WEEK HE ACTED AS A "CONDUIT" FOR INSTRUCTIONS FROM WASHINGTON, WHICH HE UNDERSTOOD TO MEAN THAT "WE WERE NOT TO GIVE THIS MAN A BREAK."

MARKS ALSO ADMITTED HE HAD MISINFORMED THE PRESS AT HIS 1973 NEWS CONFERENCE, WILDES SAID.

PROCEEDINGS AGAINST LENNON, BEGUN IN MARCH 1972 WHEN HE WAS CHARGED WITH OVERSTAYING HIS VISA, ARE STILL PENDING. PROSECUTORS CITED A 1968 BRITISH CONVICTION FOR MARIJUANA POSSESSION AS THE BASIS FOR DENYING HIM PERMANENT RESIDENCE.

WILDES SAID SEN. STROM THURMOND, R-S.C. SENT A LETTER TO MITCHELL IN FEBRUARY 1972, ENCLOSING THE COMMITTEE MEMORANDUM.

"THIS APPEARS TO ME TO BE AN IMPORTANT MATTER, AND I THINK IT WOULD BE WELL TO IT TO BE CONSIDERED AT THE HIGHEST LEVEL ... AS I CAN SEE MANY HEADACHES MIGHT BE AVOIDED IF IF APPROPRIATE ACTION BE TAKEN IN TIME," WILDES QUOTED THURMOND'S LETTER AS SAYING.

WILDES SAID OTHER DOCUMENTS SHOW KLEINDIENST SENT THE MEMO TO IMMIGRATION COMMISSIONER RAYMOND FARRELL AND THAT FARRELL'S DEPUTY INSTRUCTED SUBORDINATES IN NEW YORK TO SEEK DEPORTATION OF LENNON AND HIS WIFE, YOKO ONO.

WILDES SAID THE SUIT NAMES THE JUSTICE DEPARTMENT, MITCHELL, RICHARD KLEINDIENST, DEPUTY ATTORNEY GENERAL AT THE TIME AND MITCHELL'S SUCCESSOR, AND "VARIOUS IMMIGRATION OFFICERS."

UPI 06-17 05:39 AED

NOT RECORDED
SEP 2 1975

WASHINGTON CAPITAL NEWS SERVICE

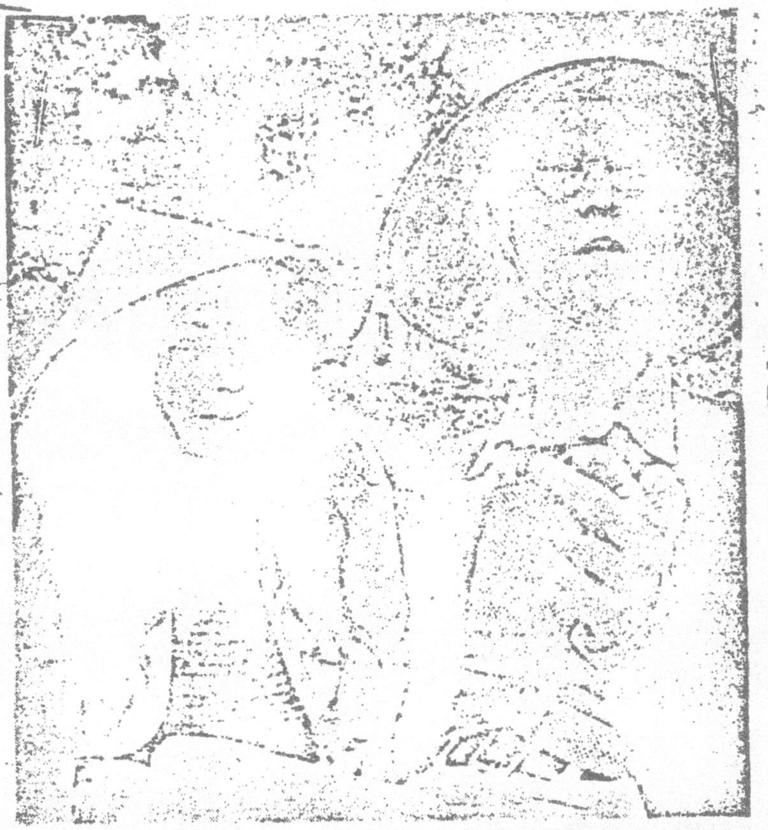

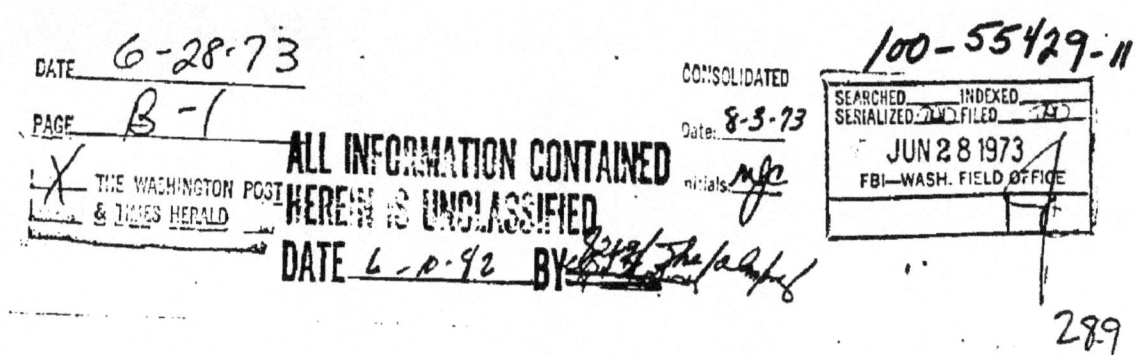

By Christopher Li—The Washington Post

ASKING PRISONER'S RELEASE — Ex Beatle John Lennon and his wife Yoko were among 20 people at the South Vietnamese embassy yesterday asking freedom for a Vietnamese "political" prisoner. The woman, Mrs. Ngo Ba Thanh, a Buddhist neutralist who opposed the war, has been held almost two years. According to Mrs. Lennon, the group was told that the woman's fate was a matter for the courts.

DATE 6-28-73

PAGE B-1

X THE WASHINGTON POST & TIMES HERALD

ALL INFORMATION CONTAINED HEREIN IS UNCLASSIFIED DATE 6-10-92 BY

CONSOLIDATED Date: 8-3-73 Initials: mjc

100-55429-11

SEARCHED ___ INDEXED ___ SERIALIZED ___ FILED ___
JUN 28 1973
FBI—WASH. FIELD OFFICE

289

0-63 (8-24-67)

TO: Special Investigative Division

FROM: ☐ Domestic Intelligence ☐ General Investigative ☐ Special Investigative

REQUEST FOR SEARCH OF SPECIAL INDICES

Date of request: 9-18-73

Requesting ████████ (b7c)

Please complete following and return one copy to:

___CD+UC___ Section Division ─ ☐ Domestic Intelligence ☐ General Investigative ☑ Special Investigative

NAMES TO BE SEARCHED	KNOWN ALIASES	Results of Criminal and Security Special Indices Search (attach separate sheet, if necessary)
John Winston Ono Lennon	—	NR

(b7c)

Searched by ████ (b7c)

Bufile: /
Date: 9-19-73

0-9 (Rev. 5-18-71)

FBI

Transmit in _____ Via ___Airtel___
     (Type in plaintext or code)   (Priority)

Date ___9/19/73___

To: SAC, New York

From: Director, FBI

ELSUR
JOHN WINSTON ONO LENNON

BUDED: 9/24/73

    Enclosed for your office is one copy of Department of Justice memorandum dated 9/18/73 requesting electronic surveillance information in accordance with specific questions set forth in the enclosed memorandum.

    Conduct check in order to answer specific questions in enclosed memorandum and Criminal Division memorandum, 4/16/69, furnished field 5/2/69. **Key answers to correspond with questions A through F.** If results reveal positive information, insure microphone sources monitoring individuals involved are identified to the Bureau.

    New York check captioned individual.

    Sutel your response to reach Bureau by COB 9/24/73. If positive, submit logs and pertinent documents by airtel.

Enclosure

Form DJ-150
(Ed. 4-26-65)

UNITED STATES GOVERNMENT

DEPARTMENT OF JUSTICE

Memorandum

TO : Director
Federal Bureau of Investigation

DATE: September 18, 1973
HEP:JLM:RPW:cn
39-51-NEW

FROM : Henry E. Petersen
Assistant Attorney General
Criminal Division

SUBJECT: In re John Winston Ono Lennon
Board of Immigration Appeals

The individual named on the attached list is the subject of a deportation proceeding before the Board of Immigration Appeals scheduled for October 29, 1973, at 2:00 p.m.

Would you please supply us with electronic surveillance information pertaining to the individual named on the attached list, following the form set forth in our memorandum to you dated April 16, 1969.

In addition, should your files reveal that the individual or the premises in which he had a proprietary interest were subjected to electronic surveillance, we would appreciate your furnishing Mr. Robert P. Weidner, Government Regulations Section, Criminal Division, with the following:

1. Logs disclosing the conversation of the individual and logs of any of the premises in which the individual is or was the owner, lessee, or licensee.

2. Any airtels which expand or summarize the portions of the logs disclosed unless fully reflected in the logs themselves.

3. Any memoranda, including reports to the Department of Justice, which expand or summarize the portions of the logs mentioned above or which demonstrate pertinent leads which may have come from the illegal electronic surveillance.

-2-

It is also requested that you advise us whether the individual has been subjected to any lawful electronic surveillance, including such surveillance where one of the parties may have consented to the surveillance, as well as such surveillance conducted pursuant to the provisions of Title III of Public Law 90-351.

If your records indicate that the individual has used names other than that given, please check your electronic surveillance indices with respect to the additional names.

Attachment

Name:	John Winston Ong Lennon
Wife:	Alien Citizen of Japan, age 40
Entry:	Entered U.S. at New York 8/13/71
Present Address:	Dakota House, Central Park West, New York City (most recent)
Prior Address:	105 Bank Street New York City
Aliases:	None Known
Date of Birth:	October 9, 1940
Place of Birth:	Liverpool, England
Citizenship:	English Citizen
Employment:	Entertainer
Last Place of Employment:	
Attorney:	Leon Wildes 515 Madison New York, New York 10022
Proceeding Date:	October 29, 1973, 2:00 p.m.

ENCLOSURE 62-318-9020

FD-36 (Rev. 5-22-64)

```
                              F B I

                              Date: 9/21/73

Transmit the following in ___CODE_____
                              (Type in plaintext or code)

Via ___TELETYPE___ ___NITEL_____
                              (Priority)
```

TO: DIRECTOR

FROM: NEW YORK (92-4564)

ELSUR, JOHN WINSTON ONO LENNON. BUDED: 9/24/73.

    REBUAIRTEL TO NEW YORK, 9/19/73.

    THE SPECIAL INDICES OF THE NYO AND CORRESPONDING RECORDS WERE REVIEWED IN ACCORDANCE WITH CRIMINAL DIVISION MEMORANDUM DATED 4/16/69, CONCERNING CAPTIONED INDIVIDUAL, WITH THE FOLLOWING RESULTS:

    (A) NO.

    (B) NO.

    (C - F) NOT APPLICABLE.

    SUCH A REVIEW FAILED TO INDICATE THAT LENNON OR PREMISES IN WHICH HE HAD PROPRIETARY INTEREST HAVE BEEN SUBJECTED TO ANY LAWFUL ELECTRONIC SURVEILLANCE.

1 - 92-4564 (SA [redacted] #53)

Approved: _____ Sent _____ M Per _____
    Special Agent in Charge

0-63 (2-24-67)

TO: Special Investigative Division
FROM: ☒ ~~Domestic~~ Intelligence ☐ General Investigative ☐ Special Investigative

REQUEST FOR SEARCH OF SPECIAL INDICES

Date of request: 9/24/73
Requesting Agent: [b6 b7C]

Please complete following and return one copy to:
Organized Crime Section, Division - ☐ Domestic Intelligence ☐ General Investigative ☒ Special Investigative

NAMES TO BE SEARCHED	KNOWN ALIASES	Results of Criminal and Security Special Indices Search (attach separate sheet, if necessary)
John Winston Ono Lennon	—	NR

4-8-83 1678 R5P

Bufile: —
Searcher: [b6 b7C]
Date: 9/24/73

9-53 (Rev. 8-19-70)

Assistant Attorney General
Criminal Division

September 25, 1973

Director, FBI

1 - Mr. Keith

JOHN WINSTON ONO LENNON

ELECTRONIC SURVEILLANCE checks

    Reference is made to your memorandum dated **September 18, 1973, HEP:JLM:RPW:cm, 39-51-NEW, requesting electronic surveillance information on captioned individual.**
On the basis of identifying data provided by the Department concerning captioned individual(s), a review has been made of appropriate records. (He was) (They were) not the subject(s) of a direct electronic surveillance nor were any of (his) (their) conversations monitored by an electronic device of the FBI. Further, this Bureau did not maintain any electronic surveillance on premises which were known to have been owned, leased, or licensed by the above individual(s).

    It is suggested that other Federal investigative agencies be contacted to determine if they had coverage of the subject(s).

NOTE: The above individual's name was cleared with SA [ ], Intelligence Division.

WAH:dsl
(4)

Return to [ ], Room 1535.

O-19 (Rev. 9-11-73)

Assoc. Dir:	
Asst. Dir.:	
Admin.	
Comp. Syst.	
Ext. Affairs	
Files & Com.	
Gen. Inv.	
Ident.	
Inspection	
Intell.	
Laboratory	
Plan. & Eval.	
Spec. Inv.	
Training	
Legal Coun.	
Telephone Rm.	
Director Sec'y	

Lennon Is Given 60 Days to Leave

The Justice Department announced yesterday that John Lennon, the former Beatle, had been given 60 days to leave the country or be forcibly deported. The order is based on a decision reached by the Board of Immigration Appeals on July 10, and Mr. Lennon's departure deadline is retroactive to that date.

Mr. Lennon, who has been living in New York and other American cities since 1971, has fought lengthy and costly legal battles, through the Immigration and Naturalization Service and the Federal courts, to have his visa extended.

Extensions have been denied because he pleaded guilty in Britain, in 1968, to a charge of possession of marijuana. In his appeals of earlier denials of extensions Mr. Lennon contended the marijuana had been planted in his home and he had pleaded guilty to the possession charge only to spare his former wife, then pregnant, the ordeal of a court appearance.

A spokesman for Mr. Lennon's lawyer said that "various avenues for appealing the order are being explored."

The Washington Post Times Herald	
The Evening Star (Washington)	
The Sunday Star (Washington)	
Daily News (New York)	
Sunday News (New York)	
New York Post	
The New York Times	29
The Daily World	
The New Leader	
The Wall Street Journal	
The National Observer	
People's World	

Date 7-18-

REC-25

NOT RECORDED
25 JUL 23 1974

55 JUL 31 1974

Date : 7-18-74

The Watergate scandal was a major political scandal in US politics that occurred as a result of the June 17, 1972 break-in at the Democratic National Committee (DNC) headquarters at the Watergate office complex in Washington, DC, and the Nixon administration's attempted cover-up of its involvement. When the conspiracy was discovered and investigated by the US Congress, the Nixon administration's resistance to its probes led to a constitutional crisis. An array of clandestine and often illegal activities undertaken by members of the Nixon administration were brought to light. Those activities included bugging the offices of political opponents and people of whom Nixon or his officials were suspicious. Nixon and his close aides ordered harassment of activist groups and political figures, using the FBI, the CIA, the IRS and, in Lennon's case, the INS. The scandal led to the discovery of multiple abuses of power by the Nixon administration.

Facing near-certain impeachment, Nixon resigned the presidency on August 9, 1974. It is the only resignation of a US President to date. The Watergate scandal also resulted in the indictment of 69 people, with trials or pleas resulting in 48 being found guilty and incarcerated, many of whom were Nixon's top administration officials.

Nixon at his desk as he announces his resignation on radio and television on August 9, 1974.

On 30 April 1975, the Vietnam War ends with the fall of Saigon. John and Yoko had been advocating against this war since the end of the sixties, participating in numerous demonstrations and peace events.

0-20 (Rev. 8-5-74)

ALL INFORMATION CONTAINED
HEREIN IS UNCLASSIFIED
DATE 2/19/81 BY SP4/SEM/mf

A299
D A
LENNON 6-16
NIGHT
NEW YORK (UPI) -- AN ATTORNEY FOR FORMER BEATLE JOHN LENNON SAID MONDAY THAT HE HAS FILED SUIT AGAINST FORMER U.S. ATTORNEY GENERAL JOHN N. MITCHELL AND OTHERS CHARGING THEM WITH "IMPROPER SELECTIVE PROSECUTION" IN SEEKING TO DEPORT LENNON IN 1972.
   THE ATTORNEY, LEON WILDES, SAID THAT IN ADDITION TO MITCHELL, THE DEFENDANTS IN THE FEDERAL SUIT INCLUDE THE U.S. DEPARTMENT OF JUSTICE, FORMER DEPUTY ATTORNEY GENERAL RICHARD G. KLEINDIENST AND "VARIOUS IMMIGRATION OFFICERS."
   THE CASE IS BEFORE JUDGE RICHARD OWEN IN MANHATTAN FEDERAL COURT.
   DEPORTATION PROCEEDINGS AGAINST LENNON WERE STARTED IN NEW YORK I MARCH, 1972. HE WAS CHARGED WITH OVERSTAYING HIS U.S. VISA, AND PROSECUTORS CITED A 1968 BRITISH CONVICTION FOR MARIJUANA POSESSION AS THE REASON FOR DENYING HIM PERMANENT RESIDENCE.
   AT A NEWS CONFERENCE IN 1973, NEW YORK IMMIGRATION DIRECTOR SOL MARKS SAID IT WAS HE WHO MADE THE DECISION TO PROCEED AGAINST LENNON
   WILDES SAID IN A STATEMENT THAT HE HAS OBTAINED DOCUMENTS SHOWING THAT LENNON'S DEPORTATION WAS ORDERED FROM WASHINGTON ON THE STRENGTH OF A SENATE INVESTIGATIVE REPORT WHICH SOUGHT TO LINK THE SINGER WITH A PLAN TO DISRUPT THE REPUBLICAN NATIONAL CONVENTION IN 1972.
   UPI 06-16 08:47 PED

WASHINGTON CAPITAL NEWS SERVICE

In June 1975, Lennon's lawyer Leon Wildes filed a suit against members of the Department of Justice and of the INS. On Tom Snyder's 'Tomorrow Show', in April 1975, he had said :

"We had some information that the deportation proceedings against John were not normally brought, certainly the procedure followed was not normal. And we had learned that rumors got to the Senate Internal Security Committee that John had some idea or was rumored to have some idea of appearing at the Republican National Convention in 1972 and leading an anti Vietnam War demonstration or the like. And that this information, in the form of a memorandum, was transmitted by Senator Strom Thurmond to the then Attorney General John Mitchell[1] who may have at the time been sitting as head of CREEP[2], the Committee to Re-elect the President [Nixon]. And we understand that a series of memoranda led all the way down to the District Director in New York [Sol Marks] and that the action he took was not as a result of John's immigration status but rather as an intention to prevent John from exercising constitutionally protected rights."

National Guard marching toward the protesters, Republican National Convention, 1972

© Dean Dexter

---

[1] See pages 97 to 99.

[2] The Committee to Re-elect the President, abbreviated CRP, but often mocked by the acronym CREEP, was a fundraising organization of Nixon's administration. Besides its re-election activities, CRP employed money laundering and slush funds and was directly and actively involved in the Watergate scandal. John Mitchell was the director of the CRP.

The CRP used $500,000 in funds raised for the purpose to re-elect President Nixon to pay legal expenses for the five Watergate burglars after their indictment in September 1972, in exchange for their silence and perjury. This act helped turn the burglary into the explosive political scandal known as *the Watergate*. The burglars, as well as G. Gordon Liddy, E. Howard Hunt, John Mitchell, and other Nixon administration figures, were imprisoned over the break-in and their efforts to cover it up.

On the same TV show, John Lennon had then added : "I think when it was started somebody didn't want me here and now they probably don't mind. It's just that it's a bureaucratic thing, it's gone on and how do we stop it, you know ? Maybe whoever makes the decision doesn't know whether it'd be politically right or what's gonna happen if we suddenly stop now what we started. I mean, it's very sort of embarrassing for everyone I guess. And half the people who started it are now having their how problems, hum hum hum, right[3]. I know there's a different lot of people in charge of my case now and I'm sure they're not as hot to get me out because they didn't even have the Republican Convention in San Diego[4] and I was not committed to go there either."

In 1975, John Lennon also recalled an unsolicited visit from a guy who said he was from the phone company and coming to fix the line. Lennon said there was nothing wrong with the phone but let him in anyway. That was in April 1972, and after that : "Everytime I picked up my phone there was a lot of noise. It began with a certain hollowness followed by soft clicking noises and the vacuum of a third person listening."

"I'd open the door and there'd be guys standing on the other side of the street. I'd get in the car, and they'd be following me in a car. Not hiding either. That's what got me paranoid. They wanted me to see I was being followed."

"I was so paranoid from them tappin' the phone and followin' me, there was a period where I just couldn't function, you know?"

Documents from pages 321 to 327 show that FBI denied any "lawful electronic surveillance" regarding John Lennon. Nevertheless, judging from the Watergate scandal revelations about methods used by the Nixon administration to spy on some of their political opponents, one shouldn't be surprised if unlawful electronic surveillance had actually been conducted.

---

[3] See page 329, about the Watergate scandal and the misuse of governmental agencies by the Nixon administration. See also note 2 on previous page.

[4] The Republican National Convention was held in Miami Beach, Florida, from August 21 to 23, 1972.

0-20 (Rev. 8-5-74)

**ALL INFORMATION CONTAINED
HEREIN IS UNCLASSIFIED
DATE** 2/19/81 **BY** ___

A054
D A
LENNON 6-17
DAY LD
NEW YORK (UPI) -- FORMER BEATLE JOHN LENNON, FIGHTING A 1971
DEPORTATION ORDER, HAS FILED SUIT AGAINST THE JUSTICE DEPARTMENT,
FORMER ATTORNEY GENERAL JOHN N. MITCHELL AND OTHER OFFICIALS,
CHARGING THEY SINGLED HIM OUT FOR "IMPROPER SELECTIVE PROSECUTION."
    LEON WILDES, LENNON'S ATTORNEY, SAID MONDAY HE HAS DOCUMENTS
SHOWING LENNON'S DEPORTATION "AS ORDERED FROM WASHINGTON BECAUSE OF
SENATE INTERNAL SECURITY COMMITTEE REPORT WHICH SOUGHT TO LINK LENNON
WITH PLANS TO DISRUPT THE 1972 REPUBLICAN NATIONAL CONVENTION.
    IN 1973, NEW YORK IMMIGRATION DIRECTOR SOL MARKS SAID AT A NEWS
CONFERENCE HE MADE THE DECISION TO PROCEED AGAINST LENNON HIMSELF.
    WILDES SAID MARKS SAID IN A DEPOSITION LAST WEEK HE ACTED AS A
"CONDUIT" FOR INSTRUCTIONS FROM WASHINGTON, WHICH HE UNDERSTOOD TO
MEAN THAT "WE WERE NOT TO GIVE THIS MAN A BREAK."
    MARKS ALSO ADMITTED HE HAD MISINFORMED THE PRESS AT HIS 1973 NEWS
CONFERENCE, WILDES SAID.
    PROCEEDINGS AGAINST LENNON, BEGUN IN MARCH 1972 WHEN HE WAS
CHARGED WITH OVERSTAYING HIS VISA, ARE STILL PENDING. PROSECUTORS
CITED A 1968 BRITISH CONVICTION FOR MARIJUANA POSSESSION AS THE BASIS
FOR DENYING HIM PERMANENT RESIDENCE.
    WILDES SAID SEN. STROM THURMOND, R-S.C. SENT A LETTER TO MITCHELL
IN FEBRUARY 1972, ENCLOSING THE COMMITTEE MEMORANDUM.
    "THIS APPEARS TO ME TO BE AN IMPORTANT MATTER, AND I THINK IT
WOULD BE WELL TO TO BE CONSIDERED AT THE HIGHEST LEVEL ... AS I CAN
SEE MANY HEADACHES MIGHT BE AVOIDED IF APPROPRIATE ACTION BE
TAKEN IN TIME," WILDES QUOTED THURMOND'S LETTER AS SAYING.
    WILDES SAID OTHER DOCUMENTS SHOW KLEINDIENST SENT THE MEMO TO
IMMIGRATION COMMISSIONER RAYMOND FARRELL AND THAT FARRELL'S DEPUTY
INSTRUCTED SUBORDINATES IN NEW YORK TO SEEK DEPORTATION OF LENNON AND
HIS WIFE, YOKO ONO.
    WILDES SAID THE SUIT NAMES THE JUSTICE DEPARTMENT, MITCHELL,
RICHARD KLEINDIENST, DEPUTY ATTORNEY GENERAL AT THE TIME AND
MITCHELL'S SUCCESSOR, AND "VARIOUS IMMIGRATION OFFICERS."
UPI 06-17 05:39 AED

NOT RECORDED
SEP 2 1975

58 SEP 5 1975

WASHINGTON CAPITAL NEWS SERVICE

On October 7, 1975, the US Court of Appeals overturned the Immigration and Naturalization Service's order to deport John Lennon. The INS had officially denied Lennon the right to live in the US because of his 1968 marijuana conviction in London, but the Court of Appeals determined that under US law John's guilty plea to possession of one ounce of cannabis resin couldn't be used as grounds to prevent him from obtaining permanent residency, and therefore that he had been prosecuted unjustly. In its thirty-page report, the court wrote : "Lennon's four-year battle to remain in our country is testimony to his faith in this American dream."

"John Liberty", 1978 - drawing by John Lennon

American Embassy
London, W. 1
July 23, 1976

Chief, Visa Unit
American Embassy

Subject: ~~John Winston Ono LENNON - IV-00034~~
~~NIV/IV Waiver Applicant~~
Adjustment of Status Applicant

Please refer to the attached application for adjustment of status pertaining to the above applicant.

According to information available to this office FBI, Headquarters in Washington D.C., has information concerning the above individual.

_____

Please let me know the decision in the cases which involve the issuance of a visa.

Cordially,

Tom Blackshear

Encl: (1)

cc : Legal Attache
w/att.

William M. McGhee

CLASSIFIED BY
EXEMPT FROM GENERAL DECLASSIFICATION
SCHEDULE OF EXECUTIVE ORDER 11652
EXEMPTION CATEGORY 5B(2)
DECLASSIFY ON

CONFIDENTIAL

BIOGRAPHIC INFORMATION

29 JUN 1976

(Family name)	(First name)	(Middle name)	☒ MALE ☐ FEMALE	BIRTHDATE (Mo.-L) 10/9/40	NATIONALITY British	ALIEN REGISTRATION NO. (If any) A17 597
LENNON	John	Winston Ono				

ALL OTHER NAMES USED (Including names by previous marriages) none	CITY AND COUNTRY OF BIRTH Liverpool, England	SOCIAL SECURITY NO. (if any)

	FAMILY NAME	FIRST NAME	DATE, CITY AND COUNTRY OF BIRTH (if known)	CITY AND COUNTRY OF RESIDENCE
FATHER	LENNON	Alfred	Liverpool, England	(deceased)
MOTHER (Maiden name)	STANLEY	Julia	Liverpool, England	(deceased)

HUSBAND (if none, so state) or WIFE FAMILY NAME (For wife, give maiden name)	FIRST NAME	BIRTHDATE	CITY & COUNTRY OF BIRTH	DATE OF MARRIAGE	PLACE OF MARRIAGE
ONO	Yoko	2/18/33	Tokyo, Japan	3/20/69	Gibraltar

FORMER HUSBANDS OR WIVES (if none, so state) FAMILY NAME (For wife, give maiden name)	FIRST NAME	BIRTHDATE	DATE & PLACE OF MARRIAGE	DATE AND PLACE OF TERMINATION OF MARRIAGE
Powell	Cynthia		8/23/62 England	11/8/68 England

APPLICANT'S RESIDENCE LAST FIVE YEARS. LIST PRESENT ADDRESS FIRST.

STREET AND NUMBER	CITY	PROVINCE OR STATE	COUNTRY	FROM MONTH	YEAR	TO MONTH	YEAR
1 W. 72nd Street	N.Y.	New York	USA	May	73	PRESENT TIME	
105 Bank Street	N.Y.	New York	USA	Nov	71	May	73
St. Regis Hotel	N.Y.	New York	USA	Aug	71	Nov	71
Tittenhurst, London Rd.	Ascot	Berkshire	England	Nov	69	Aug	71

APPLICANT'S LAST ADDRESS OUTSIDE THE UNITED STATES OF MORE THAN ONE YEAR

STREET AND NUMBER	CITY	PROVINCE OR STATE	COUNTRY	FROM MONTH	YEAR	TO MONTH	YEAR

APPLICANT'S EMPLOYMENT LAST FIVE YEARS. (IF NONE, SO STATE.) LIST PRESENT EMPLOYMENT FIRST.

FULL NAME AND ADDRESS OF EMPLOYER	OCCUPATION (SPECIFY)	FROM MONTH	YEAR	TO MONTH	YEAR
(self employed artist)				PRESENT TIME	(past five years)

Show below last occupation abroad if not shown above. (Include all information requested above)

THIS FORM IS SUBMITTED IN CONNECTION WITH APPLICATION FOR:
☐ NATURALIZATION ☒ ADJUSTMENT OF STATUS ☐ OTHER (SPECIFY)

SIGNATURE OF APPLICANT OR PETITIONER: *[signature]*
DATE: 3/31/76

Are all copies legible? ☒ Yes

PENALTIES: SEVERE PENALTIES ARE PROVIDED BY LAW FOR KNOWINGLY AND WILLFULLY FALSIFYING OR CONCEALING A MATERIAL FACT.

APPLICANT: BE SURE TO PUT YOUR NAME AND ALIEN REGISTRATION NUMBER IN THE BOX OUTLINED BY HEAVY BORDER BELOW.

COMPLETE THIS BOX (Family name)	(Given name)	(Middle name)	(Alien registration number)
LENNON	John	Winston Ono	A17 597 321

(OTHER AGENCY USE) | INS USE (Office of Origin)

100-469910-26

FORM G-325A

RIDER TO FORM G-325A

RE: JOHN WINSTON ONO LENNON
Social Security #127-52-1582

Self-employment was in connection with the following corporations:

Apple Corps, Limited
Maclen (Music) Limited
Lennon Productions Limited
Bag Productions, Limited
Joko Films, Limited
Ono Music, Limited
Subafilms, Limited
Apple Films, Limited
Apple Publishing, Limited
The Beatles, Limited

Lennon Productions, Inc.
Joko Films, Inc.
Bag Music Productions, Inc.
Yoko Ono Projects, Inc.
Ono Music, Inc.

_____
JOHN WINSTON ONO LENNON

4-750 (Rev. 4-17-85)

FEDERAL BUREAU OF INVESTIGATION
FOIPA DELETED PAGE INFORMATION SHEET

_1_ Page(s) withheld entirely at this location in the file. One or more of the following statements, where indicated, explain this deletion.

☒ Deleted under exemption(s) __(b)(3)__ with no segregable material available for release to you.

☐ Information pertained only to a third party with no reference to you or the subject of your request.

☐ Information pertained only to a third party. Your name is listed in the title only.

☐ Documents originated with another Government agency(ies). These documents were referred to that agency(ies) for review and direct response to you.

____ Pages contain information furnished by another Government agency(ies). You will be advised by the FBI as to the releasability of this information following our consultation with the other agency(ies).

____ Page(s) withheld for the following reason(s):

☐ For your information:

☒ The following number is to be used for reference regarding these pages:
__105-7-241-814   STATE DOCUMENT__

XXXXXXXXXXXXXXXXXX
X DELETED PAGE(S) X
X NO DUPLICATION FEE X
X FOR THIS PAGE X
XXXXXXXXXXXXXXXXXX

FBI/DOJ

Code (b)(3) protects from disclosure information withheld pursuant to statute, including visa and tax records.

LON-3 (Rev. 2-26-71)

UNITED STATES GOVERNMENT

Memorandum

TO : Director, FBI (100-469910)　　　DATE: 7/27/76

FROM : Legat, London (105-5492) (RUC)

SUBJECT: JOHN WINSTON ONO LENNON
IS - GREAT BRITAIN

　☒ Enclosed are __2__ copies of:

　☐ LHM ☒ Communication dated __7/23/76__, with enclosure
　classified __CONFIDENTIAL__. ☒ Conceal source.

　Source of information or communication:

　b1
　(c)

☐ Investigation requested, report results in form suitable for dissemination.

Check: ☐ Bufiles ☐ Ident. Division ☐ WFO check Passport files, Department of State.
☐ Other:

3 - Bureau (Encs. - 4)
　(1 - Foreign Liaison Unit)
1 - London
DRD:eim
(4)

ALL INFORMATION CONTAINED
HEREIN IS UNCLASSIFIED EXCEPT
WHERE SHOWN OTHERWISE.

REC-24 100-469910-26

21 AUG 6 1976

FBI INFO 2/13/96
CLASSIFIED BY: SSA9803RDD/JS
REASON: 1.5 (b)
DECLASSIFY ON: X5

CA# 83-1720

b1

ST-123   REC-71   DE-1 100-469910-0
V-18
MCT-26 22 AUG 10 1976

CA# 83-1720
CLASSIFIED DECISIONS FINALIZED
BY DEPARTMENT REVIEW COMMITTEE (DRC)
DATE: 12/10/97 SSA SLD/JS

ENCLOSURE

Notice of Classification Action
Cross Ref. File # only
File # 100-469910-25
Classified by: 1678 RFP/EOM 4-6-83
Declass on: OADR

b1

~~CONFIDENTIAL~~

ENCLOSURE
~~CONFIDENTIAL~~ 100-469910-25

100-469910-25

On the very same day this heavily blacked out FBI memorandum was issued, John Lennon was finally given his Green Card after four years of struggle to fight the deportation proceedings against him.

John with his brand new Green Card, his wife Yoko and his attorney, Leon Wildes.

From now on, John Lennon can live freely in New York City, as a permanent resident of the United States of America.

```
Routing Slip                (Copies to Offices Checked)
0-7 (Rev. 12-17-73)
TO: SAC:                                                          TO LEGAT:
☐ Albany         ☐ Houston         ☐ Oklahoma City    ☐ Beirut
☐ Albuquerque    ☐ Indianapolis    ☐ Omaha            ☐ Bern
☐ Alexandria     ☐ Jackson         ☐ Philadelphia     ☐ Bonn
☐ Anchorage      ☐ Jacksonville    ☐ Phoenix          ☐ Brasilia
☐ Atlanta        ☐ Kansas City     ☐ Pittsburgh       ☐ Buenos Aires
☐ Baltimore      ☐ Knoxville       ☐ Portland         ☐ Caracas
☐ Birmingham     ☐ Las Vegas       ☐ Richmond         ☐ Hong Kong
☐ Boston         ☐ Little Rock     ☐ Sacramento       ☐ London
☐ Buffalo        ☐ Los Angeles     ☐ St. Louis        ☐ Madrid
☐ Butte          ☐ Louisville      ☐ Salt Lake City   ☐ Manila
☐ Charlotte      ☐ Memphis         ☐ San Antonio      ☐ Mexico City
☐ Chicago        ☐ Miami           ☐ San Diego        ☐ Ottawa
☐ Cincinnati     ☐ Milwaukee       ☐ San Francisco    ☐ Paris
☐ Cleveland      ☐ Minneapolis     ☐ San Juan         ☐ Rome
☐ Columbia       ☐ Mobile          ☐ Savannah         ☐ Singapore
☐ Dallas         ☐ Newark          ☐ Seattle          ☐ Tel Aviv
☐ Denver         ☐ New Haven       ☐ Springfield      ☐ Tokyo
☐ Detroit        ☐ New Orleans     ☐ Tampa
☐ El Paso        ☒ New York City   ☐ Washington Field  AUG 13 1976
☐ Honolulu       ☐ Norfolk         ☐ Quantico
```

RE: Date _____

☒ For information   ☐ Retention optional   ☐ For appropriate action   ☐ Surep. by _____

☐ The enclosed is for your information. If used in a future report, ☐ conceal all sources, ☐ paraphrase contents.

☐ Enclosed are corrected pages from report of SA _____ dated _____

Remarks: 100-175319-62

See attached for your information. No investigation should be conducted concerning subject but your sources should be alerted to the subject's presence in the area covered by your office. Any information developed indicating activity outside the scope of the intended purpose while in the United States should be promptly furnished to the Bureau.

ALL INFORMATION CONTAINED
HEREIN IS UNCLASSIFIED
DATE 6-9-82 BY _____

SERIALIZED _____
AUG __ 1976
FBI—NEW YORK

219

That's it ! John Lennon is not wanted by the FBI any more !

Extortion

At first, a whole section of the John Lennon FBI files was not released. The reason given was : "Records or information compiled for law enforcement purposes that could reasonably be expected to constitute an unwarranted invasion of personal privacy" (code (b)(7)(c)).

The unreleased part was in fact the one you're about to read. It's related to an extortion attempt that took place in 1977-1978. John Lennon received the first letter in December 1977. It threatened him and his family and demanded 100,000 dollars in the name of the FALN. The *Fuerzas Armadas de Liberación Nacional* (Armed Forces of National Liberation, FALN) was a Puerto Rican terrorist organization that advocated complete independence for Puerto Rico. At the time of its dissolution, the FALN was responsible for more than 120 bomb attacks on United States targets between 1974 and 1983.

Lennon reported this threat to the FBI, which lead to a thorough investigation. FBI agents kept watch in the vicinity of the "Dakota" building where John & Yoko lived, as they received more threatening letters and phone calls.

This section of the John Lennon FBI files makes us more familiar with the FBI Laboratory and its scientific investigation methods. These methods had first been advocated by Hoover[5] who was convinced it would greatly help. They include fingerprint examination and typewriting comparison to try to source the sender of the letters. It actually turns into a kind of thriller when letters multiply, threatening phone calls are made, FBI surveillance is spotted... Then a composite drawing of the suspect is made thanks to the testimony of a Post Office employee[6]. But this leads nowhere and meanwhile the pressure and the violence of the threats keep increasing. Once again this makes these FBI files pleasant to read, although this threat certainly wasn't nice to deal with for John Lennon and his wife who had already had tough times during the deportation proceedings.

---

[5] John Edgar Hoover was one of the founders of the FBI in 1935, and its first director. He remained at this post until his death in 1972, at age 77.

[6] See page 399.

4-750 (Rev. 4-17-85)

XXXXXX
XXXXXX
XXXXXX

FEDERAL BUREAU OF INVESTIGATION
FOIPA DELETED PAGE INFORMATION SHEET

__207__ Page(s) withheld entirely at this location in the file. One or more of the following statements, where indicated, explain this deletion.

☒ Deleted under exemption(s) __(b)(7)(c)__ with no segregable material available for release to you.

☐ Information pertained only to a third party with no reference to you or the subject of your request.

☐ Information pertained only to a third party. Your name is listed in the title only.

☐ Documents originated with another Government agency(ies). These documents were referred to that agency(ies) for review and direct response to you.

____ Pages contain information furnished by another Government agency(ies). You will be advised by the FBI as to the releasability of this information following our consultation with the other agency(ies).

____ Page(s) withheld for the following reason(s):
_____
_____

☐ For your information: _____
_____

☒ The following number is to be used for reference regarding these pages:
__9-63510   (ENTIRE FILE)   HEADQUARTERS__

XXXXXX
XXXXXX
XXXXXX

XXXXXXXXXXXXXXXXX
DELETED PAGE(S)
NO DUPLICATION FEE
FOR THIS PAGE
XXXXXXXXXXXXXXXXX

FBI/DOJ

At first, this whole section of the John Lennon FBI files was not released. The reason given was: "Records or information compiled for law enforcement purposes that could reasonably be expected to constitute an unwarranted invasion of personal privacy" (code (b)(7)(c)).

NY0654 336Q317Z

RR HQ

DE NY 2

R 02Q15QZ EC. 77

FM NEW YORK (9-NEW) P (21)

TO DIRECTOR ROUTINE

BT

CLEAR

UNSUB, AKA [   ]; JOHN LENNON - VICTIM; EXTORTION (A),
OO: NEW YORK

ON DECEMBER 1, 1977, JOHN LENNON, MEMBER OF BEATLES ROCK GROUP, ADVISED HE RECEIVED A SPECIAL DELIVERY LETTER POSTMARKED NOVEMBER 30, 1977, JAMAICA, QUEENS, BEARING RETURN ADDRESS [   ] BROOKLYN, NEW YORK, 11229. THE LETTER THREATENED LENNON AND HIS FAMILY AND DEMANDED $100,000 TO BE READY BY DECEMBER 9, 1977.

IN LETTER PASSING REFERENCE MADE TO FALN.

NYO INDICES AND DMV NEGATIVE AND RETURN ADDRESS IS NON-EXISTENT.

ORIGINAL LETTER AND COPIES ARE BEING FOWARDED TO FBI LABORATORY AND LATENT FINGERPRINT SECTION FOR EXAMINATION.

ALL INFORMATION CONTAINED
HEREIN IS UNCLASSIFIED
DATE 4-4-83 BY 1678 RFp/EBm

PAGE TWO NY 9-NEW CLE A

NYO WILL KEEP BUREAU APPRAISED OF DEVELOPMENTS.

BT

FD- (Rev. 7-27-76)

FBI

TRANSMIT VIA:
- ☐ Teletype
- ☐ Facsimile
- ☒ Airtel

PRECEDENCE:
- ☐ Immediate
- ☐ Priority
- ☐ Routine

CLASSIFICATION:
- ☐ TOP SECRET
- ☐ SECRET
- ☐ CONFIDENTIAL
- ☐ E F T O
- ☐ CLEAR

Date 12/2/77

TO: DIRECTOR, FBI
(ATTN: ID/LFS)

FROM: ADIC, NEW YORK (9-NEW) (P) (#21)

SUBJECT: UNSUB aka
JOHN LENNON - VICTIM
EXTORTION (A)
(OO:NY)

ReNYtel, 12/1/77.

Enclosed for Identification Division is the original and two xerox copies of a letter addressed to JOHN LENNON, member of rock group The Beatles. Letter postmarked 11/29/77, Jamaica, New York, return address 16-35 East 17th Street, Brooklyn, New York 11229, a non-existent address. Letter threatens LENNON and family and demands $100,000. Letter makes reference to FALN organization.

Above letter made available on 12/1/77 by JOHN LENNON.

REQUEST OF THE BUREAU

Identification Division is requested to search the enclosed letter through the Anonymous Letter File. Also to compare with specimens previously submitted in case entitled, " - FUGITIVE (A); MOBOM; EID; (OO:NY)", Bureau File 174-7729 and other FALN related files. Further the Identification Division is requested to conduct any other examination that would help in identifying Unsub.

4 - Bureau (Encls. 3)
  (1 - ID/LFS)
  (1 - FALN 174-7729)
1 - New York (174-2667)
1 - New York
MED:jfc
(7)

ALL INFORMATION CONTAINED
HEREIN IS UNCLASSIFIED
DATE 4-4-83 BY 1678 RFP/EBM

Approved: _____ Transmitted _____ Per _____
                      (Number) (Time)

NY 9-

    2. ID/LFS is requested to conduct appropriate latent examination. If latents developed, eliminate following prints:

    JOHN LENNON, DOB 10/9/40
    USINS # A17597321

    [redacted] DOB [redacted]   b6
    USINS# [redacted]   b7C

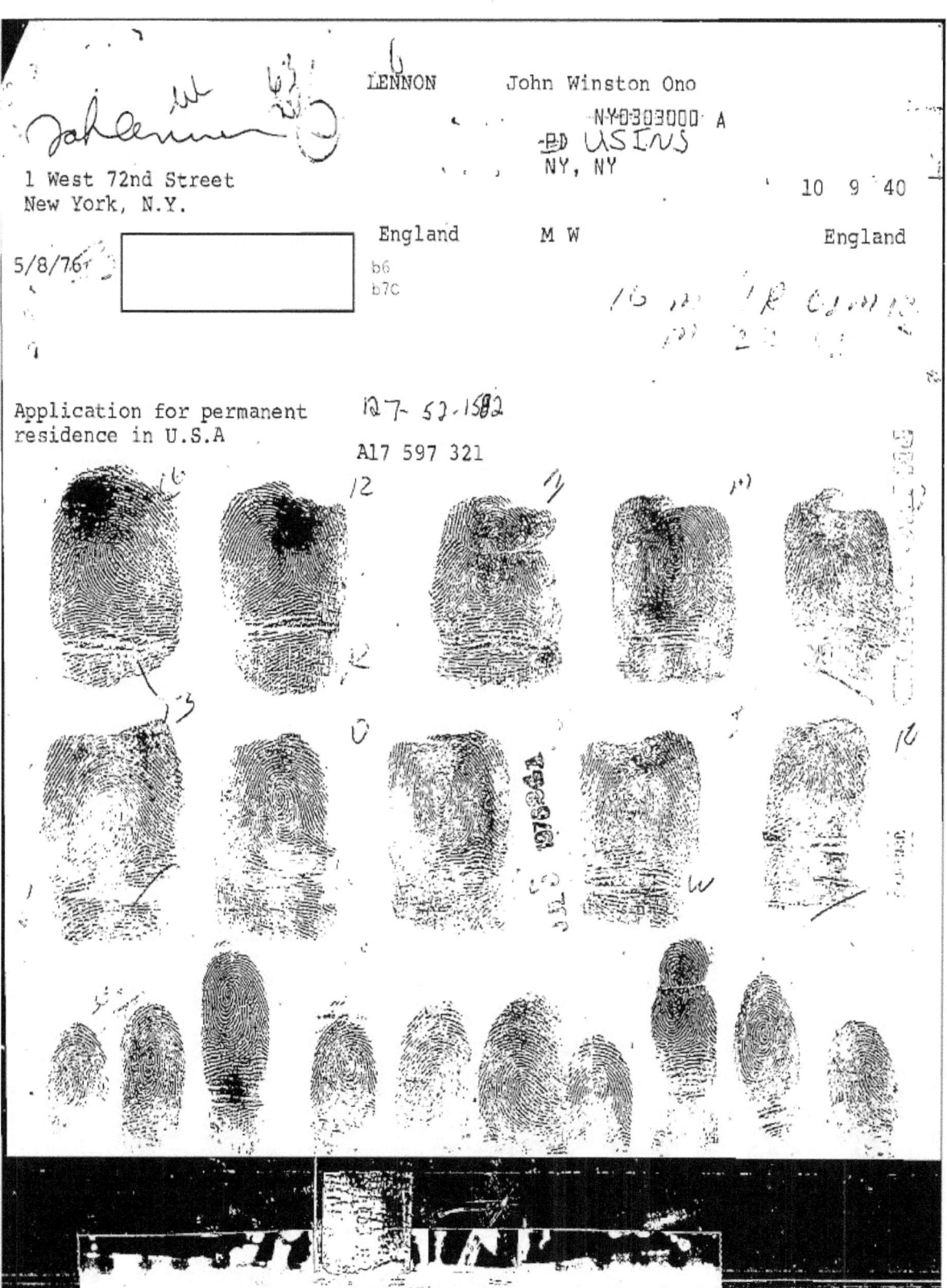

ALL INFORMATION CONTAINED
HEREIN IS UNCLASSIFIED
DATE 4-4-83 BY 1678 RFp/tem

ENCLOSURE

FROM: [b6 b7C]
BROOKLYN N. Y. 11229

JAMAICA, NY
NOV 29 PM
1977

SPECIAL DELIVERY

MR. JOHN LENNON
1 WEST 72nd STREET
NEW YORK, N.Y. 10023

SPECIAL DELIVERY

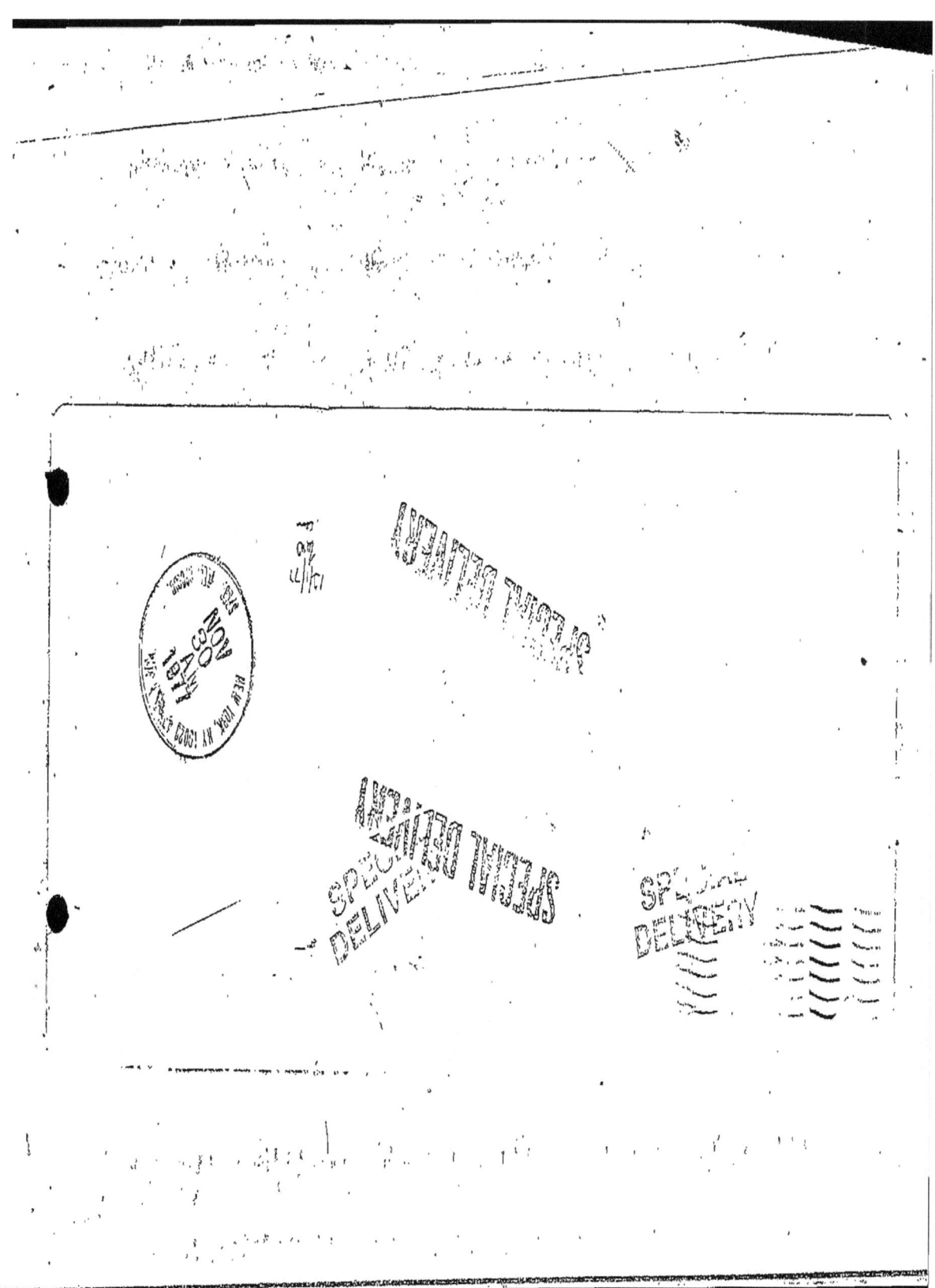

Nov. 29 _ 1977

MR. & MRS. JOHN LENNON

      This letter is not a joking, it may be one of most important and ungrateful letter that perhaps you never receive before. ********************* But everything can be happily and normal, if you follow us very careful, without wrong move..........

      This letter is a positive (THREAT) to your life, to [ ] & (SPECIAL) to [ ] life............................

WE ARE THE TERRORIST'S THE FALN PUERTO RICAN INDEPENDENCE MOVEMENT.

We are responsible for the bomb explosion, in several City's through of U. S. A. We are strong on weapon's, dynamite & munition.

      But we are weak on money problem's and we most need five million dollar's to keep our operation going on for the next three year's.

      Now how to obtain five million? Perhaps we most start from kidnap, and may be we can reach this amount in just two or three shoot's.

But the head of our organization said no; we most try it slowly, without kidnap, without asking for big ransom, without bloodiness & distress. We try do it with a (THREAT) in a simple letter.

      But if ours victim's fail our demand, then we most go ahead with our revenge and we most transform their million's in one cent worth, and the sorrow will be with them far is long they live. Also what ever we most do against them, will be without ransom.

      Now we like to inform you this? Letter's like this one, we send to over twenty four victim's in the past three month's and we are doing it so well, that we collect already two million's & four hundred thousand dollar's. No one fail's our demand, so we hope you to...

      Our demand from you, is one hundred thousand dollar's, this is the same amount that we collect from the other's. We want the money in follow way. <u>50 thousand in bill's of one hundred, twenty five thousand in fift's & twenty five thousand in twenty's.</u> We don't accept the money series number's all in order, if it come all in order it will be return to you and our negotiation will be completely off. So don't try to play any trick to us because we are good preparedly for it.

      You have exact nine day's frome the date of this letter to decide & to get the money.

      It most be put in a strong package and brought down to the <u>clerk, by front entrance</u> of the DAKOTA HOUSE. to be (pickup) by [ ]. The package most be there, Dec. 9 at two P.M. After that, any time during seven days the package will be (pickup) After seven days, you most find out if the package remain there, if it remain there it most be return to you and you'l receive new instruction about it.

Continue on second page.

ALL INFORMATION CONTAINED HEREIN IS UNCLASSIFIED
DATE 4-4-83 BY 1678 RFP/EBm

ENCLOSURE

Remember? the people who is spouse to pickup the package, they are inocent people. they don't know nothing about us or what is inside of the package. It will pass on several hand's of inocent people, before it reach our hand. But if anything comes suspicious, it mean any trap for us the package will never reach our hand and there will not be the last pickup.

But if it happen you can be sure, that you and your family, will never be free until our revenge be done and then after this, you will be free to suffer and live with sorrow far is long you live.

If you decide our demand, you most stay away from the F. B. I. or any police agents included friend's too.

But if you do not decide our demand, so there is nothing helpfully to you or to us, we will remain silence until the moment come. we will not disturb yuo with second letter nor even one telephone call.
In this case you can go ahead to the F.B.I. and show to them this letter, also you can make it public or any publicity that you like.

But don't forget, they will not protect your family for ever, but you can be sure, that we will be in every corner.

We the puerto rican terrorists.
We are responsible for this letters.
We are fighting for what we believe.
We have nothing to lose & Puerto Rico.
Some day most be independent.

T H A N K Y O U
T. F. P. R. I. M.

P.S. THE RETURN ADDRESS
OF THIS LETTER IS FALSE.

Here is some meaning reference's
We know that you live in one of most security house, in New York, City.
We know that your APT. Number, is 72 - 7th floor, with front & back door. Your APT. is face to Central Park, & South corner.
We have seen [____] many times out, with [_____] b6 b7C

You Know, that money can buy all most evrything. It mean, if for any reason we decide to go into the Dakota, you'l find out, that no place is security today.
With one or two or three thousand dollar's, we can buy any employee and get a free pass, but in case the employee refuse our offer, we take them by force and less than twenty minutes evrything be overcloud, or when you are travel expensive limousine, a grenade or something else may explode and it is it.

All this meaning, is just for you take this case very seriously, and think twice before you do any mistake.

Your problem is be rich, if you was a poor man it never happen to you.

We know, that you are very nice person and we don't want nothing happen to you or to your family, we just want the money without problem's and then you can be free for one hundred year's ahead, we will not disturb you AGAIN.

ALL INFORMATION CONTAINED
HEREIN IS UNCLASSIFIED
DATE 4-4-83 BY 1678 RFP/EPm

9-63510-1
ENCLOSURE

Logos of the FALN

FD-302 (REV. 11-27-70)

FEDERAL BUREAU OF INVESTIGATION

Date of transcription 12/6/77

_____ who is _____, furnished the following information:

At approximately 9:00 PM, on November 29, 1977, _____ received a phone call from an unknown male. The man speaking with, what sounded like a Hispanic accent, stated "Is JOHN LENNON there?". _____ asked who the caller was and he answered "Never mind who I am", then added "Tell him he is going to receive the most important letter in his life tomorrow". Again, _____ attempted to learn the identity of the caller, and he repeated "Never mind who I am", and hung up.

_____ advised _____ of the incident. The Next morning, they searched the mail and found a letter addressed to JOHN LENNON, postmarked November 29, 1977, at Jamaica, New York, with a return address of:

_____

Brooklyn, NY 11229"

_____ furnished the letter, which consisted of three typewritten pages and one blank page. In essence, the letter threatened JOHN LENNON and his family if $100,000.00 was not prepared for payment on December 9, 1977.

_____ and _____ discussed the matter, and since they had in the past received many crank letters, they hesitated turning it over to the authorities. However, combined with the phone call the previous night, they felt alarmed enough to contact the Federal Bureau of Investigation (FBI).

_____ stated that they have never received a similar type letter and have no idea who might have authored it.

Interviewed on 12/1/77 at New York, New York File # NY 9-7749-11

by SAS _____ and _____ /MED/1mm   Date dictated 12/2/77

This document contains neither recommendations nor conclusions of the FBI. It is the property of the FBI and is loaned to your agency; it and its contents are not to be distributed outside your agency.

NY 9—

[____] stated that the details regarding their residence as well as their normal habits, are generally public knowledge. [____] added that the phone number the unknown subject used to contact them, [____], is an unlisted number for [____]. [____] stated, however, that this was not the first time that fans or other individuals have managed to get that number, and to contact them. [____] explained that often people in the office will give out the number to individuals who might ask for it.

[____] advised that [____] was born on [____], and [____], JOHN LENNON, was born October 9, 1940. [____] stated that [____], who was born [____].

[____] stated that [____] would furnish the United States (US) Immigration and Naturalization Service (INS) numbers for both [____] and [____]. [____] stated further that [____] would notify the FBI immediately in the event there is any further contact made by the unknown subject.

b6
b7C

b6
b7C

b6
b7C

3

FD-302 (REV. 11-27-70)

FEDERAL BUREAU OF INVESTIGATION

Date of transcription 12/13/77

[redacted], Jamaica Post Office, Substation E, 98-34 Jamaica Avenue was advised of the official identity of the interviewing agents and the purpose of the interview. [redacted] provided the following information:

[redacted] advised that Pitney-Bowes postal meter number 159263 is located at his substation, this having been determined from physical inspection of the postal meter machine located at substation E.

[redacted] was shown a photocopy of an envelope addressed to, "Mr. JOHN LENNON, 1 West 72nd Street, New York, N.Y. 10023," post marked, "Jamaica, N.Y. 114, Nov. 29, PM 1977" with return address, "From: [redacted], 16-35 East 17th Street, Brooklyn, N.Y. 11229." [redacted] advised he returns from lunch at 12:30 pm and it was shortly after this that an individual, apparently by himself, brought the above letter into the substation. [redacted] said the individual requested it to be sent Special Delivery. [redacted] stated he noticed the return address was not in his postal zone, but did not consider this unusual. [redacted] said he weighed the letter and requested $1.38 for postage which he believes the individual obtained from his front pants pocket. [redacted] stated the only thing he recalls the individual saying was, "Special delivery." [redacted] advised he did not notice the letter was addressed to JOHN LENNON, possibly a former Beatle, until after the person posting the letter had left the substation. [redacted] stated, he does not recall having seen this individual before at the substation or in the neighborhood. [redacted] advised that he did not regard this transaction as being unusual.

[redacted] provided the following limited description based on his recollection:

Sex: Male
Race: Hispanic; possibly Puerto Rican or South American

Interviewed on 12/2/77 at Queens, New York File # NY 9-7749-6

by SAS [redacted] and [redacted] /CEM/rac   Date dictated 12/8/77

NY 9-NEW

Age	Forty
Height	5 feet 6 inches
Build	Medium
Clothing	Outer jacket
Characteristics	No glasses, no beard, no hat

[blank] advised he would contact this office if he recalled any additional information concerning this individual or the above transaction, or in the event this individual returned to the substation.

b6
b7C

FD-302 (REV. 11-27-70)

FEDERAL BUREAU OF INVESTIGATION

Date of transcription: 12/12/77

Investigation was conducted by below listed Agents in the vicinity of 16-35 East 17th Street, Brooklyn, New York, for the purpose of identifying and locating at that address a _____.

At 16-35 East 17th Street, Brooklyn, New York, a two story building was located, the first floor of which houses a florist shop and the second floor a dentist, _____. Through inquiry with the proprietor of the flower shop it was learned that both the flower shop and dentist had occupied 16-35 East 17th Street for the last few years. The proprietor advised he had never heard of any individual in the area with the name of _____ or any combination of that name.

At 16-35 East 16th Street was located a bakery which occupied both floors of the two story building there. Inquiry at that location also did not identify any individual with the name _____ or variation of the same. It was further determined that 16-35 East 18th Street, Brooklyn, New York, was a non-existant address. A neighborhood investigation was also conducted in the vicinity of these addresses with negative results.

These three aforementioned addresses are located directly off Kings Highway in the Flatbush section of the borough of Brooklyn, New York.

Interviewed on 12/2/77 at Brooklyn, New York File # NY 9-7749-5

SAS _____ /PJD/bw Date dictated 12/6/77

This document contains neither recommendations nor conclusions of the FBI. It is the property of the FBI and is loaned to your agency; it and its contents are not to be distributed outside your agency.

11

FVB:jfc
1

NY 9-7749

A surveillance was maintained by Special Agents of the Federal Bureau of Investigation (FBI) in the vicinity of the front desk at "The Dakota" building, One West 72nd Street, New York, New York, on December 9, 1978, from 1:00 p.m. to 5:00 p.m. and no contact was made by Unknown Subject (Unsub) with the desk clerk who had a package to be delivered to Unsub.

Behind John & Yoko is the "Dakota building" where they had bought an apartment in 1973 and were living at that time. The Dakota is located in the Upper West Side of Manhattan in New York City. It was to this location that the threatening letters were sent.

And it's in front of this building that John Lennon would be shot to death on December 8, 1980.

FD-302 (REV. 1-27-70)

FEDERAL BUREAU OF INVESTIGATION

Date of transcription 12/15/77

[redacted], The Dakota, 1 West 72nd Street, furnished the following information: b6 b7C

Shortly after midnight, on December 10, 1977, he received a phone call from an unknown male who spoke with a Spanish accent who asked if there were any messages for a [redacted]. [redacted] advised him that there was a letter waiting for [redacted]. The unknown male at that point told [redacted] that he could send the letter back to the apartment and hung up. [redacted] understood this to mean that the letter should be returned to the apartment of JOHN and [redacted], Apartment 72. b6 b7C

Interviewed on 12/11/77 at Westwood, New Jersey File # NY 9-7749-7

by SA [redacted] b6 b7C Date dictated 12/12/77

This document contains neither recommendations nor conclusions of the FBI. It is the property of the FBI and is loaned to your agency; it and its contents are not to be distributed outside your agency.

13

FD-302 (REV. 11-27-70)

FEDERAL BUREAU OF INVESTIGATION

Date of transcription 12/15/77

[redacted] telephonically advised of the following:

At approximately 12:05 AM, on December 11, 1977, [redacted] received a phone call. An unknown male with a Spanish accent stated that, [redacted] and asked what was the meaning of the letter that was left for him. The man then went on to say something to the effect, "You blew it". [redacted] explained that [redacted] had left the package for [redacted] with the front desk for all of Friday afternoon. When it was not picked up, they recovered it and left a letter for [redacted]. [redacted] stated that they were concerned that the package might be stolen or lost if left for an indefinite period of time with the front desk.

[redacted] explained that [redacted] and [redacted] were willing to cooperate with [redacted], but wished he would furnish new instructions.

The unknown male then stated, "Okay" and hung up.

[redacted] explained that this unknown male caller was the same individual who had contacted [redacted] by phone on November 29, 1977. [redacted] stated that [redacted] could hear no background noises during the phone call which lasted from approximately 12:05 AM, until 12:07 AM.

Interviewed on 12/11/77 at Westwood, New Jersey File # NY 9-7749

by SA [redacted] /kp Date dictated 12/12/77

FD-302 (REV. 11-27-70)

FEDERAL BUREAU OF INVESTIGATION

12/15/77
Date of transcription:

[REDACTED], The Dakota Building, 1 West 72nd Street, furnished the following information:

He does not recognize the name [REDACTED]. He stated that The Dakota has only 22 employees. He displayed a list of the current employees and there was no [REDACTED] or combination of that name on the list. [REDACTED] stated that to the best of his knowledge, there has never been anyone employed at The Dakota bearing that name.

[REDACTED] read the letter that was addressed to JOHN LENNON of Apartment 72. Upon finishing the letter, [REDACTED] stated that he did not recognize the manner of writing, but that the author apparently had some knowledge of the building.

[REDACTED] stated that every outsider, who comes into the building for work, has to have a pass and a photograph of them is taken if they do not have an identification tag. A review of the card file indicating all visitors to The Dakota during the past year was conducted. None of the cards had the name [REDACTED] or any combination thereof.

[REDACTED] stated that it would have been possible, although very difficult, for someone to obtain the LENNON's phone number from the front desk.

| Interviewed on | 12/13/77 | at | New York, New York | File # | NY 9-7749-9 |

by SA [REDACTED] /lmm   Date dictated 12/13/77

This document contains neither recommendations nor conclusions of the FBI. It is the property of the FBI and is loaned to your agency; it and its contents are not to be distributed outside your agency.

15

FD-302 (REV. 11-27-70)

FEDERAL BUREAU OF INVESTIGATION

Date of transcription 12/22/77

[redacted] New York, furnished an original envelope postmarked December 18, 1977, addressed to Mr. & Mrs. JOHN LENNON from:

[redacted]
Brooklyn, N.Y. 11229

[redacted] advised that [redacted] received the letter this date when it was hand delivered by [redacted], who is [redacted] for the Dakota. [redacted] advised that [redacted] has had no other contacts with the individual sending the letter.

Interviewed on 12/19/77 at New York, New York File # NY 9-7749-14

by SAS [redacted] and [redacted] MED/cmq Date dictated 12/20/77

This document contains neither recommendations nor conclusions of the FBI. It is the property of the FBI and is loaned to your agency; it and its contents are not to be distributed outside your agency.

16

FD-302 (REV. 3-8-77)

FEDERAL BUREAU OF INVESTIGATION

1.

Date of transcription 1/19/78

New York, New York, furnished a Special Delivery letter addressed to Mr. JOHN LENNON, 1 West 72nd Street, New York, New York. The letter was postmarked January 18, 1978, Jamaica, New York.

The letter was stamped Special Delivery and bore a return address " _____ Brooklyn, New York 11229". Inside the envelope were two typewritten pages.

A copy of the letter is attached.

Investigation on 1/19/78 at New York, New York File # NY 9-7749

by SA _____/kph Date dictated 1/19/78

This document contains neither recommendations nor conclusions of the FBI. It is the property of the FBI and is loaned to your agency; it and its contents are not to be distributed outside your agency.

19

FD-36 (Rev. 7-27-76)

FBI

TRANSMIT VIA:
☐ Teletype
☐ Facsimile
☒ Airtel

PRECEDENCE:
☐ Immediate
☐ Priority
☐ Routine

CLASSIFICATION:
☐ TOP SECRET
☐ SECRET
☐ CONFIDENTIAL
☐ E F T O
☐ CLEAR

Date __12/20/77__

TO: DIRECTOR, FBI
(ATTN: ID/LFS)

FROM: ADIC, NEW YORK (9-7749) (P) (21)

SUBJECT: CHANGED
UNSUB aka
[redacted] b6 b7C

JOHN LENNON - VICTIM
EXTORTION (A)
(OO:NY)

Title marked "Changed" to add alias [redacted] found on enclosed letter.

ReNYairtel, dated 12/2/77.

Enclosed for Ident Division is the original and two xerox copies of a letter addressed to the LENNONs. Letter postmarked 12/18/77, New York, NY. Letter turned over to FBI, 12/19/77.

REQUEST OF THE BUREAU

ID/LFS requested to conduct same examinations requested in reairtel. Further, to compare enclosed letter with previously submitted specimen.

4 - Bureau (Encls. 3)
  (1 - ID/LFS)
  (1 - FALN 174-7729)
1 - New York (174-2667)
1 - New York

MED:geg
(7)

ALL INFORMATION CONTAINED
HEREIN IS UNCLASSIFIED
DATE 4-4-83 BY 1678 RFP/EBm

Approved: _____ Transmitted _____
                    (Number) (Time)

DECEMBER, 19-1977

MR. & MRS. JOHN LENNON

You didn't pay any attention to our threat, you didn't follow any word of our letter.
In this case our promise, was we step out and break up our deal until some day.

But before we do, we have to clear up a few things that we have in suspicious or confuse.

On the date of december, 8 one day before the package was suppose to be let with the clerk, your building was under our supervision with seven training man's specialize in recognize police agents.

On Dec. 9 our man's call our headquarters, and they said we are 90 per one hundred sure that at least two police agents went inside of the building, and so very late on that day they come out.

In our figure, as the package was suppose be let there at 2 P.M. probably there was an ambush waiting for us. We are all in confuse about it, we don't believe that you will be that stupid, but in your situation, we dont believe nor even our mother's.

Our troop is number of two hundred and fifty seven man' Suppose because of you, we loss two or three man's in a shoot out with police, figure for you self how many is left be looking for you and then after how many policemans will remain with you (none)

Right Know we are going to put an strict investigation on, to find out if there was an ambush, or if you are dealing with police or if any body know about our threat. We know how to find out we have the plan made up that we will make some body talk, and let us know whatever they know.

On Dec. 9 it was the day that we plan to pickup the package. At II P.M. your building was surround by 23 armed man's of our troop, it just for in case of any ambush. At I2,I5 A.M. we call Dakota Office, and we ask if there was a package for Mr. Reviera, from Mr. Lennon. The clerk said no, we have no package, but we have a letter for you. We order him to return the letter back to Mr. Lenn. At I2,30 A. M. we call your Apt. and we spoke to [ ] for about two minutes, she try to sell us a story, but we are grownup people a nd we didn't buy it. Is you know and we know, every building like yours, all clerks they hold lots of packages to be delivery to tenants or to be pickup by people, the clerks they never Know what is inside of the package, unless you tell them.
One thing we are sure, you and [ ] are coverup something, but we will find out the true.

Our negotiation are close until Jan. 15 ± 1978
We will have a meeting on Jan. 16 at 6 P.M. in reference to your case, we will let you Know the results of this meeting.
In the meantime we like to remind you, if you are dealing with police, you better think twice because you may turn us very madly.

This is Christmas time, do your normal life, dont be afraid is no body outside looking for you, on this you can have our trust.

THANK YOU

ALL INFORMATION CONTAINED
HEREIN IS UNCLASSIFIED
DATE 4-4-83 BY 1678 13FP/sm

9-63510-2

ENCLOSURE

FD-302 (REV. 11-27-70)

FEDERAL BUREAU OF INVESTIGATION

Date of transcription: 1/25/78

[redacted], Jamaica Post Office, Substation E, 98-34 Jamaica Avenue, furnished the following information:

At approximately 2:00 or 2:30 pm, on January 18, 1978, the same individual whom he had previously described on December 2, 1977, entered the substation. This unknown male handed [redacted] a letter for special delivery mail. [redacted] noted that the letter was addressed to JOHN LENNON, 1 West 72nd Street, New York, New York 10023. [redacted] asked, "Is this the JOHN LENNON?" and the unknown male answered, "Yes." The unknown male paid the $1.38 necessary for the special delivery.

[redacted] stated that there was no other conversation, and the individual left. [redacted] stated that he did not see the individual enter or leave an automobile. [redacted] furnished the following description of the unknown individual:

Sex	Male
Race	Hispanic, possibly Puerto Rican or South American
Age	40 - 45 years
Height	5 feet 4 inches to 5 feet 5 inches
Weight	150 pounds
Build	Solid
Marks	None
Hair	Black, medium cut
Clothing	Black fur hat (Russian hat), blue 3/4 length coat, dark grey dress trousers, red plaid shirt
Characteristics	Clean shaven, wore dark glasses
Complexion	Olive or tan complexion

[redacted] stated that he would recognize the individual should he see him again.

Interviewed on 1/19/78 at Queens, New York File # NY 9-7749-18

by SAS [redacted] and [redacted]/MED/rac Date dictated 1/24/78

This document contains neither recommendations nor conclusions of the FBI. It is the property of the FBI and is loaned to your agency; it and its contents are not to be distributed outside your agency.

23

NY 9-7749

Clothing: Wearing a dark colored short jacket and brown pants.

[   ] explained that [   ] has been employed by The Dakota for approximately eleven years. He stated further that [   ] has never been the cause of any trouble in the building and is considered a reliable employee.   b6 b7C

[   ] furnished a complete listing of the employees of The Dakota.   b6 b7C

2

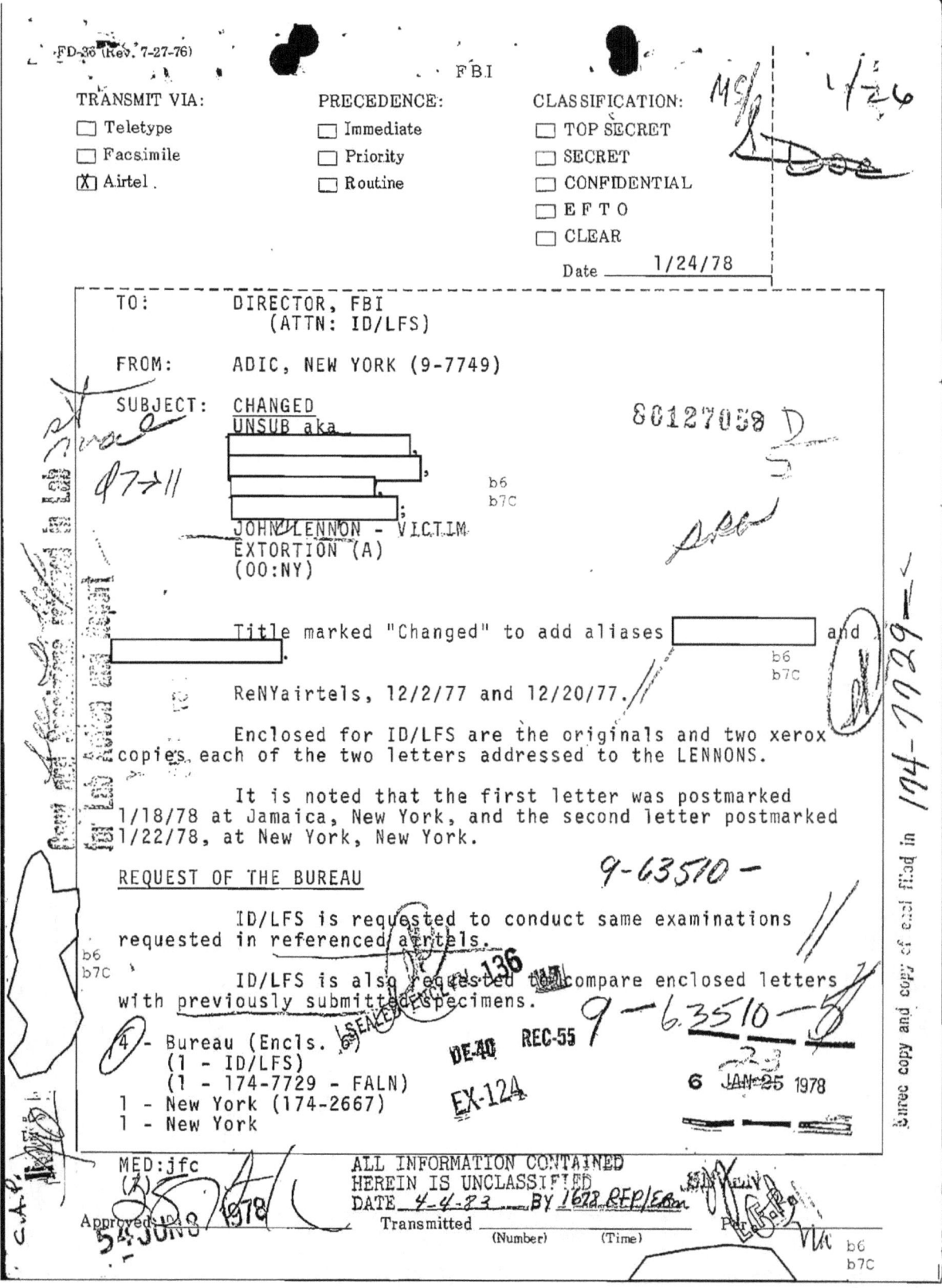

FD-36 (Rev. 7-27-76)

FBI

TRANSMIT VIA:
- [ ] Teletype
- [ ] Facsimile
- [X] Airtel

PRECEDENCE:
- [ ] Immediate
- [ ] Priority
- [ ] Routine

CLASSIFICATION:
- [ ] TOP SECRET
- [ ] SECRET
- [ ] CONFIDENTIAL
- [ ] EFTO
- [ ] CLEAR

Date 1/24/78

TO: DIRECTOR, FBI
(ATTN: ID/LFS)

FROM: ADIC, NEW YORK (9-7749)

SUBJECT: CHANGED
UNSUB aka
                                    b6
                                    b7C

JOHN LENNON - VICTIM
EXTORTION (A)
(OO:NY)

Title marked "Changed" to add aliases ⬚ and ⬚
  b6
  b7C

ReNYairtels, 12/2/77 and 12/20/77.

Enclosed for ID/LFS are the originals and two xerox copies each of the two letters addressed to the LENNONS.

It is noted that the first letter was postmarked 1/18/78 at Jamaica, New York, and the second letter postmarked 1/22/78, at New York, New York.

REQUEST OF THE BUREAU

ID/LFS is requested to conduct same examinations requested in referenced airtels.

ID/LFS is also requested to compare enclosed letters with previously submitted specimens.

4 - Bureau (Encls. 6)
  (1 - ID/LFS)
  (1 - 174-7729 - FALN)
1 - New York (174-2667)
1 - New York

MED:jfc
(7)

ALL INFORMATION CONTAINED
HEREIN IS UNCLASSIFIED
DATE 4-4-83 BY 1672 RFP/sBm

Approved _____ Transmitted _____ Per _____
                          (Number) (Time)

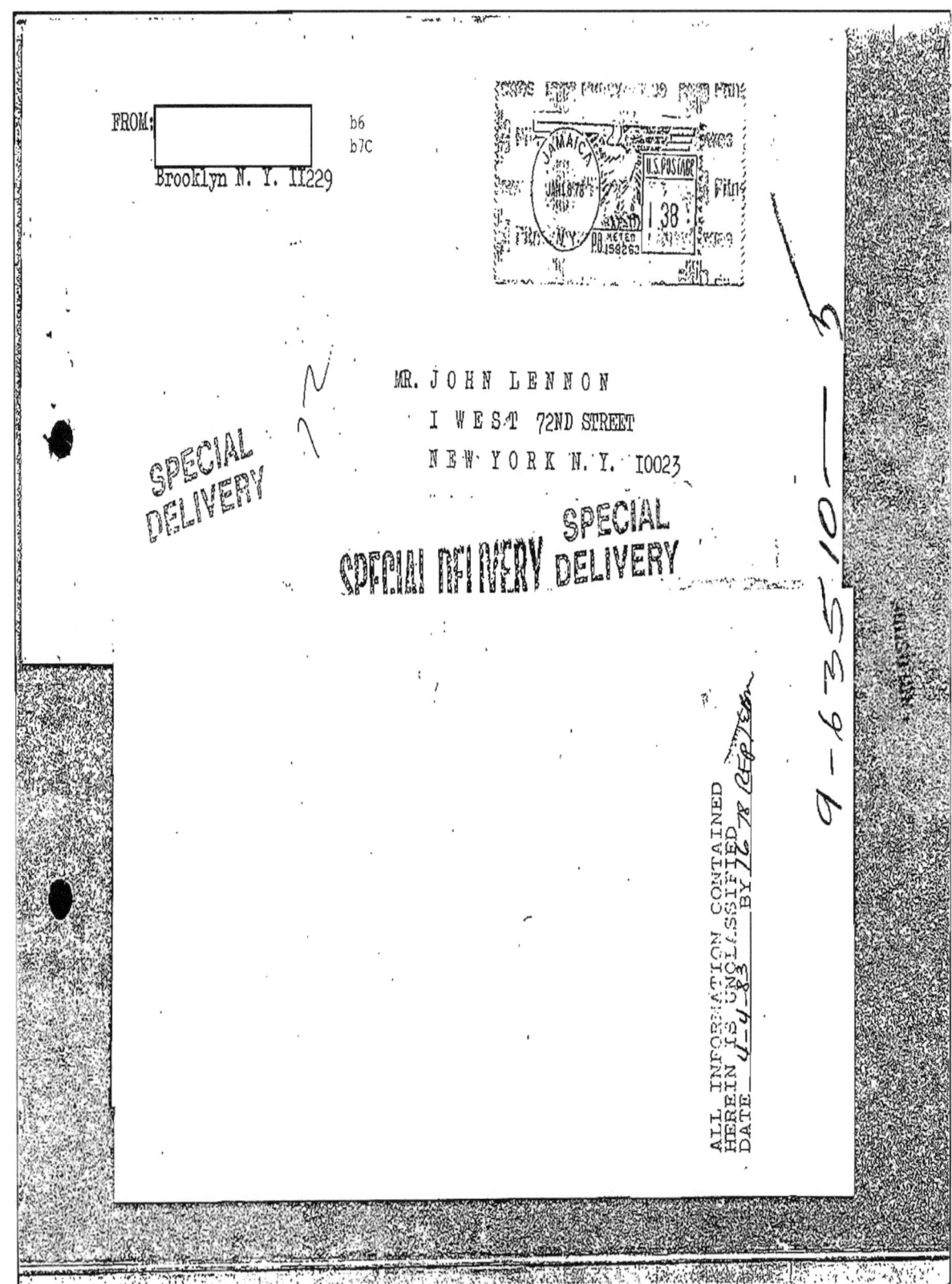

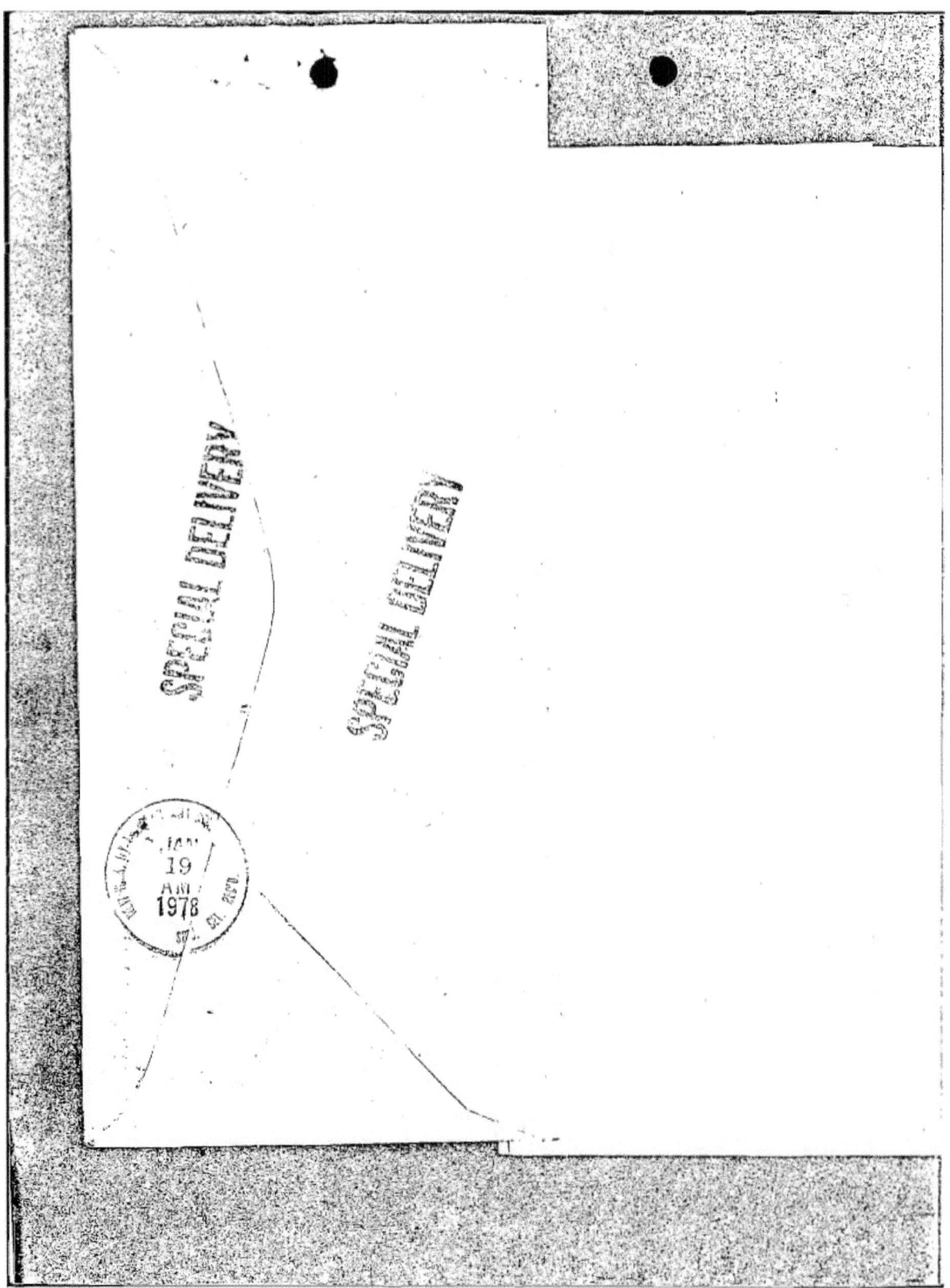

JAN 19/ 1978

MR. JOHN LENNON
         Here is the result of our meting and the termination of your case. Also the result of our investigation in police ambush waiting for us.
         But before that, we like to explain something more about us. We are a troop with 257 mans, and 97 per cent oh our mans they are worker's for many diferent trade. The five million that we need, is for to be invest for our security and the interest from it, is for to be use in pay off, to get informations and to be use in any expense that we always have in our movement. Per example, our operation on you, it cost almost nine thousand dollar's, we can't explain how because it is part of our security. If you think we are play it stupid, you are wrong. We know we are sonofvabish, or anything the worst you like to say. But we are Terrorist's fighting for what we believe to be better tomorrow. But to fight it, we need money and to get money, we most steal it, and to steal it, it may bring a conflict blood & death. But we try the most carefully to prevent it, and we try to do it in the better way.
One week before Christmas, we collect IIO thousand, from a man across the street where you live Majestic building, we ask him for IOOG ransom but he send a package with IIOG, and one simple letter with this word's? (We are sad of this demand, money is not important to mim I only have one life to live, my family is the most important thing I have, but in the same hand we are glad that you mention it before you do it. I'm send up IOG more for please stay away from my family. The money I'm sending, is not exactly in order is you demand but you can use it without fear, you can have my trust worthy nor even my wife knows about this threat. atc. atc.)
Not long ago, we threat one very rich man for IOOG. He send to us the package and when we open it, it was fill with pieces of news paper's and one letter with this word's.(Don't make me laugh because I dont like comical, if you need money you better find a job and work for it. seven day's late we call him up after we send second letter. he's wife answer the call and she said? I know all about and I'm very glad you call, I'm sorry what happen but my husband is taking it is a joke, plus he is a very sick man he suffer from heart condition. I don't want nothing happen to my grand child or to my family, I will give you the money but please give me time to prepare it, please call me up again in one month or so.) We have other man ransom for the same amount, and when we recive the package there was only 30G and a letter with this words. (This is all cash I have, I have about 500G more but it is in stocks, and my family they are living with the interest of it. New York City is fill up with so many millionnaires and why me etc etc.) We put an investigation on it, and we find out that man tell us the true. we send back the 30G to him, with our apology because we misstook him as rich man. we dont want money from the poor or middle class people.

Know let's get the point of our investigation.
All we get was this; On that time, was some police action on the Dakota Office, it was something in connection with John Lennon, something about a threat and kidnap. There was a police woman on the front, and on the next room was more police agents, waiting for a person that was supposed to come pickup a package with money, and thats all I know said the man.

                              Continue on next page
                                   9-63510-5

Mr. Lennon, we don't care more or less to Know the completely story of what happen on that day. We only like to know is this; there was or wasn't an ambush for us. So Mr. Jhon, this is unbelievable you a young and rich man with a great future ahead, and for 100G that it not make you much rich or poor, you jeopardize your family and you self.
Mr. Lennon we Know you are all confused, we Know your answer; your answer is this, why I have to give 100G to this sonofvabich, when I ever don't know who they are, why me etc etc. Our answer is this, we know all about of what is fair and what is unfair, we know that you are not a bad. But we are in underworld operation, we are out of law and we select you know more than never for the big deal, if you do not agree with our reasonable demand. We like to tell you, that we had in mind two more people for ransom in the same building of the Dakota, but because of you we call it off...   So far you are the first one who try a trap for us.
Mr. Jhon, what happen to you if we wasn't in good operation, and one or two of our man fall into police ambush, how you get out of it. You dont know yet how far a man can go, and how fast a man can die.
Mr. Jhon, any one of our man in duty, they are arm with machine gun's, grenad's etc etc. But we dont struggle with police because it don't bring profit to us, we are very very careful to stay away when police is on. We only use our arm in case we be into an ambush, So far we are holding nothing from you. but second our plan, some day you will wish no police involve because you will know what happen.
In the first letter we send to you, we mention very clear that we try it slowly, without kidnap, no big ransom, without blood or distress. our english written is poor, but we think is good enough for you understand. Know lets talk about of our meting. We was suppose to breakup our deal, and put it in silence until someday our revenge be sound exactly we promised. But some objection's of pity from some of our member's, they bring up some of your life story, that you one time you was poor. And honest you become famous and very rich from it. We all agree try to deal for second time, also reduce the ransom from 100G to 60G. If you agree with our new demand we like to have it in follow way... 30G in bill's of one hundred's and 30G in fift's. Put it in a strong package, and then replace the package inside of an shoppingbag, and write on _ To be pickup by Bloomingdle's store, send it down to the Dakota basement to be put in the package room. We find out the Dakota have the package room down in the basement. It most be there on wednesday, January 25, and it most remain there in the period of seven day's and 24 hour's a day. On Feb. 2 if it remain there, it can be return to you and we let you know why. No indemnification or signature should not be ask for the pickup, and don't worry about the package it will come to us, after that we will let you know when we have it, and then you and your family can go free we will not disturb you again. But if you do not agree with our reasonable demand, it is so simply is this; Don't send nothing down, and again do what ever you have in mind. If you have any doubt about us, you will meet us some day in ski mask, and it probably will cost you one to 1½ million dollars cash or the lost of you or some one you love. We believe you Know how to drive a car, but if [____] don't know we advice her to start taking her license because she maybe need to drive 200 mills, and at this time we don't want to see any police movement, if we see it you or [____] will never meet the end of the road, after that we do what we have to do and then we go back home. We hop you understand us at this time.

THANK YOU

T. F. P. R. I. M.

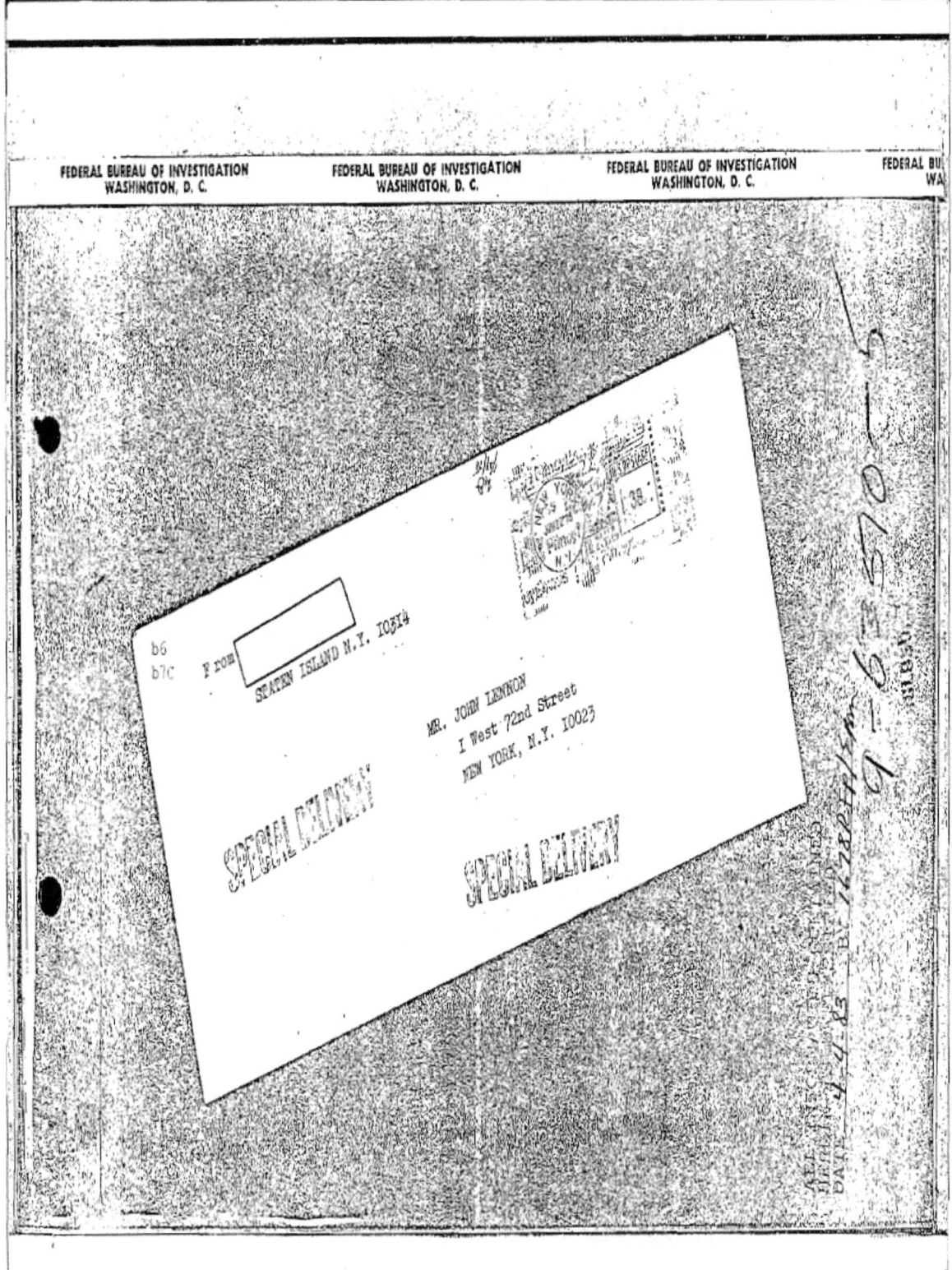

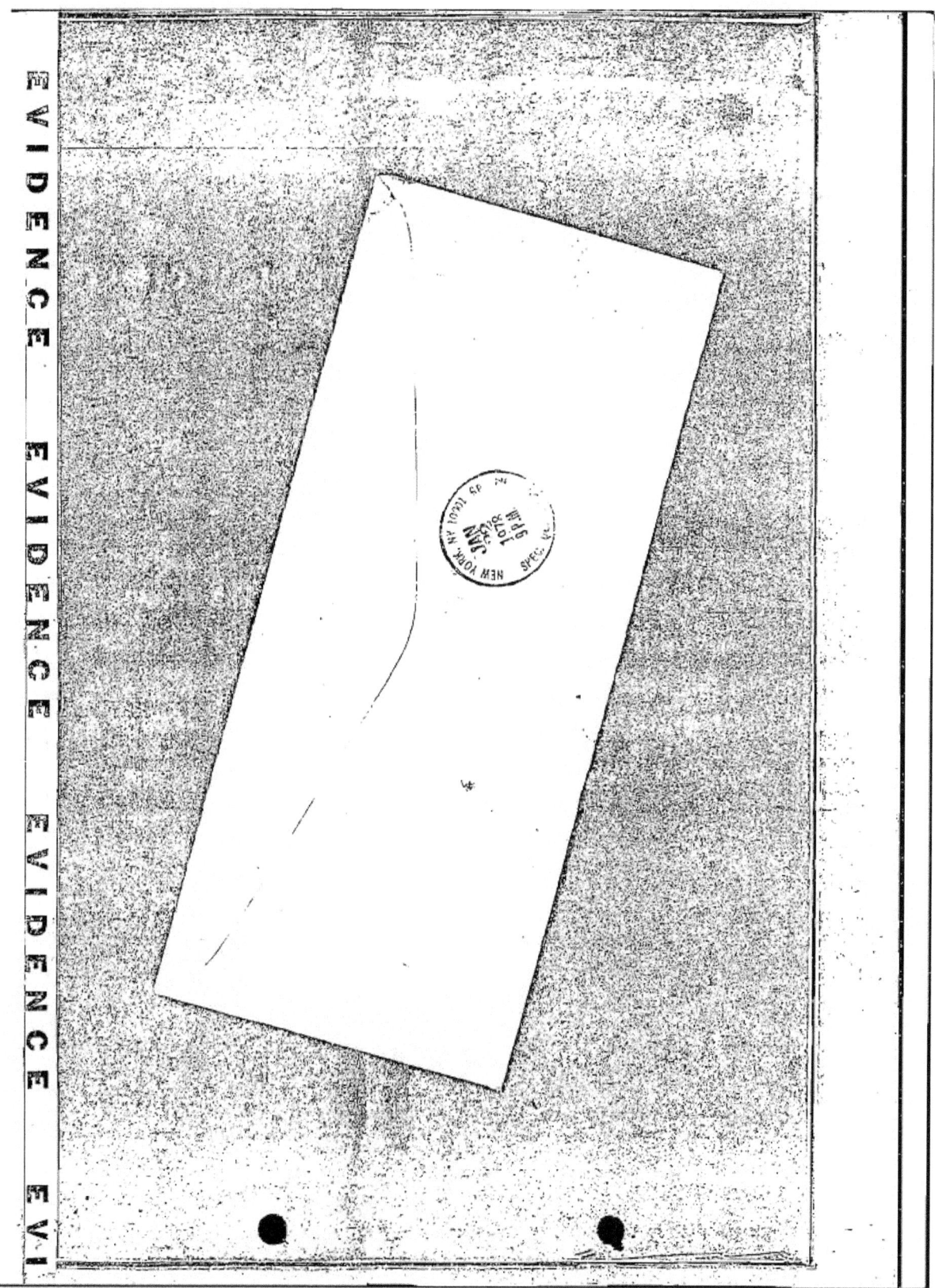

January, 22/ 1978

T. F. P. R. I. M.

Mr. LENNON

Something very important just come up, that we most postponed the date of the pickup your delivery.
At the present time we don't know what you have in mind, but if you intent to give us the money we demand, here is the new date. Please send the shoppingbag with the money down, to be put in the package room on thursday february, 2 it most remain there in the period of seven day's, and 24 hour's a day.
On Feb. 9 if it remain there, it can be return to you and we let you know why.
Also foget about the name of bloomingdale's store, and get this new one. To be pickup by Lorraine Fashions Store.

All other's intruction is effective

T.F.P.R.I.M.

ALL INFORMATION CONTAINED
HEREIN IS UNCLASSIFIED
DATE 4-4-83 BY 1678 RFP/EBm

9-63510-5

FD-302 (REV. 11-27-70)

FEDERAL BUREAU OF INVESTIGATION

Date of transcription: 1/25/78

[redacted] The Dakota, 1 West 72nd Street, furnished the following information:

He noticed a suspicious person in the vicinity of The Dakota during the past two weeks. He stated that on January 12, 1978, an unknown male driving a green Chevrolet, New York license [redacted], was parked immediately in front of The Dakota. This man was there from roughly 4:30 or 5:00 p.m. until 2:00 a.m. the following morning. [redacted], who had been in and out of the building during that period of time, asked the man what he was waiting for. The individual answered that he was waiting for JOHN LENNON. The man explained that he was hoping to get a picture of [redacted]. He added that the picture was for his wife. When asked if the picture was of [redacted], the man answered no, but of [redacted] who was visiting from England.

[redacted] noticed that the individual had some casual conversation with [redacted].

One week later on January 19, 1978, [redacted] noticed the same individual at the front of the building and again in conversation with [redacted]. [redacted] thought that the unknown male's car was parked in the alleyway and asked [redacted] about this. [redacted] stated that it was not this man's car, but a doctor who was visiting one of the resident's of The Dakota.

[redacted] described the unknown individual as follows:

Race	White
Sex	Male
Age	In his 20's
Height	5'5" or 5'6"
Weight	135 to 140 pounds
Build	Slim
Complexion	Dark

Interviewed on: 1/24/78 at New York, New York   File # NY 9-7749-17

by SA [redacted] /cmg   Date dictated: 1/24/78

This document contains neither recommendations nor conclusions of the FBI. It is the property of the FBI and is loaned to your agency; it and its contents are not to be distributed outside your agency.

25

FD-302 (REV. 11-27-70)

FEDERAL BUREAU OF INVESTIGATION

Date of transcription 1/26/78

New York City (NYC), furnished the following information:

On January 23, 1978, [redacted], JOHN LENNON, received another letter similar to those three earlier letters. [redacted] made available the original letter and envelope.

The envelope disclosed a postmark of January 22, 1978, at New York, New York (NY), and a return address of [redacted], [redacted], Staten Island, NY 10314. This letter, as with the previous three, was addressed to Mr. JOHN LENNON and marked special delivery.

Interviewed on 1/24/78	at New York, New York	File #	NY 9-7749-20
by SA [redacted] /dam		Date dictated	1/24/78

This document contains neither recommendations nor conclusions of the FBI. It is the property of the FBI and is loaned to your agency; it and its contents are not to be distributed outside your agency.

Laboratory Transmittal Form
7-7-72

FBI LABORATORY
FEDERAL BUREAU OF INVESTIGATION
WASHINGTON, D.C. 20535

To: ADIC, New York (9-7749)   January 27, 1978

From: Director, FBI

Re: UNSUB, aka
[redacted], [redacted];
JOHN LENNON - VICTIM;
EXTORTION (A)
OO: New York

FBI FILE NO. 9-63510
LAB. NO. 71206187 D MS
71227019 D MS
b6
b7C

Examination requested by: New York

Reference: Airtels dated December 2, 1977 and December 20, 1977

Examination requested: Document - Fingerprint

Remarks:

ST-135

REC-30 9-63510-4

MAILED 11
JAN 27 1978
FBI

DO NOT INCLUDE ADMINISTRATIVE PAGE(S) INFORMATION IN INVESTIGATIVE REPORT

22 JAN 27 1978

Enclosures (2) (2 Lab report)
JEL:slg (4)

ALL INFORMATION CONTAINED HEREIN IS UNCLASSIFIED
DATE 4-4-83 BY 1678 RFP/csn

ENC. BEHIND FILE

MAY 8 1978

ADMINISTRATIVE PAGE
MAIL ROOM ☑ TELETYPE UNIT ☐

b6
b7C

REPORT of the FBI LABORATORY

FEDERAL BUREAU OF INVESTIGATION
WASHINGTON, D. C. 20535

To: ADIC, New York (9-7749)　　　　　　January 27, 1978

FBI FILE NO. 9-63510—

Re: UNSUB, aka ▓▓▓▓▓▓▓, ▓▓▓▓▓▓▓;　　LAB. NO. 71206187 D MS
　　JOHN LENNON - VICTIM;　　　　　b6　　　　71227019 D MS
　　EXTORTION (A)　　　　　　　　　　b7C

Specimens received　December 5, 1977, under cover of communication dated December 2, 1977 (71206187 D MS):

　　Q1　Envelope postmarked "JAMAICA, NY 114 NOV 29 PM 1977," bearing the typewritten address "MR. JOHN LENNON I WEST 72nd STREET NEW YORK, N.Y. 10023"

　　Q2　First page of accompanying three-page typewritten letter dated 11/29/77, beginning "MR & MRS. JOHN LENNON This letter is not a joking..."

　　Q3　Second page of three-page typewritten letter beginning "Remember the people who is..."

　　Q4　Third page of three-page typewritten letter beginning "Here is some meaning reference's..."

　　ALSO SUBMITTED:

　　　　Blank sheet of paper

Page 1　　　　　　　　　　　　　　　　　　　　　　　　(over)

Specimens received December 22, 1977, under cover of communication dated December 20, 1977 (71227019 D MS):

- Q5 Envelope postmarked "New York-----G.P.O. (i.m.) 1977 Dec 18 PM" bearing typewritten address "Mr. & Mrs. John Lennon 1 West 72nd Street, New York, N.Y. 10023"

- Q6 Accompanying one-page typewritten letter dated 12/19/77, beginning "Mr. & Mrs. John Lennon You didn't pay attention..."

ALSO SUBMITTED:

Blank sheet of paper

Result of examination:

Q1 through Q6 were compared with specimens in the Anonymous Letter File, but no identification was effected. Representative photographs will be added to the file for future reference.

The typewriting on Q1 through Q6 is a style of type used on Olympia typewriters which are manufactured in West Germany. Although the typewriting on Q1 through Q6 lacks sufficient identifiable characteristics to permit a definite determination whether the same typewriter was used to prepare all those specimens, a limited number of characteristics in common were noted.

It was determined that the typewriting on Q1 through Q6 was not prepared by the use of any of the typewriters used to prepare typewritten communiques previously submitted to the Laboratory in the various FALN bombing matters.

The examinations of the submitted envelopes and sheets of paper failed to reveal any watermarks, indented writings of significance, or other significant features which might be of assistance in determining the immediate source of those items.

Q1 through Q6 were photographed. The submitted specimens will be returned to New York with the results of the requested latent fingerprint examinations.

ADIC, New York (9-7749)(P)(21) Airtel 12/2/77

Envelope + 3 page letter, Q1 thru Q4

Sheet of paper, A5

Unsub aka [redacted]

John Lennon - Victim,
Extortion

Photos of lat. prts.
2 lifts (2 lifts of chin
John Lennon)

9-63510

ALL INFORMATION CONTAINED
HEREIN IS UNCLASSIFIED
DATE 4-5-83 BY 1628 RHP/cbm

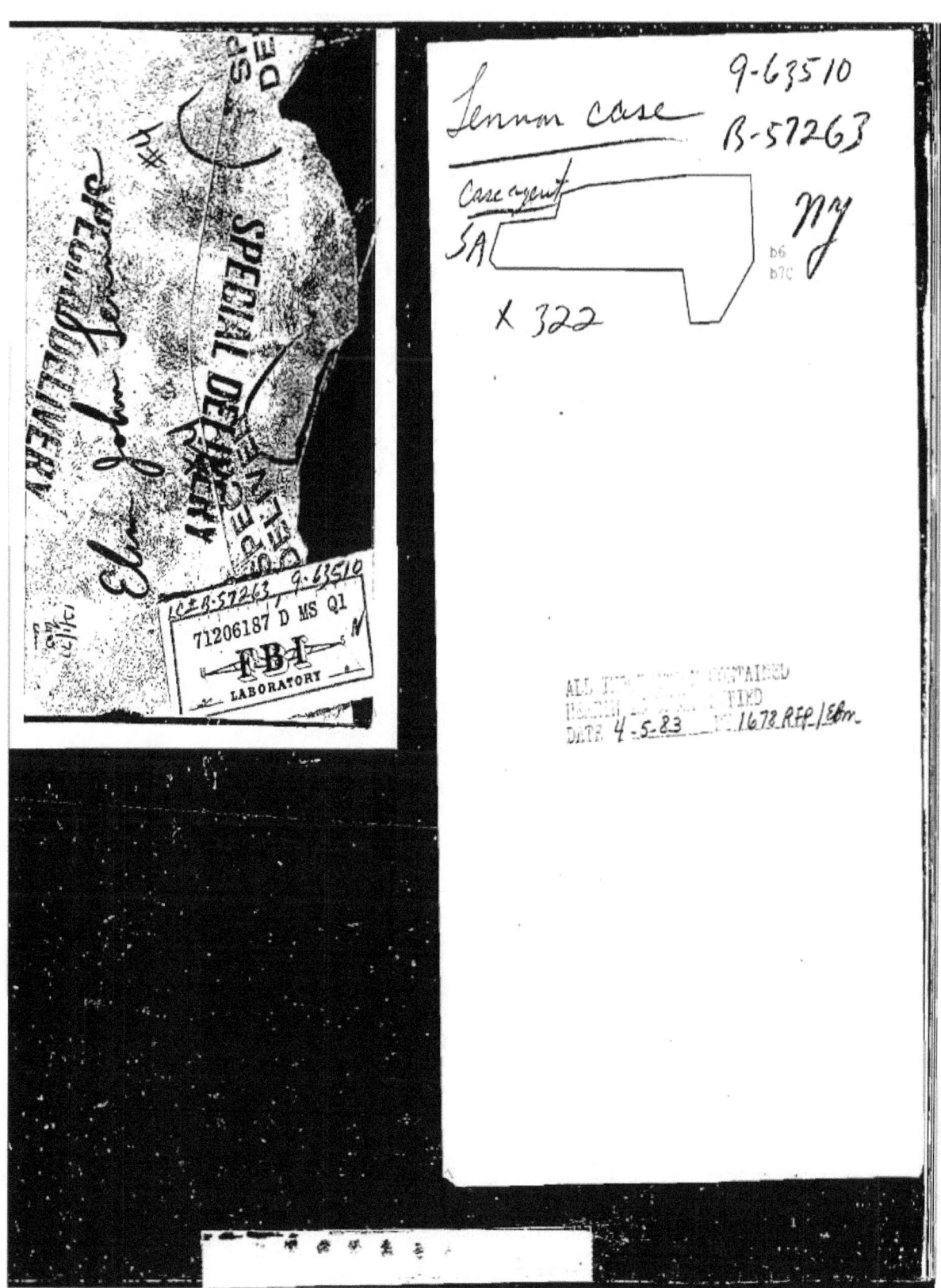

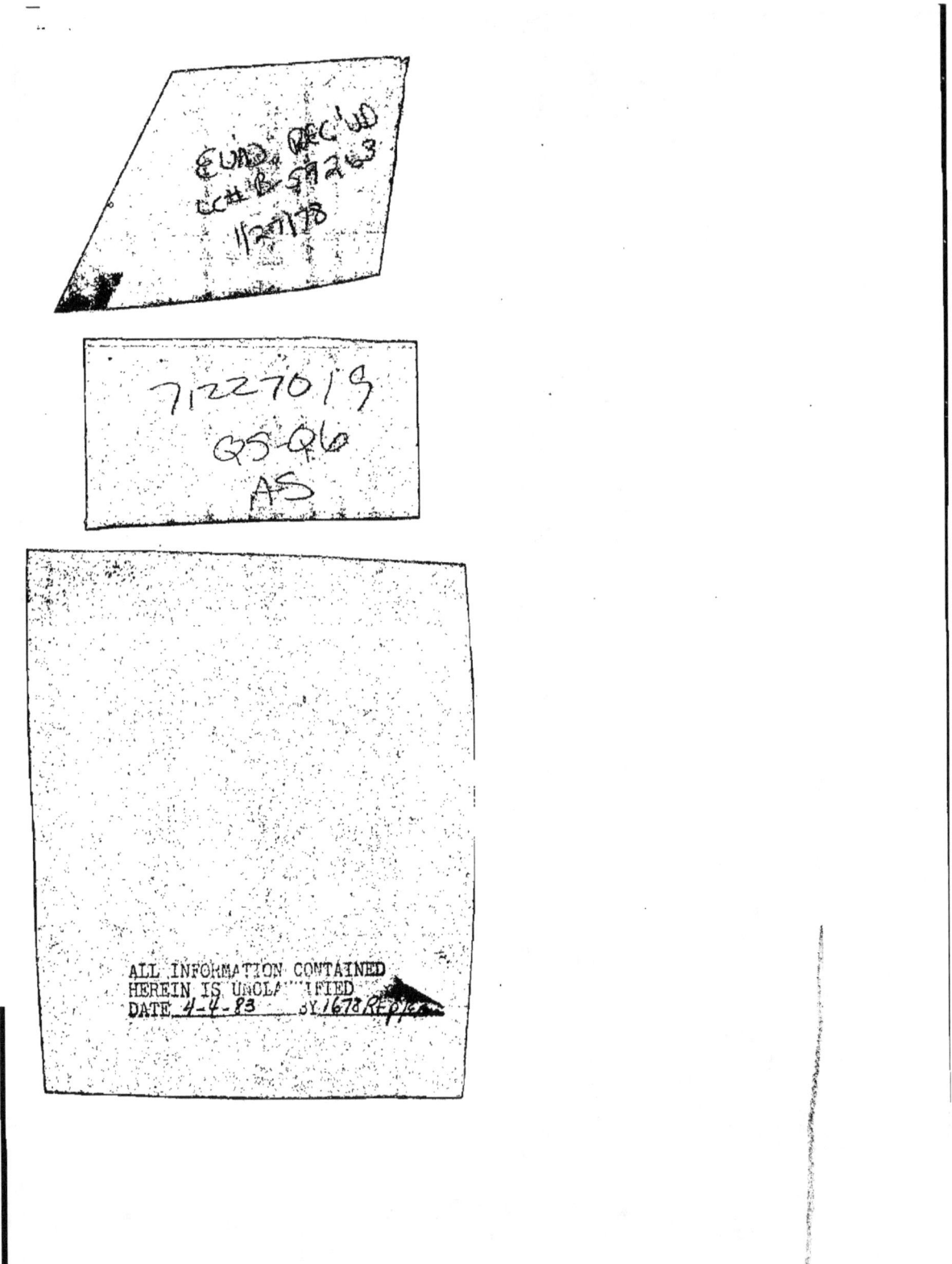

RECORDED
7-2 12/28/77
bgh

NO LAB FILE

LATENT JAN 24

FEDERAL BUREAU OF INVESTIGATION
UNITED STATES DEPARTMENT OF JUSTICE

Laboratory Work Sheet

To: ADIC, New York (9-new)

Re: UNSUB aka
JOHN LENNON - VICTIM
EXTORTION (A)
(OO: New York)

FBI FILE NO. 9-63510-4
LAB. NO. 71206187 D MS
71227019 D MS
YOUR NO.

Examination by:

1/24/78
(See reverse)

Examination requested by: New York

Reference: Airtel dated December 2, 1977

Examination requested: Document - Fingerprint

Specimens received: December 5, 1977

Q1   Envelope postmarked "JAMAICA, NY 114 NOV 29 PM 1977," bearing the typewritten address "MR. JOHN LENNON 1 WEST 72 nd STREET NEW YORK, N.Y. 10023"

Q2   First page of accompanying three-page typewritten letter dated 11/29/77, beginning "MR & MRS. JOHN LENNON This letter is not a joking. . ."

Q3   Second page of three-page typewritten letter beginning "Remember the people who is . . ."

Q4   Third page of three-page typewritten letter beginning "Here is some meaning reference's. . ."

ALSO SUBMITTED:

Blank sheet of paper

ALL INFORMATION CONTAINED
HEREIN IS UNCLASSIFIED
DATE 4-4-83 BY

Q1 white envelope

1.75±
4.1± x .0045"
9.4±

most
shift defect all UC lts ↑

Q2-Q4, AS
 white paper 8.5±" x 11±" x .0025"
 No watermarks / Indented writing
  Q1-Q4 AS

───────────────────────────

- Q1→Q6 NI, ALF added
- The Q1→Q6 is a style of type used on Olympia tw's which are mfd in W. Germany. Although the Q1→Q6 insuff chars for def diten, ltd chars in common were noted.
- Det tw Q1→Q6 not typed by any tw's used to prep commune. given subm in FALN bomb'g in others.
- Exam'd Env + sheets of paper now m's; indent writing, etc.
- P/ret w/ LFP.

7-2 RECORDED
1-4-78
BAU*

LATENTS

FEDERAL BUREAU OF INVESTIGATION
UNITED STATES DEPARTMENT OF JUSTICE

Laboratory Work Sheet

To: ADIC, NEW YORK (9-7749)

FBI FILE NO. 9-63510-4

LAB. NO. 71227019 D MS

Re: ~~CHANGED~~
UNSUB, aka
_____ b6 b7C

JOHN LENNON - VICTIM;
EXTORTION (A)
OO: New York

YOUR NO.

Examination by: [ ] b6 b7C

(See D-71206187 DMS)

Examination requested by: New York

Reference: Airtel dated December 20, 1977

Examination requested: Document - Fingerprint

Specimens received: December 22, 1977

Q5 Envelope postmarked "New York---G.P.O. (i.m.) 1977 Dec 18 PM" bearing typewritten address "Mr. & Mrs. John Lennon 1 West 72nd Street, New York, N.Y. 10023"

Q6 Accompanying one-page typewritten letter dated 12-19-77, beginning "Mr. & Mrs. John Lennon You didn't pay attention..."

Also Submitted:

Blank sheet of paper.

ALL INFORMATION CONTAINED
HEREIN IS UNCLASSIFIED
DATE 4-4-83 BY 1678 RFp/ebm

Q5 white envelope similar in observable characteristics to Q1

Q6 white paper
A5 similar in observ. charac. to Q2-Q4.

No water marks/indented writing Q5-Q6, A5

FD-302 (REV. 11-27-70)

FEDERAL BUREAU OF INVESTIGATION

Date of transcription 1/30/78

[____], United States Post Office, Station E, 98-34 Jamaica Avenue, Queens, New York, was interviewed at the New York Office (NYO) of the Federal Bureau of Investigation (FBI), 201 East 69th Street, New York, New York.

[____] advised that at approximately 2:00 pm in the later part of December, 1977, an identified white male mailed a letter at his station. This same individual had been into the post office on a previous occasion, and he had recalled that this individual had mailed a letter to Mr. JOHN LENNON. Between the first and second occasions he had been approached by Special Agents (SAS) of the FBI. On the second occasion, he asked the unknown white male if JOHN LENNON was the same JOHN LENNON with the Beatles, and the unidentified male replied, "Yes, that's him." During the time that this individual was at his window, he got change out of his pocket and upon leaving the post office, walked to the right of the main entrance down Jamaica Avenue.

[____] provided the following description of the unknown subject (unsub):

Race	White
Sex	Male
Age	40 - 45 years
Height	5 feet 3 inches to 5 feet 5 inches
Complexion	Dark
Build	Solid; medium
Eyes	Unobserved
Hair	Black
Shape of Head	Oval
Eyebrows	Thick, dark
Shape of Nose	Average
Shape of Mouth	Both lips thick
Shape of Chin	Average
Cheek and Cheek Bone	Average
Facial Lines	None
Moustache	None

Interviewed on 1/25/78 at New York, New York   File # NY 9-7749

by SA [____] /rac   Date dictated 1/30/78

This document contains neither recommendations nor conclusions of the FBI. It is the property of the FBI and is loaned to your agency; it and its contents are not to be distributed outside your agency.

NY 9-7749
2

    Beard   None
    Pock Marks   None
    Skin Irregularities   None
    Clothing   3/4 length dark blue overcoat, warn; plaid shirt, red and blue squares, open at neck; fur hat, black; sunglasses, metal framed, dark grey lenses
    Remarks   No noticeable accent; No gloves

[REDACTED] viewed the Facial Identification Catalog of the FBI and selected samples of photographs which represent a likeness to the features of the unsub. Of the photographs, a composite drawing was made by SA [REDACTED] which [REDACTED] stated resembled the unsub.

b6
b7C

图 28

FD-302 (Rev. 11-27-70)

FEDERAL BUREAU OF INVESTIGATION

Date of transcription ___1/31/78___

[REDACTED], The Dakota, 1 West 72nd Street, viewed a composite drawing of the individual who had been mailing the threatening letters to JOHN LENNON, and stated that the individual is unknown to him. [REDACTED] stated that the drawing did not resemble the individual who had been standing outside of The Dakota the previous two Thursdays and that that latter individual was much younger.

b6
b7C

Interviewed on __1/26/78__ at __New York, New York__ File # __NY 9-7749-24__

by __SA [REDACTED]__ /1mm   b6 b7C   Date dictated __1/30/78__

This document contains neither recommendations nor conclusions of the FBI. It is the property of the FBI and is loaned to your agency; it and its contents are not to be distributed outside your agency.

FD-302 (Rev. 11-27-70)

FEDERAL BUREAU OF INVESTIGATION

Date of transcription 1/31/78

JOHN LENNON [   ], Apartment 72, 1 West 72nd Street, viewed the composite drawing of the individual believed to be mailing the threatening letters and stated that the individual was unknown to them.

b6
b7C

Interviewed on 1/27/78 at New York, New York File # NY 9-7749-23

by SA [   ] /1mm b6 b7C Date dictated 1/30/78

This document contains neither recommendations nor conclusions of the FBI. It is the property of the FBI and is loaned to your agency; it and its contents are not to be distributed outside your agency.

1-336 (Rev. 6-17-76)

FEDERAL BUREAU OF INVESTIGATION
Washington, D.C. 20537

REPORT
of the
IDENTIFICATION DIVISION
LATENT FINGERPRINT SECTION

YOUR FILE NO. 9-7749 (P) (21)
FBI FILE NO. 9-63510
LATENT CASE NO. B-57263

February 2, 1978

TO: ADIC, New York

RE: UNSUB, AKA
                      b6
                      b7C
JOHN LENNON - VICTIM
EXTORTION

ALL INFORMATION CONTAINED
HEREIN IS UNCLASSIFIED
DATE 4-4-83 BY 1678 RFP/EBM

REFERENCE: Airtels 12-2-77 and 12-20-77 and telephone call 1-30-78
EXAMINATION REQUESTED BY: New York
SPECIMENS: Envelope, Q1, and accompanying three-page letter, Q2, Q3 and Q4
Envelope, Q5, and accompanying one-page letter, Q6
Two blank sheets of paper

This report supplements and confirms Bucal 1-31-78.

The Q specimens are described in a separate Laboratory report.

The specimens were examined and two latent fingerprints of value were developed on an envelope postmarked "JAMAICA, NY 114 NOV 29 PM 1977," Q1.

(Continued on next page)

Enc. (8)

ACTING ASSISTANT DIRECTOR
IDENTIFICATION DIVISION

THIS REPORT IS FURNISHED FOR OFFICIAL USE ONLY

ADIC, New York   February 2, 1978

   The two latent fingerprints on Q1 have been identified as finger impressions of John Lennon, USINS #A17597321, who was named for elimination purposes.

   The specimens are enclosed.

Page 2
LC #B-57263

7-2 RECORDED
1-4-78
baw

LATENTS

FEDERAL BUREAU OF INVESTIGATION
UNITED STATES DEPARTMENT OF JUSTICE

Laboratory Work Sheet

Recorded 1/27/78 8:30 a.m. cjw   Received 1/27/78

To: ADIC, NEW YORK (9-7749) (P) (21)

FBI FILE NO. 9-63510-

LAB. NO. 71227019 D MS

Re: ~~CHANGED~~
UNSUB, aka   b6
                          b7C

YOUR NO.
LC #B-57263

Examination by: b6
                          b7C

JOHN LENNON – VICTIM
EXTORTION ~~(A)~~

00: New York

Examination requested by: New York

Noted by:

Reference: Airtel dated December 20, 1977

Examination requested: Document – Fingerprint

Specimens received: December 22, 1977

Q5 Envelope postmarked "New York—G.P.O. (i.m.) 1977 Dec 18 PM" bearing typewritten address "Mr. & Mrs. John Lennon 1 West 72nd Street, New York, N.Y. 10023"

Q6 Accompanying one-page typewritten letter dated 12-19-77, beginning "Mr. & Mrs. John Lennon You didn't pay attention..."

Also Submitted:

ALL INFORMATION CONTAINED
HEREIN IS UNCLASSIFIED
DATE 4-4-83 BY /628 RFP/esm

Blank sheet of paper.

Specs proc min 1/27 JCS

No lat pts of val on specs (I, min sp)
Specs enclosed
Lab report ref

Ansed
2-2-78
JCS-mlk

Examination Completed 2:30 PM 1/31/78 Dictated 1/31/78

Enc (3)
               Time   Date   Date

RECORDED
7-2 12/28/77
bgl

NO LAB FILE
LATENT

FEDERAL BUREAU OF INVESTIGATION
UNITED STATES DEPARTMENT OF JUSTICE

Laboratory Work Sheet

Recorded 1/27/78 8:40 a.m. cjw   Received 1/27/78

To: ADIC, New York ( ) (P) (#21)

Re: UNSUB aka   b6
    [redacted]   b7C
    JOHN LENNON - VICTIM
    EXTORTION (A)

FBI FILE NO. 9-63510-6
LAB. NO.   71206187 D MS
YOUR NO.
LC #B-57263
Examination by: [redacted]

Examination requested by: New York   Noted by: [redacted]   b6 b7C
Reference: Airtel dated December 2, 1977 and telephone call
Examination requested: Document - Fingerprint   from SA [redacted]
Specimens received: December 5, 1977   NY on 1/30/78

Q1   Envelope postmarked "JAMAICA, NY 114 NOV 29 PM 1977," bearing the typewritten address "MR. JOHN LENNON 1 WEST 72 nd STREET NEW YORK, N.Y. 10023"

Q2   First page of accompanying three-page typewritten letter dated 11/29/77, beginning "MR & MRS. JOHN LENNON This letter is not a joking. . ."

Q3   Second page of three-page typewritten letter beginning "Remember the people who is . . ."

Q4   Third page of three-page typewritten letter beginning "Here is some meaning reference's. . ."

ALSO SUBMITTED:

    Blank sheet of paper

Continued on page 2

Examination Completed 2:30 PM   1/31/78   Dictated 1/31/78

ALL INFORMATION CONTAINED   Time   Date   Date   FBI/DOJ
HEREIN IS UNCLASSIFIED
DATE 4-4-83 BY 1678 RFP/EBm

Page 2
LC #B-57263
[redacted] b6 b7C

Names submitted for elimination purposes of:
   JOHN LENNON
   DOB 10/9/40
   USINS #A17597321

   [redacted],
   DOB [redacted]   b6 b7C
   USINS [redacted]

Specs rec'd min 1/27

Names to CJ 1/27

Q1 to photo (min) 1/30

2 lat f'p'ts of val dev min on Q1 (2 f'p'ts f. #4 elim John Lennon)

No additional lat prts of val dev on specs

Specs enclosed

Lab report sep

Enc. (5)

FD-36 (Rev. 7-27-76)

FBI

TRANSMIT VIA:
☐ Teletype
☐ Facsimile
☒ Airtel

PRECEDENCE:
☐ Immediate
☐ Priority
☐ Routine

CLASSIFICATION:
☐ TOP SECRET
☐ SECRET
☐ CONFIDENTIAL
☐ E F T O
☐ CLEAR

Date FEB 8 1978

TO: DIRECTOR, FBI
(ATT: ID/LFS)

FROM: ADIC, NEW YORK (9-7749) (P) (#21)

SUBJECT: UNSUB; aka
[redacted], Etc.;
JOHN LENNON - VICTIM
EXTORTION (A)
(OO:NY)

ReNYairtel 1/24/78.

Enclosed for ID/LFS is the original and two Xerox copies of letter, dated 2/3/78 addressed to LENNON and postmarked 2/3/78, NY, NY.

REQUEST OF THE BUREAU

ID/LFS requested to compare enclosed letter with previously submitted specimens and conduct same examination requested in referenced airtel.

EX-113

ALL INFORMATION CONTAINED
HEREIN IS UNCLASSIFIED
DATE 4-4-83 BY 1678 RFO/EBm

③ - Bureau (Encs. 3)
(1 - ID/LFS)
1 - New York
MED:nc
(5)

Approved: _____ Transmitted _____ Per _____
                          (Number)   (Time)

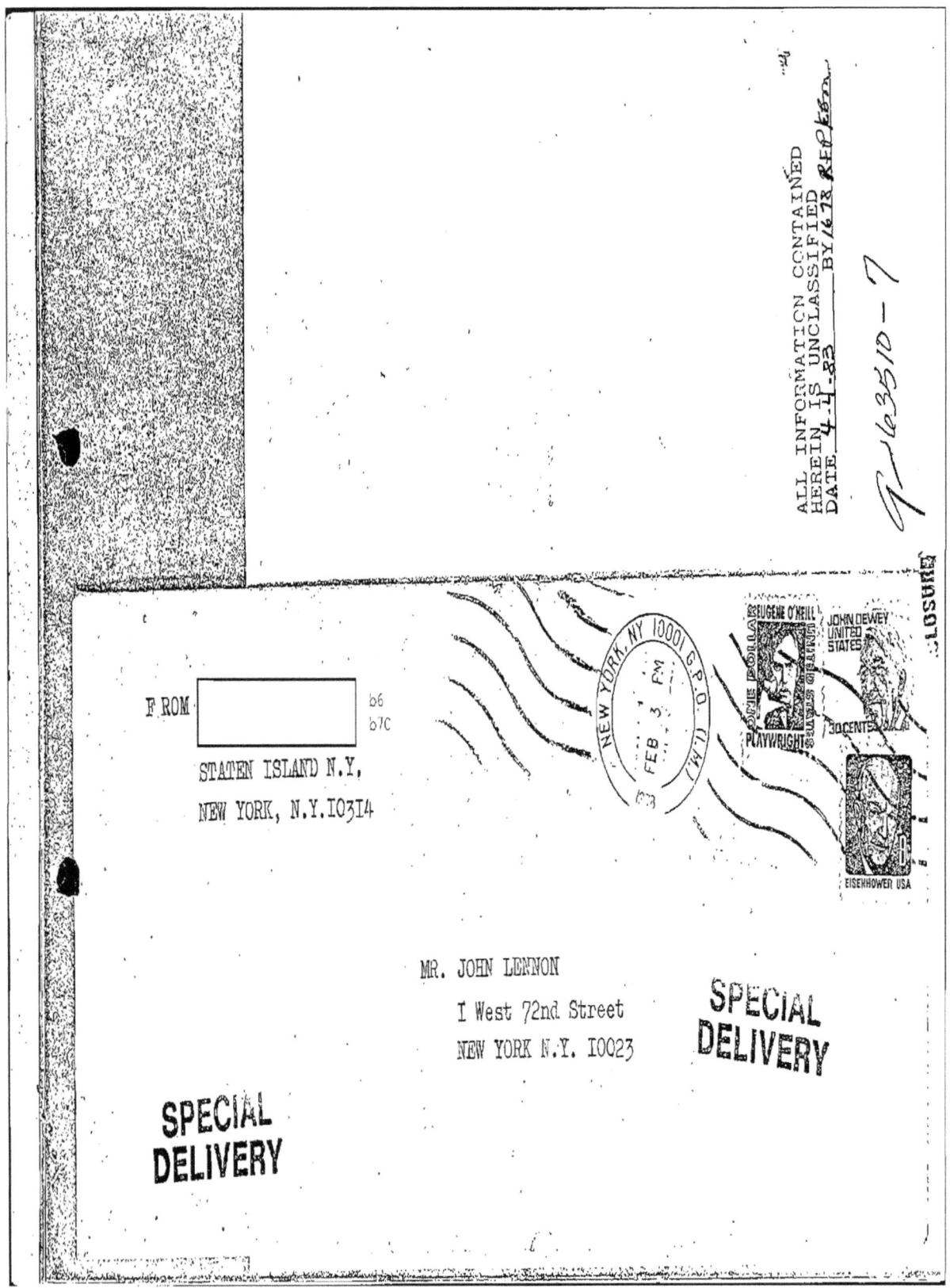

FEB. 3 1978

T. F. P. R. I. M.

Dear John.

    We are very proud of you.

Your magnificent english quality, deserve all
our respect. you are strong with a lot of courage,
people like you we love them. At last you show you
are not chickening. You are just right baby to
take it in hard way.

But in the mean time, we think you shuld call down
to the basement and tell the police to go home OK.

ALL INFORMATION CONTAINED
HEREIN IS UNCLASSIFIED
DATE 4-4-83 BY 1678 RFp/E

ENCLOSURE 9-63510-7

FD-302 (REV. 3-8-77)

FEDERAL BUREAU OF INVESTIGATION

Date of transcription 2/10/78

[redacted] New York, New York (NY), was interviewed [redacted] and voluntarily furnished the following information:

She had been notified by [redacted] at approximately 10:45 PM on February 3, 1978, that there had just been a special delivery letter addressed to JOHN LENNON, delivered at the front desk of the building.

[redacted] notified the Federal Bureau of Investigation (FBI) Agents immediately upon opening it and made the letter and envelope available to SA [redacted].

The letter was postmarked February 3, 1978, NY, NY, and specifically instructed JOHN LENNON to "Tell the police to get out of the basement."

A copy of the letter and envelope is attached.

[redacted] advised that the only three persons who handled the letter were herself, [redacted] and [redacted].

Investigation on 2/9/78 at New York, New York   File # NY 9-NEW -7749-28

by SA [redacted]   Date dictated 2/9/78

This document contains neither recommendations nor conclusions of the FBI. It is the property of the FBI and is loaned to your agency; it and its contents are not to be distributed outside your agency.

FVB:jfc
1

NY 9-7749

A surveillance was instituted in the basement of "The Dakota", One West 72nd Street, New York, New York, at 10:00 a.m., February 2, 1978, by Special Agents of the FBI near the payoff location, which was a desk located in the basement. A shopping bag with the name "Lorraines Fashions - Lennon" was placed in the bottom drawer, right side of desk, at 11:30 a.m., February 2, 1978. Surveillance was continued until 4:00 p.m. on February 6, 1978, and no contact was made by Unsub.

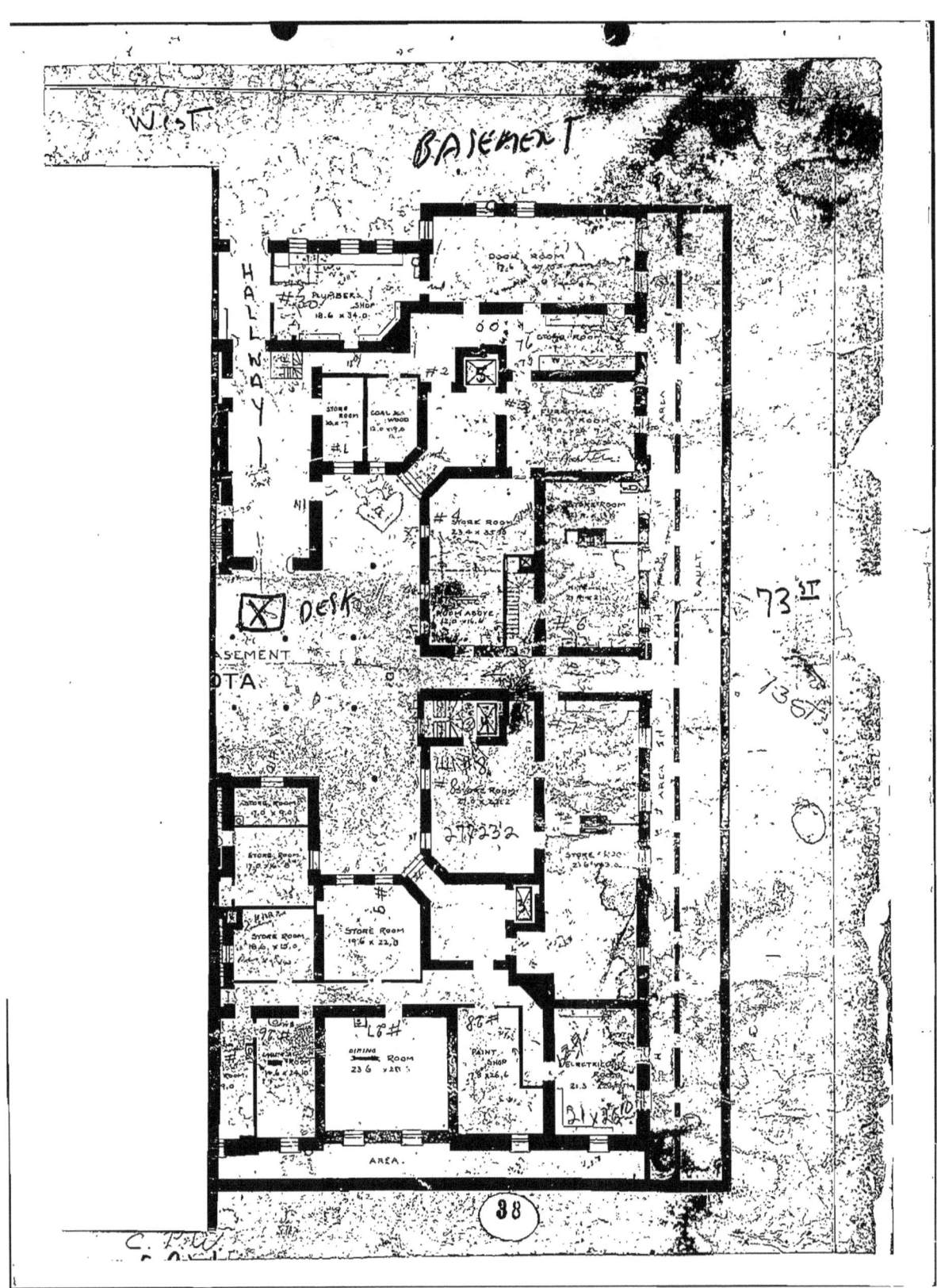

7-13 (Rev. 6/11/77)

FEDERAL BUREAU OF INVESTIGATION

2/22/78, 1977

	TL#		TL#		TL#
Mr. Kelleher	#241	Mr. Avignone	#241	Miss E. Jackson, 3372B	#241
Mr. Herndon	#241	Mr. Ball	#241	Mr. McMichael, 6823	#212
		Mr. Bodziak	#241	Assignment Clerk, 3434	#241
Mr. Kelly	#241	Mr. Buckley	#241	Assembly Locate, 10270	#343
Mr. Silas	#155	Mr. Cross	#152	Assembly Section, 10861	#343
Mr. Strain	#255	Mr. Dewan	#241	Consolidation, 4905	#125
		Mr. Dixon	#241	Reading Room, 6658	#215
Mr. Lilja	#241	Mr. Grimes	#241	Corresp. Review Unit, 6658	#215
		Mr. Hallett	#241	Data Processing, 1344	#153
Mr. Devine	#241	Mr. Harker	#152	L. F. P. S., 10955	#324
Mr. Furgerson	#152	Mr. Hayden	#241	Mail Room, 1B327	#152
Mr. Oberg	#241	Mr. Holmes	#152	Pr. & Space Mgnt., 1B879	#151
Mr. Stangel	#241	Mr. Jones	#241	Payroll, 1901	#153
		Mr. Kanaskie	#241	Photo Operations Unit, 1B903	#151
Mr. Carter	#241	Mr. Koehler	#241	Printing Unit, 1B973	#151
		Mr. Latessa	#241	Property Unit, 6132	#212
Mrs. Fox	#241	Mr. Lile	#241	Records Section	#211
Miss Sabol	#241	Mr. Lind	#152	Technical Section, 7554	#313
		Mr. Mathis	#241	Teletype Unit, 6247	#244
Mrs. Materazzi	#241	Mr. Mearns	#241	Translation Unit, 3920	#155
Miss Novotny	#241	Mr. Mones	#241	Voucher Unit, 1262	#153
Miss Prucnal	#241	Mr. Moreau	#241		
		Mr. Newbrough	#241	Mrs. Qulia, 3431	#241
See Me Please		Mr. Noblett	#241	Word Processing Center, 3431	
Initial		Mr. Paddock	#152	Attn:	
Call Me Please		Mr. Perrotta	#241		
Necessary Action		Mr. Richards	#241	Mrs. Gerken, 3434	#241
Note and Return		Mr. Senter	#241	Evidence Control Center, 3434	
Information		Mr. Smerick	#241	Any Record?	
		Mr. Sommer	#241	Place on Record	
		Mr. Spitzer	#241		
		Mr. Waggoner	#241		
		Mr. Williams	#241		

ROOM 3761

b6
b7C

From:

Room 3176

X-2988

LAB Notes

ALL INFORMATION CONTAINED
HEREIN IS UNCLASSIFIED
DATE 4-4-83 BY 1678 RFP/eBm

DOCUMENT SECTION
LABORATORY DIV.

FBI/DOJ

I does appear that the person who wrote these letters is Spanish-speaking. There are literal translations into English of Spanish idioms and there are phonic spellings of words such as "Most" for "Must" and "This" for "These" which would be consistent with a Spanish pronunciation imposed on these words.

The country of origin of this person is difficult to determine without a Spanish sample. The countries to be considered could include Puerto Rico, Cuba, Mexico, among others.

The level of education is also difficult to determine without a Spanish sample.

Laboratory Transmittal Form
7-72

FBI LABORATORY
FEDERAL BUREAU OF INVESTIGATION
WASHINGTON, D. C. 20535

1 - [ ]   b6 b7C

To: ADIC, New York (9-7749)
From: Director, FBI

February 27, 1978
FBI FILE NO.

LAB. NO. 9-63510

80127058 D MS
80214002 D MS

Re: UNSUB, aka
          b6
          b7C

JOHN LENNON - VICTIM;
EXTORTION (A)
OO: New York

ALL INFORMATION CONTAINED
HEREIN IS UNCLASSIFIED
DATE 4-4-83 BY 1678 RFO/EBm

Examination requested: New York

Reference: New York

Examination requested: Airtels dated January 24, 1978 and February 8, 1978

Remarks: Document - Fingerprint

The submitted specimens will be returned to New York with the results of the requested latent fingerprint examinations.

REC-6 9-63510-8

For your investigative assistance only, literal translations into English of Spanish idioms and phonic spellings of words such as "most" for "must" and "this" for "these" are consistent with Spanish pronunciations and would indicate that the writer (or writers) is Spanish-speaking. In the absence of a Spanish language sample by that writer, it would be difficult to determine the country of origin or educational level of the writer. However, countries to be considered would include Puerto Rico, Cuba, Mexico and perhaps others.

Enclosures (2) (2 Lab report)

DO NOT INCLUDE ADMINISTRATIVE PAGES INFORMATION IN INVESTIGATIVE REPORT

JEL:ljs* (4)

MAILED 19
FEB 27 1978
-FBI

ADMINISTRATIVE PAGE
MAIL ROOM [V] TELETYPE UNIT [ ]

FBI/DOJ

REPORT of the FBI LABORATORY

FEDERAL BUREAU OF INVESTIGATION
WASHINGTON, D. C. 20535

To: ADIC, New York (9-7749)　　　　　　February 27, 1978

FBI FILE NO.　9-63510

LAB. NO.　80127058 D　MS
　　　　　　80214002 D　MS

Re: UNSUB, aka
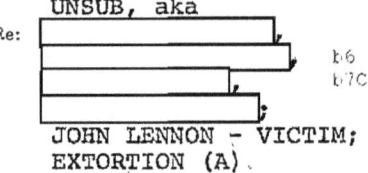
b6
b7C

JOHN LENNON - VICTIM;
EXTORTION (A)

Specimens received January 26, 1978 under cover of communication dated January 24, 1978 (80127058 D MS):

Q7　Envelope postmarked "Jamaica Jan 18 '78 N.Y. PB meter 159263" bearing the typewritten address "Mr. John Lennon 1 West 72 ND Street New York, N.Y. 10023"

Q8　First page of accompanying two-page typewritten letter dated Jan. 19 1978 beginning "Mr. John Lennon Here is the result..."

Q9　Second page of two-page typewritten letter beginning "Mr. Lennon, we don't care..."

Q10　Envelope postmarked "New York Jan 22 '78 N.Y. PB meter 643359" bearing typewritten address "Mr. John Lennon 1 West 72 ND Street New York, N.Y. 10023"

Q11　Accompanying one-page typewritten letter dated January 23 1978 beginning "Mr Lennon Something very..."

ALSO SUBMITTED:

Two (2) sheets of white paper

Page 1　　　　　　　　　　　　　　　　(over)

ALL INFORMATION CONTAINED
HEREIN IS UNCLASSIFIED
DATE 4-4-83 BY 1678 RFP/EBon

Specimens received February 16, 1978 under cover of
communication dated February 8, 1978 (80214002 D MS):

Q12   Envelope postmarked "NEW YORK, NY 1001 G.P.O.
(I.M.) 1978 FEB 3 PM" bearing typewritten
address "MR. JOHN LENNON I WEST 72nd Street
NEW YORK N.Y. I0023"

Q13   Accompanying one-page typewritten letter
dated 2/3/78 beginning "Dear John. We are
very proud of you...."

ALSO SUBMITTED:

    Blank sheet of paper

Result of examination:

    The submitted envelopes and sheets of paper
are similar in observable physical characteristics
to those previously submitted in this matter. No
significant features were noted which would assist
in determining the immediate source of those items.

    It was determined that the typewriting on
Q7 through Q13 is the same size and style of type
as the typewriting on specimens previously submitted
and contains limited characteristics in common. However,
there are an insufficient amount of identifiable characteristics to permit any definite determination whether the
same typewriter was used.

    The submitted specimens were photographed
and will be returned separately.

Page 2
80127058 D MS

RECORDED
7-2 2/3/78
bgk

LATENT

FEDERAL BUREAU OF INVESTIGATION
UNITED STATES DEPARTMENT OF JUSTICE

Laboratory Work Sheet

To: ADIC, New York (9-7749)

Re: UNSUB, aka
                                                                b6
                                                                b7C

JOHN LENNON - VICTIM;
EXTORTION (A)

OO: New York

FBI FILE NO.   9-63510-8
LAB. NO.   80127058 D MS
YOUR NO.   80214002 DMS

Examination by: ☐   b6
                                                                b7C
                            2/23/78

Examination requested by: New York

Reference: Airtel dated January 24, 1978

Examination requested: Document - Fingerprint

Specimens received: January 26, 1978

Q7   Envelope postmarked "Jamaica Jan 18 '78 N.Y. PB meter 159263" bearing the typewritten address "Mr. John Lennon 1 West 72 ND Street New York, N.Y. 10023"

Q8   First page of accompanying two-page typewritten letter dated Jan. 19 1978 beginning "Mr. John Lennon Here is the result . . ."

Q9   Second page of two-page typewritten letter beginning "Mr. Lennon, we don't care . . ."

Q10 Envelope postmarked "New York Jan 22 '78 N.Y. PB meter 643359" bearing typewritten address "Mr. John Lennon 1 West 72 ND Stre/t New York, N.Y. 10023"

ALL INFORMATION CONTAINED
HEREIN IS UNCLASSIFIED
DATE 4-4-83 BY 1678 RPL/EBm

PAGE 1   OVER

Q7-Q11, AS Physicals similar w/observable characters. to Q1-Q6 no WM end. writ 2/3 photo'd

Q11   Accompanying one-page typewritten letter dated
       January 22 1978 beginning "Mr Lennon Something
       very..."

ALSO SUBMITTED:

   Two (2) sheets of white paper

Results: — The envelopes & sheets of paper are sim. in obsv. phys. char. to those prev subm. in this matter.

— Det that the two Q7→13 is same sign & style as two specimens subm & contains ltd char in common. However, w/o indent. char. it is diff. determ. if same two.

— P. t not'd sep.

T.F. Sub spec to N.Y. w/ lab results.

— For your invest. assist., literal translations into Eng. of Spanish idioms and phonic spelling of words such as "most" for "must" & "this" for "these" are consistent with Spanish pronunciations and would indicate that the writer (or writers) is Spanish-speaking. In the absence of a Spanish language sample by that writer, it would be difficult to determ the country of origin or educational level of the writer. However, countries to be considered would include Puerto Rico, Cuba, Mexico, and perhaps others.

PAGE 2
80127058 D MS

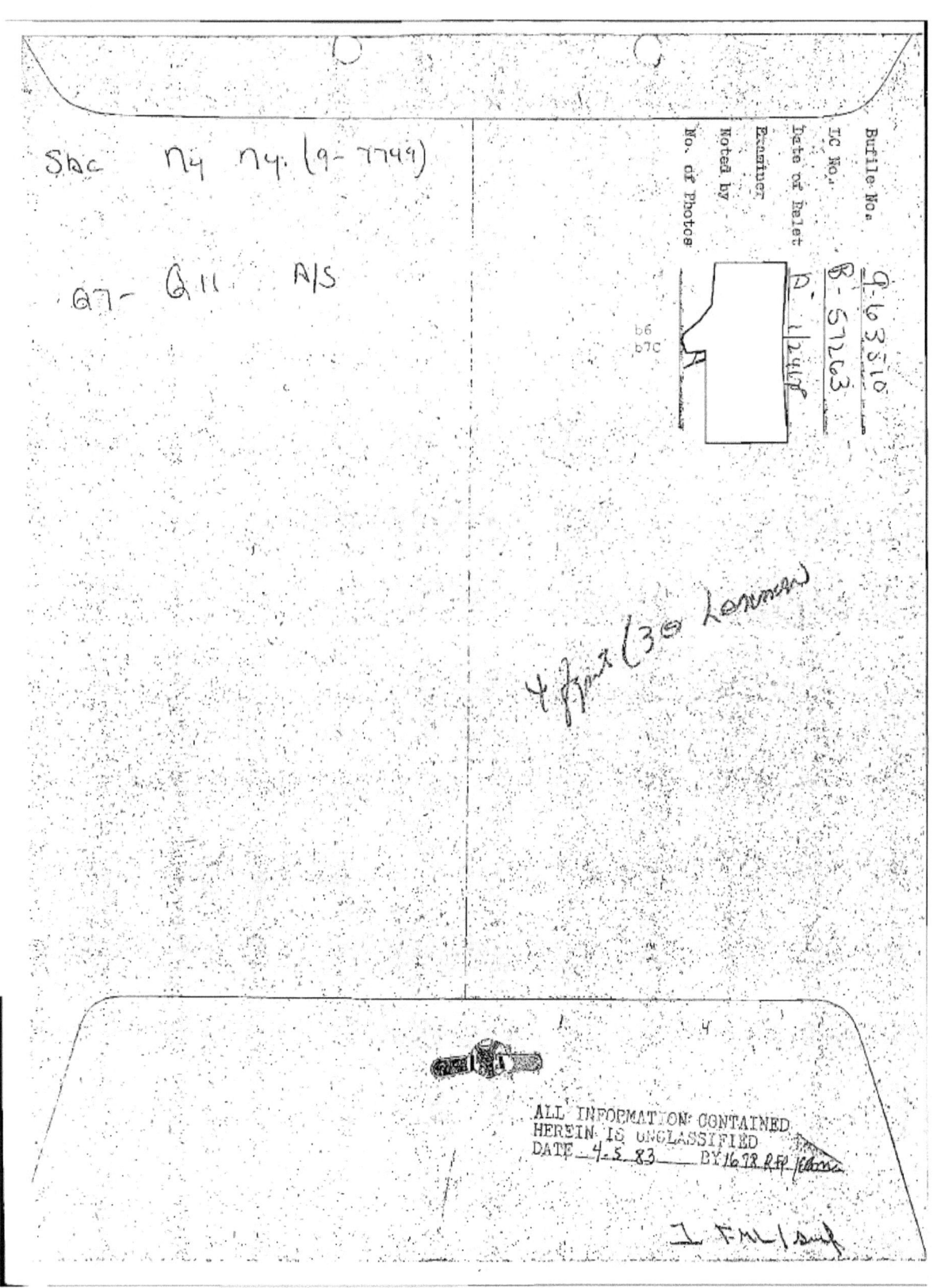

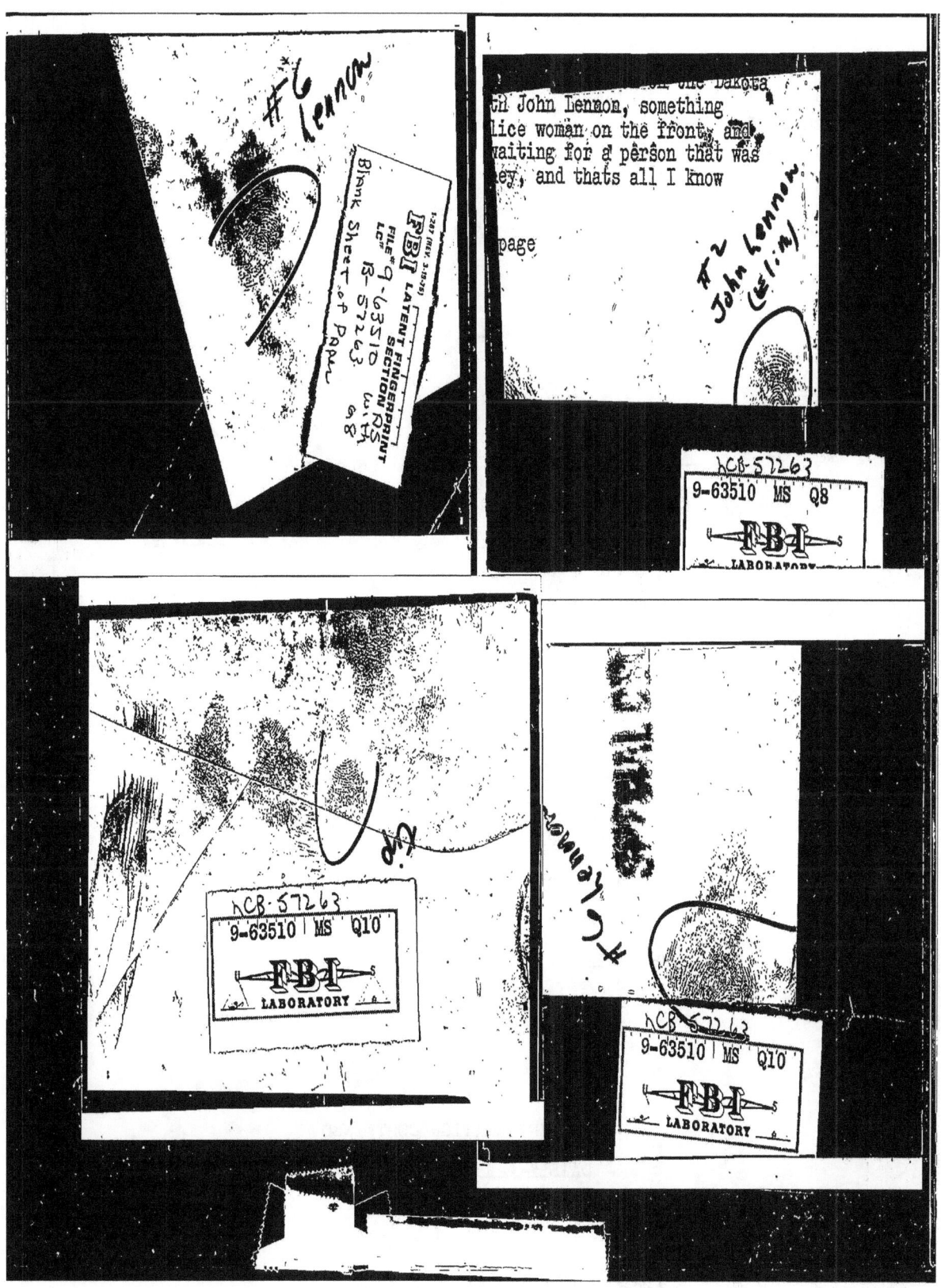

7-2 RECORDED
2/17/78
Hmc

LATENTS

FEDERAL BUREAU OF INVESTIGATION
UNITED STATES DEPARTMENT OF JUSTICE

Laboratory Work Sheet

To: ADIC, New York (9-7749) (#21)

FBI FILE NO. 9-63510

Re: UNSUB; aka _____, Etc.; b6 b7C
JOHN LENNON - VICTIM;
EXTORTION (A)
OO: New York

LAB. NO. 80214002 D MS

YOUR NO.

Examination by: ____ b6 b7C

(See 80127058 DMs)

Examination requested by: New York

Reference: Airtel dated February 8, 1978

Examination requested: Document - Fingerprint

Specimens received: February 16, 1978

Q12 Envelope postmarked "NEW YORK, NY 1001 G.P.O. (I.M.) 1978 FEB. 3 PM" bearing typewritten address "MR. JOHN LENNON I WEST 72nd Street NEW YORK N.Y. I0023"

Q13 Accompanying one-page typewritten letter dated 2/3/78 beginning "Dear John. We are very proud of you . . ."

ALSO SUBMITTED:

Blank sheet of paper

ALL INFORMATION CONTAINED
HEREIN IS UNCLASSIFIED
DATE 4-4-83 BY 1678 RFp/Eom

Q12-13. Physicals same as
as previous Q's — nothing else sig
noted — no indent. writings

FBI/DOJ

SAC NY (9-7749)(P) #21

GIL-G13 D/S

Unsub;
AKA [redacted] (ct)
John Lennon - Victim
Extortion

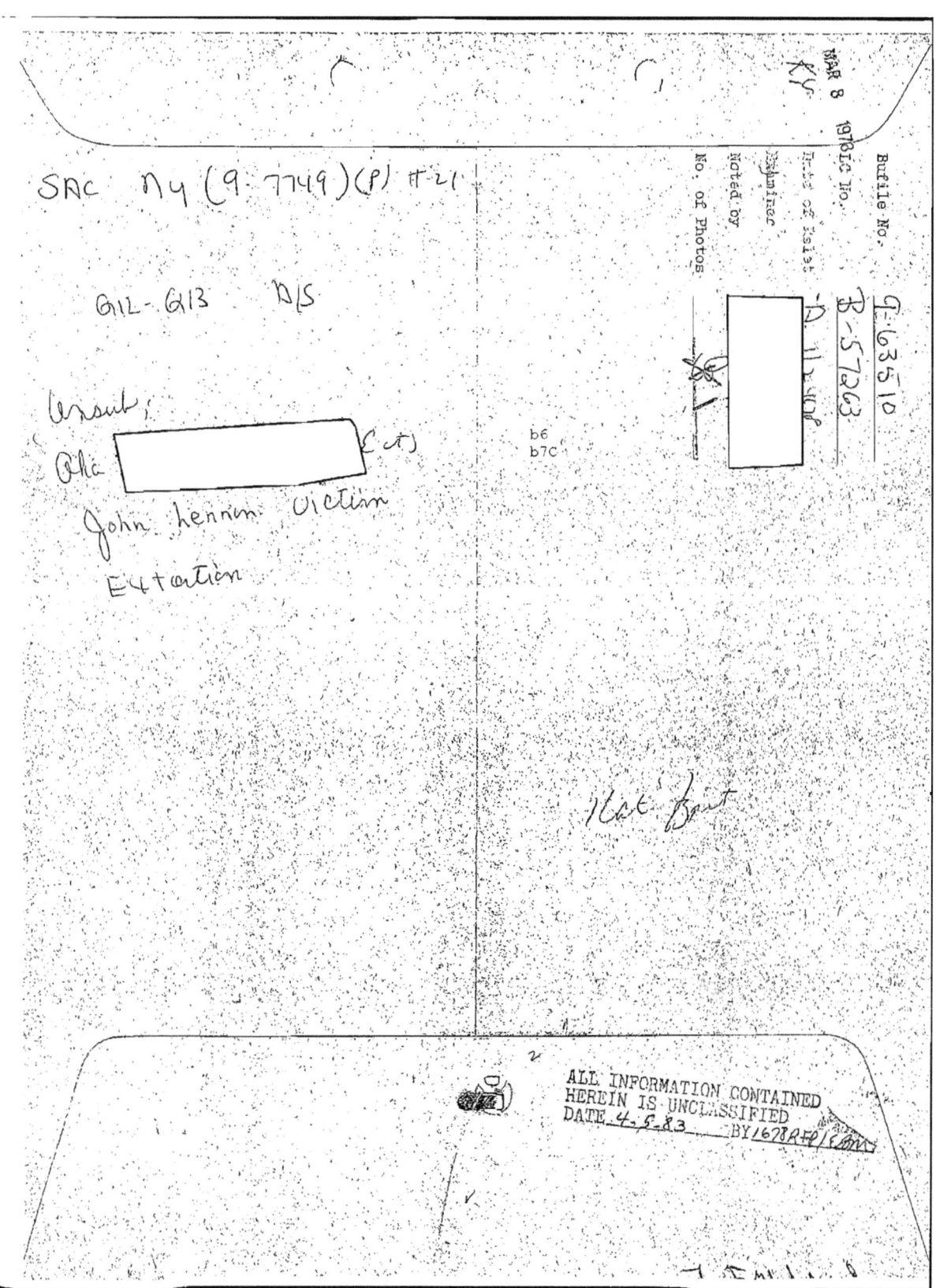

ALL INFORMATION CONTAINED
HEREIN IS UNCLASSIFIED
DATE 4-5-83 BY 1628 RFP/EAW

1-336 (Rev. 2-2-78)

FEDERAL BUREAU OF INVESTIGATION
Washington, D. C. 20537

REPORT
of the
IDENTIFICATION DIVISION
LATENT FINGERPRINT SECTION

YOUR FILE NO. 9-7749 (P) (#21)
FBI FILE NO. 9-63510
LATENT CASE NO. B-57263

March 7, 1978

TO: ADIC, New York

RE: UNSUB., AKA
[redacted]
ET AL.;
JOHN LENNON - VICTIM
EXTORTION

b6
b7C

ALL INFORMATION CONTAINED
HEREIN IS UNCLASSIFIED
DATE 4-4-83 BY 1672RFP/ebm

REFERENCE: Airtels 1-24-78 and 2-8-78
EXAMINATION REQUESTED BY: New York
SPECIMENS: Three envelopes, Q7, Q10 and Q12
Four pages of typewritten letters, Q8, Q9, Q11 and Q13
Three blank sheets of paper (designated A through C in the LFPS)

The specimens are further described in a separate Laboratory report.

The specimens were examined and five latent fingerprints, one of which is from the extreme tip area of a finger, were developed on Q8, Q10, Q12 and the sheet of paper designated A.

Three latent fingerprints developed on three specimens, have been identified as finger impressions of John Winston Ono Lennon.

(Continued on next page)

Enc. (10)
DRW:dep
(4)

Robert E. Kent
Acting Assistant Director, Identification Division

THIS REPORT IS FURNISHED FOR OFFICIAL USE ONLY

b6
b7C

FBI/DOJ

ADIC, New York   March 7, 1978

One of the latent fingerprints is not identical with the fingerprints of Lennon. The remaining latent fingerprint was compared, insofar as possible, with the available fingerprints of this individual, but no identification was effected. Fully recorded inked impressions of the extreme tip areas of the fingers are necessary for a conclusive comparison.

The specimens are enclosed.

Page 2
LC #B-57263

RECORDED
2/3/78
bgh

LATENT

FEDERAL BUREAU OF INVESTIGATION
UNITED STATES DEPARTMENT OF JUSTICE

Laboratory Work Sheet

Recorded 2/24/78   12:50 p.m.   cds   Received 2/24/78

To: ADIC, New York (9-7749) (P)(21)

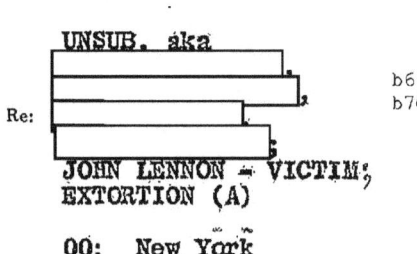

Re: UNSUB. aka
    b6
    b7C

JOHN LENNON - VICTIM;
EXTORTION (A)

OO: New York

FBI FILE NO. 9-63510-9
LAB. NO. 80127058 D MS
YOUR NO. LC#B-57263

Examination by:

Noted By:
    b6
    b7C

Examination requested by: New York
Reference: Airtel dated January 24, 1978
Examination requested: Document - Fingerprint
Specimens received: January 26, 1978

Q7   Envelope postmarked "Jamaica Jan 18 '78 N.Y. PB meter 159263" bearing the typewritten address "Mr. John Lennon 1 West 72 ND Street New York, N.Y. 10023"

Q8   First page of accompanying two-page typewritten letter dated Jan. 19 1978 beginning "Mr. John Lennon Here is the result . . ."

Q9   Second page of two page typewritten letter beginning "Mr. Lennon, we don't care . . ."

Q10   Envelope postmarked "New York Jan 22 '78 N.Y. PB meter 643359" bearing typewritten address "Mr. John Lennon 1 West 72 ND Stret New York, N.Y. 10023"

ALL INFORMATION CONTAINED
HEREIN IS UNCLASSIFIED
DATE 4-4-83 BY 1678 RFP/EBm

Ans'd 3-7-78

PAGE 1   OVER

FBI/DOJ

2/24 Lab rep. sup.
   Spers. pur NIN

2/27 Spers respur NIN to photo
3/2 1 lat fprt dev on Q8, Q#2 for John Winston Ono Lennon
3/: 2 lat fprts; 1g. which [?] pan extreme tip g fpr)
    dev on Q10 - 10 #6 for John Winston Ono Lennon
  1 lat fprt dev on blank sheet of paper 1. A, Q #6 for Lennon.
  No lats g cal dev remi spers.
  Rem lat fprt comp. insofar as poss fprts Lennon.
  No o e fl fully recorded inked imps of tip
  areas of fprs nec. for cond. comp.

3/3 Spers pur sv re add'l lats dev dest.
    Spers dest. [?]

(7end)

7-2   RECORDED   LATENTS
      2/17/78
      hmc

                    FEDERAL BUREAU OF INVESTIGATION
                    UNITED STATES DEPARTMENT OF JUSTICE
                           Laboratory Work Sheet

          Recorded 2/24/78   12:45p.m.   cds   Received 2/24/78

To: ADIC, New York (9-7749) (#21) (P)

                                        FBI FILE NO.   9-63510
      UNSUB; aka
Re: Etc.; b6   LAB. NO.   80214002 D MS
      _____   b7C
      JOHN LENNON - VICTIM;   YOUR NO.   LC#B-57263
      EXTORTION (A)
      OO: New York
                                        Examination by:

                                                                   b6
                                                                   b7C

Examination requested by: New York
                                            Noted By:
Reference: Airtel dated February 8, 1978

Examination requested: Document - 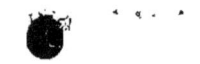Fingerprint

Specimens received: February 16, 1978

      Q12   Envelope postmarked "NEW YORK, NY 1001 G.P.O.
              (I.M.) 1978 FEB 3 PM" bearing typewritten
              address "MR. JOHN LENNON I WEST 72nd Street
              NEW YORK N.Y. 10023"

      Q13   Accompanying one-page typewritten letter dated
              2/3/78 beginning "Dear John. We are very
              proud of you . . ."

      ALSO SUBMITTED:

              Blank sheet of paper (C)

                                        ALL INFORMATION CONTAINED
                                        HEREIN IS UNCLASSIFIED
                                        DATE 4-4-83 BY _____

Examination Completed _____ Dictated _____
                        time   date   date

3/2 Let. fgrnt not o fgrnts John Lennon.
3/3 Specs pur s/v no addl lots dev. dest.
   Specs. end.
          DW
3End.

FD-36 (Rev.)

FBI

TRANSMIT VIA:
☐ Teletype
☐ Facsimile
☒ Airtel

PRECEDENCE:
☐ Immediate
☐ Priority
☐ Routine

CLASSIFICATION:
☐ TOP SECRET
☐ SECRET
☐ CONFIDENTIAL
☐ E F T O
☐ CLEAR

Date 3/9/78

TO: DIRECTOR, FBI
(ATTN: ID/LFS)

FROM: ADIC, NEW YORK (9-7749) (P)

SUBJECT: UNSUB: aka
─────────────, Etc.,
JOHN LENNON - VICTIM
EXTORTION (A)
(OO:NY)

ReNYairtel, 12/2/77.

Enclosed for ID/LFS is the original and two xerox copies of letter postmarked 3/7/78, at New York, New York, addressed to JOHN LENNON. Documents include two page letter, the envelope, a blank sheet, and a newspaper clipping.

REQUEST OF BUREAU

ID/LFS requested to compare enclosed letter with previously submitted specimens, and conduct same examination requested in referenced airtel.

③-Bureau (Encs. 3)
(1-ID/LFS)
1-New York

MED:dar
(5)

ALL INFORMATION CONTAINED
HEREIN IS UNCLASSIFIED
DATE 4-4-83 BY 1678 RTP/ebm

REC-79 9-63510-10
ST-131

17 MAR 10 1978

Approved: _____ Transmitted _____ Per _____
                              (Number) (Time)

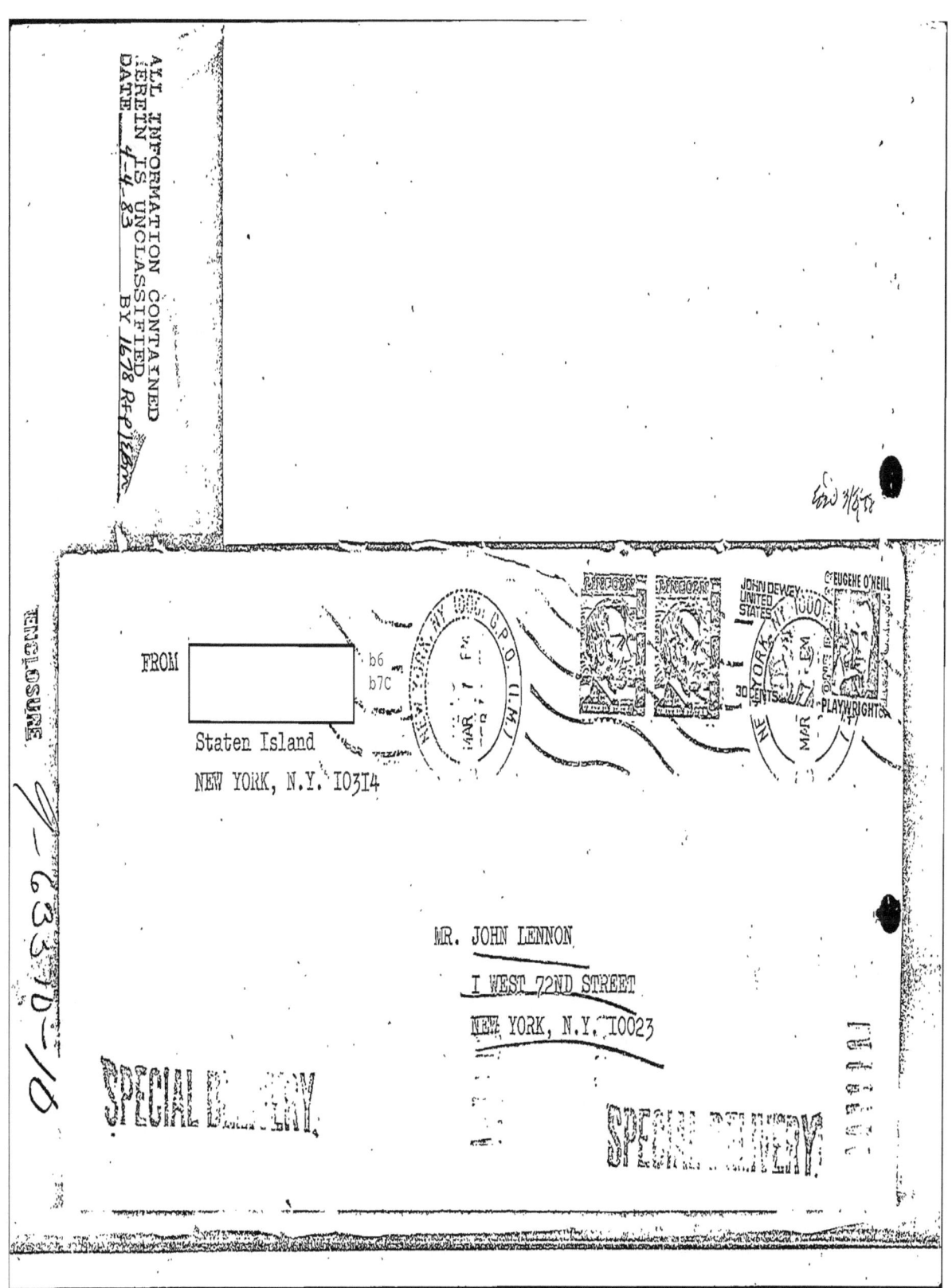

T.F.P.R.I.M.   March, 7/1972.

MR. JOHN LENNON

On a very slow motion evrything looks like nice and cool, like nothing never happen. But this is the away we do things, and on many case's we end things in the same way.

On Feb. 3 we call our people to stand off and clear up the area. On feb. 4 we had just one very quick meting that so far it result that you lost for completely the ground and the opportunity to deal with us again......It mean that we don't need your money any more. We don't need money and having the F.B.I. looking for it. But let us tell you this; it never happen yet to us receive money marked bill's, but if it happen we will know it before we start use it, and if it is marked bill's it only will be good to us, to throw fire on every bill and burn to dead who ever give it to us, this is our plan for who ever try do it to us. Also we like to inform you that is completely off of our plan any attempt of kidnap for a smal or big ransom on you or on your family, you are worth not one penny to us, revenge is all our plan same day in coming future. This is all so far what we get from our quick meting, we will have soon a final meting for revenge, it will be made up with a vote against you and in favor of you. You only will hear from us if anything c... up in your favor, but if the vote number against you be greater you will not hear from us any more, we will turn you over to 12 man's that they name them selfs in a deathblow, and then you will be part of our war. We did advice you from the first to the last letter, what you should do and what you shouldn't do, but all we get in trust of it is you did try to fish us twice supported by the F.B.I. We Know plenty about your deep involvement with the F.B.I. included we have two recorded conversation's of your wife and the F.B.I. We think that we give you more than time enough to satisfy your self with your reven... aganst us. Know the time is up, the F.B.I. give up and you are left with all your money. What you need know is the time to enjoy all of it. Also you are left by the F.B.I. with a nice promise; for any time you need them, they will be right of way for search, and in the mean time they will call you up some times just to see how is evrything, but is very nice of them. But your problem is we are not behind bars, and the time needed for you call them you may haven't. We have lots of many plan's to be presented on our final meting. But nothing can be done

till it be approve by our staff. According to many of our opinion you are the worse enemy of the T.F.P.R.I.M.
So far, we have four persons that they refuse to give our demand. But we stil negotiate with them, but so far no one did try call the police because they know all threat's come with a warning, but is no warning for revenge. You pushover evrything real deep in a badly situation. But in the mean time, you have some chance to step out free from it because you still have sympathy from some of our man's included [redacted], the fifth chief of our organization. Telephone call's between us and threat victim's, is not allow by our people. We only do it from public telephone booth to telephone booth when is needed. But [redacted] is allow, and he will call you soon. You will have exactly 75 second's to say anything in your defense if you have any to be use in our final meting. [redacted] is not allow to answer any question or to talk, if there is any question to be answer, we will do it by letter. No more special delivery be send out destined to you, if we have to answer any question we do it by duplicate letter and we send it to you by regular mail. Also if evrything turns against you, we have no plan for any attempt where you live; but anyway we will send a letter to the superintendent of the Dakota, for him to advise all the employees for in case of any attempt, all most obey orders all most stay still, any one who try to move will be shoot. We know you have all the sympathy from all the employees of the Dakota, but it will help you nothing.

T.F.P.R.I.M.

TERRORISMO

Andrei Gromiko, Ministro de Asuntos Exteriores de Rusia, saluda efusivamente a Yasir Arafat, líder de la Organización de Liberación Palestina.

posible? Aún está fresco en la mente el recuerdo de los 11 muertos y decenas de heridos que produjo una bomba colocada en los armarios para equipaje, supuestamente, por un fanático miembro de las Fuerzas Armadas de Liberación Nacional de Puerto Rico (FALN). ¿Quién puede pasar caminando lentamente junto al lugar que ocupaban los armarios en la estación subterránea de Gran Central sin sentir temor al recordar la explosión del artefacto explosivo colocado allí por los terroristas croatas?

CANCER MUNDIAL

El terrorismo ha sentado bases en todo el mundo y, como un cáncer, va destruyendo paulatinamente la salud política

Haya, Holanda, y secuestrado al embajador y a otros diez funcionarios de la misión diplomática. A cambio de sus vidas, habían demandado la libertad de un miembro de la organización terrorista japonesa, Yutuka Furuya, que había sido arrestado en el parisino aeropuerto de Orly cuando trataba de pasar ciertos mensajes secretos sobre futuras acciones terroristas.

En sus negociaciones con los terroristas, el Gobierno holandés trata de mantener la calma y efectuar las negociaciones lentamente con el definido propósito de tratar de capturar a los comandos o hacerlos desistir de sus planes. Pero los franceses son menos pacientes y "Carlos" lo sabía. La

Cuando estas dos últimas etapas estén un poco más avanzadas, la acción terrorista no se limitará a la captura o secuestro de un edificio o un avión, sino que se podrá poner en peligro e incluso controlar ciudades enteras y por ellas el país completo.

ARMAS ADICIONALES

Los grupos terroristas -principalmente los de izquierda- han demostrado sobradamente que les resulta excesivamente fácil el lograr presionar a los gobiernos occidentales y al mismo tiempo, han hecho patente que los servicios de inteligencia y policíacos de todas estas naciones son totalmente ineficaces.

En la actualidad, los terroristas tienen a su favor un 80 por ciento de probabilidades de li-

"Vivimos en una era de violencia como sacar un calculado provecho ristas, los mercaderes del terror sus territorios, han hecho que ambas naciones se conviertan en el "paraíso de los mercaderes del terror".

El caso que más fácilmente demuestra la posición francesa, es el del terrorista palestino Uchmed Daoud Mechamed Auda, cuyo nombre de guerra es "Abu Daoud".

Daoud es un miembro -a nivel intermedio- de la Organización de Liberación Palestina (PLO) y hace algún tiempo fue una de las figuras claves de la temible organización terrorista conocida como "Septiembre Negro". Sin embargo, Daoud no fue el "cerebro" de la masacre de los atletas israelitas en la Villa Olímpica de Munich, en 1972, como inicialmente se creyó. Este desgraciado galardón le corresponde a Alí-Hassan Salameh, jefe de planificación de "Septiembre Negro" y el hombre que encabeza la lista de los asesinatos ordenados por la agencia de contrainteligencia israelí, Mossad.

El papel de Daoud en la "masacre de Munich" fue el de coordinador de logística. Él se encargó de hacer llegar las armas al comando árabe y los proveyó con pasaportes falsos, con los que algunos de los ocho hombres que integraron el comando burlaron a las autoridades alemanas. Días antes de que se efectuara la operación abandonó Munich, pero meses más tarde era arrestado por la Policía Secreta Jordana, mientras se encontraba en una misión de espionaje para el PLO. Allí, las autoridades lo "convencieron" de que se presentara ante las cámaras de televisión y narrara todo lo sucedido en la Villa Olímpica de Munich y denunciara a los que había planificado la lamentable acción comando.

Pocos días después de la comparecencia de Daoud ante las cámaras de televisión, un comando de "Septiembre Negro" atacaba la embajada de Arabia Saudita en Khartoum, asesinando a dos diplomáticos norteamericanos que se encontraban de visita, en un intento

"De las granadas y ametralladoras están pasando a los cohetes dirigidos por rayos infrarrojos y algunos están ya adentrándose en la utilización de material atómico, mientras otros dan sus primeros pasos en el proceso de la guerra bacteriológica..."

mundial. Los enfermos más graves son: Irlanda del Norte, Líbano, Argentina, Brasil, Puer-

granada que el mismo lanzara causó el efecto deseado. El miedo corrió por París y llegó a

brarse de ser capturados o resultar muertos en el transcurso de una acción; un 80 por ciento de

FD-302 (REV. 11-27-70)

FEDERAL BUREAU OF INVESTIGATION

Date of transcription: 3/16/78

[redacted b6/b7C] furnished a letter addressed to Mr. JOHN LENNON, 1 West 72nd Street, New York, New York. The letter was postmarked "3/7/78 New York, New York", "GPO" for General Post Office.

The letter was stamped Special Delivery and bore a return address: [redacted b6/b7C], Staten Island New York, N.Y. 10314." Inside the envelope were two typewritten pages, a blank sheet of paper and a newspaper clipping from a Spanish-language newspaper bearing the word "Terrorismo."

[redacted b6/b7C] stated the letter was received late in the evening March 7, 1978.

Interviewed on: 3/8/78 at New York, New York   File # NY 9-7749-47

by SA [redacted b6/b7C] jmj   Date dictated: 3/14/78

This document contains neither recommendations nor conclusions of the FBI. It is the property of the FBI and is loaned to your agency; it and its contents are not to be distributed outside your agency.

FD-302 (REV. 11-27-70)

FEDERAL BUREAU OF INVESTIGATION

Date of transcription: 3/16/78

New York, New York, telephonically advised as follows:

At about 9:00 PM on both March 11 and 12, 1978, she received phone calls from a man who stated ▭▭▭▭▭. On both occasions she asked the caller to hold on, placed his call on hold and left it there until he hung up.

(Telephonic)
Interviewed on 3/12/78 at Washington Township, New Jersey NY 9-7749
by SA ▭▭▭▭ :jmj   Date dictated 3/15/78

FD-302 (REV. 11-27-70)

FEDERAL BUREAU OF INVESTIGATION

Date of transcription 3/20/78

[REDACTED], New York, New York, Apartment [REDACTED] an employee of the United States Postal Service, was interviewed at the United States Post Office, General Post Office (GPO), West 33rd Street, New York City. Present at the interview was Postal Inspector [REDACTED].

[REDACTED] observed a composite drawing of an individual who had mailed letters to JOHN LENNON, 1 West 72nd Street, New York City. She stated that the individual is unknown to her. [REDACTED] stated she was working at [REDACTED] (Special Delivery), GPO, on Sunday, [REDACTED] 1978. She added that under normal circumstances the window would be closed by 5:00 PM and customers would not have access to a postal meter.

Interviewed on 3/15/78 at New York, New York File # NY 9-7749-53

by SA [REDACTED]/jmj Date dictated 3/17/78

This document contains neither recommendations nor conclusions of the FBI. It is the property of the FBI and is loaned to your agency; it and its contents are not to be distributed outside your agency.

FD-302 (REV. 11-27-70)

FEDERAL BUREAU OF INVESTIGATION

Date of transcription __3/20/78__

                                                                               New York,   b6
New York, Apartment ▇▇▇ advised as follows: b7C

    At approximately 7:00 PM, Tuesday, March 14, 1978, she took a call from an unknown male who stated "This is ▇▇▇." He said nothing else for the three to four minutes they were on the line together. He would occasionally respond "hmm hmm."

    The operator cut in signalling the end of their initial period. ▇▇▇ asked ▇▇▇ if he had a nickel and apparently he did not because they were disconnected. ▇▇▇ spoke the full time stating she did not understand why he had picked on them since ▇▇▇▇▇▇▇▇▇ stand for love and peace.

    ▇▇▇ stated ▇▇▇ apparently had called at about 4:00 PM the same date asking for ▇▇▇." ▇▇▇, the governess, said she was not in and ▇▇▇ hung up.

Interviewed on __3/16/78__ at __New York, New York__   File # __NY 9-7749__ 54

by SA ▇▇▇▇▇▇▇▇▇▇:jmj   Date dictated __3/17/78__

48

This document contains neither recommendations nor conclusions of the FBI. It is the property of the FBI and is loaned to your agency; it and its contents are not to be distributed outside your agency.

FD-36 (Rev. 7-27-76)

FBI

TRANSMIT VIA:
☐ Teletype
☐ Facsimile
☒ Airtel

PRECEDENCE:
☐ Immediate
☐ Priority
☐ Routine

CLASSIFICATION:
☐ TOP SECRET
☐ SECRET
☐ CONFIDENTIAL
☐ E F T O
☐ CLEAR

Date 3/22/78

TO: DIRECTOR, FBI (9-63510)
(ATTN: FBI LAB AND ID/LFS)

FROM: ADIC, NEW YORK (9-7749) (P) (#204)

SUBJECT: CHANGED
UNSUB aka
                                    , b6
                                      b7C
Et Al;
JOHN LENNON - VICTIM
EXT (A)
(OO:NY)

Title is marked "CHANGED" to show the additional alias of   as used by unsub in letter postmarked 3/20/78.

ReNYairtels to Bu, 12/2/77 and 3/9/78.

Enclosed for the Bu is the original of a typewritten letter and two xerox copies of a letter postmarked 3/20/78, NY, NY, to   NY, NY, with the return address of   ,   , Brooklyn, NY, 11229. Letter is a "Special Delivery" letter that was received by the LENNONS on 3/21/78 and made available to the NYO on the same date. Letter is threatening in nature. Letter is one typewritten page, however, one blank page was enclosed with letter.

REQUEST OF THE BUREAU

FBI Lab is requested to compare enclosed letter with letters previously submitted in this case.

ID/LFS is requested to conduct appropriate examination to develop any latents of value and to compare with latents previously found on other letters.

Investigation continuing at NY.

④ - Bureau (Encls. 3)
   (1 - FBI Lab)
   (1 - ID/LFS)
3 - New York
FVB:csc

ALL INFORMATION CONTAINED
HEREIN IS UNCLASSIFIED
DATE 4-4-83 BY 1678 RPP/cbm

Approved   Transmitted   (Number) (Time)

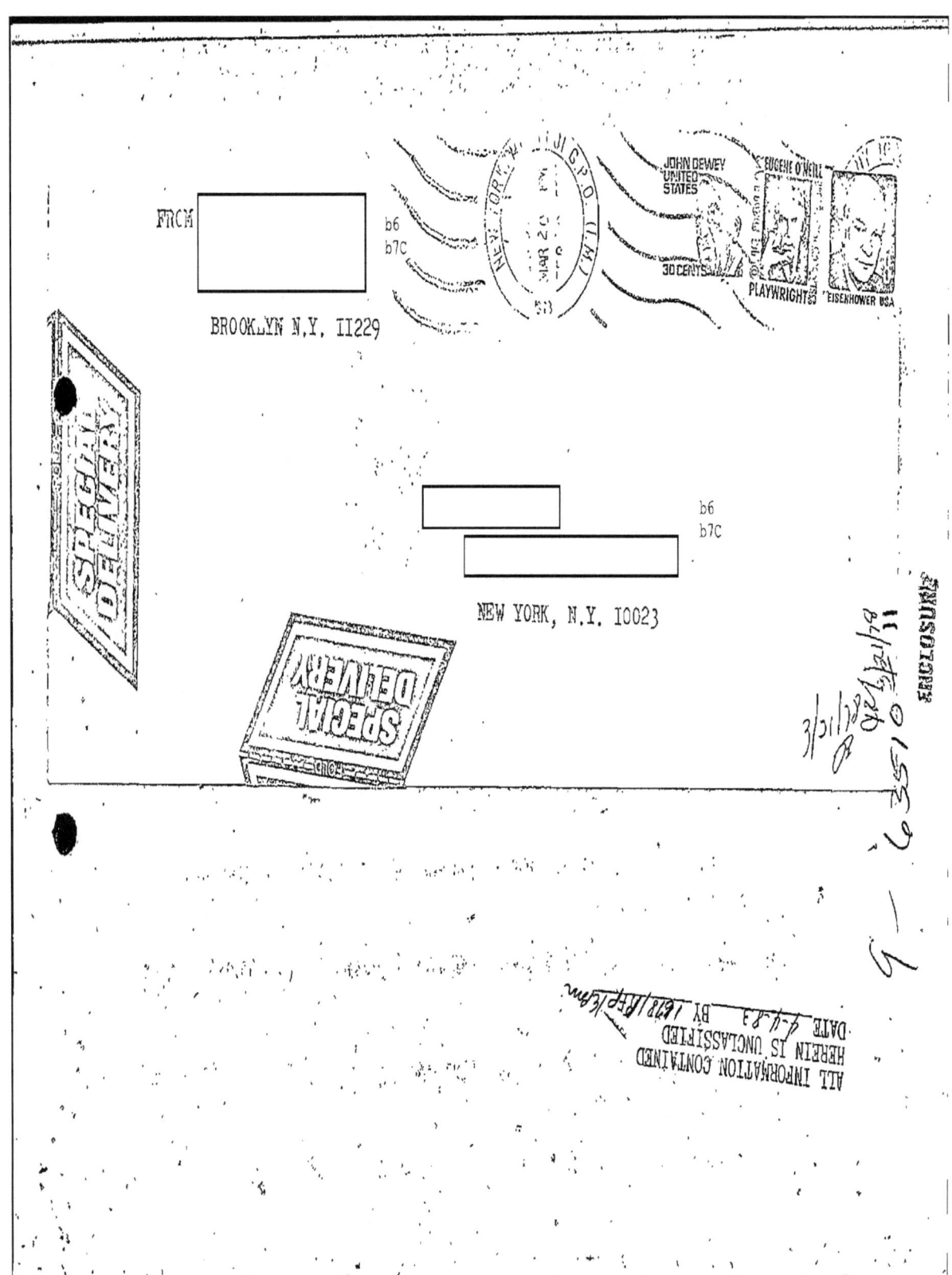

MARCH, 20 - 1978

[   ]. This letter, is in reference to our talk on telephone March, 14. I am [   ], the fifth chief of T.F.P.R.I.M. TERRORIST ORGANIZATION.

I, and one third of our members we are much sympathizers to your family, and because of my sympathy for all of you, I'm been put over everything in a difficult conclusion, and thats why we go ahead for a final meting with votes against, and in favor. Now I am in charged to carry some good reson from you, to speak in your behalf in our final meting. I don't have any. Everything you said by the telephone, is comprehensive by me but it don't accomplish much to them. What ever you said it was recorded to be listen by all of us in our final meting.

[   ], you are in a very serious situation because they are very angry they want revenge because we lost over 23 thousands dollars on this operation with you, and hundreds of hours lost for nothing. The problem now, is they don't want any part of your money anymore, they only want is all of you be part of our war. Part of our war it mean, that all of you will blowup in somewhere, and then they will send a letter to the F.B.I. claiming responsibility for the act.

[   ], this letter is only between you and me, I will never jeopardize any one of our man's, but I will try to help all of you, but you must follow my instructions exatly in what I say.
FIRST. I'm going to call you up again soon, what ever you say it will be recorded. SECOND. I only say by the telephone, I'M [   ], and then you say? YES [   ], I REAL DON'T KNOW WHAT TO SAY, BUT WE ARE VERY SORRY FOR WHAT WE DID, BUT WHEN WE RECIEVE YOUR FIRST LETTER, IT TURN US IN PANIC AND WITHOUT THINKING GOOD , WE DECIDE CALL THE F.B.I. BUT LATER WE REALIZE IT WAS A MISTAKE CALL THE F.B.I. BUT IN OTHER HAND WE ARE RICH BUT WE DONT HAVE THAT MUCH CASH, WE HAVE EVERYTHING INVESTED BUT WE MAY CAN HELP YOU WITH 24 THOUSENDS, I PROMISE THIS TIME I WILL NOT CONTACT THE F.B.I., AND THE MONEY WILL BE CLEAN, NO MARKED BILL'S. PLEASE LET ME KNOW IF YOU AGREE WITH OUR REQUEST, WE DON'T LIKE VIOLENT WE LOVE PEACE.

THANK YOU.

[   ], This is my best idea to try put you off of revenge, I do believe with this my idea, they will calm down and they will accept the request, but if they don't accept the request, at least I have more card's and good reson to try make them to forget everything. One thing that I like to clear up is this, I'm not demand of what you have to do, I'm just giving you my best idea. But if you have better idea made up of your own better than mine, please give it to me and what ever you give to me I'll have to put it on the table.

In anyway I'll give my vote in favor of you, I'll speak in favor of you and I do what I can do for all of you.

Good Lack

ALL INFORMATION CONTAINED
HEREIN IS UNCLASSIFIED
DATE 4-4-83 BY 1678 RFP/som

63510-11

ENCLOSURE

FD-302 (REV. 3-8-77)

FEDERAL BUREAU OF INVESTIGATION

Date of transcription: 3/24/78

On March 21, 1978, ▇▇▇▇▇▇▇▇▇▇▇▇▇▇▇▇ was contacted and advised that on the morning of March 21, 1978, she received in the United States Mail a special delivery letter addressed to her with the return address ▇▇▇▇▇▇ ▇▇▇▇▇▇▇▇▇▇▇▇, Brooklyn, New York 11229. The letter is postmarked 3/20/78 PM New York GPO. The letter is a one page typewritten letter addressed to ▇▇▇▇▇ dated 3/20/78.

b6
b7C

The letter states that ▇▇▇▇▇▇ will be in further contact with ▇▇▇▇▇.

b6
b7C

▇▇▇▇▇ made the envelope and letter available.

Investigation on 3/21/78 at New York, New York   File # NY 9-7749

by SAS ▇▇▇▇▇▇▇▇▇ and ▇▇▇▇/FVD/ahh   Date dictated 3/23/78

b6
b7C

This document contains neither recommendations nor conclusions of the FBI. It is the property of the FBI and is loaned to your agency; it and its contents are not to be distributed outside your agency.

49

FVB:jfc
1

    The previously mentioned letters were forwarded to the FBI Lab and Latent Fingerprint Section in communications dated 12/2/77, 12/20/77, 1/24/78, 2/8/78, 3/9/78, and 3/22/78.

    In communications dated 1/27/78, 2/27/78, and 5/16/78, the FBI Lab and in communication dated 2/2/78, 3/7/78, and 5/4/78, the Latent Fingerprint Section furnished results of their examination.

I-336 (Rev. 2-2-78)

FEDERAL BUREAU OF INVESTIGATION
Washington, D. C. 20537

REPORT
of the
IDENTIFICATION DIVISION
LATENT FINGERPRINT SECTION

YOUR FILE NO. 9-7749 (P) (#204) May 4, 1978
FBI FILE NO. 9-63510
LATENT CASE NO. B-57263

TO: ADIC, New York

RE: UNSUB, AKA  b6
   ETC.; b7C
   JOHN LENNON - VICTIM
   EXTORTION

REFERENCE: Airtels 3/9/78 and 3/22/78
EXAMINATION REQUESTED BY: New York
SPECIMENS: Two envelopes, Q14 and Q17
   Three pages of typewritten letters, Q15, Q16 and Q18
   Two blank sheets of paper
   Newspaper clipping

The specimens are further described in a separate Laboratory report.

Fourteen latent fingerprints and one latent palm print of value were developed on six specimens, Q15, Q16, Q17, Q18 and two blank sheets of paper. No latent prints of value were developed on the remaining specimens.

Ten of the latent fingerprints have been identified as finger impressions of John Winston Ono Lennon.

(Continued on next page)

Enc. (8)

Robert E. Kent
Assistant Director, Identification Division

THIS REPORT IS FURNISHED FOR OFFICIAL USE ONLY

FBI/DOJ

ADIC, New York   May 4, 1978

The remaining latent fingerprints are not identical with the available fingerprints of Lennon. No palm prints are contained in our Identification Division files for this individual.

The currently reported unidentified latent prints were compared with the comparable areas of the previously reported unidentified latent prints in this case, but no identification was effected.

The specimens are enclosed.

Page 2.
LC #B-57263

7-2

RECORDED
3/21/78

FEDERAL BUREAU OF INVESTIGATION
UNITED STATES DEPARTMENT OF JUSTICE

LATENTS
3/13/78

Laboratory Work Sheet

slg*   Recorded 4/25/78   12:05p.m.   mcl   Received 4/25/78

To: ADIC, New York (9-7749) (P) (#204)

FBI FILE NO. 9-63510-12

LAB. NO. 80315081 D MS

Re: UNSUB; aka
    _____, Etc., b6 b7C
    JOHN LENNON-VICTIM;
    EXTORTION
    OO: New York

YOUR NO.
LC# B-57263

Examination by: ____ b6 b7C

Noted By: d

Examination requested by: New York

Reference: Airtel dated March 9, 1978

Examination requested: Document - Fingerprint

Specimens received: March 13, 1978

Q14 Envelope postmarked "NEW YORK, NY 10001 G.P.O. (I.M.) MAR 7 PM" bearing typewritten address "MR. HOHN LENNON I WEST 72ND STREET NEW YORK, N.Y. X0023"

Q15 First page of accompanying two-page typewritten letter dated 3/7/78 beginning "MR. JOHN LENNON On a very slow motion..."

Q16 Second page of two-page typewritten letter beginning "till it be approve..."

ALSO SUBMITTED:
    AI...
    HEREIN IS UNCLASS...
    DATE 4-4-83 BY 1678 RFP/EAM

    Blank sheet of paper
    Newspaper clipping

anso
5-4-78
DRW.lr

Specs proc min 4/25 88
4 paper specs to photo 4/26 (N)
(over)

Examination completed 11:30 AM   5/2/78   Dictated 5/2/78 DRW

              Time   Date   Date

FBI/DOJ

DOCUMENT(S) CANNOT
BE SCANNED

DESCRIPTION:

PHOTO NEGATIVES

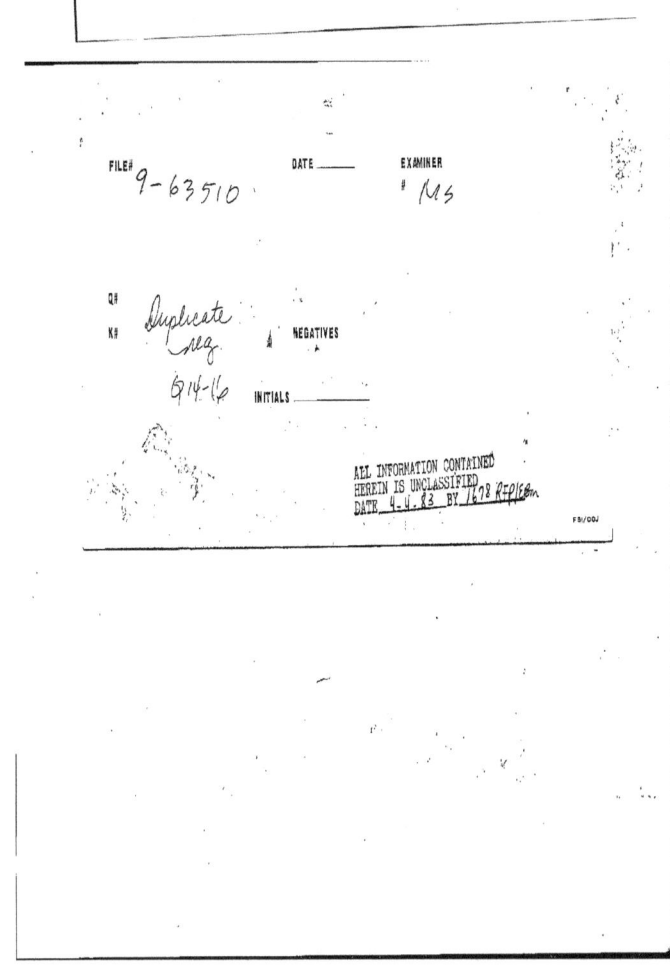

5/1/78 — 9 lat fpts g val dev on 3 specimens

2 lat fpts g val dev. on Q15 —
    1@#1, 1@#2 — John Winston Ono Lennon

4 lat fpts g val dev. on Q16 —
    1@#2 — John Winston Ono Lennon

3 lat fpts g val dev. on a blank sheet g paper (A/S)
    2@#2 - 1@#7 — John Winston Ono Lennon

No lats g val dev. on remaining specs. (nine)

Remaining lat fpts comp'd insofar as possible, fpts g Lennon, but No g effected. Need fully & clearly recorded inked impressions g the extreme tip and side areas g the fingers for a conclusive comparison.

Current un g lat fpts not g lat fpts prev. reported in this case.

5/2/78 —
Proc'd specs S.N — No lats g val dev.
Detached.
Specimens enclosed.
Enclosures (5)
    LCA.

7-2

RECORDED
4/6/78
bam

FEDERAL BUREAU OF INVESTIGATION
UNITED STATES DEPARTMENT OF JUSTICE

LATENT

Laboratory Work Sheet

Recorded 4/25/78 11:55a.m. mcl   Received 4/25/78

To: ADIC, New York (9-7749) (#204) (P)

FBI FILE NO. 9-63510—12
LAB. NO. 80327075 D MS

Re: UNSUB aka
[redacted b6 b7C],
Et Al;
JOHN LENNON - VICTIM;
EXT
OO: New York

YOUR NO.
LC# B-57263

Examination by: [redacted]

Noted By: [redacted b6 b7C]

Examination requested by: New York

Reference: Airtel dated March 22, 1978

Examination requested: Document - Fingerprint

Specimens received: March 24, 1978

Q17 Envelope postmarked "NEW YORK, NY 10001 G.P.O. (I.M.)   b6
     March 20 PM 1978" bearing typewritten adress '[redacted]   b7C
     [redacted] NEW YORK, NY 10023".

Q18 Accompanying one-page typewritten letter dated 3/20/78,
     beginning '[redacted]'. This letter is in reference to
     our talk ..."

ALSO SUBMITTED:

ALL INFORMATION CONTAINED
HEREIN IS UNCLASSIFIED
DATE 4-4-83 BY 1678RFP/[initials]

Blank sheet of paper

Examination completed 11:30AM 5/2/78   Dictated 5/2/78

             Time   Date   Date

FBI/DOJ

5/1/78 — 5 lat f.p.ts + 1 lat p.p dev. on 3 specimens

1 lat fpt q ual dev. on Q17

3 lat fpts + 1 lat pp q ual dev. on Q18 - 2¢'s #6, 1¢ # 7 - John Winston Ono Lennon.

1 lat fpt q ual dev. on a beach shirt of proper (R/S) 1¢ #2 - John Winston Ono Lennon.

remaining lat fpt not fpts of Lennon.

No pp's located here for Lennon.

remaining no & lat fpts not & lat fpts prev. reported in this case.

5/2/78 —

Proc'd specs S.N — No lat q ual dev.

detained

Specimens enclosed.

Enclosures (3)

    LCA

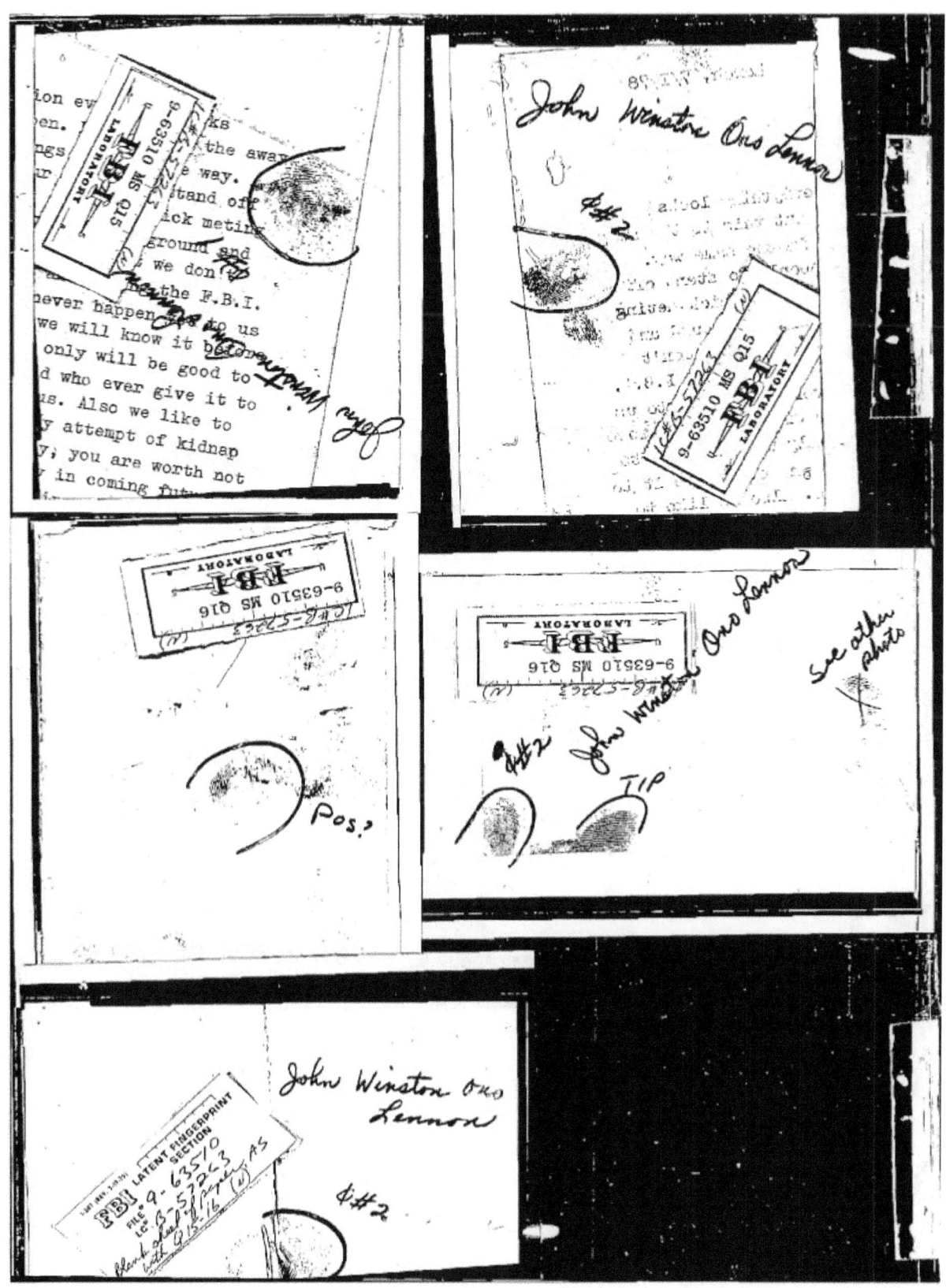

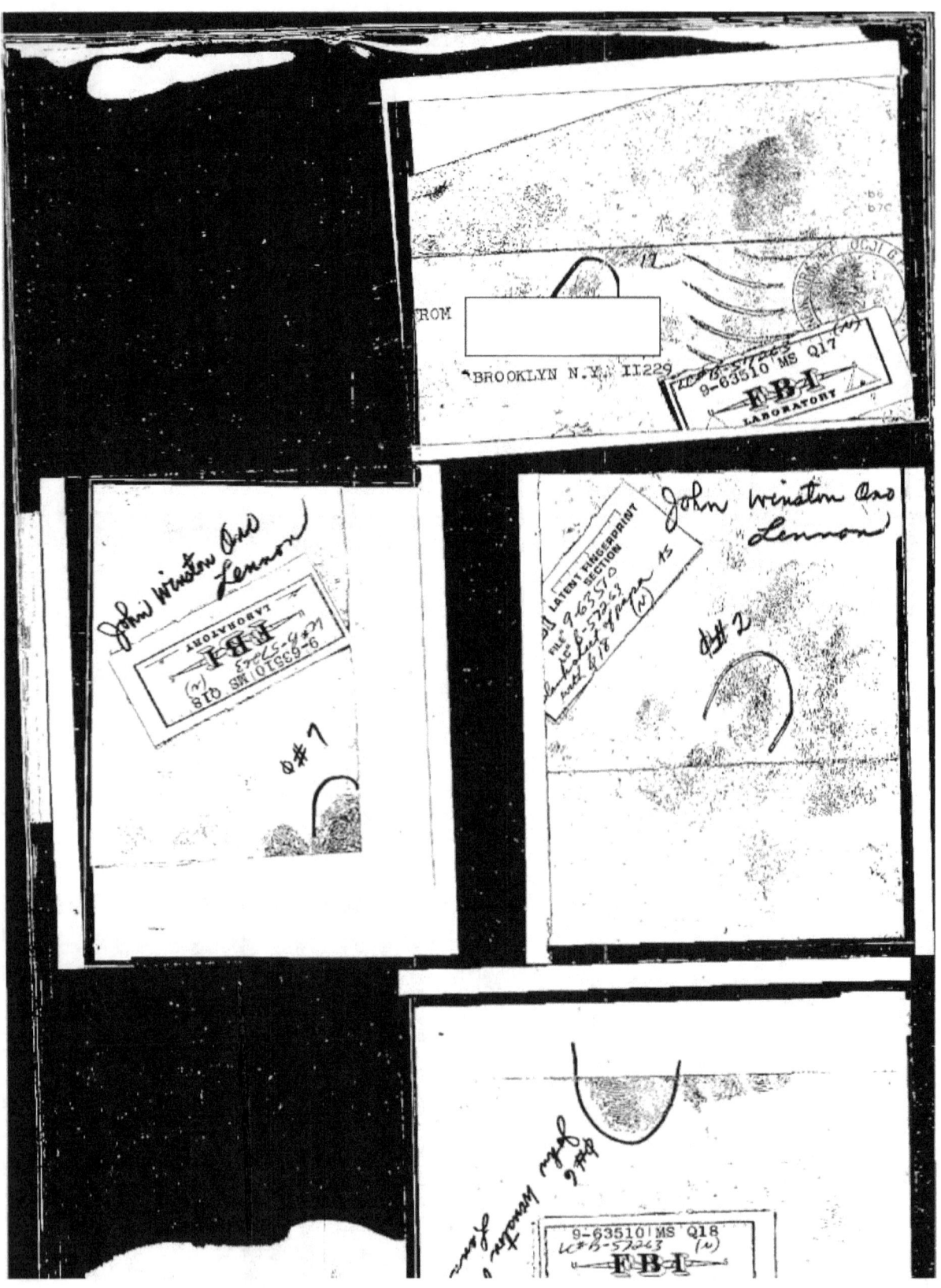

for all of you, I'm been
on, and thats why we go
, and in favor. Now I am
ou, to speak in your behalf
rything you said by the
on't accomplish much to
o be listen by all of us in

tion because they are very
er 23 thousends dollars on
ours lost for nothing.
rt of your money anymore,
r war. Part of our war it
here, and then they will
nsibility for the act.
, and me, I will never
l try to help all of you,
 in what I say,
, what ever you say it will
ephone, I'M ▮
DON'T KNOW WHAT TO SAY, BUT
N WE RECIEVE YOUR FIRST
HINKING GOOD , WE DECIDE CALL
ISTAKE CALL THE F.B.I. BUT
 THAT MUCH CASH, WE HAVE
U WITH 24 THOUS
F.B.I., AND T
KNOW IF YOU A

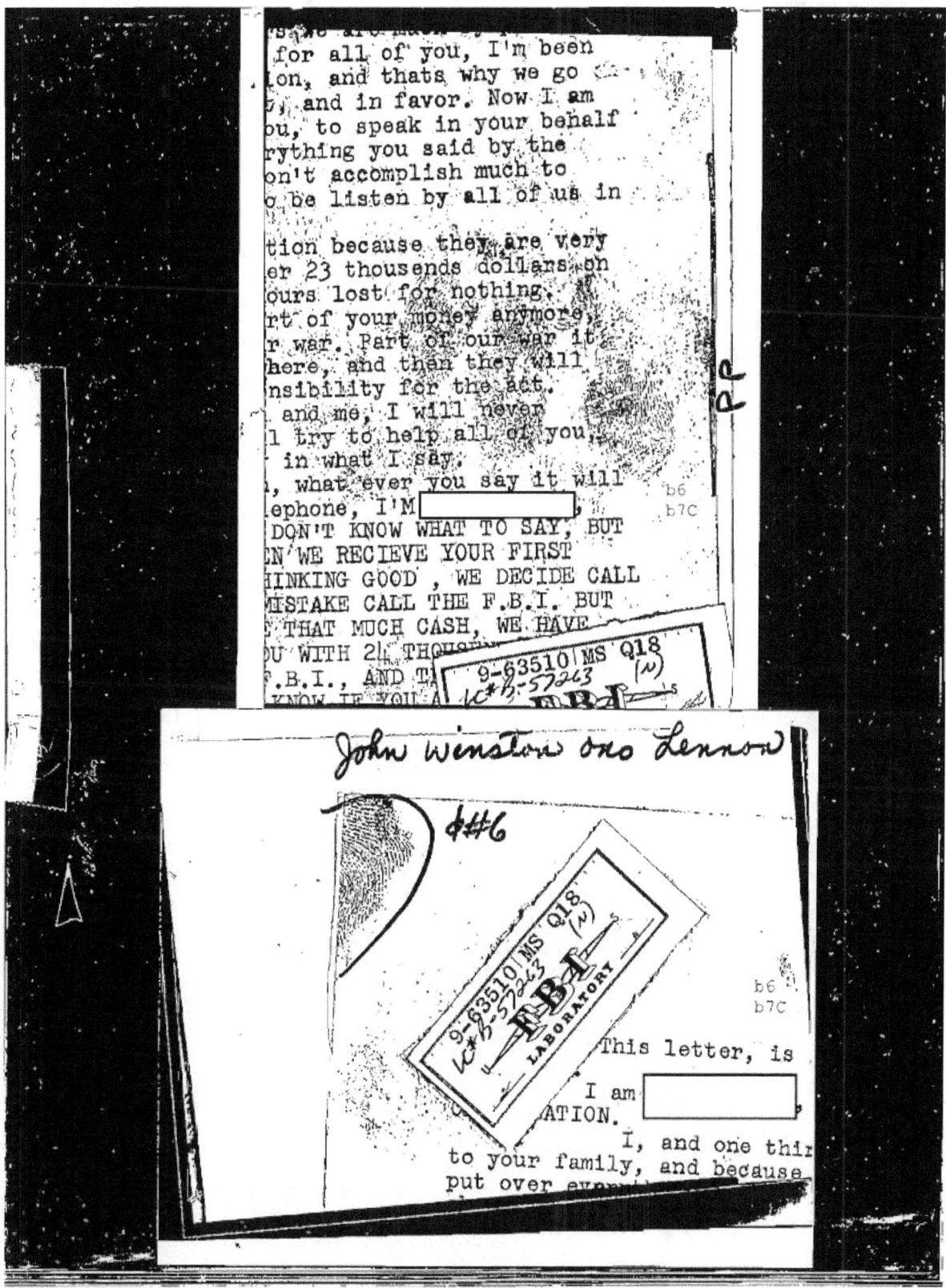

John Winston Ono Lennon

$#6

This letter, is
I am ▮
ATION.
I, and one thir
to your family, and because
put over ev

Laboratory Transmittal Form
7-72

FEDERAL BUREAU OF INVESTIGATION
WASHINGTON, D. C. 20535

May 16, 1978

To: ADIC, New York (9-7749)

From: Director, FBI

FBI FILE NO. 9-63510
LAB. NO. 80315081 D MS
80327075 D MS

Re: UNSUB; aka
[ ], Etc., b6 b7C
JOHN LENNON - VICTIM;
EXTORTION

OO: New York

Examination requested by: New York

Reference: Airtels dated March 9, 1978 and March 22, 1978

Examination requested: Document - Fingerprint

Remarks:

Enclosures (2) (2 Lab report)

ALL INFORMATION CONTAINED
HEREIN IS UNCLASSIFIED
DATE 4-4-83 BY 1678 RFP/ebm

JEL/tap* (4)

EX-121 REC-72 9-63510-13

MAY 17 1978

MAILED 5
MAY 17 1978
FBI

DO NOT INCLUDE ADMINISTRATIVE
INFORMATION IN
INVESTIGATIVE REPORT

ADMINISTRATIVE PAGE
MAIL ROOM ☑ TELETYPE UNIT ☐

FBI/DOJ

REPORT of the FBI LABORATORY

FEDERAL BUREAU OF INVESTIGATION
WASHINGTON, D. C. 20535

To: ADIC, New York (9-7749)

May 16, 1978

FBI FILE NO. 9-63510-13

LAB. NO. 80315081 D MS
80327075 D MS

Re: UNSUB; aka
 ███████████, Etc.,   b6
JOHN LENNON - VICTIM;   b7C
EXTORTION

Specimens received

March 13, 1978, under cover of communication dated March 9, 1978 (80315081 D MS):

Q14 Envelope postmarked "NEW YORK, NY 10001 G.P.O. (I.M.) MAR 7 PM 1978" bearing typewritten address "MR. JOHN LENNON I WEST 72ND STREET NEW YORK, N.Y. I0023"

Q15 First page of accompanying two-page typewritten letter dated 3/7/78 beginning "MR. JOHN LENNON On a very slow motion..."

Q16 Second page of two-page typewritten letter beginning "till it be approve..."

ALSO SUBMITTED:

Blank sheet of paper

Newspaper clipping

ALL INFORMATION CONTAINED
HEREIN IS UNCLASSIFIED
DATE 4-4-83 BY 1678 RFP/E

Page 1   (over)

Specimens received March 24, 1978, under cover of communication dated March 22, 1978 (80327075 D MS):

Q17   Envelope postmarked "NEW YORK, NY 10001 G.P.O. (I.M.) March 20 PM 1978" bearing typewritten address "☐ ☐ NEW YORK, NY 10023".

Q18   Accompanying one-page typewritten letter dated 3/20/78 beginning ☐. This letter is in reference to our talk..."

ALSO SUBMITTED:

   Blank sheet of paper

Result of examination:

   The Q14 through Q17 envelopes and sheets of paper and the ALSO SUBMITTED sheet of paper accompanying Q14 through Q16 are similar in observable physical characteristics to the envelopes and sheets of paper previously submitted in this matter. The Q18 sheet of paper and the ALSO SUBMITTED sheet of paper accompanying Q17 and Q18 bear the watermark "EATON'S CORRASABLE BOND USA BERKSHIRE 25% COTTON FIBRE." Paper bearing that watermark is manufactured by the Eaton Paper Company, a division of Textron, Inc., Pittsfield, Massachusettes.

   The examinations of Q14 through Q18 and the ALSO SUBMITTED items failed to reveal any additional watermarks, indented writings of significance, or other significant features which might be of assistance in determining the immediate source of those specimens.

   It was determined that the typewriting on Q14 through Q16 is the same size and style as typewriting on specimens previously submitted in this matter and contain limited characteristics in common and no significant differences with that previous typewriting. However, there are an insufficient amount of identifiable characteristics in that typewriting to permit a definite determination whether the same typewriter was or was not used.

   The typewriting on Q17 and Q18 is a style of pica type, spaced ten characters to the horizontal inch, used on Royal typewriters. That typewriting is different from the typewriting on the remainder of the specimens submitted in this matter.

(over)

The typewriting on Q17 and Q18 was compared with specimens in the Anonymous Letter File, but no identification was effected. Representative photographs will be added to the file for future reference.

Q14 through Q18 were photographed. You are being advised separately of the results of the requested latent fingerprint examination and the disposition of the submitted specimens.

RECORDED
4/6/78
bam

FEDERAL BUREAU OF INVESTIGATION
UNITED STATES DEPARTMENT OF JUSTICE

LATENT

Laboratory Work Sheet

To: ADIC, New York (9-7749) (#204)

FBI FILE NO. 9-63510-13
LAB. NO. 80327075 D MS

Re: UNSUB aka
    [b6 b7C]
    Et Al;
    JOHN LENNON - VICTIM;
    EXT (A)
    OO: New York

YOUR NO.

Examination by: [b6 b7C]

Examination requested by: New York

Reference: Airtel dated March 22, 1978 (See 80315081 DMS)

Examination requested: Document - Fingerprint

Specimens received: March 24, 1978

Q17 Envelope postmarked "NEW YORK, NY 10001 G.P.O. (1 M.) March 20 PM 1978" bearing typewritten adress, "[____] ONE WEST 72ND STREET NEW YORK, NY 10023".

Q18 Accompanying one-page typewritten letter dated 3/20/78, beginning '[____]. This letter is in reference to our talk ..."

ALSO SUBMITTED:

Blank sheet of paper

ALL INFORMATION CONTAINED
HEREIN IS UNCLASSIFIED
DATE 4-4-83 BY 1678 RFP/Elm

Q18, AS, paper:
 8.5 × 11± × .0035±   no Indented writings
 Watermark   Q17-18, AS
  EATON'S
  CORRASABLE   Eaton Paper Co.
  BOND   Div. of Textron, Inc.
  USA   75 S Church St.
  BERKSHIRE   Pittsfield, Mass. 01201
  25% COTTON FIBRE

```
7-2
```

RECORDED   FEDERAL BUREAU OF INVESTIGATION   LATENTS   b6
3/21/78   UNITED STATES DEPARTMENT OF JUSTICE   3/13/78   b7C

Laboratory Work Sheet

slg*

To: ADIC, New York (9-7749)

FBI FILE NO. 9-63510-13

LAB. NO. 80315081 D MS

Re: UNSUB; aka
     [redacted], Etc.,   b6 b7C
JOHN LENNON-VICTIM;
EXTORTION (A)
OO: New York

YOUR NO. 803270750

Examination by:

Examination requested by: New York

Reference: Airtel dated March 9, 1978

Examination requested: Document - Fingerprint

Specimens received: March 13, 1978

Q14   Envelope postmarked "NEW YORK, NY 10001 G.P.O. (I.M.) MAR 7 PM" bearing typewritten address "MR. JOHN LENNON I WEST 72ND STREET NEW YORK, N.Y. 10023"

Q15   First page of accompanying two-page typewritten letter dated 3/7/78 beginning "MR. JOHN LENNON On a very slow motion..."

Q16   Second page of two-page typewritten letter beginning "till it be approve..."

ALSO SUBMITTED:

    Blank sheet of paper

    Newspaper clipping

ALL INFORMATION CONTAINED
HEREIN IS UNCLASSIFIED
DATE 4-4-83 BY 1678RFO/em

TW same size & style
Q14-16 A/s paper same in observable
physical characteristics as Q1-Q13
No e/w/ watermarks, 76th dbl sig. noted

- The Q14→18 envs + sheets of paper are sim in obsv. phys. chars to the + the AS sheet of paper accompanying Q14→16
envs. + sheets of paper prev sub in this matter. The Q18 sheet of paper + the AS sheet of paper accompanying Q17&Q18 bear the WM "EATON'S CORRASABLE BOND USA BERKSHIRE 25% COTTON FIBRE". Paper bearing that WM is mfld by the Eaton Paper Co., a Div of Textron, Inc., Pittsfield, Mass.

- Exams Q14→18 + AS int’vs failed to reveal any add’l WMs, indents of sig or other signif features which might be of assistance in determ. the immed. source of these specs.

- Det the tw on Q14→16 is in same s+s as tw on specs prev sub this matter + contains ltd chars in common + no signif diffs. However, insuff amt of rel wt. chars to permit def determ of same tw used.

- The tw on Q17&Q18 is a style of pica type, 10→inch, used on Royal tws. It differs in tw'g from tw on of papers sub this matter. Q17&Q18 NJALF added.

- Q14→18 photo'd. admin exp CFP + dispo.

UNITED STATES GOVERNMENT

Memorandum

TO : DIRECTOR, FBI (9-63510) DATE: AUG 2 1978

FROM : ADIC, NEW YORK (9-7749) (P) (#212)

SUBJECT: UNSUB, aka
  ,
  ET AL;
  JOHN LENNON - VICTIM
  EXTORTION (A)

ReNYlet to the Bu, dated 3/22/78.

Last letter received by _____ on 3/21/78, and subsequently forwarded to FBI Laboratory.

There have been no contacts by unknown subject either by letter or telephone since the letter of 3/21/78.

The LENNON family went to Japan for summer months and are not expected to return to the US until September, 1978. Contact being maintained with their secretary in NYC and the manager of The Dakota, 1 West 72nd Street, New York, New York (LENNON's residence). No contact had with unknown subject.

Bureau will be kept advised of any new developments in this matter.

ALL INFORMATION CONTAINED
HEREIN IS UNCLASSIFIED
DATE 4-4-83 BY 1678 RFP/EBm

EX-110
REC 62 9-63510-14

AUG 3 1978

2 - Bureau
1 - New York

FVB:kp
(3)

Buy U.S. Savings Bonds Regularly on the Payroll Savings Plan

FVB:jfc
1

NY 9-7749

On May 1, 1978, JOHN LENNON advised that they have had no contact with Unsubs either by letter or telephone since the receipt of their last letter on March 21, 1978. He stated that they will be going to Japan on May 8, 1978 for three or four months (Summer vacation). Mr. LENNON stated that their secretary will contact the New York Office of the FBI should any letters be received.

On October 4, 1978, JOHN LENNON advised that they (his family) returned to the United States during the latter part of September, 1978. He stated that no letter or contact was made by the Unsubs during this time. He advised he will call the New York Office if he receives any information.

On December 15, 1978, JOHN LENNON advised that no contact has been made by Unsubs with him since their last letter of March 21, 1978.

FD-263 (Rev. 7-15-78)

FEDERAL BUREAU OF INVESTIGATION

REPORTING OFFICE	OFFICE OF ORIGIN	DATE	INVESTIGATIVE PERIOD
NEW YORK	NEW YORK	DEC 28 1978	12/1/77 – 12/15/78

TITLE OF CASE	REPORT MADE BY	TYPED BY
UNSUBS aka	b6 b7C	jfc
[redacted]		
JOHN LENNON – VICTIM	CHARACTER OF CASE: EXTORTION (A)	

REFERENCES

New York teletype to Bureau, 12/1/77
New York airtels to Bureau, 12/2/77, 12/20/77, 1/24/78, 2/8/78, 3/9/78, and 3/22/78.
New York letter to Bureau, 8/2/78.
FBI Lab letters to New York, 2/27/78, 2/27/78, and 5/16/78.
FBI LFS letters to New York, 2/2/78, 3/7/78, and 5/4/78.

-C-

ADMINISTRATIVE

It is noted that the investigative period has been extended, however, contact has been maintained with victim. Victim and his family were in Japan for the Summer months and returned to U.S. during the latter part of September, 1978.

ACCOMPLISHMENTS CLAIMED [ ] NONE

CASE HAS BEEN:
PENDING OVER ONE YEAR [X] YES [ ] NO
PENDING PROSECUTION OVER SIX MONTHS [ ] YES [X] NO

COPIES MADE:
1 - Bureau (9-63510)
1 - New York (9-7749)

ALL INFORMATION CONTAINED
HEREIN IS UNCLASSIFIED
DATE 1-5-83 BY 1678 RFP/ebm

9-63510-15   REC-80
SI 109
15 DEC 29 1978

62 JAN 11 1979

COVER PAGE

-A-

NY 9-7749

ADMINISTRATIVE (CONTINUED)

A complete list of employees of "The Dakota", One West 72nd Street, NY, NY, was furnished by [_____]. Background investigation and criminal checks on these individuals are not being set forth in report, but are maintained in the files of the NYO.

b6
b7C

[_____]

b3

Surveillance of the drop site at "The Dakota" was maintained by SAs of the FBI on 12/9/77 and 2/2-6/78 with negative results.

All logical investigation has been conducted and no prime suspects developed. Since there has been no contact by Unsubs either telephonically or by letter since 3/21/78, no further investigation being conducted by the NYO. If additional information is received, this case will be re-opened and the Bureau immediately advised.

-B*-
COVER PAGE

FD-204 (Rev. 3-3-59)

UNITED STATES DEPARTMENT OF JUSTICE
FEDERAL BUREAU OF INVESTIGATION

Copy to:

Report of: [redacted b6 b7C] Office: New York, New York
Date: DEC 28 1978

Field Office File #: 9-7749 Bureau File #: 9-63510

Title: UNKNOWN SUBJECTS;
JOHN LENNON - VICTIM

Character: EXTORTION (A)

ALL INFORMATION CONTAINED
HEREIN IS UNCLASSIFIED
DATE 4-6-83 BY 1673 REP/ebm

Synopsis: Seven special delivery letters sent to JOHN LENNON, One West 72nd Street, NY, NY, from unknown individuals. Two letters received in December, 1977, two in January, 1978, one in February, 1978, and two in March, 1978. Letters postmarked Jamaica, New York, 11/29/77; GPO NYC, 12/18/77; Jamaica, NY, 1/18/78; GPO, NY, 1/22/78; GPO NY, 2/3/78; GPO, NY, 3/7/78; GPO, NY, 3/20/78. Letters had return address of [redacted], Brooklyn, NY; [redacted], Brooklyn, NY; and [redacted], Staten Island, NY. Letters threatened life of JOHN LENNON, [redacted], and [redacted], if $100,000 was not paid to Unsubs. Several telephone calls made by Unsubs to residence of JOHN LENNON during this period. Composite photo of individual who mailed special delivery letter at Jamaica Post Office on 1/18/78, exhibited with negative results. Surveillance of drop site maintained on 12/9/77 and from 2/2/78 to 2/6/78, with negative results. FBI Lab and LFS reports set forth. No contact by Unsubs since 3/21/78.

-C-

DETAILS:

This case is predicated upon telephonic contact to the New York Office of the Federal Bureau of Investigation (FBI) on December 1, 1977, by [redacted], telephone [redacted], who advised that [redacted] received a special delivery letter, in which the writer threatened to kidnap or kill [redacted]. [redacted] requested to see an agent immediately.

This document contains neither recommendations nor conclusions of the FBI. It is the property of the FBI and is loaned to your agency; it and its contents are not to be distributed outside your agency.

U.S.GPO:1975-O-575-841

The dream is over

On December 1980, shortly before 11pm, John Lennon, was shot 4 times in the back by Mark David Chapman at the entrance of the Dakota building in New York as he was coming home with Yoko Ono after a recording session. He was only forty.

This is how the life of one of the most influential artists of his time came to an abrupt end. John Lennon gained worldwide fame with the Beatles, whose music remains a reference for all, more than forty years after their breakup. The Beatles sold more than one billion records worldwide. He also had a successful solo career, with international hits like "Imagine", "Woman" ou "Instant Karma", used his skills and image to advocate peace, was involved in anti Vietnam War activism. He wrote acclaimed books, painted and drew a lot, and never stopped experimenting with all kinds of artistic means : video, performance...

Or, as Paul McCartney put it : "John was a great man who will be sadly missed by the world, but remembered for his unique contribution to art, music and world peace".

The news of Lennon's death spread rapidly and thousands of people gathered instantly outside the Dakota building, wanting to pay tribute to John Lennon, his music and activism for peace and freedom. One week later, on 14th December, millions of people around the world responded to Yoko Ono's request to pause for ten minutes of silence to remember John.

So here are the last few FBI documents in John Lennon's file, dating from after his death. The first ones refer to an investigation regarding the use of a restricted access photograph of John Lennon's body at the morgue on the cover of the *New York Post*. Then, in 1983, the FBI checked if the fingerprints found on the letters and envelopes threatening Lennon for money in 1977-1978 were the same as those of an individual whose name is blacked out but who most probably is Mark Chapman.

John Lennon signing an autograph on a "*Double Fantasy*" LP handed to him by Mark Chapman (on the right), only a few hours before he would shoot the ex-Beatle to death...

But I'm one of your biggest fans, 1979 - drawing by John Lennon.

JOHN LENNON shot dead in New York Dec 8 1980
DEATH OF A HERO

Fan gathered near the Dakota building to pay tribute to John Lennon

IG 199

THE CITY OF NEW YORK
DEPARTMENT OF CORRECTION
100 CENTRE STREET
NEW YORK, N.Y. 10013

BENJAMIN WARD
COMMISSIONER

LOCAL & STATE

May 18, 1981

ROBERT GOLDMAN
INSPECTOR GENERAL

Honorable William H. Webster
Director
Federal Bureau of Investigation
U.S. Department of Justice
Washington, D.C. 20535

Attention: FBI Laboratory
Re: _____ John
Lennon deceased victim

Dear Mr. Webster:

On December 15, 1980, an exclusive photo appeared in the New York Post showing _____ singer John Lennon, _____.

Preliminary investigation indicates that the copy depicted in the news photo was copied from one of the photos attached to official New York City Department of Correction documents. Since the enclosed photos can be identified with specific documents, a positive identification as to the photo copied would help to narrow the scope of our investigation as to the individuals having access to said documents.

I am sending you, by registered mail, a package containing the following evidence:

1. News photograph of _____.

2. Six (6) New York City Department of Correction photographs from official documents.

It would be appreciated if you would examine the photographs to determine which one was used to obtain the copy shown in the New York Post.

This evidence, which we would like to have returned to us, has not been examined by any other expert.

Sincerely,

Robert Goldman
ROBERT GOLDMAN
Inspector General

RG:hjc
Enclosures

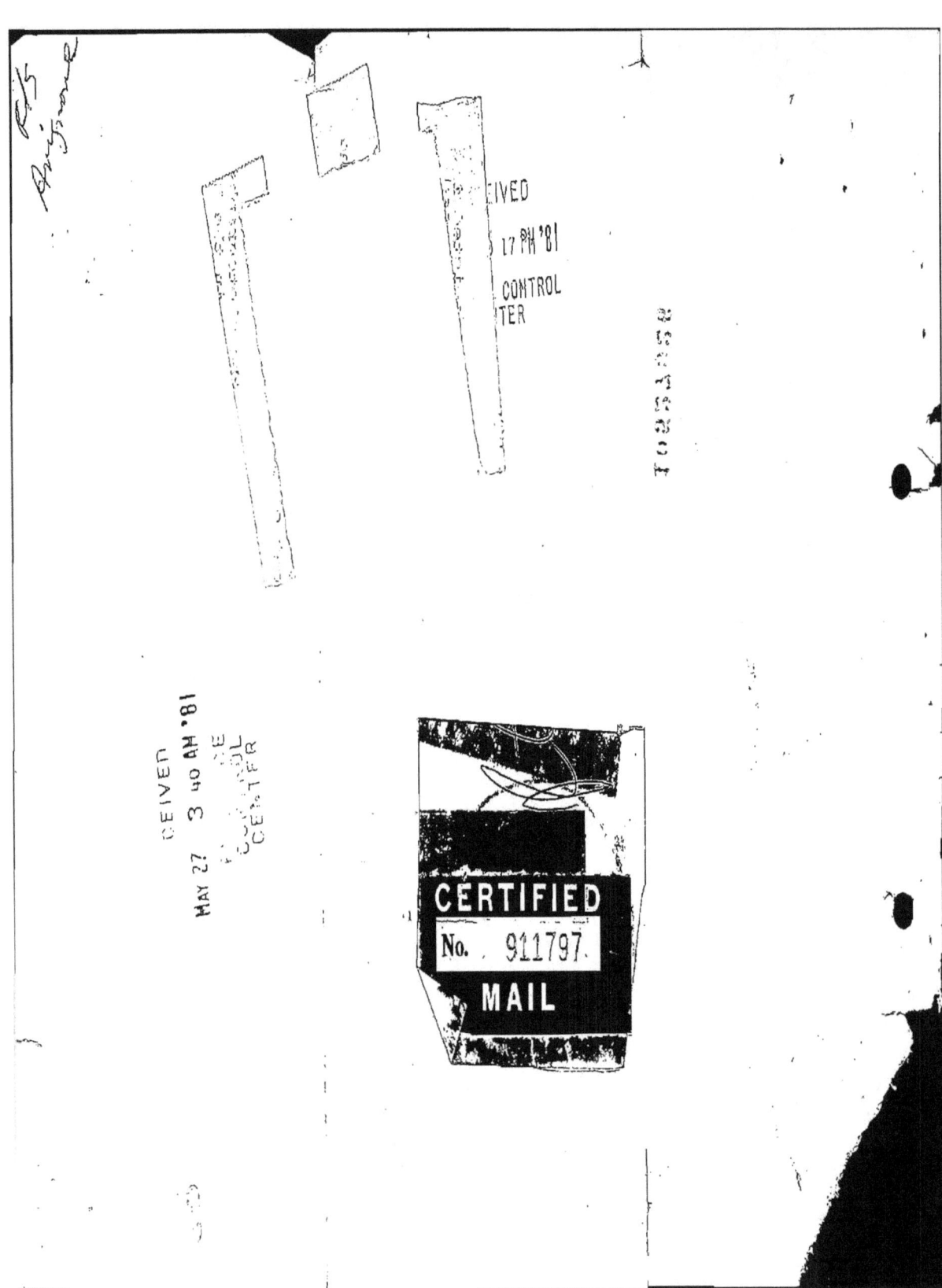

We chose not to publish the photo printed in the *New York Post* that is mentioned in the previous document. It is a photograph of Lennon's dead body at the morgue. If you wish, you can easily find it on the Internet though.

Instead, here is an article related to this event published in the *Bulletin Journal* dated December 14, 1980 :

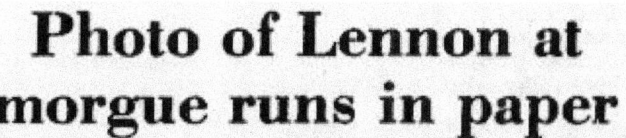

Photo of Lennon at morgue runs in paper

NEW YORK (UPI) — Someone snapped a photograph of John Lennon's body in the city morgue and officials are determined to find out how their security measures were circumvented.

A spokeswoman for Mayor Edward Koch said Thursday chief Medical Examiner Dr. Elliot Gross "and his inspector general are trying to check the matter out as quickly as possible."

"I personally am really distressed," the spokeswoman said. "Security measures were taken, but somehow they weren't enough."

Whoever was responsible for the security lapse will be dismissed immediately, she said.

The photo, showing only Lennon's head, appeared on the front page of Thursday's New York Post and was distributed by the news agency Sygma.

The paper and the agency refused to disclose anything about the origin of the photo.

The spokeswoman speculated that a morgue worker was offered a "whole lot of money," which proved to be "too tempting for somebody."

An autopsy was performed by Dr. Gross and two assistants on Tuesday. The body was released Wednesday afternoon and cremated at Ferncliff Crematorium in Hartsdale, N.Y.

Lennon was shot to death Monday night outside his home in the exclusive Manhattan Dakota Apartments, allegedly by a deranged fan, Mark Chapman, 25, of Honolulu.

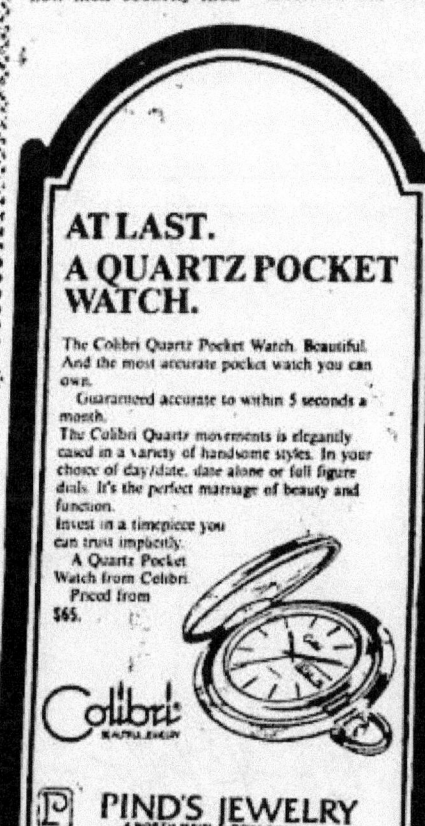

7-1a (Rev. 4-26-78)

REPORT of the
FBI LABORATORY
FEDERAL BUREAU OF INVESTIGATION
WASHINGTON, D. C. 20535

LOCAL & STATE

To:
Commissioner
Department of Correction
100 Centre Street
New York, New York 10013

Re: Attention: Mr. Robert Goldman
Inspector General

July 15, 1981

FBI FILE NO. REGISTERED
95-243496
LAB. NO. 10527026 P MG
YOUR NO.

MISUSE OF OFFICIAL DOCUMENTS -
UNAUTHORIZED DISCLOSURE OF
PHOTOGRAPH OF ███████ b6 b7C

Examination requested by: Addressee

Reference: Letter dated May 18, 1981

Examination requested: Photographic

Specimens:

Q1   News photograph of ███████ which appeared in the New York Post 12/15/80.

Six New York City Department of Correction photographs further described as follows:

SPECIMEN	NUMBERED
K1	3 and 4
K2	5 and 6
K3	7

Enclosures (7)
Page 1

This examination has been made with the understanding that the evidence is connected with an official investigation of a criminal matter and that the Laboratory report will be used for official purposes only, related to the investigation or a subsequent criminal prosecution. Authorization cannot be granted for the use of the Laboratory report in connection with a civil proceeding.

SPECIMEN	NUMBERED
K4	8
K5	9
K6	10

Result of examination:

It was concluded that Q1 was not prepared from K1, K2 or K4 through K6. Similarities were noted when Q1 was compared with K3 indicating that K3 could have been used to make Q1.

The submitted evidence has been photographed and is returned herewith.

RECORDED FEDERAL BUREAU OF INVESTIGATION 5/26/81
6/2/81   UNITED STATES DEPARTMENT OF JUSTICE

Laboratory Work Sheet

ACK 7-32
6/4

To: Commissioner
Department of Correction
100 Centre Street
New York, New York 10013

FBI FILE NO. 95-242496-2

LAB. NO. 10527026 P MG

Attention: Mr. Robert Goldman
Inspector General

Re: YOUR NO.

—————————— - SUSPECT;
JOHN LENNON - VICTIM;
HOMICIDE

Examination by:

Misuse of Official Documents - Unauthorized Disclosure of Photographs of

Examination requested by: Addressee

Q, K1-6 SPU 6/8

Reference: Letter dated May 18, 1981

Examination requested: Photographic

Specimens received:

Specimens:

Q1 News photograph of _____ which appeared in the New York Post 12/15/80

Six New York City Department of Correction photographs further described as follows:

SPECIMEN	NUMBERED
K1	3 and 4
K2	5 and 6
K3	7

Page 1   (over)

conc Q, not from K1, K2 and K4-K6.
is not noted, when cup/K3 w/ofc K3
could be been used to make Q

7-1a
7-15-81
JMA:ar

SPECIMEN	NUMBERED
K4	8
K5	9
K6	10

Memorandum

To: ▢

From: O. B. Revell

Subject: UNSUBS;
AKA ▢

JOHN LENNON - VICTIM
EXTORTION (A)
OO: NEW YORK
BU FILE 9-63510
NY FILE 9-7749

Date 5/16/83
1 - Mr. Revell
1 -
1 -
1 -
1 -
1 -

b6
b7C

PURPOSE: To determine if latent prints of unsubs in this matter are identifiable to prints of ▢.

RECOMMENDATION: That latent prints obtained in this matter be compared with those of ▢ FBI number ▢ who was ▢

APPROVED: ...

DETAILS: The investigative period of captioned matter was 12/1/77 - 12/15/78. The case was predicated upon telephonic contact to the New York Office by ▢. ▢ advised Bureau Agents that ▢ had received a special delivery letter in which the writer threatened to kidnap or kill ▢. A total of seven threat letters were received by the Lennon family beginning December 1, 1977, and ending in March, 1978. The letters threatened the life of each member of the John Lennon family if a $100,000 demand was not paid. The case was closed on 12/15/78 since all investigative leads had been exhausted and the captioned victim family had not been contacted by unsubs since 3/21/78.

Identification Division latent case number B 57263 indicates that fourteen latent fingerprints and one latent palm print of value were developed on six specimens in this matter by the Latent Fingerprint Section, Identification Division.

ARG:htg (8)

CONTINUED - OVER

Memo from O. B. Revell to [   ] b6
RE: UNSUBS; AKA; JOHN LENNON - VICTIM b7C

Ten of the latent fingerprints were identified as finger impressions of John Winston Ono Lennon. No identification was effected of the remaining four latent fingerprints or the palm print previously mentioned.

[   ] the murder of b6
John Lennon on 12/8/80 and [   ]. b7C

The Personal Crimes Unit, Criminal Investigative Division, requests that [   ] fingerprints and palm prints be compared to those aforementioned unidentified prints in this matter. b6 b7C

FEDERAL BUREAU OF INVESTIGATION
Washington, D. C. 20537

REPORT
of the
LATENT FINGERPRINT SECTION
IDENTIFICATION DIVISION

YOUR FILE NO.   9-7749 (P) (21)   May 24, 1983
FBI FILE NO.   9-63510
LATENT CASE NO.   D-57263

TO: ADIC, New York

RE: UNSUB.; AKA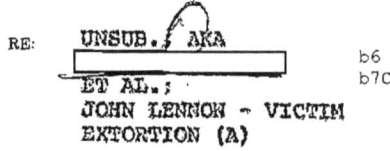
       ET AL.;
       JOHN LENNON - VICTIM
       EXTORTION (A)

REFERENCE: Bureau letter 5/16/83
EXAMINATION REQUESTED BY: Bureau
SPECIMENS:

       Three of the previously unidentified latent fingerprints are not the fingerprints of _____, FBI # ____. The remaining three previously unidentified latent fingerprints were compared, insofar as possible, with the available fingerprints of this individual, but no identification was effected. Complete comparisons were not possible since the extreme tips of the fingers were not fully recorded. There are no palm prints in the Identification Division files for _____.

1 - SA _____, Room 5096, TL #233
CGR:bj
(4)

THIS REPORT IS FURNISHED FOR OFFICIAL USE ONLY

1-36 (Rev. 11-6-63)

FEDERAL BUREAU OF INVESTIGATION
LATENT FINGERPRINT SECTION WORK SHEET

Recorded: 5/18/83   bcq   Reference No: 9-7749 (P) (21)
                                  FBI File No: 9-63510
Received: 5/18/83   Latent Case No: B-57263

Answer to: ADIC, New York

Examination requested by: ~~Addressee~~ BUREAU

Copy to:

RE: UNSUBS.;
    AKA [redacted]
    [redacted];
    JOHN LENNON - VICTIM
    EXTORTION (A)

b6
b7C

Date of reference communication: ~~Bureau~~ Letter 5/16/83
Specimens:
    Named Suspect: [redacted], FBI# [redacted]

Result of examination: Examination by: [redacted]
                                      Evidence noted by:

(21 LAT FGRPS & 1 PP PREV REPORTED — 15 Ø ELIM PRINTS LENNON)
3 PREV UNIDENT LAT FGRPS NOT [redacted] — REMAINING 3 PREV UNIDENT
LATS COMPD INSOFAR AS POSS NO Ø — TIPS NEEDED 5/19 eh
NO PP's here FOR [redacted]
([redacted] ADVISED 5/19 eh
 SA [redacted]   DIV 6 ADVISED 5/19 eh)

b6
b7C

Examination completed 12:10 PM   5/18/83   Dictated 5/17/83
                       Time   Date   Date

1 SA [redacted]   Rm 5096, Tl 233
                                              b6
                                              b7C

FBI/DOJ

GENERAL GLOSSARY

Airtel : Urgent FBI internal communication sent by airmail on the day it is written.

BU File or Bufile : Bureau file. File located and kept at FBI headquarters in Washington, DC.

CALREP : FBI code referring to the 1972 Republican National Convention before it was scheduled to take place in Miami.

DID : Domestic Intelligence Division of the FBI.

Director : Refers to FBI director, John Edgar Hoover till May 1972.

EYSIC : Election Year Strategy Information Center, far-left activist group advocating for peace in Vietnam and against President Nixon's re-election. When John Lennon contributed money to EYSIC, the FBI intensified its surveillance on him and Nixon's administration began harassing him on visa and immigration issues.

FALN : The *Fuerzas Armadas de Liberación Nacional* (Armed Forces of National Liberation, FALN) was a Puerto Rican terrorist organization that advocated complete independence for Puerto Rico. The FALN was responsible for more than 120 bomb attacks on United States targets between 1974 and 1983.

FOIA : Freedom Of Information Act. Its is under the FOIA that the Lennon FBI files were released. Jon Wiener, Professor of History at the University of California and author of several books on John Lennon, was the investigator of a judicial procedure against the FBI that had first withheld much of the material. This litigation lasted 14 years (!) and it is what enables us to have access to some previously blacked out parts of the FBI documents on John Lennon. Many thanks to Jon Wiener and his attorneys Dan Marmalefsky and Mark Rosenbaum !

Informant : Someone who provides information to the FBI and is paid for that.

INS : Immigration and Naturalization Service. It administrated the permanent residence, naturalization, visa and asylum issues. It was replaced by the US Citizenship and Immigration Services (USCIS) in 2003.

IS : Internal Security. Classification category for FBI files and investigations.

Legat : The FBI has offices around the globe. These offices—called *legal attachés* or *legats*—are located in US embassies.

LHM : Letterhead Memorandum. This is a FBI report summing up the knowledge about an investigation, done for dissemination to other federal agencies. Theses documents conceal confidential sources.

LNS : Liberation News Service. Independent US news network that provided the alternative and underground media with news stories.

MI : The Miami FBI office.

MIDEM : FBI code for the 1972 National Convention of the Democrats, to be held in Miami.

MIREP : FBI code for the 1972 National Convention of the Republicans, to be held in Miami.

New Left : Refers to antiwar activists in the late 60s and the 70s. **NL** is the corresponding FBI code.

NYO : The New York FBI office.

OO : Stands for Office of Origin. It's the FBI field office that mainly manages an investigation. In Lennon's case, the OO was New York City.

OS or **O/S** : Outside the scope. Marginal notation by the FBI on the released documents indicating that the section is withheld because the information it contains has nothing to do with the subject of the FOIA request.

PCPJ : People's Coalition for Peace and Justice. An antiwar organization.

REVACT : FBI code for "revolutionary activities".

RM : Code for racial matter.

SA : Special Agent. Name given to FBI agents.

SAC : Special Agent in charge.

SM : Security Matter. FBI classification code for files and investigations about potential threats to US internal security. John Lennon's activities were considered a security matter.

Source : someone who provides information to the FBI without being paid (unlike the informant).

Teletype : An encrypted message sent over FBI's secure communication network.

USSS : US Secret Service.

WPP : White Panther Party. A far-left anti-racist political organization led by John Sinclair.

YES : Youth Election Strategy. A group planning antiwar protests during the 1972 presidential campaign.

YIP : Youth International Party. New Left movement founded by Jerry Rubin.

Explanation of FOIA Exemptions

(Source : FBI / US Department of Justice)

When a portion of a record is withheld from public release, the subsection of the FOIA law describing that exemption(s) may be found listed in the margin next to the space where the withheld text would have been found. The list below describes the type of material withheld under each subsection of the FOIA.

(b)(1) Specifically authorized under criteria by an executive order to be kept secret in the interest of national defense or foreign policy[7].

(b)(2) Related solely to the internal personnel rules and practices of an agency.

(b)(3) Specifically exempted from disclosure by statute, provided that such statute (A) requires that the matters be withheld from the public in such a manner as to leave no discretion on issue or (B) establishes particular criteria for withholding or refers to particular types of matters to be withheld.

(b)(4) Trade secrets and commercial or financial information obtained from a person and privileged or confidential.

(b)(5) Inter-agency or intra-agency memorandums or letters that would not be available by law to a party other than an agency in litigation with the agency.

(b)(6) Personnel and medical files and similar files, the disclosure of which would constitute a clearly unwarranted invasion of personal privacy.

(b)(7) Records or information compiled for law enforcement purposes, but only to the extent that the production of such law enforcement records or information:

- (a) Could reasonably be expected to interfere with enforcement proceedings;
- (b) Would deprive a person of a right to a fair trial or an impartial adjudication;
- (c) Could reasonably be expected to constitute an unwarranted invasion of personal privacy;
- (d) Could reasonably be expected to disclose the identity of confidential source, including a state, local, or foreign agency or authority or any private institution that furnished information on a confidential basis, and, in the case of a record or information compiled by a criminal law enforcement authority in the course of a criminal investigation or by an agency conducting a lawful national security intelligence investigation, information furnished by a confidential source;
- (e) Would disclose techniques and procedures for law enforcement investigations or prosecutions or would disclose guidelines for law enforcement investigations or prosecutions if such disclosure could reasonably be expected to risk circumvention of the law; or
- (f) Could reasonably be expected to endanger the life or physical safety of any individual.

OS or **O/S** : Outside the scope. Marginal notation by the FBI on the released documents indicating that the section is withheld because the information it contains has nothing to do with the subject of the FOIA request.

---

[7] The "national security" classification is based on an executive order on classification issued by the US President defining the restrictions placed on release of information under the FOIA.

Listen to

LIVERPOOL REVOLUTION LIVE

the ultimate Beatles webradio

www.liverpoolrevolution.com

We broadcast Beatles' music 8 days a week and 24 hours a day
100% Fab Four flavour non stop

On this webradio you can listen to every single song ever recorded by the Beatles. Studio versions, lives, rarities, alternate takes, previously unreleased material !

With LIVERPOOL REVOLUTION LIVE, in the beautiful Beatles' sound you dive !

(Re)discover all the Beatles' songs and follow each step of the evolution of their music that would set new standards for the decades (and probably centuries) to come.

We broadcast a lot of exclusive material, never commercially released on record : live sessions from concerts all over the world, alternate takes, rehearsals and jams by the Beatles and much more rarities you can hear nowhere else.

LIVERPOOL REVOLUTION LIVE, all Beatles' music all day and all night
Enjoy !

www.ingramcontent.com/pod-product-compliance
Lightning Source LLC
Chambersburg PA
CBHW060503300426
44112CB00017B/2532